HINDUS, Michael Stephen. Prison and plantation: crime, justice, and authority in Massachusetts and South Carolina, 1767-1878. North Carolina, 1980. 285p (Studies in legal history) bibl index 79-19493. 20.00 ISBN 0-8078-1417-2. CIP

Hindus, currently an attorney and formerly a teacher of history and criminal justice at the University of Minnesota, has written the first comparative study of the development of the criminal justice system in two very different states in the 19th century. While the system in quickly industrializing, "modern" Massachusetts was vastly different from that in rural, "traditional" South Carolina, he yet argues that in overall conception they were quite similar. In elaborate detail he compares and contrasts the development of their court and legal systems, types of crimes, punishments, and attempts at legal reforms. The crux of the argument is that South Carolina had little need for prisons and extensive punishments for whites because of slavery, which effectively controlled the "dangerous" black population. Crimes by and among whites, on the other hand, were considered to be personal, not social, problems. In Massachusetts, on the other hand, the dangerous classes were the poor and the immigrants, mostly in cities, who had to be controlled and hopefully transformed by an impersonal criminal justice system. Both states, in their different ways, were concerned about maintaining order. His research, both in primary and secondary sources, is impressive. This study

adds significantly to our understanding of the topic, broadened in recent years by such studies as Morton J. Horwitz's *The transformation of the American law, 1780-1860* (CHOICE, June 1977). Must reading for those interested in social change in the 19th century. Extensive footnotes and bibliography. Level: advanced undergraduate through professional.

Prison and Plantation

Prison and Plantation

Crime, Justice, and Authority in Massachusetts and South Carolina, 1767–1878

by Michael Stephen Hindus

232987

The University of North Carolina Press

Chapel Hill

For Lynne

© 1980 The University of North Carolina Press
All rights reserved
Manufactured in the United States of America
Library of Congress Catalog Card Number 79-19493
ISBN 0-8078-1417-2

Library of Congress Cataloging in Publication Data

Hindus, Michael Stephen, 1946–
   Prison and plantation.

   (Studies in legal history)
   Bibliography: p.
   Includes index.
   1. Criminal justice, Administration of—South Carolina—History.
2. Criminal justice, Administration of—Massachusetts—History.
3. Crime and criminals—South Carolina—History. 4. Crime and
criminals—Massachusetts—History. I. Title. II. Series.
HV8145.S6H55   364'.9759   79-19493
ISBN 0-8078-1417-2

Contents

Tables

Figures

Acknowledgments

In the preparation of this book I have benefited from the assistance and encouragement of many people and institutions. First, I want to single out those people who made walking into a strange archive or library a less forbidding experience. Special thanks to Mrs. Granville T. Prior (South Carolina Historical Society), Allen Stokes (South Caroliniana Library), Julian Mims (Local Records, South Carolina Archives), and Charles Lee (director, South Carolina Department of Archives and History). This study would have been quite a different one if not for the counsel of R. Nicholas Olsberg, formerly of the South Carolina Archives and currently (appropriately for this study) archivist of Massachusetts. Stephen T. Riley, formerly director of the Massachusetts Historical Society, helped me exploit its resources. To the tireless staffs of the Houghton Library of Harvard University and the Huntington Library, I wish also to extend my gratitude.

Support for this research originally came from the Center for the Study of Law and Society at the University of California and the graduate schools of the University of California and the University of Minnesota. I was especially fortunate to have been a fellow of the Center when I began this study. I want to extend particular thanks to Jerome Skolnick, director of the Center, for his friendship, patience, and confidence in this project.

A Russell Sage Foundation Residency in Law and Social Science and a Liberal Arts Fellowship from Harvard Law School enabled me to broaden my sights in legal history. Were this study to benefit fully from that experience, it might not see the light of day for another decade. Support for additional research came from the American Bar Foundation, the National Endowment for the Humanities, and the American Philosophical Society.

Finally, as is so often the case in the academic world, the counsel of many scholars improved this manuscript, even while often seeming to delay it. James Kettner gave the text a thorough reading; Estelle Freedman shared with me her considerable insights into the social history of crime and punishment. My former colleagues at Minnesota, George Green and Paul Murphy, offered useful suggestions for my preliminary revision. Eric Monkkonen and I met weekly over lunch one autumn to discuss the significance of crime rates. Morris Arnold offered valuable criticisms in preparing this book for publication in the Studies in Legal History Series. Meryl Weinreb assisted in the research on crime statistics and pardons.

Parts of Chapter 3 appeared as "The Contours of Crime and Justice in Massachusetts and South Carolina, 1767–1878," in the *American Journal of Legal History* 21 (1977): 212–37; Chapter 6 appeared as "Black Justice under White Law: Criminal Prosecutions of Blacks in Antebellum South Carolina," *Journal of American History* 63 (Dec. 1976): 575–99. My thanks to the editors for permissions to reprint. Readers should be aware that the South Carolina Archives is in the process of reorganizing many of the collections referred to in the notes. Nevertheless, the notes do contain adequate information for scholars who wish to use those sources.

Far and away my greatest debt is to Lynne E. Withey. As my staunchest booster and most astute critic, she sacrificed time from her own extremely heavy workload to help see this project to completion. And she knows that that is only one of the reasons why this book is dedicated to her.

Cambridge, Massachusetts   M.S.H.
October 1978

Abbreviations

BPDS	Boston Prison Discipline Society
MBSC	Massachusetts Board of State Charities
MHS	Massachusetts Historical Society
SCA	South Carolina Department of Archives and History
SCHS	South Carolina Historical Society
SCL	South Caroliniana Library
SCMF	Spartanburg District Court of Magistrates and Freeholders
Statutes at Large	Thomas Cooper and David McCord, eds., *The Statutes at Large of South Carolina* (Columbia, S.C., 1836–73)

Introduction

The modern criminal justice system developed in America during the nineteenth century. Many of the institutions and practices that are now familiar to us, such as police forces, prisons, indeterminate sentencing, parole, and probation, had their origins in that century. Some parts of the story are well known. We have studies of the growth of urban police, of the rise of the penitentiary, of legal and penal reform, and of the dangerous class itself.[1] But we have few studies of the criminal justice system *as a system.*[2] And we have none that attempts to place this system within the context of a locality's social and legal history.

Although histories of individual components of the criminal justice system are useful, we must remember that the pieces were meant to fit together. It would be pointless, for example, to study prisons without knowing something about criminal statutes, capital punishment, sentencing discretion, police, and the courts. Similarly, it would be futile to study crime without knowing something about the legal tradition and legal culture of the locality and the social tensions that produce both crime and the means of repressing and punishing it. Whether disjointed, incoherent, or well integrated, elements of the criminal justice system functioned as a system— and those components can best be understood by looking at the systemic results. This study integrates the various elements of the criminal justice system and describes their interaction during this formative period.

During the century from the Revolution to the Gilded Age, an era of great social change, American society diversified, perhaps to a greater extent than in any subsequent period in American history. The English domination of colonial society was strained and diluted by successive waves of immigration. The nonwhite segment of the

1. James Richardson, *The New York Police* and *Urban Police in the United States;* Roger Lane, *Policing the City;* David J. Rothman, *The Discovery of the Asylum;* W. David Lewis, *From Newgate to Dannemora;* Richard Ellis, *The Jeffersonian Crisis;* Maxwell Bloomfield, *American Lawyers in a Changing Society, 1776–1876;* Eric H. Monkkonen, *The Dangerous Class.*

2. Ironically, one of the few state studies for this period is for South Carolina, Jack Kenny Williams, *Vogues in Villainy.* Aside from its frequently laudatory and anecdotal approach to the South Carolina criminal justice system, this study by intent left out blacks. An older study of unusual value is Howell M. Henry, *The Police Control of the Slave in South Carolina.*

population was proportionately greater than at any other time. And, unlike any other period of American history, the nineteenth century witnessed the flourishing of two highly sophisticated systems of production. While the Northeast was experiencing rapid industrialization and urbanization, the South refined its plantation system with significant economic success.

But why belabor the apparently obvious? Quite simply, because in order to understand the relationship between crime, justice, and society in nineteenth-century America, it is necessary to look at more than one type of society. To appreciate the uniqueness of certain developments in the Northeast, for example, we need to know not merely what preceded them, but also what was happening elsewhere.

From the revolutionary era to Reconstruction, the most important regions of the country were the North and the South. United in independence, they became the protagonists in the bloodiest organized conflict this nation has experienced, a fact that alone demands comparative analysis. But such comparative history is rare. David Rothman, in his penetrating study, *The Discovery of the Asylum*, reduced the South to a footnote.[3] But Rothman's dismissal was not unique; on the contrary, he was acting in a time-honored tradition. Almost a century and a half before, in their classic report on the penitentiary system of the United States, Gustave de Beaumont and Alexis de Tocqueville did exactly the same thing.[4] The one comparative study in the literature on crime and law is transatlantic.[5]

It is easy to see why historians of crime, justice, and law should have slighted the South. Steeped in a northeastern experience that almost seems normative, the historian searches in vain for the southern counterparts. In crime and law, the external contrasts cannot be ignored. Few southern states had penitentiaries that would be recognizable to the northern traveler or scholar. The vast network of reform societies, with their widely circulated annual reports, often tumultuous meetings, and distinct evangelical fervor, simply did not exist below Mason and Dixon's symbolic boundary. Accustomed to a different political style, legislatures—and particularly the one in South Carolina—failed to produce the reams of documents pertaining to penal matters that were a staple in the

---

3. Rothman, *Discovery*, p. 328.
4. Gustave de Beaumont and Alexis de Tocqueville, *On the Penitentiary System in the United States and Its Application in France*, p. 12n. This note was written by Francis Lieber, as editor and translater, but the authors made the same point in the text (p. 15).
5. Wilbur Miller, *Cops and Bobbies*.

North. And when southerners did write about crime and justice, it was frequently to deny the value of northern solutions and institutions to this different region.

The absence of familiar turf is further confounded by the presence in the South of one decidedly unfamiliar institution—that is, of course, slavery. Slavery altered all relationships based on class and authority, relationships that are critical to the legal and criminal justice systems. Slavery made it ideologically difficult to acknowledge the existence of a white criminal class and to legislate for its control (or for its benefit, for that matter). Blacks, who by southern ideology fit the requirements of a criminal class, were as slaves already confined for life in an institution that deprived them of their liberty. This effect of slavery was vital to the development and understanding of southern justice.

Slavery has made it easy for historians to conclude that the region lacked the complex structures of authority and justice that were emerging in the North in the nineteenth century to become the prototype for America. But obviously this is far from the case—it simply means that we must use a different focus to understand crime, justice, and authority in the South, a focus that is not dependent on northern normative notions. If there were no penitentiaries in South Carolina, we have to consider the ways in which slavery and deference perhaps eliminated the need for this sort of control.

Before we can begin this comparative enterprise, therefore, we must understand how to identify these functional equivalents and what consequences, if any, flow from these apparent dissimilarities. A functional alternative is obviously not an exact substitute, but rather an arrangement in the social structure that appears to serve a similar purpose in society. The most obvious are the plantation for the penitentiary, slaves for the criminal class. But there are others that are as striking. Police forces are an example. If Charleston did not rush to establish a Boston-style professional police force, it was in part because the object of such surveillance and control was the black population; all whites, by virtue of their skin, had "police power" over all blacks.

Functional alternatives existed in other areas of life less directly touched by slavery. For a certain class of whites, dueling was a more satisfactory way of settling grievances than was the legal system. In parts of rural South Carolina, the competency of the courts was diminished as if to promote the use of informal means of dispute settlement. Vigilantism replaced formal law enforcement in the backcountry and supplemented slave control in the years of racial tension before the secession crisis. These equations do not imply that such alternatives were superior to formal institutions of law and justice; rather, they show that societies tend to develop mechanisms for achieving a certain degree of order and providing for dispute resolution.

In order to appreciate these alternatives, however, we must use a comparative approach. Monographs in social, cultural, and economic history have made implicit comparisons between North and South. Studies of slavery have compared the bondsman's condition to that of the northern worker; studies of free blacks have compared their status to that of slaves. The economies of the two regions have been contrasted in an attempt to find an economic interpretation of the Civil War. But most of the literature to date has been comparative in an indirect sense; that is, contrasting material is usually left to notes or parenthetically included as a point of interest. There are no studies, for example, that spend equal time on northern workers and southern slaves. No one has done for social history what William R. Taylor tried to do for cultural and intellectual history.[6]

If external criteria are to be determinative, then a comparison between these two particular states becomes extraordinarily elusive. In the area of legal and penal reform, for example, few northern states were as innovative as Massachusetts, few southern states as recalcitrant as South Carolina. Massachusetts, therefore, cannot represent the typical northern state, nor South Carolina the typical southern state. But, in making a regional comparison, regional patterns are evident. The building of prisons and the proliferation of reform groups characterized the Northeast. Similarly, slavery, plantation justice and slave codes, a high number of capital offenses, and difficulty in obtaining divorce characterized southern states. Factories, cities, and immigrants typified the North; slaves and farms the South. Obviously, states, unlike towns and cities, are too distinctive for any one to serve as a prototype. But regional trends and characteristics can be identified. We can use these two states to show how two distinct systems of criminal justice evolved in the United States, and we can go one step further. We can take these outward, striking contrasts and see whether the actual functions and purposes of law in each society were as different as we may at first glance suspect.

While the most important contrasts in the study are the regional ones, significant changes occurred over the century. During this time, the Massachusetts penal system evolved, with police forces, a state prison, and legal revision. Even South Carolina was not static.

6. William R. Taylor, *Cavalier and Yankee.*

By the Civil War, the state had reduced the number of capital offenses, begun court reorganization, and reformed somewhat the system of trying slaves. Nevertheless, the most striking contrasts are not the ones over time, but the ones between the two states, both at the beginning and at the end of the period studied.

With this comparative approach, we can trace the development of criminal justice in American history, place the criminal justice system in the context of both the social structure and the legal system, and contrast crucial developments in crime, law, and justice for an urbanizing, industrializing free state and a rural slave state. These contrasts permeated every aspect of life in the two states. But we should not let contrast turn into stereotype. Both states were common law jurisdictions and ostensibly followed the rule of law, a collection of post-Enlightenment principles proclaiming universality of laws, procedural rights, and neutral judges. If formal adherence to the rule of law was mechanically maintained in each state, however, little illumination would be gained by a comparative study. But such concepts are ideal types. The legal systems in both Massachusetts and South Carolina were far from ideal, and we can find elements of both traditional and bureaucratic justice present in each of them. But traditional authority played a greater role in the legal system of South Carolina than in Massachusetts, in part because of slavery, in part because of the state's historical legal culture, and in part because it seemed to be well suited to that particular society. Actual operation of a legal system is, of course, more important that the formal ideals it may espouse.

There are, as I have indicated, different ways of exercising authority in a society. By studying the legal system, I have chosen to emphasize the formal, bureaucratic system of law and authority that seemed suitable to the emerging modern state which Massachusetts with its complex economy and diverse population was becoming in the nineteenth century. But, although it clearly is easy to contrast these two states on the basis of differences in their economic and social structures, this study is concerned less with those contrasts per se than with the suitability of each legal system for its particular society. To this end, we must consider the importance of elements of customary law. In contrast to the impersonal, virtually autonomous, bureaucratic authority, customary authority is personal and individualistic. Rigid norms yield to an intricate if less articulated system based on personal contact, on relative positions in the status hierarchy, and on certain immediate and frequently symbolic needs to be served.

Although we find that many obvious and external symbols of

bureaucratic authority were present in Massachusetts and lacking in South Carolina, our interpretation cannot be complete until we have considered what alternate forms of authority flourished in South Carolina instead. As important as the key structural and institutional contrasts revealed in this study is the discovery that in many ways, the legal system that developed in each society was not only well suited to the particular needs of that society, but also, and less obviously, served the same functional ends.

The historical study of crime is of special importance. Criminal laws are enacted to embody, preserve, and enforce societal values. Punishment indicates the importance of the preservation of those norms. There are other ways in which society registers disapproval of behavior. Churches in colonial New England disciplined and excommunicated violators of religious norms. Artisan guilds and merchant organizations policed their professional codes. Parents punished children (and occasionally each other), and communities ostracized those who overstepped certain boundaries.

But the criminal sanction is unique. Criminal laws are intended to embody the most general norms of a society, whereas the other sanctions are parochial (in the case of the church), limited in scope (as in business and commerce), or local (families and neighborhoods). Furthermore, violators of the criminal law are dealt with by the institutions that, in theory at least, represent the entire collective will of a society. Therefore, the criminal justice system is intended to deal with those offenses that are both so significant that the other forms of control and sanction are not sufficiently effective and so threatening that the entire resources of the state may be marshaled against them.

The history of crime and justice is also part of legal history, and the findings here are compatible with the major synthesis of nineteenth-century legal history. This synthesis stresses the relationship between law and the economy that helped pave the way for large-scale commercial and industrial development.[7] The same values that the legal system endorsed for the sake of economic growth —certainty, predictability, and rationality—can be found in the criminal justice system of Massachusetts. In South Carolina, where a different economy demanded only that the legal order protect the slave system, these economic goals were not incorporated into the criminal justice system. On the other hand, the legal system of the South was a major linchpin of the slaveholding regime.

---

7. The best-known formulation of this view is J. Willard Hurst, *Law and the Conditions of Freedom in the Nineteenth-Century United States.*

The most influential book in legal history in recent years has described a transformation of American law in roughly the same years covered by this current study.[8] Looking at every state, Morton Horwitz suggests that this transformation was a national phenomenon; local variations are noted, but are not considered significant. Even within this majestic and stimulating scope, however, we can note that South Carolina stands out as an aberration and Massachusetts as perhaps the norm. Although this study does not concern doctrine, it is noteworthy that while Massachusetts under Joseph Story and Lemuel Shaw forged the synthesis of law and economic growth, an interpretation of South Carolina doctrine remains more complex. Although its commercial decisions were in the vanguard of American law, South Carolina maintained a medieval marriage and property law, out of step with the rest of the country, but compatible with the dynastic aspirations of its leading planters.

Massachusetts and South Carolina are natural cases to use in order to illustrate regional differences. Both were founded as colonies in the seventeenth century, and their legal histories are indigenous. By the nineteenth century, however, they symbolized totally different ways of life. In fact, on the eve of secession, the two states seemed to have had almost their own private civil war. When Samuel Hoar arrived in Charleston from Massachusetts to attempt to mediate the dispute over the Negro Seaman's Acts, he was hounded out of town under the threat of personal violence. And certainly it was no accident that a senator from Massachusetts so incensed a congressman from South Carolina that the latter felt driven to caning his adversary to insensibility. When South Carolinians deplored the anarchy of the North, their favorite examples were the burning of the convent and the rescue of fugitive slaves, both chapters in the Bay State's history. The southerners lumped these two events together, but in Massachusetts they were viewed quite differently. The burning of the convent was a capitulation to bigotry, superstition, and fear, but the fugitive slave rescues represented the triumph of liberty.

The differences between the two states were very real in terms of population, ethnicity, and culture. Massachusetts was the most heavily urbanized state in the country; South Carolina was one of the most rural. But even that contrast only touches the surface. Both states had major cities that were regional centers. But in addition Massachusetts had several lesser cities of considerable importance, such as Worcester, Salem, New Bedford, and Fall River. In South

8. Morton J. Horwitz, *The Transformation of American Law, 1780–1860.*

Carolina, beyond Charleston, there was only Columbia, a sleepy college town that was also the state capital. Columbia had 8,069 residents in 1860; Massachusetts had eighteen places with at least that population.

Massachusetts was also one of the major magnets for foreign and domestic migrants. In 1860, 21 percent of the population was foreign-born and 35 percent was born outside the state. South Carolina, by contrast, was no magnet at all. Only 3 percent of the white population was foreign-born; 8 percent were born out of state, and the most salient fact about the state's migration trends was that native South Carolinians were leaving in huge numbers. Of course, the ethnic component of the state's population was far less significant than its racial makeup. South Carolina was 59 percent black in 1860; no other state had that large a proportion. Individual districts were up to 86 percent black. In Massachusetts, by contrast, less than 1 percent of the population was black.

The economies of the two states were very different. Historically a commercial center, Massachusetts became the American prototype for industrialization. The labor system at Lowell attracted almost as many visitors as did the state's prisons. South Carolina, by contrast, had some of the most highly developed forms of plantation organization, and slavery, too, attracted the inquisitive visitor.

The two states can be contrasted culturally as well. In Massachusetts, Horace Mann established a uniform statewide system of public education. South Carolina had no free school system at all, although there were small state educational subsidies to the districts. Formal education in South Carolina was a class-based privilege. Massachusetts was a hotbed of agitation for all sorts of social issues; South Carolina had virtually no social reform societies. Yet, Nullification and secession galvanized the state into action. South Carolina citizens were the only ones in the Union who did not vote for presidential electors; the legislature chose the electors and the governor as well. With no opportunity for choice, South Carolina spawned no competing political parties.

In short, despite their common participation in the growing nation, despite their common English tradition, despite their unity in the relatively recent struggle for independence, it is obvious that South Carolina and Massachusetts were different in ways that were not merely cosmetic but fundamental.

Criminal justice evolved differently in the two states for three reasons: tradition, economic and social development, and slavery. From the days of Puritan holy watching in the seventeenth century, law played a significant role in the lives of Massachusetts citizens.

Much of colonial South Carolina, by contrast, was a frontier society, where alternatives to formal authority had to be found. These traditions influenced subsequent developments in both states, causing Massachusetts authority to remain activist, while South Carolina valued a laissez-faire approach. This traditional pattern was suited not so much to the backcountry (where the extreme lack of formal authority led to the Regulator rebellion in the 1760s) but to the plantation areas where aristocrats could live like manor lords.

Tradition, evolving from conditions of settlement as well as from the ideas of those who settled each colony, explains why divergences between Massachusetts and South Carolina are clear even in the colonial era, preceding the massive social changes of the nineteenth century. For example, by the Revolution, South Carolina had ten times as many capital offenses in its criminal code as did Massachusetts. Massachusetts had been gradually (if slowly) revising its seventeenth-century Mosaic code, but South Carolina had already shown great reluctance to alter its 1712 penal code. Each state had a frontier rebellion over courts, the Regulators in South Carolina (1766–67) and Shays's Rebellion in Massachusetts (1785). But while the South Carolina protesters demanded more courts to tame the backcountry, the Massachusetts rebels wanted to stem the oppressive encroachment of centralized authority into the Berkshires. Each state's legal heritages, then, were significant in shaping their subsequent legal histories.

A second reason why criminal justice evolved differently can be found in the contrasting needs of the new economic order in Massachusetts and of the South Carolina plantation. The manorial authority of the planter was supported, not superseded, by the state. An ideology of deference—whether it be among whites or across races—obviated the need for meticulous legal regulation of the affairs of society. In Massachusetts, by contrast, the pace of social change outstripped the ability of traditional mechanisms of control and order. Family, church, and community proved inadequate guardians of virtue and morals in an increasingly transient and anonymous society. State authority was exercised on behalf of capital and property. A laboring class of immigrants and migrants required the inculcation of the new factory-inspired values of hard work, self-control, and self-denial.

The impersonal and complex society produced by social and economic change had to deal with deviance on a large-scale basis. Criminal justice had to be routinized. Institutional controls—permanent, universalistic, and dependable—were seen as the only way to keep the lid on crime and disorder.

Tradition and economic development are important to understanding differences in the use of extralegal authority, the rise of the penitentiary, and the like. But perhaps the single most important factor was slavery. Above all, as Charles Sydnor pointed out decades ago, slavery created a class that was virtually beyond the law.[9] South Carolina whites became accustomed to dealing with a majority of that state's population without any serious restrictions. Moreover, slavery altered all class relations in the South. Rather than wishing to inculcate middle-class virtues in the criminal, dangerous, and laboring classes, as was the goal in Massachusetts, South Carolinians conceived of their dangerous and criminal class as one which by its innate inferiority could not be salvaged. This meant, of course, that no reformatory sentence was ever contemplated for South Carolina slaves.

But slavery altered relations among whites as well. Although a fifth of the state's white population was living at a subsistence level, no poor, dangerous, or laboring class of whites was ever officially recognized. The only serious notice taken of the mass of poor whites appeared in the ill-fated attempt to reopen the slave trade in the mid-1850s, the purpose being to broaden the slaveholding base, already the broadest in the nation. This plan would have taken care of the ambiguous status of the poor whites by ensuring that the society consisted solely of two classes, masters and slaves.

These three basic contrasts—tradition, social development, and slavery—pervade all aspects of the study. The first section contrasts the ways in which authority was exercised in the two states. Massachusetts consistently sought to bolster the role of formal authority by strengthening its courts, establishing police, and curbing extralegal violence. In South Carolina, however, plantation aristocrats mocked court laws, took their quarrels to the dueling field instead of the courthouse, belatedly established police, supported permanent vigilante organizations, and actually encouraged citizens to find extralegal accommodations rather than increase strife through lawsuits.

The pattern of crime, prosecution, and punishment in the two states shows how crime was related both to the social order and to the differences between the two societies. In Massachusetts, crimes against property and propriety were the most common. Both types of offenses challenged the demand for order in the new industrial

9. The classic analysis of southern attitudes toward law is Charles Sydnor's "The Southerner and the Laws."

era. In South Carolina, by contrast, crimes of violence were the most common among whites. Crime against property was seen almost exclusively as the work of slaves. Because white crime was seen as the product of passions, not hunger, it was hardly a cause for alarm or action. As a result, archaic statutes and conscience-stricken juries freed over two-thirds of those arraigned. In Massachusetts, where crime and disorder appeared to threaten the fragile new order, conviction rates were twice as high.

If white crime created little alarm in South Carolina, slave crime had almost the opposite effect. Slaves were prosecuted for crimes against property, convicted at rates comparable to those in Massachusetts, punished severely, and executed at shocking rates. On the other hand, slaves were afforded little protection against white abuse.

Slavery may not have been a "total institution," but it was still the one to which most black South Carolinians were confined. The only equivalent in the North was the penitentiary, repository for the most dangerous of the dangerous class. While the plantation represented commercial agriculture in a slave society in its most highly developed form, the Massachusetts State Prison took its cue (and its system of labor and discipline) from the new industrial order.

Finally, this study examines the impetus for legal and penal reform. In Massachusetts, efforts to render the legal and penal system rational, responsive, and predictable received widespread support. Proponents of statute reform, penal reform, and abolition of the death penalty realized many of their desired goals, although all stopped short of complete success. In South Carolina, even the most modest proposals for eliminating some of the more bizarre and antiquated features of the legal and penal systems were summarily rejected.

Reform failed in one state and gained a hearing in the other for many reasons. Chief among them was the existence (or absence) of a culture of reform, the extent to which the aims of reform varied from the status quo, and the views of society and of the classes in it held by each state. Environmentalist thought in Massachusetts, spurred by religious fervor, led to a penal policy that stressed rehabilitation. Only a small minority of even the dangerous class was considered beyond hope. In South Carolina, by contrast, the association of crime with race meant that rehabilitation was impossible, unnecessary, and undesirable. Ironically, Massachusetts began to move away from its optimistic posture after decades of penal reform failed to alter the crime problem. By the 1860s, environmentalism, with its promise of reclamation, began to yield to the less flexible and less optimistic tenets of heredity and stock.

It should be clear that, although I view the Massachusetts experience as the prototype of our modern criminal justice system, there is little in that system to cheer about. Furthermore, although the structure, laws, and institutions are those of Massachusetts, some of the values—particularly the association of crime with race or nativity—are those of South Carolina. And that, most certainly, is nothing to cheer about. Massachusetts would hardly be eager to accept credit for the criminal justice system as we know it today, but the South Carolina experience clearly shows that there was no virtue in intransigence, nor in a legal and penal system based on extralegal terror, fatal notions of honor, and racial supremacy. By offering a contrasting model with which to view the institutions so familiar to us, this study demonstrates that there was nothing inevitable, linear, or progressive about our history of criminal justice. And perhaps this study should begin on a cautionary note, recalling the words of Samuel Gridley Howe, who warned over a century ago that "institutions . . . so strongly built, so richly endowed . . . cannot be got rid of so easily." Not in 1865, when those words were written, and apparently not now.

Part I
The Contours of Authority

Crime and criminal justice are important components of a society's system of authority. The criminal sanction is the state's way of dealing with undesirable behavior; family, church, and neighborhoods have other ways that are often more effective. The formal quality of the state's response distinguishes crime from other undesirable behavior. But criminal justice is only part of the larger legal order; indeed, to many it is a relatively unimportant part. To appreciate the institutional context of crime and justice, we must look at the legal system as a whole. After all, the same court system heard both civil and criminal cases, and the same judges presided. Issues in court organization and the configuration of authority may have been prompted primarily by the demands of the law in the civil, private realm, rather than the public, criminal arena, but the end result affected criminal proceedings as well.

By looking at the formal structures of authority, we can begin to see what role the rule of law played in ordering the affairs of society in the two states studied here. In South Carolina, that role was minimal; the law did not reach many areas of life, institutions such as courts were kept weak, and local instruments of law enforcement ranged from ineffective to incompetent. The meaning of the South Carolina experience is not that the state was relegated to medieval barbarity (as some proponents of change were wont to describe it). Rather, if we must use a crude historical metaphor, the more appropriate one would be feudal order, the maintenance of authority and control by the dominant elite over the subordinate population by means of custom and deference. South Carolina, with its extraordinary capital investment in commercial agriculture, was far from a feudal society, but it was a society in which the classical notions of the rule of law had very little appeal. To the extent that it was a well-ordered society, South Carolina was not predominantly ordered by formal, legal structures of authority. South Carolina had only some of the form and very little of the substance of the democratic rule of law.

In Massachusetts, by contrast, formal authority played a large role. Judicial authority was centralized, and attempts were made to keep the courts efficient. Disorder was controlled by the first professional police force in the United States. And law figured prominently in the private affairs of the state's citizens, regulating personal conduct in ways that South Carolina law failed to touch.

In both states, the legal systems were imperfect. As independent bases of power, courts were particularly troublesome for the governing elite. South Carolina's solution was to reduce the role of courts to prevent their becoming a power base that could threaten planter hegemony. Although life tenure for judges appeared to guarantee judicial independence in Massachusetts, court reorganization could serve as a pretext for installing judges of the proper political stripe, thus accomplishing in the name of reform what in other branches of government was achieved by the traditional patronage route (and, it might be noted, rout). In Massachusetts we see form: strong courts and agencies of law enforcement, statutory intervention to order private affairs. But substance is another matter. Police frequently placed class control ahead of crime control, legislation seemed to proscribe the habits of the politically powerless lower classes, and clogged dockets and protracted delays reduced the efficacy of this neatly designed authority structure.

In this first section I will probe the systems of formal authority in each state and will try to assess the relative strengths of the formal and informal systems of authority. The first chapter looks at courts and law enforcement. The next chapter defines the penetration of law in daily life through a comparison of the reach of statutory criminal law and the role of extralegal and informal means of law enforcement and dispute settlement.

Chapter 1.
The Structures of Authority

In the decades following the American Revolution, many states reorganized their judicial systems as part of the general overhaul of the political system demanded both by the rebels and by the fact of independence. Finding the proper relationship between courts and citizens was crucial. Experience had shown that the judiciary was an extremely dangerous and a potentially repressive institution. More important, the judiciary was the most significant contact between citizen and government in the early republic; frequently it was the only contact. Not surprisingly, therefore, the structure of the judiciary was a crucial issue in both Massachusetts and South Carolina.

Since courts mediated between conflicting parties and interests in society, court organization naturally was a cause for concern. Where courts were located, how often they sat, and for how long determined popular accessibility to formal justice and authority. The quality of talent on the bench influenced public respect for the judiciary and therefore its willingness to use courts to settle disputes. Finally, the degree to which disputes were resolved by the courts ultimately determined the utility of the court system. Appeals, errors, and delays could undermine its value.

The Structure of the Courts

Over the course of the period from the Revolution to the Civil War, South Carolina and Massachusetts both experimented with different forms of court organization. South Carolina was mired in tradition and easily influenced by parochial political considerations, whereas Massachusetts appeared to move toward efficiency and rationality, consistent with contemporary trends in law. Nevertheless, despite the obvious structural differences, the results in each state were similar. By the eve of the Civil War, neither state's court system had solved completely the problems of political interference, accessibility, and delay.

Courts provided the setting for severe and frequently violent struggles over the nature of authority in the late eighteenth century.[1] Two of the most significant backcountry rebellions involving courts occurred in Massachusetts and South Carolina. Protesting the lack of formal authority in the crime-ridden upcountry of South Carolina, leading citizens formed the Regulators and in 1767 used vigilante action to fill the vacuum of authority. Less than two decades later, in western Massachusetts, followers of Daniel Shays took to arms to protest the oppressiveness of local courts directed from Boston.

These two armed rebellions can be compared for what they reveal about the role of the judiciary in society. In each case the protesters were settlers to somewhat newly organized areas in a state and a colony with centralized political authority. In the Regulator era, South Carolina had only one court, sitting in Charleston. The refusal to extend courts into the backcountry was symptomatic of the attempt of the lowcountry planters to prevent any challenge to their autonomy. Lowcountry manor lords feared that additional courts would be the opening wedge to the political organization of the backcountry that in turn would lead to demands for the sharing of political power. This is exactly what happened, but by the time it did, lowcountry planters realized that hegemony need not depend on political power alone. The Regulator affair was only the beginning of a century-long and ultimately unsuccessful attempt in South Carolina to find the appropriate relationship between courts and the citizenry.

Shays's Rebellion sought to curb rather than extend the authority of the courts. This revolt, like the Regulator episode, marked a critical juncture in the history of authority in the state. Like the Regulators, who protested the concentration of authority in Charleston, the Shaysites protested Boston's domination of the state's judicial affairs. The western Massachusetts rebels believed that the courts were responsive only to the commercial interests of the metropolis. In the interest of establishing a credible currency and credit system, Massachusetts courts offered no relief to the hordes of debtors victimized by economic circumstances beyond their control.

The agrarian rebellions in both South Carolina and Massachusetts were symptomatic of the problems of establishing authority on the

1. Many of the changes described in this chapter apply specifically to courts handling civil business only. The focus of this section is primarily on authority, however, and patterns of authority in general affect how citizens relate to criminal justice. In South Carolina particularly, problems of court organization in the civil area affected criminal courts as well.

frontier. But the aftermath in South Carolina was uncertainty, as the state groped with a number of different schemes in an attempt to create a court system that would be neither too distant to be of any use nor too near to be oppressive, neither too subservient to be credible nor too independent to be troublesome. In Massachusetts, by contrast, the Shaysites' banner was never again raised. The state would constantly grope for the proper balance of jurisdictions, but the desirability of a strong, centrally directed judiciary was no longer doubted.

The proper distance between courts and citizens was an issue that continued to plague South Carolina long after the Regulator affair. Prerevolutionary South Carolina suffered from too few courts; postrevolutionary South Carolina seemed to have too many. Two events in the last two decades of the eighteenth century typified the state's inability to find a suitable posture between courts and the citizenry. The first was the Camden court protest of 1785, an uncanny miniaturization of Shays's Rebellion. The second was the birth and premature death of the county court system.

The new court system that followed the Regulator protest was hardly established before the Revolution disrupted all judicial functions. After the Revolution, attempts to establish a court system were influenced by current conditions. Just like their counterparts in western Massachusetts, rural South Carolinians, in the words of Judge Joseph Brevard, "were deeply involved in debt."[2]

Beginning in 1783, the aristocratic, planter-dominated legislature passed several measures that were not merely unsympathetic, but demonstrably hostile to the debtors' plight. The first was a depreciation table that stipulated that debts had to be paid in currency equivalent to the value of the obligation when originally contracted, depriving the debtor of the classic benefit of inflation. In the following year the jurisdiction of the Charleston Court of Wardens was expanded to include nonpayment of debts. Finally, in March 1785, quarterly county courts were established in this state, where any courts outside of Charleston were a recent and (because they were closed during the Revolution) inconclusive experiment.

These courts were composed of each county's justices of the peace meeting *en banc.* South Carolina also had biannual district circuit courts, equivalent to *nisi prius* terms, conducted by the individual appellate judges. District courts were further divided into General Sessions (criminal), and Common Pleas (civil, with separate ses-

2. Reprinted in 1 *Statutes at Large,* p. 434.

sions for law and equity). The county courts had long been the pet project of Judge Henry Pendleton, who modeled them after those of his native Virginia, and the timing may have been coincidental. South Carolina had been the only colony without county courts.[3] But debtors could hardly have taken solace in the title of the bill that established the courts "for the more expeditious determination of suits and controversies and the recovery of debts."[4] Debtors in 1785 faced new and repressive measures of repayment and a legislature more interested in easing the conditions of foreclosure than in alleviating their plight.

This was the setting of the Camden court protest of 1785, a significant event not only for its similarity to the Shaysite struggle, but also for shedding light on the subsequent fate of the county courts. News of the new courts may not have even reached the upcountry town of Camden by late April, but the government's lack of sympathy for the debtor was well known. On 23 April 1785, Judge John Faucheraud Grimké rode into town expecting to convene the spring term of the district circuit court. He was confronted by a group of citizens who presented him with a memorial "in consequence of the very great grievance that the citizens of this district labor under on account of the many law suits which are brought against them and the very great scarcity of money which renders them unable to discharge their debts with cash." The protesters demanded that the forthcoming court session not handle any debt cases, that no executions already ordered be completed, and that property be accepted as full payment provided that three-fourths of its assessed value satisfy the debt. Recognizing that "in all probability the law will for some time be dormant," the protesters promised to "suppress every species of villainy that shall be committed during the suspension" and agreed to support the court in criminal matters. The aristocratic judge would have no part of this protest, complaining that the whole affair "had wounded the credit of the District." Although Grimké held his ground, he was unable to compel the appearance of any jurors and was forced to adjourn the court.[5]

The Camden debtors accomplished their two main goals. The court session was blocked, and six months later the legislature passed the Pine Barrens Act. This measure enacted one of the spe-

3. James W. Ely, Jr., "American Independence and the Law," pp. 958–62; the County Court Act is 7 *Statutes at Large*, pp. 211–42; John M. Murrin, "Anglicizing an American Colony," p. 163n.

4. 7 *Statutes at Large*, p. 211.

5. Memorial to the Governor Respecting the Disturbances at Camden April Court, 1785, Grimké Family Papers, SCHS.

cific demands of the protesters—that land could be tendered as payment for debts.[6] By their support of the court in criminal matters and their promise to treat officers of the court "with the utmost civility"[7] the dissidents showed their basic acceptance of authority, but resistance to its oppressive encroachment.

The Camden affair illustrates the hostility directed at the judiciary during these years. The conditions under which the county courts were established help to explain why this system lasted only slightly longer than a decade. The courts met quarterly in thirty-four county seats and were staffed by seven justices of the peace elected by the legislature. The county system itself was an unwelcome innovation, threatening to impose local government onto the rural backcountry; the districts, by contrast, had virtually no political significance. Although civil jurisdiction was limited and the criminal jurisdiction did not extend to felonies, these courts were important fixtures in the state's legal apparatus.[8]

The justices of these courts were generally an untalented lot, and the premature demise of the system was attributed to their incompetence. In an effort in 1788 to improve the quality of these tribunals, Judge Grimké published his manual, *The South Carolina Justice of the Peace*. Grimké noted "the strange and illegal irregularities which have been committed by magistrates and the officers of the several criminal courts," but charitably attributed this situation to the lack of a current digest of laws and procedures. He doubted that more than half a dozen complete copies of the state's laws were extant.[9]

Grimké's efforts seem to have been to little avail; the quality of the courts showed no improvement. Judge Joseph Brevard called their justice "tedious and defective . . . loose and imperfect."[10] The courts prompted Judge Adamus Burke to comment, "The law ought to be like a wall through which the lions . . . could not break, but now it is . . . rotten."[11] Even Henry Pendleton, the founder of these courts, soured on them. They were "too much dependent upon ignorant and rough men," he conceded. "That mistakes, prejudice,

6. 4 *Statutes at Large*, pp. 710–12; Ely, "American Independence," p. 942.

7. Memorial to the Governor, Grimké Papers.

8. 7 *Statutes at Large*, pp. 211–42.

9. John F. Grimké, *The South Carolina Justice of the Peace*, p. v; the most recent compilation before Grimké's had been published in 1761, William Simpson, *The Practical Justice of the Peace*.

10. Joseph Brevard, *An Alphabetical Digest of the Public Statute Law of South Carolina*, 1 : xvi.

11. Quoted in John Belton O'Neall, *Biographical Sketches of the Bench and Bar of South Carolina*, 1:38.

and gross errors should have been the result . . . ought to have been expected." That they were extremely unpopular in some counties is evident. When the court for Winton was abolished, the citizenry celebrated by burning down the courthouse.[12]

The poor quality of these tribunals is too readily documented to be seriously questioned, but other factors also contributed to their demise. The courts were subjected to frequent changes in their operation and jurisdiction. Such measures were not merely symptoms of dissatisfaction, but were also attempts to cripple them by whittling away their authority. In the same year in which it established the courts, the legislature considered changing the mode of selecting the justices. In 1786, their jurisdiction in larceny cases was increased, but thereafter their functions and fortunes declined. In 1790, justices were ordered to sit without pay, a move that did nothing to improve their quality. The following year civil suits for assault and battery were removed from their jurisdiction because "great mischiefs have arisen . . . from the power vested in justices of the peace." Seven years later the courts were stripped of all judicial functions, retaining only the supervisory ones. Finally, in 1799, the legislature dropped the other shoe and abolished the county courts while vastly expanding the district circuit courts.[13]

All these measures point to substantial dissatisfaction with the way these courts were run and with the local justices who staffed them. But another current runs through the history of the county courts that goes to the heart of the nature of authority in South Carolina. This is the massive refusal of parts of the state, particularly the coastal plantation areas, to have anything to do with these courts—and the subsequent sanction given to this resistance by the legislature in making such courts a matter of local option. In 1788, before the legislature had formally responded to this resistance, Grimké stated that the coastal areas refused to accede to the county court act: "The maritime districts adher[ed] to the old method of conducting their legal proceedings . . . , and the interior districts revolt[ed] therefrom, and embrac[ed] the new measure of dividing the country into counties and establishing an inferior court of justice in each of them[. This] has created two sorts of magistrates and two species of law."[14]

Resistance to the county courts eventually became so widespread that it cannot be ascribed to lowcountry planter autocracy alone.

12. Ibid., pp. 31–33.
13. *South Carolina House Journal*, 1785; 7 *Statutes at Large*, pp. 243, 266, 268, 287, 291.
14. Grimké, *South Carolina Justice*, p. vi.

But this resistance took two forms. The most extreme originated in the lowcountry areas; many districts refused to have anything whatsoever to do with the new system. The legislature freely recognized this fact; rather than enforcing the county court act, it merely extended the jurisdiction of magistrates and justices of the peace "where there are no county courts established." By 1791, the legislature adopted a policy of permitting the abolition of the courts in counties where a majority of the citizens were clearly opposed to them.[15]

In applying this principle, the legislature seemed more responsive to lowcountry discontent than to upcountry reservations. In 1791, it suspended the county courts in Beaufort and Georgetown "because the majority of the inhabitants . . . are desirous that the court . . . not be continued."[16] But the legislature, unconvinced that the opposition represented majority sentiment, rejected similar appeals from the interior districts of Newberry, Fairfield, and Clarendon. At least one legislative committee declared that majority sentiment should not determine judicial policy—an acceptable position, but one that created a double standard between the two regions. In 1792, in response to new remonstrances from Newberry and Fairfield, the legislature noted significant opposition to the courts resulting from the "maladministration of justice" and called for remedial action. Although hostility to the county courts was widespread, the most effective opposition to the county courts came from the lowcountry. The solitary defense of the county courts came from the extreme upcountry district of Ninety-Six, whose grand jury complained about "the late attempt by the enemies of the County Courts to destroy that valuable institution."[17]

Since lowcountry districts, if Grimké's tone is any guide, simply resisted such courts, judicial incompetence cannot explain all the opposition. More likely, the county courts—ill-staffed to be sure—were caught in a dispute between the old colonial parishes and the newly settled upcountry districts over the nature of centralized authority. Over half a century later a South Carolina legislator blamed the downfall of the county courts on "inherent objections to that sort of tribunal."[18] Undoubtedly, the problem was a product of the difference between coastal and inland society. Each section had conflicting conceptions of the role of formal authority. Lowcountry planters likened themselves to manor lords. Not only did they as-

15. 7 *Statutes at Large*, pp. 246–49.
16. Ibid., p. 266.
17. Presentment of the Grand Jury of Ninety-Six (n.d., but probably 1790s), SCHS.
18. *South Carolina Legislative Times*, p. 245.

sume control over their households and slaves, they resented and opposed the intrusion into their own affairs which the quarterly courts represented. Staffed by people of generally lower status and limited to petty jurisdiction, those courts could have only been considered a nuisance.

By the turn of the century, South Carolina had not established a suitable relationship between courts and citizens. Events during the previous third of a century had demonstrated how strongly its residents felt about the proper posture of courts. Courts were both established and closed by force or the threat of force. Lowcountry planters could decide to have nothing whatsoever to do with certain courts—and get away with it. This paradoxical behavior demonstrates the lack of consensus on the role of formal authority and shows how poorly entrenched such authority was when it conflicted with the wishes of the dominant planters. Force soon disappeared as a significant element in South Carolina's judicial history, but the legitimacy of a strong, independent judiciary was never on firm ground in the antebellum years, in large part because of the indifference and hostility of planters, who resisted any competing claim of authority.

The demise of the county courts must also be understood in the context of the state's legal tradition. Since such traditions were powerful forces in shaping the structure and operation of the courts, it is hardly a coincidence that the structure of the judiciary in both states remained remarkably similar to that which was erected in the early nineteenth century. South Carolina lacked a tradition of local, low-level courts and treated their creation as an intrusion on local authority patterns. In Massachusetts, by contrast, quarterly county courts existed from the onset of settlement; centralized control was not a burning issue in Massachusetts, but delay and efficiency were. Shays's Rebellion, in addition to being a protest against metropolitan domination, was also directed against the way the legal system was run. Many of the problems first attacked by Shays were never settled.

Farmers in western Massachusetts after the Revolution were, like their South Carolina counterparts, deeply in debt. Confronted by several courts of overlapping jurisdiction, extra taxes on legal paper, and an unsympathetic bar with an oppressive fee system, they, too, turned their wrath toward the judiciary. Almost from the time courts tried to resume business following the Revolution, groups of debtors delayed, harassed, and obstructed the proceedings.[19] Shays's Rebellion culminated these years of dissent, but, whereas the Cam-

---

19. Robert J. Taylor, *Western Massachusetts in the Revolution*, pp. 75–76, 103, 116.

den protesters achieved some success, the Shaysites received nothing other than pardons for their convictions of treason. The hated fee schedule was not appreciably altered. Attorneys charged for every day they sat in court for a client, represented several clients, and charged this daily fee to each one. One response to the complaints of judicial harassment was to reduce the number of court sessions. Apparently, the legislature overreacted. By 1789, Governor John Hancock recommended additional sessions: "I am inclined to believe that the plan lately adopted of drawing but two courts of Common Pleas, and two courts of Sessions annually in each county, will not have the salutory effects which were expected from it; and that more courts, in nearly all the counties, will be of great advantage to the people."[20]

The problems plaguing the Massachusetts courts were similar to those confronted by courts in South Carolina. In both states, civil cases routinely took years to settle. The lawyers' fee system offered no incentive for speeding up the process. Cases took so long to be heard that each client incurred a substantial bill simply from "waiting time."[21]

A judicial system ought to be final arbiter of disputes. At the close of the eighteenth century, the vital elements of certainty and decisiveness were missing from the judiciary of both South Carolina and Massachusetts. The problems were similar—long delays, frequent (and frivolous) appeals, and lack of a final decision—but causes varied in each state. In South Carolina, the situation was a product of crowded dockets, overworked judges, and political interference. In Massachusetts, these problems were exacerbated by an appellate procedure that granted new trials with unusual ease, a system by which juries decided both fact and law, and seriatim charges by judges.

Although the problems were similar in each state, the responses were very different. South Carolina did not make headway on these structural problems until 1868, although improvements were made in 1824 and 1859. Massachusetts, on the other hand, undertook elaborate court reform in the first decade of the nineteenth century.[22] In taking this course, Massachusetts vastly increased the role

20. *Laws and Resolves of Massachusetts, 1788–89*, p. 751.

21. A good discussion of these problems can be found in Richard E. Ellis, *The Jeffersonian Crisis*, pp. 184–87.

22. Ibid., pp. 184–229; F. W. Grinnell, "The Constitutional History of the Supreme Judicial Court of Massachusetts from the Revolution to 1813," pp. 495–507, 519–41; Richard E. Welch, Jr., "The Parsons-Sedgwick Feud and the Reform of the Massachusetts Judiciary," pp. 171–87.

and influence of the judiciary in society; systematic neglect in South Carolina had the opposite effect.

Court reform in Massachusetts involved not only reorganization but also substantive changes in judicial procedure. The need for change was obvious. At the turn of the century, observed Isaac Parker, Massachusetts courts were "inadequate to the establishment of a course of proceedings and uniformity of decisions so necessary to the safe and satisfactory administration of justice."[23] The court system of postrevolutionary Massachusetts was inefficient and chaotic. Every county had a court of General Sessions, composed of the county's justices of the peace sitting collectively. Similar in form to South Carolina's ill-fated county court, it reflected the common English legal heritage.

But just as the South Carolina county courts were weakened before their ultimate demise, so, too, General Sessions progressively lost its criminal jurisdiction. Its second major function was the administration of county government—roads, taverns, poor relief, and bastardy cases. Here, too, Sessions went into eclipse, as standardized procedures for poor relief (such as institutionalization) replaced the highly individualized system of warning out. Furthermore, as judicial control of sexual behavior became moribund after the Revolution, Sessions lost much of its justification for continued existence.[24]

The main trial courts were the Court of Common Pleas (in its various incarnations) and the Supreme Judicial Court (which had substantial original jurisdiction in addition to its appellate jurisdiction). A system of virtually automatic appeals and trials *de novo* sapped this arrangement of any efficiency or rationality. Initially, all justices of the Supreme Judicial Court had to hear civil cases invoking its original jurisdiction. A case decided within two years was considered exemplary. A modification in 1799 enlarging the Supreme Judicial Court to seven justices and requiring that only three hear such cases did little to alleviate the delays.[25] New trials were easily obtainable on facts as well as points of law, and the losing party in an appeal had the right to a second appeal, providing he had not already lost in an inferior court. The system, then, consisted of inferior courts that were poorly staffed and possessed limited jurisdiction and the state's highest court that was hopelessly engulfed in endless appeals and new trials.

23. Quoted in Theophilus Parsons, *Memoir of Theophilus Parsons*, p. 410.

24. Hendrik Hartog, "The Public Law of a County Court," pp. 282–329.

25. Grinnell, "Constitutional History," p. 477 and passim; William E. Nelson, *The Americanization of the Common Law*, p. 84.

Organization was only part of the problem. Well into the nineteenth century, juries were empowered to decide both fact and law, a practice that ran counter to attempts to professionalize bench and bar. The power of the jury conflicted with the demands of a commercial economy for predictability, rationality, and stability in the law. Equally troublesome was the seriatim charge to the jury. From three to five judges presided over jury trials in the Supreme Judicial Court. Each one charged the jury separately, and, not surprisingly, judges frequently contradicted one another. Juries had to determine both fact and law according to conflicting guidelines. All this, lamented Chief Justice Lemuel Shaw, promoted the "glorious uncertainty of the law."[26]

Given this state of confusion, it is not surprising that the most important impetus for change in both organization and procedure came from the bench. Theodore Sedgwick was a central figure in this effort. Appointed to the Supreme Judicial Court in 1802, Sedgwick instituted strict discipline in the courtroom, insisted on polite relations between bench and bar, and ruthlessly rejected what he considered to be ill-founded and frivolous motions. Almost singlehandedly he tried to professionalize the Massachusetts bar.[27]

In addition, Sedgwick published a series of letters suggesting ways to reorganize the judiciary. The most important of these, signed by four other justices, was written in 1804. Sedgwick's efforts, described below, are in marked contrast to those of the South Carolina judges. Sometime after 1796, Judge Grimké wrote a letter to the governor on behalf of the judiciary. The complaints were similar to those cited by Sedgwick—crowded dockets and unconscionable delays. But Grimké's solution was far more parochial. Unlike Sedgwick, who outlined a total restructuring of the court system, Grimké wanted the legislature simply to appoint a fifth judge, a position authorized but not filled. The vacant position, he argued, amounted to an unconstitutional pay cut, because the four sitting judges were doing the work of five.[28] The contrast highlights the growing professional elan of the Massachusetts bench and the parochialism of the South Carolina judiciary. Sedgwick proposed raising judicial salaries in order to attract more qualified people, streamlining the Supreme Judicial Court, allowing justices of the peace to

26. Grinnell, "Constitutional History," p. 475.
27. Welch, "Parsons-Sedgwick Feud," p. 174; Ellis, *Jeffersonian Crisis*, pp. 187–91.
28. *Letters of the Justices of the Massachusetts Supreme Judicial Court to His Excellency the Governor*, Massachusetts Legislative Documents; Letter from the Judges to the Governor, n.d. (but after 1796), Grimké Papers (the letter is in John F. Grimké's handwriting).

serve on juries, curbing the power of the jury to determine law, and publishing appellate opinions. He also proposed reducing the Supreme Judicial Court to five justices. Jury trials would be heard by a single judge in a *nisi prius* term; the entire bench would hear appeals and trials of capital crimes. This proposal meant that both phases of the judicial process could be handled more expeditiously while eliminating (except for capital trials) the seriatim charge.

The most important part of Sedgwick's program, the reorganization of the Supreme Judicial Court, was enacted almost immediately in 1804. A previous modification in 1803 required that only two justices hear criminal cases and deprived General Sessions of its criminal jurisdiction.[29] This system was virtually unchanged for the next quarter century; in 1830, Lemuel Shaw could look back to the system created by 1805 as the one he knew.[30]

In both states the special needs of urban society were recognized by the judicial system. Regular courts sat longer in Boston and Charleston, and each city had special courts to handle the greater caseload. But even the functions of these courts reflected the subtle differences between these two cities. Unlike most seaport cities, where crime rates were well above average, Charleston's need for extra court capacity came from the civil side. The Charleston Court of Wardens and the municipal court that replaced it in 1801 were civil courts with limited criminal jurisdiction.[31] The court could hear assaults and larcenies, the most minor but most common offenses. In Boston, on the other hand, a higher incidence of crime spurred the creation of a specialized urban court. The Boston Municipal Court was established in 1800 precisely because of "the peculiar circumstances of the town of Boston, as a metropolis and great seaport, [which make] the usual mode of enforcing the laws and administering justice in criminal cases, . . . attended with great delays and burthensome expenses."[32]

By the early nineteenth century, Massachusetts and South Carolina had fashioned the court systems that, with minor modification, persisted until the eve of the Civil War. Experiments with county courts staffed by peace justices had failed; variations on the English *nisi prius* system were introduced; delays and appeals remained serious problems; and city courts had been established. But reorgani-

29. Grinnell, "Constitutional History," p. 477; Thomas C. Amory, *Life of James Sullivan with Selections from His Writings,* 2:208.

30. Quoted in Grinnell, "Constitutional History," p. 477.

31. James W. Ely, Jr., "Charleston's Court of Wardens, 1783–1800," p. 658.

32. *The By-Laws and Orders of the Town of Boston,* p. 166 (the law was passed in 1800).

zation and procedure, though significant, do not totally describe the role of the judiciary in society. Other indicators include the caliber of the bench, degree of judicial independence, and general attitudes toward the courts. It is in these areas that the clearest contrasts emerge.

Politics, Incompetence, and the Judiciary

The idea of an independent judiciary was one of the fundamental principles upon which the American republic was founded. Massachusetts and South Carolina both enacted constitutional provisions that, it was hoped, would protect that independence. South Carolina's constitution provided that a judge's salary could not be altered while he was on the bench. This clause guarded judicial independence; judges whose rulings were favorably received would not be rewarded nor would others be penalized. Inflation, understandably, made this feature unrealistic, and in 1817 all but two judges resigned in order to be reelected at a higher salary. Although some of the remaining judges invited the legislators to use this pretext as an opportunity to pass on their performance in office, all who resigned were reelected.[33]

Despite its Enlightenment era deference to the principle of an independent judiciary, South Carolina was uncomfortable with that concept—and not without cause. In a society in which personal authority was more important than political or institutional power, an independent judiciary posed a threat to planter autonomy. Court reorganization and harassment through politically inspired impeachment attempts were used to try to impede the growth of an independent power base. The fate of the first statewide appellate court illustrates the state's discomfort with an independent judiciary.

In 1824, after nearly two decades of prodding by governors, South Carolina established a single appeals court of three judges without circuit duties.[34] This move was a response to increasing unhappiness with crowded dockets and the dual system of law and equity in

33. O'Neall, *Biographical Sketches*, 1:122, 126, 129, 135, 241, 246, 275; 2:13; Thomas Waties to the House of Representatives, 13 Dec. 1817, W. D. James to House of Representatives, 13 Dec. 1817, Legal System Papers, Letters, SCA; James W. Ely, Jr., " 'That no office whatever be held during life or good behavior,' " p. 188. The exceptions were Elihu Bay and John F. Grimké. Bay was ailing and feared that his infirmity would disqualify him, whereas Grimké, who had been the subject of two impeachment attempts, was sufficiently unpopular that reelection was risky.

34. 7 *Statutes at Large*, p. 325; Henry W. DeSaussure to Langdon Cheves, 28 Dec. 1824, Langdon Cheves Papers, SCHS; see also Donald Senese, "Building the Pyramid," pp. 362–65.

which no final tribunal resolved conflicts between the two jurisdictions. This new court was composed of jurists of unusual distinction —John Belton O'Neall, William Harper, and David Johnson. Yet in 1835 it was abolished and the old system was reinstituted so quickly that it caught the legal profession by surprise.[35]

The immediate cause of the court's demise was its ruling in the test oath case, *McCready* v. *Hunt*. One legacy of the Nullification crusade was the oath of allegiance to which all state officers were forced to swear. Edward McCready, a militia officer, refused; his case rekindled all the passions of the recent struggle. The most prestigious legal talent in the state lined up on opposing sides— Thomas Smith Grimké, James Louis Petigru, and Abram Blanding for the Unionists and Robert Barnwell Rhett for the Nullifiers. In 1834, a majority composed of O'Neall and Johnson declared the oath unconstitutional, outraging the strong Nullifier faction and sealing the court's fate. Further proof of the court's heresy was provided the following year when it decided a case in favor of federal power.[36] Decades later, when opponents of a plan to resurrect the appeals court claimed that the court would have failed on its own, they had to concede that "it may be true that the decision [in the test oath case] . . . hastened its downfall."[37]

Political interference of a most obvious sort was thus responsible for a major restructuring of South Carolina's judiciary. Two decades later, amid similar political turmoil, Massachusetts reorganized its court system at least in part to wreak vengeance on one relatively minor probate judge. In South Carolina in the 1830s, the Nullification struggle polarized the state; in the 1850s, enforcement of the Fugitive Slave Act had the same effect on Massachusetts. In 1854, United States Commissioner Edward G. Loring shocked Boston by ordering Anthony Burns back to Virginia as a slave. His federal position placed Loring beyond the Bay State's wrath. But he was also a Massachusetts probate judge and in that capacity was not invulnerable. Loring was eventually removed from the bench, ostensibly for holding two offices, but actually for his role in the Burns affair, a role one historian characterized as "a mockery of the canons of judicial neutrality."[38]

35. David J. McCord to Langdon Cheves, 28 January 1836, Cheves Papers.

36. The decision in the test oath case was reported in 2 Hill 1 (1834); see also Senese, "Building the Pyramid," pp. 368–69; William W. Freehling, *Prelude to Civil War*, pp. 316-17.

37. *Legislative Times*, pp. 27–29.

38. Leonard W. Levy, *The Law of the Commonwealth and Chief Justice Shaw*, p. 105; Grinnell, "Constitutional History," pp. 515–16.

The end result was a complete restructuring of the court system. Just as the South Carolina Appeals Court was abolished for its substantive rather than its structural infirmities, court reorganization in Massachusetts appeared more the result of political whim than a serious effort to solve the problems plaguing the judiciary. The Superior Court that replaced Common Pleas in 1859 retained the identical jurisdiction of its predecessor and maintained with one exception the statewide unified structure. The one change was the inclusion of Suffolk County in the scheme. But Suffolk had been taken out of Common Pleas only four years previously, so even this one modification was hardly a significant innovation. The functional impact of this change was so slight that clerks continued to record cases in the same bound volumes they had used for Common Pleas, noting the change in nomenclature at the opening of the first sessions.[39]

Because the structural change was so relatively insignificant, we must look for motives other than efficiency or reform to determine the reasons for this alteration. And, not surprisingly, the motive was partisan—to replace the hidebound Whig justices with those more responsive to the new Democratic regime in the state. Like South Carolina, Massachusetts did not value an independent judiciary over immediate political considerations.

The reforms of 1859 were intended, in the words of their sponsor, Benjamin Butler, "to prevent delays in the administration of justice . . . whether civil or criminal." But a major step in streamlining the administration of justice—converting the Supreme Judicial Court to appellate business only—was gutted while still in legislative committee. Although Governor Nathaniel P. Banks left office in 1861 convinced that the Superior Court was a "marked improvement" and proclaiming that "no complaint of unreasonable delay is heard," his gloating was short-lived. By 1876, a legislative committee repeated the familiar complaints, particularly with regard to criminal trials.[40]

In retrospect, we can see that the great reform of 1859, born out of political interference with the judiciary in the Loring case, was a political expedient. Banks's satisfaction with the new court system might well have been influenced by the opportunity it gave him to appoint all the new judges. Indeed, his view of the old Common

39. Michael S. Hindus, *The Records of the Massachusetts Superior Court and Its Predecessors*, p. 18.

40. Governor's Address (Nathaniel Banks), Massachusetts *Acts and Resolves* (1858–59), p. 473; *Public Document No. 32* (1876); see also Alan J. Dimond, *The Superior Court of Massachusetts*.

Pleas system was apparently so negative that he declined to appoint a single Common Pleas judge to the Superior Court, despite the virtually identical jurisdiction of the two! The opportunity to use the reorganization plan as a stepping stone to judicial rationalization was lost when the Supreme Judicial Court retained almost all of its original trial jurisdiction.

It was naive to expect that even a rational redistribution of jurisdiction would have reduced delays and expenses. Those, after all, are caused both by the nature of criminal and civil litigation and by the refusal of the commonwealth to supply sufficient resources for the courts. Changes in jurisdiction were no panacea. In the century after the 1876 legislative report, specialized courts were created and enlarged to help make the Supreme Judicial Court an appellate court and the Superior Court the major trial court of the commonwealth, but the Massachusetts dockets remained among the most crowded in the country.[41]

Political considerations, then, led to major changes in court organization in both states. But the impact in Massachusetts was much less extreme. To be sure, some judicial deadwood was removed, although perhaps at the cost of an ideal notion of judicial independence. But the court system that resulted—for better or worse—was remarkably like the one it replaced. In South Carolina, it is not clear whether the state needed the two-tiered, unified court system that was frequently proposed. Nevertheless, as in Massachusetts, decisions were not made in the interests of efficiency and rational justice, but for political expediency. By refusing to acknowledge that its motives were political, the South Carolina legislature committed itself to rejecting the notion of separate appeals courts.[42] The issue, of course, was not the merits of one particular form of court organization, but the motives for preserving that form. Despite the apparent merits of separate appeals courts and specialized trial courts, both South Carolina and Massachusetts rejected this form of legal rationalization throughout most of the pre-Civil War era.

Both states had difficulty attracting the best-qualified people to the bench. In the early nineteenth century, heavy workloads and low salaries were poor inducements to accept posts of uncertain prestige. Recognizing this problem, Sedgwick argued that "the salary ought to be such that the office may be accepted without much

---

41. Archibald Cox, *Report on the State of the Massachusetts Courts.*

42. Another issue lurking in the background involved equity courts; some legislators objected to equity because of the absence of a jury; others, however, holding to a pure English system, objected to an appeals court that mixed law and equity; see *Legislative Times*, pp. 28, 29, 40.

pecuniary sacrifice by any man in successful practice."[43] Massachusetts was able to lure onto the bench such people as Theophilus Parsons and Lemuel Shaw, despite their reservations about salary, but in South Carolina, Benjamin F. Perry turned down a judicial post solely for that reason.[44]

After the court reform of 1805, the judiciary of Massachusetts was one of the more distinguished in the nation. Parsons and Sedgwick helped professionalize bench and bar, while Lemuel Shaw fashioned a court that guided Massachusetts into the modern world through decisions on tort, contracts, railroad law, corporate liability, and criminal responsibility.[45] South Carolina judges, on the other hand, were a mixed lot. The state's most distinguished jurist, Henry W. DeSaussure, was known not for his brilliance, but for his stamina. The widely noted fact that he wrote 924 of the court's 2,173 equity opinions reflects overcrowded dockets and mediocre colleagues more than it does his stature in American legal history.[46]

Complaints about the South Carolina judiciary were both frequent and severe. Many judges rode to the courthouse late, arrived intoxicated, or failed to show up at all. Having appeared, judges were not beyond reproach. "Judges have been known," noted one grand jury, "to take an unnecessary and strange course in charging a jury."[47] Criticism of crowded dockets and unconscionable delays were common. One grand jury blamed delays in the courts not on the backlog of new cases, but on the failure of the bench to dispose of old ones.[48]

But grand juries were not the only critics of the South Carolina bench. One traveler noted that little talent seemed necessary for one to hold a judicial post.[49] Edward Pringle complained in 1850 that opinions were studded with "illogical deductions . . . and most startling outrages upon the King's English."[50] According to O'Neall,

43. *Letters of the Justices.*

44. Levy, *Law of the Commonwealth*, pp. 12, 17; Elizabeth Perry to Benjamin F. Perry, 7 Dec. 1843, Benjamin F. Perry Papers, SCL.

45. In general see Levy, *Law of the Commonwealth*, and Stanley I. Kutler, *Privilege and Creative Destruction.*

46. O'Neall, *Biographical Sketches*, 1:249.

47. Richland District Grand Jury Presentment, Fall 1827, Presentments, Legal System Papers, SCA.

48. Presentments of the following grand juries: Abbeville (Spring, Fall 1817), Chesterfield (1814), Chester (1823, 1825), Charleston (1824), Edgefield (1811), Fairfield (1818), Laurens (1802), Marion (1856), Newberry (1813, 1814, 1822, 1829, 1828), all in Presentments, Legal System Papers; the grand jury quoted is Richland District (Fall 1827).

49. William Faux, *Memorable Days in America*, p. 80.

50. Edward J. Pringle, "The Judiciary System of South Carolina," p. 467.

Elihu Bay, author of South Carolina's earliest published decisions, was partial to female defendants and was deaf, senile, and infirm during his last years on the bench. Upcountry attorney Benjamin F. Perry recalled that Judge Richard Gantt frequently took sides in criminal cases.[51] Some South Carolina judges participated in duels even though dueling was a crime punishable by removal from public office.[52]

Impeachments of high court judges for cause, relatively rare in Massachusetts, were to some extent indicative of the quality of the South Carolina judiciary, although they also illustrate some concern over this problem and were frequently the result of political rivalry. Revolutionary war hero William Dobein James was removed from office in 1828 for intemperance, eighteen years after his fitness was first questioned. Waddy Thompson, impeached that year for the same reason, had a drinking problem that went back several years.[53] The impeachment of John Smyth Richardson in 1847 illustrates the interplay of many problems of the South Carolina judiciary. The seventy-year-old jurist, on the bench since 1818, was charged with being too old and infirm to discharge his duties. Richardson blamed the legislature for failing to create new judgeships to handle the rapidly increasing workload, maintaining that he had performed "well, [rather] than rapidly."[54] Although the legislature acquitted Richardson, it failed to act on his grievances. Three years later, citing the same problems, Pringle wrote that "decided improvement . . . is necessary to save [the judiciary] from falling into contempt." Pringle feared that poor conditions would cause the bench to lose status and that as a consequence the best legal talent would stay at the bar.[55]

Why, in the face of delays, crowded dockets, and incompetent judges, was there no significant improvement? The answer involves the place of the judiciary in South Carolina, a state in which government was kept at an arm's length whenever possible. The legislature maintained elaborate procedures to ensure that it and the executive (which it controlled) did as little as possible. Local government was so skeletal and powerless as to be nearly nonexistent. But the judi-

51. Benjamin F. Perry, Autobiography (1849), Perry Papers; O'Neall makes the same point, *Biographical Sketches*, 1:130; on Bay, see ibid., 1:54, 59.

52. Freehling, *Prelude to Civil War*, p. 85; O'Neall, *Biographical Sketches*, 1:183.

53. South Carolina House Journal, 1810, p. 110 (SCA); letter dated 30 Jan. 1828, Legal System Papers, Letters; letter (n.d.) in "miscellaneous," R. F. W. Allston Papers, SCHS.

54. Quoted in the account of the proceedings reprinted in O'Neall, *Biographical Sketches*, 1:142–79 (the quote is from p. 169).

55. Pringle, "Judiciary System," pp. 464, 468.

ciary posed special problems. Courts for both civil and criminal business were a necessity and perhaps were the organs of government with the greatest and most obvious utility. But life tenure made the judiciary independent of the patterns of power and control in the state. By dismissing demands for judicial reform, the legislature attempted to keep the place of the judiciary as narrow and as limited as possible. If courts were necessary, this attitude seemed to imply, they were also a necessary evil.

The Debate over Equity Courts

There was one way in which South Carolina judges already had more discretion than their Massachusetts counterparts. The state had parallel courts of law and equity, whereas Massachusetts resisted all but piecemeal equity jurisdiction until the mid-nineteenth century. Sitting without a jury, equity courts vested considerable discretion in judges. For this reason, equity courts were favored by mercantile interests who distrusted popular juries. Naturally, legal populists were strongly hostile to equity. With the bar and mercantile interests allied in support of equity courts, the failure of Massachusetts to establish such tribunals shows the power of tradition over professional and economic interests.

The positions of each state on equity in the nineteenth century were due less to the influence of mercantile interests or the desire to curb judicial power than to conditions in the seventeenth century. South Carolina, as a royal colony, had no cause to deviate from the seventeenth-century English pattern. Yet Puritan New England could hardly have trusted the king's conscience. Legal traditions die hard, and even though Massachusetts judges successfully curbed the power of the jury, the state, despite attempts by bench and bar, did not significantly expand equity jurisdiction until midcentury. In South Carolina, by contrast, where any aggrandizement of judicial power was resisted, tradition kept the courts of equity almost completely unscathed.

Massachusetts and South Carolina approached the question of equity jurisdiction from different directions. In South Carolina, equity was totally separate from law and had its own bench. No single court resolved possible differences between the two parallel systems. In 1808, Governor Charles Pinckney urged the creation of a separate appeals court to hear cases in both law and equity, and for the next sixteen years, governors regularly repeated this litany. Finally, Governor John Lyde Wilson's spirited attack on the equity system in 1822 spurred the creation, two years later, of the long-desired appeals court.[56]

Chancellor DeSaussure blamed the unpopularity of equity for this innovation. Differences between law and equity, the stated reason for the change, "did not exceed five or six points" in forty years. The true reason for this "revolution in our judiciary system" was "the nature and organization of the Court of Equity." Not "sufficiently popular to be in harmony with our other institutions" and lacking the "shield of a jury to protect it," the independent equity system succumbed to the attacks of its critics. As a final insult, no chancellor was appointed to the newly created high bench.[57]

The appellate court's judgment in the test oath case, the immediate cause of its dissolution, was seized upon by the defenders of equity as a pretext for reestablishing the pre-1824 system. A legislator who flatly denied that the notorious decision had anything to do with the dissolution of the appellate court claimed the court lost popular confidence because of "its mongrel mix of law and equity."[58] The strongest defense of the pure equity system came from James L. Petigru and the well-entrenched commercially oriented Charleston bar. The upcountry bar was forced into a more populist stance. Led by Benjamin F. Perry, they sought to reduce equity power to help break the stranglehold on the state's legal affairs held by the urban oligarchy.[59]

In Massachusetts, as in South Carolina, equity was favored by the legal establishment, which was uncomfortable with the discretion of the jury. In 1808, Joseph Story proposed creation of an equity court, but republican hostility to such a large grant of judicial discretion doomed that plan.[60] In 1825, William Sullivan, in a well-known address to the Suffolk bar (itself an example of the bar's increasing professionalism and self-awareness) called for the estab-

56. Message of the Governor, 1808, SCA; John Lyde Wilson, *Review of the Court of Equity;* Senese, "Building the Pyramid," pp. 360–62. Two contemporary pamphlets on this issue were *A Letter Addressed to His Excellency John L. Wilson Governor of the State of South Carolina on the Subject of the Judiciary* and *A Short Review of the Project for Uniting the Courts of Law and Equity in This State.* Good discussions of equity law and equity courts in Anglo-American law can be found in Stanley Katz, "The Politics of Law in Colonial America," pp. 257–84, and Lawrence M. Friedman, *A History of American Law,* pp.21–23, 130–31, 346–47. Katz makes the cogent point that equity courts were far more controversial than equity jurisdiction. This was certainly true in both states under consideration here.

57. Henry W. DeSaussure to Langdon Cheves, 28 Dec. 1824, Cheves Papers.

58. *Legislative Times,* p. 39.

59. Benjamin F. Perry to Elizabeth Perry, 12 Dec. 1836, in Hext Perry, ed., *Letters of My Father to My Mother,* p. 16.

60. Ellis, *Jeffersonian Crisis,* p. 223.

lishment of an equity court. But even Sullivan admitted that "it is not to be denied that in . . . [England] the practice [of equity] is dilatory, expensive, perplexing, and is, in fact, a science by itself."[61] Massachusetts resisted such proddings, although it granted its courts equity jurisdiction in certain limited areas.[62] In the last analysis, the fate of equity courts depended more on tradition than on political or professional power. After the Civil War, however, the two states took a similar middle course. Separate equity courts were abolished in South Carolina in 1868; Massachusetts granted its Supreme Judicial Court full equity jurisdiction in 1877.

The Quest for Efficiency

Both states grappled with the relationship between appellate and local courts, and throughout most of this period, justices from the appellate court heard cases in local court terms. In Massachusetts, the original jurisdiction of the circuit sessions of the Supreme Judicial Court was limited; much was shared with the Court of Common Pleas. Justices of the state's highest court presided over only a fraction of all original trials. South Carolina, by contrast, had only one system of courts of original jurisdiction, staffed by the judges who collectively comprised the appeals courts in law and equity.

The significance of this contrast becomes clear when dealing with the response of each court system to overcrowded dockets. In Massachusetts, jurisdiction was shifted piecemeal from the Supreme Judicial Court to the Courts of Common Pleas. Common Pleas was infinitely expandable because the justices never sat collectively. Because all its judges comprised the appeals court, South Carolina was unable to respond to increased demands on its judiciary.

That the notion of a separate appellate court was controversial in South Carolina is itself indicative of the attitude toward the judiciary. A curious sort of legal populism underlay the defense of the circuit system. Judges, it was argued, should not be aloof. Appellate judges without circuit duty, in the words of one legislator, "will know nothing of the judiciary system . . . they will be so far removed from the people that they will know nothing of the legal wants of the state."[63] At times the hostility could border on the

---

61. William Sullivan, *Address to the Members of the Bar of Suffolk Massachusetts*, pp. 44, 44–45n.

62. William J. Curran, "The Struggle for Equity Jurisdiction in Massachusetts," pp. 280, 284n, 287–91.

63. *Legislative Times*, p. 109.

ridiculous. One legislator feared that the appeals court would be a judicial aristocracy "at war with the interests of all the other classes of the community." A chief justice, no less, was anathema in a republican state! The most basic fear, however, was one of power. The appeals court, without the check apparently provided by overwork, would have "a most irresponsible power."[64]

This argument was not necessarily wrong or ill-considered. It represents instead a conception of the role of law and of the judiciary that was suited to a society in which disputes were often resolved informally. In such a system, law represents a relatively fixed and known set of values and principles; a judge is a referee, imparting the rules of the game to both sides and to the jury. Law is not intended to be severed from the public will, but juries and legislators, not judges, are the vehicles for such input. Fears of judicial aristocracies and unlimited power indicate that not everyone in South Carolina shared or appreciated this classic conception of the judge's role.

The major function of civil courts is the impartial resolution of conflicts according to specific rules and standards. Since courts are the creation of the state, the state seemingly has an interest in accomplishing this goal. But the attitude toward the judiciary occasionally expressed in South Carolina makes one wonder if the state really had such expectations from its courts. South Carolina consistently declined to remove any of the structural barriers to the resolution of conflicts through legal means. In 1855, for example, some citizens of Claremont asked the legislature to split the district in half and create the new district of Clarendon. As in the communitarian towns of seventeenth-century New England, the populace in one rapidly growing part of the district found it too inconvenient to attend court in the older section. A new district, with a more centrally located courthouse, would make justice more accessible. That this issue was the single most hotly debated question in the South Carolina legislature in 1855 reveals the state's extreme disinclination to alter existing authority relationships. But even more revealing was one reason given for resisting the division: creating another court district would only lead to increased litigation. "As you multiply Court Houses, you multiply the means of litigation. In overgrown districts, where they are at a distance from the Court Houses, parties are more likely to make a compromise before they will go to a court of justice, and then they will give up the law."[65] In other

64. Ibid., pp. 110, 111, 113, 109.
65. Ibid., p. 157.

words, delays and inconveniences were desirable because they kept people from resorting to the courts. Rather than utilize the legal processes designed for dispute settlement, citizens should be encouraged to "give up the law." No more explicit statement of the reduced role of courts and law in South Carolina should be expected.

In 1855, a proposed appeals court was defeated, but even if the measure had passed, not much certainty would have been introduced. The court would have had four judges, and evenly split votes might well have rendered that institution powerless. South Carolina did establish an appeals court in 1859 and installed John Belton O'Neall as chief justice, but even this tribunal was not the ultimate arbiter. In cases involving constitutional questions, split opinions, or disagreements between law and equity, all the circuit judges, chancellors, and appeals judges sat as a grand court of error. Not until 1868 did South Carolina finally create a single and supreme court.

Although Massachusetts engineered several seemingly significant changes in its court system, as we have seen, most of these measures had little impact on the delays and expenses that were the object of dissatisfaction. Some alterations, such as the shift from Courts of Common Pleas to Superior Courts in 1859, were politically inspired and substantively cosmetic. The abolition of the Court of General Sessions, which took over a decade in the early part of the century, was virtually a *de facto* ratification of the disuse into which these bodies had already fallen.

Courts in Massachusetts were at best an imperfect embodiment of the idea of equal justice under law. But unlike South Carolina, Massachusetts never appeared to challenge the importance of the judiciary in ordering the affairs of the commonwealth. Reorganizations that attempted to strengthen the role of the courts, particularly in appellate matters, were regularly enacted. Where Massachusetts courts failed was not in their centrality to the public order, but rather in the obstacles they presented to those who relied on the promises and premises of the legal system for justice. While Massachusetts fashioned the pyramidlike court structure essential to definite statements of doctrine and precedent, its dockets were hopelessly overcrowded and access to them was costly, time-consuming, and frustrating.

The history of the judiciary in nineteenth-century Massachusetts was marked by the shifting of jurisdictions from higher to lower courts, the beginnings of specialization in the judiciary. These shifts were not always to the overall benefit of the court system. In 1832, for example, the bulk of criminal circuit jurisdiction was transferred from the Supreme Judicial Court to the inferior Courts of Common Pleas. Since no accommodation was made for Common Pleas to deal with the increased workload, this reorganization in the name of efficiency apparently resulted in further delays. Moreover, state officials complained that the administration of justice was not uniform from county to county; minor errors too frequently invalidated convictions.[66] Common Pleas was abolished in 1859 partly to eliminate deadwood from the bench.[67]

Concern for efficiency and certainty was a response to the needs of those who used the law in their daily business and professional lives. The judicial system was not made any more accessible, however, to ordinary citizens. "There is no justice . . . for that class of the poor," complained Judge Josiah Quincy in 1822, "who cannot afford to [appeal]."[68] As in all too many areas of law, therefore, the benefits of the Massachusetts judicial system were not uniformly distributed.

In contrasting the courts and judiciary of the two states, it is immediately obvious that the differences are both of degree and of kind. Both states grappled with similar problems of court organization; indeed, both responded in similar ways, but often the results were different. Nevertheless, it is possible to isolate and identify what seem to be the most salient contrasts between the states. In Massachusetts, we can see an attitude that tended to reinforce and strengthen the role of formal institutions in society. In South Carolina, a policy of inaction and intransigence seemed at times to be a deliberate attempt to minimize and undermine the role of such bodies. It should be clear that South Carolina did not lack strains of authority, nor was it anarchic; it was simply that the structural underpinnings of the rule of law were weak, frequently replaced by informal systems of authority based on custom, deference, and race.

Local Justice

If courts were the arm of government with which citizens most frequently came into contact, magistrates, sheriffs, and justices of the peace most likely were responsible for this contact. Such local

66. James T. Austin, *Report and Opinion of the Attorney General on the Subject of the Expenses of Criminal Justice*, p. 25; *Report of the Attorney General,* 1861, Public Document 18, p. 4.

67. William T. Davis, *History of the Judiciary of Massachusetts,* p. 252.

68. Josiah Quincy, *Remarks on Some of the Provisions of the Laws of Massachusetts Affecting Poverty, Vice, and Crime,* pp. 8–9.

officials represented formal authority on a day-to-day basis. They handled official business and were charged with keeping order in a general way. These local officials had a differential impact in the two states. In Massachusetts, town government was the unit of authority with which the citizenry was most frequently in contact. In South Carolina, where there was little or no town government, sheriffs, justices, and magistrates served similar functions.

The South Carolina situation merits some attention because of the interaction of honor, self-interest, and incompetence in the administration of justice. Unlike Massachusetts, where local government was organized around the unit of the town, in South Carolina the district was the central political entity. Justices and magistrates in the Palmetto State were appointed by the legislature; after 1808 sheriffs were elected.[69] Throughout the nineteenth century, local officials were the source of much discord and dissatisfaction.

One problem was financial. Sheriffs performed execution sales that frequently involved large sums of money, and financial irregularities were common. The problems created by entrusting such sums to local officials of questionable competence are illustrated by the following examples. One person, citing the "deranged state" of a sheriff's office, took $6,240 in execution proceeds home with him for safekeeping. A meeting with the sheriff to return the funds never materialized.[70] Nathaniel Greene Cleary, sheriff of Charleston District, apparently found the temptations of the office too great. The details of Cleary's financial entanglements reveal the problems inherent in the organization of the office. Cleary left office bankrupt, owing $3,720 to the state. He had used the proceeds of execution sales to pay daily bills connected with the office because reimbursement was annual. But Cleary claimed he never received all his fees; some people simply refused to pay. Other fees Cleary termed inadequate, such as the standard $64.29 paid for setting up a jury. To avoid bankruptcy, Cleary sought repeal of the statute forbidding reelection to the office. The complex web of finances left by Cleary was not straightened out until 1839, over a decade after he left office. Cleary's experiences may have inspired a bill to punish criminally any public official converting to private use monies entrusted to him.[71]

---

69. 5 *Statutes at Large*, p. 569.

70. R. B. Scriven to Walter Blake, 25 April 1821, SCL.

71. Report of the Judiciary Committee, n.d.; N. G. Cleary file, Petitions; Petition of B. F. Hunt and Lance Aiken, all in Petitions, Penal System Papers, SCA; *South Carolina Reports and Resolutions* (1839), pp. 92–93. Cleary had filed a claim with the state for the full amount he was in arrears, claiming this was due him for services

A bizarre problem arising from sheriff's fees began inauspiciously in 1809, when young Robert Turner arrived in Laurens District, South Carolina, from Maryland. Since the lad appeared to be in distressed circumstances, Sheriff John Clark took him in as a boarder. In September 1809, Clark discovered that the proceeds of execution sales—some $800, for which he was personally responsible—had disappeared. The money was kept in the house, so Clark suspected his boarder. Clark and several other men found Turner and extracted a confession from him. Turner was convicted, confined to jail, and sentenced to be branded for grand larceny.

Far from settling things, this conviction only caused more complications. Turner claimed that he had been tortured into confessing to a crime he did not commit and charged that Clark and his posse had used exceedingly brutal means in order to extract this admission.[72] This treatment was brought to light only because Turner, despite his apparent indigence, came from a substantial family in Maryland. Turner's father, upon hearing of these atrocities, complained to Governor John Drayton.[73] The older Turner carried a letter verifying the story from the young Laurens attorney John C. Calhoun.[74] Turner, meanwhile, petitioned Drayton for a pardon, a request that was backed by the report of the presiding judge. Turner was pardoned; Clark was impeached and convicted.[75]

Obviously, this case illustrates the brutality of which local officials were capable. But more significantly, Clark's defense shows the pressures of the office, particularly when filled by ordinary folk imbued with South Carolina's peculiar sense of honor. Without denying Turner's allegations, Clark staunchly defended his actions. The money taken was that which the sheriff "was in daily expecta-

---

rendered, but the claim was rejected. Hunt and Aiken held the bond on Cleary and sought to have their loss compensated.

72. Turner's hand was placed in a severely tightened vise for over an hour. Next he was dragged outside and whipped. Five days later he was tied to a log and placed in a fire, "burning his feet to a crisp." Finally, he was thrown into a cell and prevented from standing until his trial.

73. Thomas Waties to Governor Drayton, 20 April 1810; deposition of Robert Turner, Testimony Given before the Committee Appointed on the Governor's Message Number 4 in the Case of John Clark, 4 Dec. 1811, Clark File, Impeachments, Legislative System Papers.

74. John C. Calhoun to Governor Drayton, 21 April 1810, ibid.

75. Waties to Drayton, 20 April 1810; Clark deposition; Bill of Impeachment (10 Dec. 1811); Joseph Turner to Governor of South Carolina, 11 Sept. 1811; Petition of Robert Turner, all in ibid.; Drayton to Joseph Turner, 20 Aug. 1810, Executive Letter Book; Pardon in Miscellaneous Records, Book BBBB, p. 285, SCA; South Carolina House Journal, 1811, pp. 76–77.

tion of being called on for." Clark claimed that because of "the pressure and effects of a severe indisposition, the loss of money for which he was responsible and unable to pay, being poor and solely depending on the scanty profits of his office, his mind was very much agited [*sic*] and disordered." The loss "involved [Clark] not in ruin only, but in disgrace." Turner was merely a scapegoat; Clark's honor was at stake. This was the justification for "making the most vigorous execution, if not to recover his loss, to show and convince the world that however unfortunate, he yet had his honor and integrity whole."[76] Clark was hardly the first South Carolinian to place honor above the law.

Criticism of sheriffs, as these examples demonstrate, was usually based on financial irregularities. Problems with the magistrates went deeper. Magistrates and justices had broad powers as conservators of the peace until the court convened. They, too, were ordinary folk, dependent on fees. Grand juries frequently charged that magistrates initiated frivolous prosecutions solely for fees that would accrue regardless of outcome. Magistrates lacked the training and had no incentive to distinguish between legitimate and meritless actions. They were accused of instigating strife and conflict in order to benefit from the inevitable legal residue. Complaining that the total fees paid in Columbia had risen fifteenfold in the space of a few years, the Richland grand jury accused the justices of "prostituting" their appointments by taking "an active role in riots and public disturbances with the sole view . . . of increasing their bill of fees." A Charleston grand jury charged that the magistrates encouraged a "litigious spirit among the poor and ignorant" and sought to "rescue this class . . . from unnecessary oppression and illegal charges, and drive from the court house a number of trifling cases, calculated only to harass the court and clog the wheels of justice." In short, such officials were "encouragers of strife," not "conservators of the peace."[77]

The problem of frivolous prosecutions was particularly troublesome in assault and battery cases, the most common criminal prosecution. The claim that many of the cases were without merit was hardly unjustified. Two-thirds of all assault and battery bills were either rejected by the grand jury or not prosecuted by solicitor or

---

76. Clark Deposition, Clark File, Impeachments, Legislative System Papers.

77. Richland District Grand Jury, Fall 1823; Charleston District, Fall 1826; Greenville District, Fall 1823; other grand juries that addressed themselves to this problem included Chester (Fall 1820), Charleston (Fall, Spring 1824, 1856), Pickens (1829, 1830), all in Presentments, Legal System Papers.

complainant.[78] Clearly, many of these prosecutions were ground-less.

Besides being greedy, magistrates were incompetent, notoriously untrained in the law. Governor James Hammond complained that "much inconvenience and sometimes serious evil arise from the ignorance of the common magistrates."[79] Not all of this was their fault, as indicated by an 1822 grand jury proposal that magistates be informed of all new legislation. In 1844, B. C. Pressley published his *Law of Magistrates,* but that manual did nothing to stem the tide of criticism. Over a decade later, a legislator stated that "some magis-trates are entirely incompetent," a charge even their defender chose not to deny.[80]

Some grand juries felt that the sheer number of such officials encouraged abuse of the office. In 1846, there were 1,128 magistrates for a white population of 259,084 and a total population of 594,398. Admittedly, these were part-time posts; nevertheless, the ratio of approximately one magistrate per 500 persons exceeded that of most urban police departments in the nineteenth century—and this was for only one office. Sheriffs, constables, and peace justices lowered that ratio even further, showing that there were many local officials with little to do in what was clearly not a policed society.[81] Yet, though some districts had too many magistrates, others demanded more. A Marion grand jury asked for more magistrates, and in 1856 citizens of Bluffton in Beaufort District petitioned the governor for a magistrate, "there being none in less than twenty-five miles of this place."[82]

Attitudes toward the magistrates and peace justices reveal a fun-damental ambivalence in South Carolina's conception of authority. On the one hand, the magistrates were avaricious, ignorant men with few principles and even less training. On the other hand, they were a necessary convenience in a society where courts were expen-sive, met only twice a year, and were unlikely to finish a civil case in less than several years. Not surprisingly, therefore, at the same time that some grand juries complained about frivolous prosecu-tions and ignorant magistrates, others advocated expanding their

78. See Chapter 4.

79. James H. Hammond, *Selections from the Letters and Speeches of the Hon. James H. Hammond of South Carolina,* p. 91.

80. *Legislative Times,* pp. 106–7; one legislator suggested no change, claiming that "if you give them no business you will always leave them ignorant."

81. Report of the Judiciary Committee (1846) filed with Marion Grand Jury Pre-sentment 1850, Presentments, Legal System Papers.

82. Marion Presentment (1850), ibid.; Citizens of Bluffton to Governor J. H. Adams, 27 May 1856, Governor's Correspondence, SCA.

authority,[83] such as granting them summary jursidiction in assault cases. Whatever abuses these officials tolerated or encouraged would be less expensive and disruptive in such a proceeding than in court.

The contradictory complaints and suggestions do not indicate so much a fundamental conflict over the office of magistrate as total frustration with the legal system. Given the attitudes of the legislature—that courts multiply conflict and litigation—and a policy designed to reduce or limit the effectiveness of the only formal institutions of authority in South Carolina society, it is hardly surprising that citizens wishing to utilize the legal system would have to choose between the lesser of two evils. On the one hand were incompetent magistrates dispensing quick but limited justice; on the other were overcrowded, expensive, and clogged courts. Perhaps the governing elite really hoped that people would choose to do nothing.

It is difficult to know how similar this problem was in Massachusetts. Grand jury presentments—the most consistent guide to local thought about the legal system in South Carolina—were not made in Massachusetts. There are some indications that the temptations offered by fees were interfering with justice in the Bay State as well. At least one magistrate was impeached for bribery.[84] John Augustus, the pioneer of probation, insisted that opposition to his efforts to release juveniles without jail terms came from the court officials who resented losing their *mittimus* fees for transferring suspects and convicts to jails.[85] In 1859, Governor Nathaniel Banks charged that arrests had increased primarily because of a new fee system under which the state reimbursed towns.[86]

The structures of authority in Massachusetts and South Carolina appear to have been quite different. But were they? Neither state was free from political interference with the judiciary, neither solved the problems of delay and expense in litigation, and both

83. Presentments from Laurens (Fall 1824), Darlington (1855), Lancaster (1830), Chester (1825), Kershaw (1823), and others, Presentments, Legal System Papers; in 1846, the legislature, in response to these complaints, passed a bill entitled "An Act to Diminish the Number of Magistrates," which reduced their numbers outside the coastal area. In three separate instances (12 *Statutes at Large*, pp. 712, 782, 814) the legislature authorized more magistrates in specific areas. The 1846 measure is 11 *Statutes at Large*, pp. 359–60.

84. Massachusetts *House Journal*, 1807, pp. 151–52, 123–24; ibid., 1808, p. 23.

85. John Augustus, *A Report of the Labors of John Augustus for the Last Ten Years in the Aid of the Unfortunate*, p. 19.

86. *Address of His Excellency Nathaniel Banks*, pp. 39–40.

wrestled with finding a proper posture for authority, to make it neither distant nor oppressive. It seems evident, then, that substance does not invariably follow form.

Although it would be absurd to hinge an interpretation on the presence of a distinct appeals court or court of equity, we can see some subtle differences in the way structures of authority were treated. In Massachusetts, the courts were slated to play a large role in ordering the affairs of this increasingly complex society. This certainly did not mean, for example, that commercial interests dominated the judicial process or dictated their demands to a compliant legislature. It does mean, though, that the goals necessary to achieve efficiency and legal rationalization were seriously pursued.

By contrast, in South Carolina resistance to expanding the role of the courts was substantial. Arguments based on efficiency were countered with fears of judicial power. The periodic crises that produced overdue changes in the Massachusetts judiciary were based on overcrowded dockets; in South Carolina, crises were produced by politically unpopular decisions. In the two states there were different attitudes toward formally constituted authority and different conceptions of the role of the state. This theme will become clearer as we explore the actual operation of the legal and justice systems.

But as important as it is to recognize that these different conceptions of state authority existed, it is also important to realize that these attitudes did not always translate into substantive contrasts. Bound by the Anglo-American legal tradition, South Carolina was not as free to emasculate judicial authority as it might have been if forced to consider that authority from the start. And, conversely, the limits of the public commitment to justice and the frustrating nature of much of the judicial process itself kept the Massachusetts courts from being the models of efficiency and rationality that their champions undoubtedly desired.

Chapter 2.
The Boundaries of Authority:
Extralegal Activities and the
Enforcement of Morals

In 1858, reflecting on South Carolina's chronically ineffective system of formal authority, James L. Petigru remarked, "The want of justice that gave rise to the Regulators is still a desideratum attested by the prevalence of lynch law."[1] The distinguished attorney realized that whenever a demand for authority existed but was not satisfied by officially constituted mechanisms, extralegal forms were likely to emerge, whether spontaneous or premeditated, individual or collective, justified by the claim that they provided a remedy not obtainable by law. This was the classic justification of extralegal authority. One Boston rioter, for example, explained his conduct in an 1825 attack on a notorious brothel by complaining that "the law was full of delay, that it was not meted out equally."[2] Since the role of formal authority was much smaller in South Carolina than in Massachusetts, the Palmetto State was more prone to the exercise of extralegal authority. Moreover, extralegal and informal authority was actually encouraged as part of the state's overall reluctance to maintain a strong system of formal authority. Extralegal authority was not unknown in Massachusetts, but its impact on the state's legal system was far less significant, and it almost never received sanction or encouragement from formally constituted authority.

Before discussing specific instances of extralegal and informal authority, we should consider a few general observations about the phenomenon. First, authority patterns in any society are mixed. Formal, legally constituted authority is of most concern in studying the legal system, but other wielders of authority such as the family, the church, or even the neighborhood are more powerful in their

1. James Louis Petigru, "Oration Delivered on the Third Anniversary of the South Carolina Historical Society," pp. 19–20.
2. *Commonwealth* v. *Charles Jenkins and others* (1825), *Thacher's Criminal Cases* 118 at 199.

respective domains. These latter groups and institutions all wielded nonlegal authority. Extralegal authority attempts to substitute for that which is formally constituted. Family, church, neighborhood, and the master-servant nexus were important examples of competing forms of authority, but their relationship to the formal legal system was only tangential. Dueling, rioting, and vigilantism substituted for such legal activities as litigation and policing.

Secondly, there is nothing especially normative about a particular mix of legal and extralegal authority, but certain relationships between the two categories may exist. A society may determine that extralegal authority is more responsive or reliable than formal authority and may tacitly encourage such activity. Or extralegal activity may be a response to a deliberate or inadvertent weakness of formal authority. Legal and extralegal authority usually do not mix very well; frequently they stand in tension to each other. But unless the boundaries of each authority system are clear, the one used less often will wither through nonuse. Thus, if extralegal authority is relied on to keep the peace, law enforcement will be difficult when extralegal authority proves either ineffective or excessive.

The particular mix of legal and extralegal authority is also useful in charting the boundaries of formally constituted authority in a given society. Again, there is no normative position on the proper extent of formal state intervention into the lives of the citizens; indeed, this issue is as problematical today as it ever was in American legal history. In addition to the particular matrix of legal and extralegal authority in the two states, one further area provides an interesting test case of the penetration of law. This is state regulation of moral behavior, an important discretionary bellwether. We will see that the boundaries of formal authority and the mixture of formal and informal authority in the two states were quite different. Neither mix was absolutely satisfactory, but each was reasonably appropriate for its society.

Any society will have a combination of legal and extralegal authority, just as customary elements coexist within the rule of law. But this does not mean that custom and law exist in the same proportions or that differences in degree are not crucial to the role of formal authority. These caveats must be kept in mind during this discussion. Both South Carolina and Massachusetts were formally organized under legal authority. Extralegal authority existed in both states, but its role was far greater in South Carolina.

Furthermore, the interplay between formal and informal authority was strikingly different in the two states. In Massachusetts, extralegal authority was seen as a damaging challenge to legally constituted order, and the state tried vigorously to minimize the influence of this competing form of authority. South Carolina, by contrast, in many cases tolerated and in some cases actually encouraged the growth of extralegal and informal authority, preferring notions of honor and popular justice to the strengthening of formally constituted authority. In Massachusetts, in order for the legal system to have maximum impact in ordering society, all challenges had to be defeated. In South Carolina, however, in order to keep the formal legal order weak and to prevent the rule of law from eviscerating the planter aristocracy, extralegal and informal authority was nurtured.

Not only were such contrasting forms reflective of legal traditions and political realities, they were also suited to prevailing economic modes. In South Carolina, despite the existence of international commerce, much enterprise was conducted in the traditional face-to-face manner. Honor was an important part of the state's economic life and formed the basis of its legal life as well. When the legal system proved ill-equipped to protect honor, South Carolinians took matters literally into their own hands. By contrast, the Massachusetts economic order was more impersonal, disruptible, and dependent on routine expectations. Such a society is particularly vulnerable to riots, a common form of extralegal activity. As Karl Polanyi noted, "The market system was more allergic to rioting than any other economic system we know."[3] In addition, the complexities of a modern economy demanded the acceptance of a commonly acknowledged ultimate source of authority. The competing claim to this authority posed by extralegal forms was intolerable. It is not surprising, therefore, that Massachusetts took strong measures to prevent extralegal activity. In less commercially or politically complex societies, disruption was more easily tolerated and less easily suppressed, the legitimacy of legal and formal authority was not always well established, and competition with extralegal forms was possible. Extralegal authority lost an important pretense to legitimacy when official authority claimed to embody all the values of a society. But until or unless that happened, the lynch mob was preferred to the courthouse.

Extralegal authority creates two problems. First, it coexists very poorly with the legal order, for its continued existence is a reminder of the failures of the legal order to maintain its legitimacy. Thus the persistence of forms of extralegal authority is virtually equivalent

3. Karl Polyani, *The Great Transformation*, p. 186; see also Allan Silver, "The Demand for Order in Civil Society," pp. 1–24.

to the growth of that authority at the expense of the legal order. Second, extralegal authority is not limited in its capriciousness; it attempts to embody not the moral consensus of the community, but only that of its adherents or leaders. Instead of codifying general principles, as the law is intended to do, lynching and rioting are frequently responses to specific situations. Consistency, while not precluded, is not guaranteed. Thus the South Carolina Regulators, after arresting and trying backcountry criminals, sought to suppress all behavior of which they did not approve, even if that behavior was not illegal but only undesirable in their eyes. Official justice is not necessarily free from arbitrariness, as police activity in antebellum Boston showed.[4] But formally constituted authority is limited in its discretion and must acknowledge the rules by which it operates. That these restrictions fall far short of the ideal is well known, but hardly means that extralegal justice is more equitable. On the contrary, rioters and lynch mobs have usually chosen as their victims precisely those who were protected by laws, no matter how defective the laws may have been.

Extralegal activity took many forms. In South Carolina, there was an extralegal counterpart to nearly every major element of the legal and criminal justice system: plantation justice handled much slave crime; dueling substituted for some forms of litigation; mob activity policed city streets; vigilantes patrolled country bounds. This analysis of extralegal activity will focus on dueling, vigilantism, and rioting; only the last was endemic to both states, indicating the larger role of extralegal authority in South Carolina.

The Legacy of the Mob

From the Revolution to the Civil War, both states experienced serious urban rioting related to political and social issues. In both Boston and Charleston, ethnic violence spurred the creation of permanent police forces. Although the most serious urban violence occurred in the nineteenth century, the revolutionary mobs of both Boston and Charleston were significant because they portended the major themes in the history of crime and authority in each state. In both cities, the radicalism of the mob exceeded that of its leaders. But in Boston the perceived threat was a disruption of property

4. Michael S. Hindus, "A City of Mobocrats and Tyrants," pp. 74–76. On this pattern as a general characteristic of vigilantism, see Richard Maxwell Brown, "The American Vigilante Tradition."

relations; in South Carolina, it was the fear of inciting a slave insurrection.[5] Appropriately, in the nineteenth century criminal law in Massachusetts had as a central concern the protection of property, but in South Carolina it was the maintenance of race control.

In the early national period, Boston experienced a type of rioting endemic to northern cities, characterized by political, racial, religious, and ethnic clashes. Boston responded—as did other cities—by establishing a professional police force. The specific impetus for this move was the Broad Street riot of 1837, a Yankee-Irish battle that involved almost a fifth of the city's adult population. Ethnic clashes were hardly new in Boston; three years earlier, an anti-Catholic mob had destroyed the Ursuline Convent.[6]

This type of rioting was not unknown in Charleston, but was much less frequent throughout most of the antebellum years. Both cities, however, experienced political rioting in the 1830s. Nullifiers in Charleston in 1832 and antiabolitionists in Boston in 1835 clashed with their opponents. Many of South Carolina's political leaders led the raid on the Charleston post office (to destroy abolitionist literature) in the same year that their archenemy, William Lloyd Garrison, was the mob's victim in Boston. Yet despite the passions that produced these confrontations, neither posed a serious threat to life, property, and order in the city.[7]

The seriousness of these incidents should not be underestimated. Obviously, the attempt to stifle political debate was a serious threat to democratic rights and procedures, and both episodes steeled the determination of the antislavery movement. But ethnic conflict of the sort exhibited in the Broad Street riot was the impetus to establishing a police force in Boston. Charleston, by contrast, did not experience for many years the ethnic conflict that was so potentially injurious to the social order as to demand new forms of policing, even though it did tolerate duelists and brawling sailors. As long as Charlestonians believed that blacks were the sole threat to order, white supremacy served in lieu of a police force. In such a racially

5. See the two articles by Pauline Maier, "Popular Uprisings and Civil Authority in Eighteenth-Century America" and "The Charleston Mob and the Evolution of Popular Politics in Revolutionary South Carolina."

6. Hindus, "Mobocrats and Tyrants," pp. 68–72.

7. In Charleston, Petigru was struck by an object, and in Boston, Garrison was paraded through the streets with a noose around his waist, but even contemporaries agreed that lives were not at stake, only principles. See H. P. Rutledge to E. C. Rutledge, 13 Oct. 1832, 10 Oct. 1843, 6 Sept. 1832, Rutledge Family Papers, SCL; James Louis Petigru, *Life, Letters, and Speeches of James Louis Petigru, the Union Man of South Carolina*, pp. 100–105; Hindus, "Mobocrats and Tyrants," pp. 72–73.

stratified society, with few legal rights accorded the black man, every white person, by virtue of his skin, had sufficient authority over blacks. As James H. Hammond saw it, "Our vigilance . . . does not arise from fear, but from the fact that we ourselves . . . constitute our own police."[8] An elaborate city guard and militia system kept alert for insurrection, but no full-time professional force was specifically concerned with black or white crime and routine disorder until the 1850s. Only when policing problems concerned the white population—as in tension between immigrant groups or in controlling the grog shops catering to blacks (where the policing problem was more the whites who ran the shops than the black patrons)—was a police force seen to be necessary.

Conveniently forgetting the street battles of the Nullification era, Charlestonians prided themselves on avoiding the type of mob violence that resulted in the burning of the convent in Boston. But in 1849, a narrowly averted confrontation involving racial policy portended an end to the city's complacency. On 13 July 1849, thirty-seven blacks escaped from the Charleston workhouse.[9] The day after the workhouse escape, a large mob tried to destroy the Calvary Episcopal Church, under construction for free blacks and slaves. Moderation—and the threat of igniting a citywide conflagration Charlestonians knew only too well—prevailed. A committee was formed to decide the fate of the structure; endless meetings followed; but the church was constructed.[10]

The timing of the clash at the church could hardly have been coincidental. The structure had been under consideration for years; the workhouse escape was a reminder of the unsettled state of race control that revived the city's uneasiness about a separate black church. The workhouse escape signaled a clear lapse in race control, and the black church undoubtedly was seen as possibly contributing to the spirit of rebelliousness that triggered the escape. Taken together, the two events challenged the city's complacency about the effectiveness both of race control and of the city guard. But the ideology expressed so succinctly by Hammond was not easily abandoned. Rather than acknowledge the threat to the peace of the city that the attempted burning represented, Charleston residents con-

8. James H. Hammond, *Selections from the Letters and Speeches of the Hon. James H. Hammond of South Carolina*, p. 37.

9. Jacob Schirmir Diary, 13–20 July 1849, SCHS (Schirmir noted that the workhouse escape was "badly managed"); Carson, *Petigru*, pp. 280–81; Charleston *Mercury*, 13–25 July 1849.

10. Charleston *Mercury*, 21 July 1849.

gratulated themselves on having averted a more serious confrontation.[11] Within a few years, however, the threat became a reality.

Charleston experienced subtle changes in the 1850s. Observers believed that immigrant artisans were filling positions previously held by blacks because the number of slaves in the city fell sharply.[12] Demographic evidence does not show a large increase in the foreign-born population, but the emergence of a strong nativist political movement and agitation by white artisans indicates increased popular awareness of and hostility to immigrants.[13] Charleston in the 1850s, with its newly visible foreign-born population, was thus subjected to the same tensions and conflicts between whites that had plagued Jacksonian Boston. In 1857, 69.4 percent of the persons committed to the house of correction were of Irish nativity and 83.5 percent were foreign-born.[14] The indefatigable chronicler of Charleston life, Jacob Schirmir, recorded almost no ethnic affrays or murders before 1850; in the following decade, however, there were five murders by Irishmen, five by Germans, one murder of an Irishman by a German, and two riots between Irish and city guards.[15] Charleston's mayor, William Porcher Miles, appreciated the changing situation when he told his constituents to "consider the growing size and population of the city, continually receiving accessions from a laboring class who require the check which only a regularly organized police, removed from them and independent of them, can supply." In 1856, nearly two decades after Boston, Charleston formed a professional police force.[16]

In both states, then, endemic urban violence in the antebellum

11. Interestingly, Charlestonians made no connection between the workhouse escape and the attempted burning of the church. The operations of the workhouse were sharply criticized, and this incident spurred the construction of a new building in 1851.

12. The slave population of the district dropped from 19,532 in 1850 to 13,909 a decade later, but the foreign-born population increased by only 10 percent (from 5,954 in 1850 to 6,533 in 1860) (United States census figures, 1850 and 1860).

13. *Report of the Committee on the Colored Population on the Petition of the South Carolina Mechanics Association.*

14. *Mayor's Report on City Affairs,* percentages computed from information on p. 64. The comparable figures for Boston (1858–63) were 49.2 percent and 63.6 percent respectively (Oscar Handlin, *Boston's Immigrants,* computed from information on p. 257).

15. Jacob Schirmir Diary, 15 May 1850, 13 June 1852, 10 March, 25 April, 7 Aug., 13 Nov., 15 Dec. 1855, 24 Oct. 1857, 5 May 1858, 25 Jan., 31 March, 4 July 1860.

16. *Mayor's Report,* pp. 14–23; see also Edward P. Cantwell, "A History of the Charleston Police Force." The police force was apparently modeled on that of Savannah, Georgia.

years spurred the establishment of professional police forces. But the significance of urban violence in predominantly rural South Carolina should not be overestimated. Far more revealing was a form of extralegal authority with no counterpart in Massachusetts, the organized, rural vigilante society. Unlike urban mobs that could be spontaneous or called to action on relatively short notice, the vigilante society required organization. Problems of communication in rural plantation areas made regular meetings, elaborate rituals, membership lists, and written constitutions a necessity. Organized at time of racial or political crisis, these societies were a response both to the lax enforcement of South Carolina patrol and militia laws and to the demographic facts of lowcountry life. In the tidewater, where blacks outnumbered whites by huge ratios, laws requiring the physical presence of one white for every ten slaves were frequently disregarded, as were regulations requiring militia and patrol duty. Most of the time, such laxness provided the measure of flexibility essential to the South Carolina system of slave control. But in times of crisis, new arrangements were necessary.

The first societies were formed as a result of the Vesey panic of 1822. The South Carolina Association, founded by Charleston aristocrats, was actually an urban vigilante group.[17] In nearby St. John's Parish the durable Pineville Association was established in 1823 to apprehend runaway slaves accused of violence or robbery. Supported by assessments on nearby slaveholders (who paid a fixed amount per slave owned), the Pineville Association paid the costs of prosecuting runaways and in 1827 set up a bounty system. The Association was revived in 1839, this time to suppress "all traffick with slaves." Vigilante groups were also formed to enforce the Negro Seaman's Act, ensuring that black crewmen remained quarantined in jail or aboard ship while in port.[18]

During the secession crises of 1849–51 and 1859–61, vigilantism became a general phenomenon throughout South Carolina. Two upcountry districts, Union and Spartanburg, sparked the first wave in 1849,[19] and the South Carolina Association was revived as the Charleston Vigilance Society. Most of the activity was directed against innocent free blacks and alleged violators of trading and patrol laws. These years have been described as a reign of terror for

17. William W. Freehling, *Prelude to Civil War.*, p. 113, and Marina Wikramanayake, *A World in Shadow*, p. 165.

18. Pineville Association Secretary's Book, SCHS; see also Howell M. Henry, *The Police Control of the Slave in South Carolina*, pp. 132–33.

19. Henry, *Police Control*, p. 159; A Copy of the Proceedings of the Committee of Vigilance for Union County, 8 Nov. 1849, McLean Family Papers, SCL.

blacks, but they were not the only victims.[20] A movement that began as a typical attempt to supplement South Carolina's ineffective patrol and militia system and to enforce the frequently ignored prohibitions on trading with blacks soon followed the classic vigilante pattern. Crossing the fine line between filling a vacuum of authority and outright terrorism, this second type of vigilantism also focused on suspected abolitionists. Using the same mock trial procedures of the Regulators and other vigilante movements, these self-appointed guardians of order tarred and feathered and even drove out of the state anyone considered soft on slavery.

Inevitably, the societies disposed of anyone they found offensive. Anyone with a northern background was particularly suspect; two northern schoolteachers were expelled from their homes in Kingstree in 1859 even though there was no proof that they were abolitionists.[21] In 1854, James L. Petigru won $2,500 for his client, a Yankee woodchopper, who was a victim of lowcountry vigilantism. As Petigru explained, "The vigilance committee had determined that no Yankees should come among them and, in pursuance of this determination, seized this man, . . . tied him . . . carried him to jail, and under the ridiculous pretense that he had stolen a piece of rope, whipped him publicly."[22] This incident illustrates the type of "violation" that could trigger vigilante justice. Petigru's victory, on the other hand, shows that such activities had to be kept within community or customary norms or they would not be sanctioned or protected.

The response to mob violence and vigilantism in each state demonstrates fundamentally divergent concepts of the role of formal law and authority. Massachusetts tried to reduce such challenges to official authority by expanding law enforcement, whereas South Carolina not only tolerated challenges to state authority, but frequently encouraged them on the not unreasonable pretext that they served a necessary function.

In Massachusetts, mob violence presented a challenge to the social order that could not be ignored. New antiriot legislation was passed after the convent burning; the police force was established primarily to prevent similar episodes and only secondarily to apprehend criminals. In South Carolina, by contrast, patrol and militia laws had become such dead letters that vigilantes could justifiably claim to be filling a societal need. Because authority was ineffective or nonexistent, extralegal methods posed no serious threat to it. An

20. Steven Channing, *Crisis of Fear,* pp. 29, 36.
21. Ibid., pp. 31–32.
22. Carson, *Petigru,* pp. 350–51.

example of official approval of extralegal action occurred in 1854. A private citizen, J. Malachi Ford, asked the legislature for compensation for arresting two slave murderers. The committee on claims granted him $200 to encourage this sort of action "when the ordinary officers of the law shrink from its performance."[23] Vigilantism was a necessary component of South Carolina's system of authority; not simply tolerated, it was acknowledged and encouraged until or unless it got out of hand—and sometimes was not even stopped then.

The Code of Honor

Both vigilantism and rioting represented collective responses to societal problems. But in South Carolina a significant element of extralegal activity pitted individual against individual. This element was the duel, an alternative to litigation practiced widely in the state. Dueling deserves special attention because it vividly illustrates an important aspect of South Carolina life. The persistent notion of honor in South Carolina explains to a large degree the refusal of citizens to allow the legal system to play a large role in their lives. The best way to understand South Carolina's sense of honor is to look at dueling, the Code of Honor.

Dueling was a form of extralegal activity that was far more widespread and symbolically more significant than vigilantism. The duelist's challenge went to the very foundation of formal authority, confronting not only a combatant, but also the notion of a society based on law and reason. Dueling had never been a way of life in Massachusetts or in the North. Declared illegal in 1784 in Massachusetts, it virtually disappeared in the North in the general revulsion that followed the death of Alexander Hamilton.[24] The last major duel in Massachusetts was fought in 1806—ironically, over legal reform. In the nineteenth century, the duel was primarily a southern insitution.[25]

The significance of dueling in South Carolina lies not in the actual practice, although duels were strikingly frequent. Rather, the importance lay in their public nature, in the class of people who

23. *South Carolina Reports and Resolutions,* 1854, p. 251.

24. Massachusetts *Acts* of 1784, ch. 9.

25. Richard E. Ellis, *The Jeffersonian Crisis,* p. 218. On dueling in the South, see in general Daniel J. Boorstin, *The Americans,* pp. 206–12, and John Hope Franklin, *The Militant South, 1800–1861,* pp. 33–60. On dueling in South Carolina see Jack Kenny Williams, "The Code of Honor in Ante-Bellum South Carolina."

participated in them, and in the concepts of law espoused by the defenders—and opponents—of the practice. Were it not for these other factors, dueling might have become simply another aspect of plantation era folklore, a chivalric curiosity, a remnant of an earlier civilization.

More than the functional equivalent of litigation among the upper classes, dueling was the only way for gentlemen to settle disputes or to avenge insults. The very name attached to the proceedings—the Code of Honor, a particular irony in a state that lacked codes of law—attests to its legalistic pretensions.

The duelist sought a negation of the law, and he claimed this as a natural right for his privileged class. Alexander Moultrie noted in 1787 that dueling is "a part of the residuum of natural liberty left in a society—but 'tis to protect that, the Law can't."[26] Duelists claimed that they could achieve no satisfaction in the courts, that no laws existed to avenge honor. Although South Carolina law provided no criminal penalties for libel and slander, the latter was actionable in civil proceedings. At bottom, it was these proceedings that were objectionable. In "Modern Honor," John Blake White's five-act tragedy on the evils of dueling, this argument is clearly expressed.[27]

>   let cowards take
> Your Dull routine of courts—Your writs, your pleas
> Rejoinders and Demurrers—A Gentleman
> Should scorn to follow in this idle round
> And sue for through the tedious lapse of year
> What in a moment he should grasp.
>
> What is a court but a record of disgrace?

The irony of this claim, of course, is that the lawmakers themselves often participated in duels. South Carolina law provided that dueling disqualified a man from holding public office.[28] In reality, participation in a duel seemed almost a prerequisite for such office.

The public nature of duels by prominent citizens further eroded the law. One traveler was shocked when two lawyers dueled in

---

26. Alexander Moultrie's Commonplace Book, SCL.

27. John Blake White, "Modern Honor: A Tragedy in Five Acts," manuscript in SCHS.

28. 5 *Statutes at Large* 671. An argument developed over whether this law violated the provision of the South Carolina constitution permitting each house to decide the qualifications of its own members. Futile efforts to enforce this provision by constitutional amendment appear as late as 1844 (Bills, 1844, SCA).

Charleston and "no notice" was taken.[29] Although the combat was often private, the challenges and preliminary correspondence were frequently published in the local press. The duels themselves were well reported; indeed, opponents charged that "our very newspapers have given publicity to duels." Such a complaint was not as repressive of press freedom as it may appear on first glance; South Carolina's newspapers withheld or delayed publication of news deemed harmful to public safety.[30]

In 1812, South Carolina mandated a heavy fine and up to a year in jail for all participants in duels, including seconds. If the duel was fatal, the survivor could be prosecuted for homicide. Seven years later, this act was gutted when the state's appellate court held that survivors and seconds could not be forced to testify in such prosecutions because to do so would violate their right against self-incrimination. Since the only witnesses to a duel were likely to be involved in some capacity and therefore liable to prosecution themselves, it was almost impossible to prosecute. In 1823, the law was changed to give immunity to such witnesses,[31] but continued disinterest in prosecuting showed that legal technicalities were hardly the major bar.

Although only gentlemen engaged in duels, the notion of honor permeated all white classes of southern society.[32] This fact, not the constitutional objections, made prosecution for dueling "a mere mockery of justice."[33] The juries' propensity to acquit overcame the prosecutors' perseverance. Although two of five duelists were convicted in selected districts—a respectable rate by South Carolina standards—the more telling figure is the small number of prosecutions initiated.[34] Moreover, magistrates were virtually powerless to prevent duels, because few citizens "from the impulses of public or

29. James Silk Buckingham, *The Slave States of America*, 1:552.

30. Charleston Anti-Dueling Association Petition to the Senate, Penal System Papers, SCA (this petition is marked 1819, but it is probably misfiled; the society was not formed until 1826. Charleston *Courier*, 19 Oct. 1826). Newspapers withheld information during the Vesey crisis, and the attempt to fire the Calvary Church was not reported until a week after the events and then only when a North Carolina newspaper reported it in an inflammatory manner (Charleston *Mercury*, 12 July 1849).

31. Attorney General Robert Y. Hayne to Governor, 6 Nov. 1819, Dueling File, Legal System Papers, SCA. The case was *State* v. *John Edwards* 2 Nott and McCord (1819) 13; the change in the law was 6 *Statutes at Large* 208.

32. Franklin, *Militant South*, pp. 36, 44.

33. Charleston Anti-Dueling Association Petition, Dueling File, Legal System Papers.

34. Districts included Richland (1800–1835), York (1800–1839), Lexington (1800–1824), Laurens (1806–35), Chester, Spartanburg (1800–1839), and Horry (1800–1835).

private regard or common humanity . . . give information."[35] Given popular hostility to legal interference with private vengeance, the watering down of the dueling law in 1834 hardly seemed necessary.[36]

Although the most serious threat posed by dueling was to the concept of law, other principles were also at stake. Since many duels resulted from remarks made in political debate, the potential threat of a challenge had a stifling effect on politics in a state where political divisions were little valued. Politicians caught without their dueling pistols were appropriately distraught.[37] Many duelists were newspaper editors, challenged by those they had offended in columns. Even an editor who had merely published someone else's article was likely to be a victim of the code; many editors, including Benjamin F. Perry, believed such duels seriously threatened freedom of the press in antebellum South Carolina.[38]

Duelists claimed they were not above the law at all, but guided by another law. The etiquette of dueling was every bit as elaborate as courtroom ritual. In one duel, the report of the attending surgeon, usually concerned with injury or death, was devoted entirely to a breach of dueling etiquette.[39] Duelists relied on John Lyde Wilson's *The Code of Honor*, a codification of the rules of dueling in a state that ironically had no code of its own statute law. Wilson's pamphlet is a clear expression of the ideology of dueling. Because the author was a prominent South Carolina politician—and something of a legal reformer—*The Code of Honor* is of unusual interest.

As governor, Wilson had urged the humanization of the slave trial system in 1824 while most of the state was still engulfed by post-Vesey hysteria. His criticism of the equity appeals system led to a major court reorganization, and his brief for codification was published in the same year as Thomas Smith Grimké's much better-known oration. Wilson's interest in legal matters undoubtedly inclined him toward writing *The Code of Honor*, but he also had a personal motive: he was married to Aaron Burr's ward.[40]

35. Charleston Anti-Dueling Society Petition, Dueling File, Legal System Papers.

36. 6 *Statutes at Large* 515.

37. See, for example, the increasingly desperate pleas of J. P. Dickinson for return of his dueling pistols, Dickinson to J. L. Manning, 3, 4, 20 Jan. 1844, John L. Manning Papers, SCL.

38. Benjamin F. Perry Autobiography (1874), Benjamin F. Perry Papers, SCL; Charleston *Mercury*, 15 Sept.–9 Oct. 1856.

39. Report of J. G. McWhorton, Dec. 1822, George McDuffie Papers, SCL.

40. Governor's Message, 1824, SCA; John Lyde Wilson, *Review of the Court of Equity* and *Codification*; Wikramanayake, *World in Shadow*, p. 166; O'Neall, *Biographical Sketches*, 2:319.

Wilson believed unequivocally in the principles of honor. Specifically denouncing a turn-the-other-cheek mentality as "repugnant to those feelings which nature and education have implanted in the human character," Wilson declared that if antidueling laws were enforced, "all the honorable [men] in the community would quit the country and inhabit the wilderness with the Indians." Wilson thus neatly turned the arguments of opponents of dueling on their heads. Whereas dueling had been criticized as a barbaric custom, Wilson declared that a society without dueling would be barbaric; his noble savage, in contrast to the opponents of dueling, was also a man of honor. Despite his crusade for legal reform, Wilson believed that in some cases the laws could give no redress.[41] Yet he was uncomfortable with blatantly extralegal activity. Although a leader in the raid on the Charleston post office, for example, Wilson sought to legitimize that action by popular vote.[42] Similarly, Wilson sought to cloak dueling with a legalistic veneer by codifying the custom.

Wilson insisted that life under the Code of Honor would result in fewer injuries caused by dueling because satisfaction, rather than the infliction of injury, was the true goal of the injured party. Any implication, Wilson protested, that he was "an advocate of duelling and wished to introduce it as the proper mode of deciding all personal difficulties and misunderstandings . . . would . . . [be a] great injustice."[43] Wilson sought to retain the ritual and principle of defending one's honor, but to end its most objectionable feature, the tendency toward homicide. Believing that ninety-nine out of one hundred duels occurred from lack of experience and knowledge by the seconds in handling disputes in their early stages, Wilson directed his efforts at their enlightenment. If seconds used more finesse in the preliminary negotiations of a duel, they could prevent bloodshed. Honor, the rock on which dueling was founded, itself could be invoked to end duels. Merely teach gentlemen that nothing was "more derogatory to the honor of a gentleman than to wound the feelings of anyone, however humble," and provocations would not occur.[44] Wilson's rules were used in duels, but his advice on ending the practice went unheeded.[45]

By staking out a monopolistic claim to principle and honor, the

41. John Lyde Wilson, *The Code of Honor*, p. 7.

42. John Belton O'Neall, *Biographical Sketches of the Bench and Bar of South Carolina*, 2:29.

43. Wilson, *Code of Honor*, pp. 3–4.

44. Ibid., pp. 8–9.

45. Record of a Duel between Davidson Legare and John Dunovant, 2 Aug. 1853, SCL: "In all respects not herein provided for, the parties will be guided by Wilson's *Code of Honor*."

duelist forced his opponent to accept the challenge or face "the ruin of all a man's hopes, interests, and enjoyments as a member of society."[46] Some duelists carried a certificate attesting that there had been "no want of firmness" in their hostile encounters.[47] Even some of those who deplored the practice recognized and accepted its rationale. "This duelling is a shocking business," William Ford DeSaussure told his brother, but "to be sure they cannot always be avoided. A man must never submit to insult, but he should take care never to insult others, and to be temperate tho' firm in the vindication of his own rights."[48]

A persistent theme in the opposition to dueling was that it was inimical to modern civilization. Opponents charged that "it originated in a dark and barbarous age."[49] Just as defenders of the *code duello* justified their views by a wholesale criticism of the administration of justice, so, too, the opponents collectively presented a telling indictment of the South Carolina legal system. They did not always understand, however, the extent to which dueling and similar alternatives to formal authority were integral parts of the total matrix of authority, of which the legal system was only part.

Opponents of dueling feared that the practice contained the seeds of anarchy. Dueling threatened the "security of property" by undermining the "paramount influence of the laws."[50] An antidueling sermonist claimed that dueling "has effected a practical subversion of the law of the land . . . the absolute overthrow and destruction of the criminal code."[51] But what dueling proved most emphatically about the legal system was its blatant class bias. The immunity of the duelist showed that the penal laws existed "for but one class of citizens and those are the weak . . . the ignorant and the defenseless." The privileged classes have established for themselves a "higher law," complained the sermonist. "They may and do not commit murder with impunity."[52]

Cognizant of how the criminal justice system operated, critics found that employing it for desirable ends was difficult. Charleston petitioners, for example, rejected the death penalty for duelists, but

46. Nathaniel Bowen, *Duelling under Any Circumstances the Height of Folly*, p. 14.
47. Certificate, 20 May 1831, Landgon Cheves Papers, SCHS.
48. William Ford DeSaussure to John F. DeSaussure, 31 Jan. 1829, DeSaussure Family Papers, SCL.
49. Petition on Dueling, 1805, Dueling File, Legal System Papers.
50. Robert Henry, *Discourse Occasioned by the Death of Edward P. Simons, Esq. and Archy Mayson, Esq.*, p. 5.
51. Arthur Wigfall, *A Sermon upon Duelling*, p. 9.
52. Ibid.

not for philosophical reasons. Quite pragmatically, they realized that only people of wealth and influence participated in duels. Because there would be irresistible pressure to acquit or pardon such people, any punitive laws would quickly become a nullity. One grand jury called for a penalty "less severe but more sure." Out of despair, an essayist suggested legalized dueling. Such an act would be a reversion to "a dark, bloody, ignorant age," but would at least end the contempt for government that the practice and current law fostered.[53] Caught between the demands of a proper legal order and a strong belief in honor, the state was no more ready to legalize dueling than it was to prosecute the duelist.

The survival of the *code duello* provides a significant clue to the nature of criminal justice in antebellum South Carolina. The rationale behind dueling is a clear expression of the South Carolina attitude toward authority. Having declared the law inadequate for achieving satisfaction, duelists discarded the law and placed themselves above it. Content with the law's inadequacies, they sought no changes. Dueling itself by no means explains South Carolina's 150-year failure to alter its legal system in any meaningful way. But the attitude of the duelist is so consistent with the policy of neglect as to be expressive of a concept in which official authority was seen as secondary to traditional relationships and expectations. The type of satisfaction sought by the duelists—the restoration of wounded honor—could no more be accomplished by a revision of the libel and slander laws than could Boston rioters rid their city of the unwelcome presence of Irish Catholics or blacks.

Dueling, mob violence, and vigilantism represented attempts to satisfy grievances where legal remedies were seen as inadequate. But the extent of human activity touched by the law was not similar in each state. Just as the role of courts and law enforcement was more narrowly circumscribed in South Carolina than in Massachusetts, so was that area of life touched by the law itself. One branch of criminal law in particular serves as a compelling indicator of the role of formal authority in society; these are crimes against chastity, morality, and decency.

The Regulation of Morals

Protection of life and property is one main object for forming political societies. Regulation of morals, on the other hand, is strictly

53. Charleston Anti-Dueling Association Petition, SCA; Reports of Dueling and Carrying Concealed Weapons, Report on the Presentment of the Abbeville Grand Jury, 8 Dec. 1846, Legislative System Papers, SCA; "The Duel," p. 443.

discretionary. Obviously, a society has an interest in controlling the economic consequences of morally proscribed behavior, such as enforcing child support for bastards and alimony for deserted and dependent spouses. But it is not essential that official authority become the guardian of morality, a function that can be filled in many societies by family and religion. Nor is it clear how moral guidelines are to be formed in a state. Moreover, lack of state supervision of morals hardly poses the threat to the existence of a society that murder and robbery do, although it may disturb stability. Therefore, since state action in this area can be regarded as gratuitous, the public enforcement of morals provides an index of the willingness—or insistence—of a state to intervene in the personal lives of its citizens and, accordingly, of the extent of penetration of formal authority into the lives of citizens.

On this score the two states represent polar extremes, with Massachusetts taking an activist approach and South Carolina a laissez-faire attitude. Massachusetts persisted in trying to regulate moral behavior, changing the particular emphasis to reflect new standards and behavior patterns. In South Carolina, such regulation was not considered a proper exercise of state authority, despite popular insistence that the state enter this arena.

The insistence with which colonial Massachusetts punished violations of sexual norms is well known. Laws were harsh and at the outset were strictly enforced. Sodomy and adultery were capitally proscribed; Sabbath-breaking, fornication, and profane swearing were among the more serious misdemeanors. The history of the enforcement of such laws is quite a different matter. Colonial court records reflect the decline of Puritanism and the simultaneous erosion of the efficacy of legal sanctions. In the seventeenth century, fornication was strictly punished; 60 percent of all premaritally pregnant couples were prosecuted in Essex County from 1671 to 1680. As the volume of offenses exploded during the sexual revolution of the eighteenth century, the penalties decreased and the nature of the prosecution shifted. By the mid-eighteenth century, married couples were no longer prosecuted for an early birth. By the Revolution, the only fornication convictions were of mothers of bastards, and by the 1790s child support, not moral disapproval, was the primary incentive to such proceedings.[54] By the nineteenth century, Massachusetts acknowledged the new

54. George Lee Haskins, *Law and Authority in Early Massachusetts*, pp. 80, 131, 145–47; Daniel Scott Smith and Michael S. Hindus, "Premarital Pregnancy in America, 1640–1971," pp. 537–80; William E. Nelson, "Emerging Notions of Modern Criminal Law in the Revolutionary Era," pp. 452–58.

reality and concentrated on prosecuting prostitutes and their employers.

The decline in prosecutions for fornication did not indicate community approval. The formal proscription remained in the statutes (as it does today). But the shifting emphasis illustrates two important themes in Massachusetts legal history. First, it represents the legal accommodation to reality. The pattern of prosecution shifted because the volume of offenses dictated choosing among different degrees of sexual offenses. Moreover, the type of community "holy watching" that could ferret out such offenders was no longer possible in a growing, heterogeneous society. Second, the continued regulation of sexual activity shows that this type of intrusion into the personal lives of its citizens was considered in Massachusetts to be a proper, even necessary, exercise of authority. Fornication, adultery, and bastardy were prosecuted throughout the entire period under study, even though the proportion of prosecutions represented by those offenses never regained their colonial significance. This interventionist posture extended to other areas of moral behavior as well. Well into the nineteenth century, Sabbath-breaking was a source of consternation. Not surprisingly, Massachusetts was the last state to jail a person for blasphemy.[55]

The actions that were banned in Boston, however, were not always unlawful in South Carolina. South Carolina did not punish fornication and proscribed bastardy only because of the potential economic threat of bastards as public charges. Although the penalty for fathering bastards was severe, the impetus was clearly financial. There was no penalty for mothering them, providing the child did not become a public charge.[56] Although the state inherited the English strictures against Sabbath-breaking and blasphemy, these were generally not enforced. A postrevolutionary vagrancy statute received its greatest usage in the 1850s to rid the countryside of suspected abolitionist incendiaries.[57]

Perhaps most revealing is the contrast between the two states in

55. *Remarks on the Existing State of the Laws in Massachusetts Respecting Violations of the Sabbath;* Leonard W. Levy, *The Law of the Commonwealth and Chief Justice Shaw,* pp. 43–58.

56. 2 *Statutes at Large* 270. During the Regulator era, licentiousness was apparently rampant in the Carolina backcountry, according to the colorful account of Charles Woodmason, *The Carolina Backcountry on the Eve of the Revolution,* pp. 15, 52, 56, 256–57, 281–82. Woodmason alleged that all but six of one hundred women whom he married as itinerant minister were pregnant (pp. 99–100); he also complained about wifeswapping (pp. 225–26).

57. Branchville Vigilance Association, Dec. 1860, SCA; Channing, *Crisis of Fear,* pp. 30, 51.

their attitude toward divorce. Again, the formal difference is not great. Massachusetts granted divorces only for adultery and impotence. Even for those who qualified, divorce was difficult to obtain and required tenacity, legal sophistication, and the services of an attorney.[58] Although Massachusetts was by no means a divorce haven, it stood in marked contrast to South Carolina's absolute prohibition on divorce, unique among all the states.

Despite the ban, several people petitioned the South Carolina legislature for divorce in the early nineteenth century. Fraud, adultery, and insurmountable suffering notwithstanding, no relief was granted. One couple emphasized that the "petition is a *joint* one seeking *unitedly* a relief indispensable to *their* future peace and happiness." Another petitioner told of being abandoned by his wife after less than five months of marriage. He complained that he was forced to choose between leaving his home state or a "life of celibacy," as foreign divorces were not recognized in South Carolina. Despite his wife's consent and the signatures of twenty-five citizens, including South Carolina College President Thomas Cooper, the petition was summarily rejected.[59] Appeals to the courts brought no relief. The judiciary denied jurisdiction, claiming that only the legislature could grant such authority.[60]

Characteristic of the state's tendency to utilize extralegal accommodations, many South Carolinians found a way out of the divorce debacle. They left their spouses and cohabited with other men or women. South Carolina did not prosecute adultery or fornication, and such arrangements were widespread. Although grand juries complained of this "growing evil," attempts to proscribe fornication or adultery were rebuffed in 1822, 1844, and 1856.[61] The sole legis-

58. *Revised Statutes of the Commonwealth of Massachusetts*, ch. 76, sec. 5. William O'Neill makes the point that permitting divorce in the first place is more important than the number of causes (*Divorce in the Progressive Era*, p. 26).

59. Petitions from Benjamin Harrison (1823), Drucilla Evans (1819), Henry and Nancy Gable (quoted, 1810), Elizabeth Hamilton (1813), Richard Hembree Hughes (1818), Rachel Teagle (1802), Mary Wilson (1821), and Curtis Winget (1830), Legal System Papers.

60. Women were entitled to alimony, but not divorce, in cases of desertion. *Olly Mattison* v. *Mary Mattison*, 1 Strobhart Equity 387 (1847); *DeVall* v. *DeVall*, 4 DeSaussure Equity 79 (1809). See also Joel Prentiss Bishop, *Commentaries on the Law of Marriage and Divorce and Evidence in Matrimonial Suits*, pp. 470–74. In the colonial period, the absence of ecclesiastical courts made divorce nearly unobtainable in the South; see George Elliott Howard, *A History of Matrimonial Institutions*, 2:367–68.

61. Bills, 1822, 1844, 1856, SCA; Presentments from Barnwell (1823, 1830), Chesterfield (1814), Darlington (1830), Edgefield (1805), Newberry (1813), Orangeburg (1828), Pendleton (1814), and Union (1822), Legislative System Papers.

lative response to this situation, interestingly, was to limit to one-quarter the amount of one's estate that could be left to concubines and bastards.[62] The response in South Carolina, then, was not to try to regulate behavior, but rather to assert the primacy of the natural and monogamous family by protecting wives and children from the economic consequences of the husband's behavior.

Even prostitution was not an area of major concern. Although keeping a bawdy house was illegal, most of the concern was focused on keeping such institutions beyond a ten-mile radius of South Carolina College. Prostitution was widespread in Charleston, but no moral crusade arose to eradicate it.[63]

The refusal to permit divorce or to proscribe adultery was consistent with the southern sanctification of family and womanhood, and is illustrative of the sexual and legal double standard in this planter-dominated state. The divorce ban was intended to be protective of women, who, in the words of Judge John Smyth Richardson, "have their charms destroyed and their constitutions wrecked in childbearing . . . the justification for which agony and bloody sweat is the security of the attentions of the one man for whom all was borne."[64] South Carolinians boasted of their state's moral stance, decrying all other states as "un-Christian" for permitting divorce. "The endurance of partial suffering" was considered "an evil vastly less . . . than that which arises . . . from the facility with which divorces are granted."[65] Even the few court decisions in this area seemed to place the economic relationship of marriage and the chivalric desire for security for the wife at the heart of marriage. Marriage was viewed as a life contract between competent parties, a contract based on economic interest, not on love.[66]

Taken together, the refusal to prohibit adultery or to permit divorce did not represent official sanction of extramarital sexual activity, but rather expressed a consistent sense that these areas were not appropriate to the exercise of state jurisdiction. But there was a disturbing element in this situation that shows not simply South Carolina's reluctance to intervene into private lives, but also the class-based nature of this laissez-faire attitude. Lowcountry planters, with their slave concubines, were beyond the law on their plantations. Divorce was not necessary, as marriage with a slave was

---

62. 5 *Statutes at Large* 271; see also *Hull* v. *Hull*, 2 Strobhart Equity 174.
63. Charleston Grand Jury Presentment 1820, Legislative System Papers.
64. Legal Notes, John Smyth Richardson Papers, SCL.
65. "Marriage and Divorce," p. 345; *Carolina Law Journal* vol. 1, no. 3.
66. *DeVall* v. *DeVall*, p. 83.

unthinkable. But not all of the state consisted of plantations. In the upcountry, adultery as a form of poor man's divorce was unsettling, especially to that region's militant Presbyterians. Every present-ment calling for laws against adultery came from the inland areas; only one complained of interracial liaisons.[67] One such presentment declared that "a strict observance of the rule of morality is indis-pensable and necessary for the good order, peace, and harmony of any community" and that "adultery destroys marriage" and is "pro-ductive of ruin and disgrace." To this grievance, the committee on religion (an interesting choice!) declined to legislate, "believing that such aberrations from divine laws . . . will be restrained by the si-lent admonitions of religion . . . and the indignations and contempt . . . of the community."[68] A clearer statement of the rationale be-hind South Carolina's disinclination to legislate morality could hardly be found: the planter's wife had her security, the planter his freedom, and everyone else had religion!

The extent of discretionary intervention in the area of sexual be-havior shows that neither state's experience can be seen as norma-tive. In Massachusetts, the continued obsession with sexual offenses confused law with a particular moral code, causing those who did not share that identical set of values to question the legiti-macy of authority. The South Carolina stance was equally consis-tent. Sexual matters, this posture implied, were not a subject of state concern; formal authority was to be used sparingly and only where necessary. By refusing divorce but openly encouraging alter-native arrangements, South Carolina left moral issues—as it did those of honor—as matters of individual responsibility and judg-ment.

This contrast between the two states is consistent in many areas of law and authority, although the suitability of these solutions for problems more pressing than fornication and divorce is far less clear. By reorganizing its courts, giving free rein to activist judges, con-straining mob violence with the first professional police force in America, and maintaining a strict watch on moral behavior, Mas-sachusetts exemplified a state in which law and the institutions of formal authority were intended to play a large role. The same legal philosophy that employed the law and the judiciary as vehicles for

67. See the presentments listed in note 61. The one complaint about interracial cohabitation is from Barnwell, 1830.
68. Union Grand Jury Presentment, Fall 1824; Report of the Committee on Reli-gion, Benjamin James, Chairman, 1824, both in Legislative System Papers.

the expansion of enterprise in the economic realm was mirrored in the criminal justice area as well. Massachusetts was an activist state that sought to regulate and routinize large areas of human endeavor in the name of the commonwealth. One may dispute the ulterior motives of such actions, how widely the benefits and costs of such enterprises were distributed, and the value of such a model for other and contemporary societies, but one can hardly disagree with this characterization.

In South Carolina, on the other hand, law was constricted. Courts were understaffed, laws were allowed to become and then remain obsolete, and local officials did their best to repel any use citizens might want to make of the instruments of justice and authority. Little attempt was made to supplant the apparently necessary services provided by the vigilante society and the Code of Honor. Local law enforcement was nonexistent until Charleston found through northern-style conflicts that its social problems could no longer be dealt with in traditional southern ways. Even in the area of moral legislation, where the legislature was faced with conduct of which it could hardly officially approve, and where there was sufficient precedent for action even within the comfortable English common-law tradition, the state would rather condone adultery than permit any alteration of its philosophy of law and authority.

In reviewing the structures of formal authority extablished by each state and the role of extralegal alternatives to that authority, we can identify a correlation between the effectiveness of those structures (such as statutes and courts) and the role of authority in that society (especially when contrasted to extralegal authority). But does this correlation have a causal component as well? This is far less clear, for the answer involves solving a classic chicken and egg problem. In South Carolina—to state the case in its clearest form —did weak institutions encourage extralegal authority or did the strength of such forms of authority inhibit the development of strong structures of law and authority? What is the role of tradition and values in determining whether a society will promote formal authority or its extralegal, informal, or traditional alternatives?

It is clear that neither state was either autocratic or anarchic. Both states had an elaborate base of social cohesion, apparently appropriate to each context. And yet the patterns of authority and the area of life touched by the law were vastly divergent. Perhaps what is most important is to recognize that whatever the source, by the end of the eighteenth century, the cause of this contrast was not as important as the consequence. By then, each state had an ongoing tradition of handling problems of conflict and control either primarily through the legal system or primarily through other forms of authority. Each state, then, struck a balance between formal and informal, legal and extralegal. In the following chapters we will explore the implications of these balances to determine the suitability of each to the society that maintained it.

Part II
The Contours of Crime and Justice

In the previous chapters we have seen how the structures of law, authority, and justice in the two states diverged during the late eighteenth and nineteenth centuries. Despite their common English legal heritage, despite the common experience of rebellion and constitution making, despite similar structural problems, the two states erected and maintained dissimilar systems of justice and authority.

These differences extended not simply to courts, justices, magistrates, and law enforcement personnel, but to the nature of law and authority as well. In Massachusetts, the rule of law played a central role in the ordering of society; institutional arrangements reflected this centrality and reinforced the legal order. But in South Carolina, the legal order was but one alternative among many. Notions of honor, class deference, and race control all encouraged the growth of extralegal and informal arrangements, sometimes at the expense of the formal exercise of authority. And, in certain important discretionary areas, even the extent of life touched by law was significantly different.

Neither state's experience was prescriptive in that regard; the extent of interference with private morals in Massachusetts clearly represented the imposition of elite values upon a seemingly less socialized, largely immigrant population. And South Carolina's laissez-faire attitude stemmed from a fundamental hostility to official state power in any form that was so extreme that it prevented the state from educating even its white inhabitants.

For the most part, these structural contrasts are of greater significance for civil than for criminal law. The debt cases that closed courts in both states, the debate over equity, even the relative status and duties of appellate and lower court judges were all primarily aimed at certainty and consistency in the formation and application of legal doctrine. Such arrangements are important to criminal law insofar as they are indicative of general attitudes toward formal law and authority, but they do not necessarily affect criminal justice directly.

Now we look at the criminal justice system itself, but not through structures or institutions. Rather, this section will statistically analyze thousands of criminal cases in the aggregate, concentrating on those stages from which systematic patterns can be drawn. Chapter 3 considers the patterns of criminal prosecutions from the seventeenth to the nineteenth centuries. It is comparative on two levels —chronological as well as cross-sectional changes are considered. This method of comparison demonstrates that prosecution patterns remained totally disparate in the two states, even though the pattern of prosecutions in Massachusetts underwent considerable change in the two-hundred-year period.

The contrasts in the pattern of prosecutions, refined but not otherwise altered in the analysis of urban and rural trends, undoubtedly shaped the development of criminal justice in each state. To oversimplify, but by way of preview, white crime in South Carolina primarily involved individual violence. Not the result of societal conditions or of some predatory or dangerous class, such crime was a function of honor and a high level of sustained personal contact in this highly individualistic society. In Massachusetts, on the other hand, crime posed a threat to society, not simply to individuals within it. Drunks and vagrants harmed few passersby, but threatened to rip a social fabric based on diligence and self-control. Theft and burglary threatened the very foundation of private property in the state and promised to undermine individual incentive to acquire property.

These very different crimes, therefore, fueled similarly divergent views on what to do about crime, and we shall explore these later as we look at punishment and reform. But even within the criminal justice system, the crime patterns had significant implications. These can be seen in the way various types of prosecutions were disposed, the subject of Chapter 4. The last chapter in this segment focuses on punishment, the final end of justice.

Through this statistical portrait of the cases that clogged the courts in each state, we can see what crimes triggered such a different response in each state.

Chapter 3.
The Dimensions of Crime

Different concepts of law and authority prevailed in Massachusetts and in South Carolina. Central to any study of crime and justice is knowledge of the types of crimes prosecuted and the behavior of the criminal justice system in handling cases. Here, too, the contrasts are striking. By the nineteenth century, the types of offenses committed in the two states were distinctly correlated with economic, social, and cultural patterns. Massachusetts's prosecution of crimes against property and propriety well served the needs of its urbanizing, industrializing society, but also reflects the severe dislocations that accompanied these processes and in turn stimulated deviant behavior. In South Carolina, by contrast, the absence of a distinct predatory class of whites and the strength of the notion of honor seem to account for the extraordinary level of prosecutions of crimes of violence; crimes against property and propriety were of far less frequency relative to those of violence.

Numerous conceptual and methodological problems are associated with any statistical study of crime. All historians of crime have wrestled with them, but most have chosen to use statistical material to some degree. I will not repeat the litany—both of difficulty and of utility—except to add that my use of these data conforms to most of the caveats in the existing literature. Only long-term, large-scale differences are accorded significant explanatory value. Rates generated by the data are not taken literally, but are used comparatively, both over time and cross-sectionally, whenever changes in reporting and collection do not invalidate the results.[1]

1. Several recent studies in the history of crime have used statistics. Despite individual reservations about the validity of the data, all the scholars (except Tobias) have used criminal statistics. Some, such as John Beattie, are satisfied that the "dark figure," or crimes that will never be known to the historian, is a fairly constant multiple of reported crimes. Therefore, he implies, statistics do register significant changes in criminality over time. Gatrell and Hadden maintain that if the jurisdiction is sufficiently large and the time span sufficiently long, local changes in police manpower and policy will not interfere with analysis of the trends. Tobias, however, disagrees, and in the only statistical part of his monograph, shows that reported crime is affected by policy matters. The most significant works on the history of crime are John M. Beattie, "The Pattern of Crime in England" and "Towards a Study

One central question can never be fully resolved, given the lack of available data. This is the extent of correlation between officially recorded crime and actual levels of criminal behavior. To say, for example, that crime in Massachusetts was characterized by a high level of offenses against property and propriety refers only to crimes officially reported. But rather than ignore this material, and rather than separate it completely from behavioral reality, we can find a common-sense solution.

Crime statistics are not totally divorced from reality, just as they are not totally reflective of it. The emphasis on property and order offenses reflects not only the perceived threat to the social order presented by such crimes, but also the changed conditions that both facilitated such offenses and increased their visibility. For example, the same economic changes that increased the potential disruption of theft and white collar crimes also made them easier to commit. The growth of a commercial economy was accompanied by increased concern about crimes against property that threatened the fragile market economy. But another effect of the rise of large-scale commercial enterprises was the emergence of specialized institutions and buildings, such as stores and warehouses. These made theft easier because the separation between residence and business reduced the likelihood that anyone would witness the crime. Furthermore, as goods became more fungible, tracing and identifying stolen property became more difficult. As commercial transactions became both more numerous and more impersonal, it became impossible for every businessman to know the reputation for honesty and integrity of all those with whom he had to deal. This situation, in turn, facilitated the commission of such white collar crimes as fraud and forgery.

An increase in prosecutions of certain crimes against order is also related to social change. The growing density of settlement made

---

of Crime in 18th Century England"; V. A. C. Gatrell and T. B. Hadden, "Criminal Statistics and Their Interpretation"; Joel B. Samaha, *Law and Order in Historical Perspective*; and Abdul Qaiyum Lodhi and Charles Tilly, "Urbanization, Crime, and Collective Violence in Nineteenth-Century France." An earlier attempt to deal with American crime statistics can be found in Roger Lane, "Crime and Criminal Statistics in Nineteenth-Century Massachusetts." One scholar who rejected crime statistics (though using a statistical argument) is J. J. Tobias, *Urban Crime in Victorian England.* Perhaps the most elaborate statistical study of criminality in America is Eric H. Monkkonen's *The Dangerous Class.* Monkkonen uses matching techniques to identify the criminal class of Columbus, Ohio. Concerned with offenders, not offenses, Monkkonen successfully avoids the problem of the dark figure. A good statistical overview of female criminality in this period can be found in Estelle Brenda Freedman, "Their Sisters' Keepers," pp. 6–39.

people more aware of their neighbors. Most crimes against order were prosecuted only if they actually offended or bothered other people. Given the close quarters of life in early nineteenth-century cities, it is not surprising that behavior that would go largely unnoticed in rural areas was characterized as a public nuisance in the metropolis.

The pattern of identifiable offenses, therefore, is not the mere creature of the criminal justice system. Constables in nineteenth-century Massachusetts did not suddenly begin arresting hordes of thieves whom they had ignored in the eighteenth century in the search for fornicators. The relationship between social values and criminal prosecutions includes actual behavior. The full extent of the relationship between all three factors is far from completely understood, but mechanistic explanations based on the observable response of the criminal justice system must not be substituted simply because of their conceptual convenience.

Finally, there is another reason for looking at the data collected in the past. This information frequently served as the basis of popular perception and attitudes and thereby influenced public policy. The spread of news through widely circulated media such as newspapers increased the awareness of crime. In Massachusetts, the annual reports of jails, correction houses, state prison, and the attorney general stimulated discussion of the crime situation. Such analysis was frequently shortsighted—annual increments overshadowed the more elusive long-term trends—but public policy was determined to a large extent by such reports and the perceptions of increased or decreased criminality contained in them.

There are several reasons why comparing the incidence and type of crime in Massachusetts and South Carolina must be inexact. Of major importance is slavery. Slaves and free blacks were subjected to an entirely different penal code and mode of trial than were whites; their crimes are analyzed separately. But whites could be prosecuted for crimes involving slaves; such crimes have no counterpart in Massachusetts. Second is the problem of jurisdiction. Both states had two levels of criminal proceedings. The first was summary, or trial without a jury. In South Carolina, these trials were conducted by a justice of the peace or a magistrate. Some town councils also heard minor cases. In Massachusetts, summary proceedings were conducted by a peace justice, trial justice, or police court. Since complete records of summary jurisdiction do not exist, such cases are excluded from the comparison. Only the second type of proceeding, cases originally presented to the grand jury and (if brought to trial) heard by a petit jury, are considered.

But this limitation does not ensure perfect comparability. The jurisdiction of trial courts in the two states was not equivalent. Assaults and larcenies were almost invariably tried before a jury in South Carolina; in Massachusetts they could be heard by either justices or juries. Including summary jurisdiction when known in Massachusetts changes the absolute incidence of offenses, of course, but does not significantly alter the general pattern.[2] Summary jurisdiction was less important in South Carolina (because the types of cases that could be heard in that manner were limited) so that the absence of such records is not as crucial.

These problems could be avoided by studying only felonies, but even that solution would leave two problems unsolved. First, many official records in Massachusetts made no distinction between felonies and misdemeanors for such crimes as larceny. More significantly, felonies were an extremely small part of the total crime picture. To understand the concern about crime, to appreciate the impetus for building penitentiaries and correction houses and for establishing police, one must look at the entire spectrum of criminal behavior.

For South Carolina, complete data are unavailable. Consistent with the manner in which justice in South Carolina was administered, there are no centralized judicial statistics. Many court records have not survived. In 1838, in an attempt to justify the state's need for a penitentiary, Benjamin F. Perry asked each district to prepare summaries of criminal trials since 1800.[3] Surviving compilations for districts that complied have been incorporated here. Other sources include court journals and grand jury findings. I have used most of the records and transcripts that have been centrally collected. All rates are computed with the appropriate population base. The coastal counties, however, are severely underrepresented because few records survived. A fragment of Charleston records is extant, so this vital urban district was included.

The Massachusetts data are more complete and more varied. In order to gain the broadest possible vantage point, centrally compiled statistics, rather than county court dockets and files, were used for the statistical base. There were two annual compilations. The first was by the attorney general (except for 1843–48 when the office was

2. The pattern remains similar because liquor-related offenses were the most significant in either jurisdiction. For summary jurisdiction, drunkenness was the most common offense. For jury trials, it was violations of the license law. Arrests for these offenses varied with the passage of liquor legislation.

3. Benjamin F. Perry, *Report of the Special Committee Appointed at the Session of 1838 on the Subject of the Penitentiary System*, pp. 18–21.

abolished). The other was the annual reports of the keepers of the jails and houses of correction. The latter source fails to distinguish between jury trials and summary judgment, so it cannot be used comparatively. Commitment figures are useful because they include everyone incarcerated at any stage in the criminal process from arrest to punishment. Although they present a more comprehensive picture of incarceration than is available from almost any other source, commitment figures are influenced by such class-based factors as ability to make bail.

The data show that the first striking difference in the two states is the pattern of crime. A simple frequency distribution by category and offense illustrates the types of crime dominant in each state independent of rates of incidence. In South Carolina, in both the eighteenth and nineteenth centuries, assaults dominated the dockets, comprising nearly three-fifths of the nineteenth-century cases (Tables 3.1 and 3.2). In Massachusetts, crimes against morality dominated in the colonial era; over three-fifths of eighteenth-century prosecutions involved such offenses. In the nineteenth century, property crimes—particularly those involving theft—increased to almost a third of all prosecutions. White collar, financial crimes also increased in importance. But the single largest category in nineteenth-century Massachusetts was liquor-related offenses. This general description includes both violations of the licensing laws (the offenses prosecuted most frequently in trial courts) and drunkenness (the offense for which the largest number of people were committed to jails and correction houses). There were more prosecutions for liquor offenses in Massachusetts than for property offenses.

In South Carolina, it is clear that some form of violence usually triggered an encounter with the criminal justice system. In this sense, the state looks very different from Massachusetts. But although underlying conflicts resulted in violence more frequently in South Carolina than they apparently did in Massachusetts, it does not follow that the underlying antagonisms themselves were totally different. It is impossible to quantify the reasons for which people assaulted each other in a state characterized by short fuses. The degree of information in surviving prosecutions is too eclectic to withstand systematic and quantitative scrutiny. Most prosecutions omit any mention of the provocation, and it is impossible to know whether the omissions were random.

Of the cases for which the provocation is known, some patterns emerge. There are four general categories, two of which are hardly unique to South Carolina, one of which is sui generis, and only one

Table 3.1. Colonial Crime Patterns, Massachusetts and South
Carolina (percentage of total prosecutions by category)

	Location		
Crime	Essex Co. Mass., 1651–1680	Middlesex Co., Mass., 1760-1774	Charleston, S.C., 1769–1776
Crimes against Persons			
Murder		1.2	5.1
Assault			48.3
Rape			.2
Total		9.5	53.6
Crimes against Property	20.8		
Larceny		12.9	28.8
Arson		.3	.4
Other			8.6
Total		13.2	37.8
Crimes against Order and Morals			
Bastardy, fornication	16.8	57.6	1.6
Riot, vagrancy	6.6	n.a.	1.6
Total	23.4	57.6	3.2
Forgery, fraud, counterfeit	n.a.	1.2	2.4
Slave-related	n.a.		3.1
Crimes against the church	32.7	7.3	
Contempt of authority	23.1	11.1	
Total	100.0	100.0	100.1*
Number of Cases		370	597 (includes 48 misc.)

Sources: Essex County: Kai T. Erikson, *Wayward Puritans*, recomputed from data
on p. 175. Middlesex County: William E. Nelson, "Emerging Notions of Modern
Criminal Law in the Revolutionary Era," pp. 452–53. South Carolina: South
Carolina Court of General Sessions, Journal (Charleston Sitting), 1769–76, SCA.
   *Rounding error.

Table 3.2. Criminal Prosecutions in Nineteenth-Century
Massachusetts and South Carolina

Crime	Massachusetts Prosecutions, 1833–1859*		South Carolina Prosecutions, 1800–1860†	
	Number	Percent‡	Number	Percent‡
Crimes against Persons				
Murder	149	.5	283	2.2
Assault	5,106	17.2	7,018	55.8
Rape	44	.1	37	.3
Total	5,299	17.8	7,338	58.3
Crimes against Property				
Theft, receiving	8,911	29.9	1,573	12.5
Arson	258	.9	73	.6
Total	9,169	30.8	1,646	13.1
Crimes against Order and Morals				
Nuisance, riot, vagrancy	1,477	5.0	1,210	9.6
Drunkenness	657	2.2		
License law	9,901	33.3	336	4.4
Sexual offenses	2,079	7.0	336	2.7
Other			166	1.3
Total	14,114	47.4	2,268	18.0
White collar	1,147	3.9	92	.7
Slave-related	—	—	1,240	9.8
Total	29,769	99.9	12,584	99.9
Other	3,084		932	
Grand Total	32,853		13,516	

Sources: Massachusetts: *Reports of the Attorney General,* Legislative Documents. South Carolina: Richland County Grand Jury Findings, York Cases, Spartanburg Sessions Index, Charleston Sessions Journal, Lexington, Horry, Chester, Laurens, Edgefield, Greenville, Newberry, Kershaw, Union, miscellaneous manuscripts and WPA sessions transcripts, SCL.

*1833–1838, 1849–1852, 1854–1859.

†Spartanburg (1800–1860), Horry (1800–1835; 1855–1860), Richland (1800–1835), Lexington (1810–1824), Laurens (1800–1860), Charleston (1857–1860), Chester (1806–1835), Edgefield (1807–1860), York (1800–1860), Greenville (1817–1822; 1836–1860), Newberry (1822–1834; 1858–1860), Kershaw (1810–1814; 1830–1835; 1840–1855), Union (1840–1860).

‡Rounding error.

of which is clearly supportive of the notion that this was a violent society, even though a violent reaction was involved in all these prosecutions.

The first category includes assaults resulting from disputes over property. Although South Carolina prosecuted a relatively small percentage of offenders for property crimes, many assaults resulted from disputed ownership. For example, in 1815, Lavinia Taylor (also known as Lavinia Smith) was prosecuted for assaulting Sarah Gannon; the dispute concerned change of a $10 bill. Two assault prosecutions resulted in arrests for thievery. Still others resulted from alleged bad dealings or swindles or failing to pay gambling debts. Thus, assault cases may in part explain the low incidence of property-related prosecutions.[4]

Class control was an important element of law enforcement in Boston. But the second characteristic type of assault prosecution shows that this was significant in Charleston as well. As an important international port, Charleston at almost any given time had a huge number of sailors either in port or waiting to ship out. These sailors were probably the closest white group to a criminal class in the city, and they were constantly involved in assault prosecutions both on ship and near the waterfront.[5]

A third major category of assault prosecutions involved interracial and slavery-related issues. Leaving aside the various racial slurs that resulted in altercations, slavery itself seemed to inspire a certain pugnacity. Four men were accused of assaulting Tenis Vanholten when they entered his property and carried away an unidentified "mulatto." Another man was charged with assault when he tried to stop a man from beating his father's slave. Some of these prosecutions crossed categorical lines. For example, one man was assaulted by the captain of the ship he had entered for the purpose of retrieving a slave he claimed as his. The slave, if he was one, had signed on as a crew member.

Finally, many assault prosecutions resulted from attacks on one's honor. These were often the response to a verbal insult, and many of these insults were race-related. Still other assaults resulted from being called everything from a "rascal" to an "infernal Bitch." Consistent, too, with the chivalric notion of honor, men resorted to violence to defend southern womanhood. John B. White (conceiv-

4. See *State* v. *Taylor* (1815), *State* v. *Deas* (1817), *State* v. *Martin* (1839), *State* v. *Dickhoff* (1839), and many similar prosecutions, Charleston District Court of General Sessions, Indictments, SCA.

5. See *State* v. *Maxsayk* (1816), *State* v. *Hines and Brush* (1822), and other similar cases, ibid.

ably the John Blake White who wrote on dueling) confessed to assaulting John Summers after Summers accused White of taking liberties with Summers's sister. John Thomas assaulted Maurice O'Flynn after O'Flynn had insulted Thomas's wife.[6]

Thus, many assault prosecutions represented South Carolina's peculiar response to the insecurity of property in the urban setting. Assault prosecutions linked to race and slavery show how the existence of large numbers of blacks seemed to contribute to an aura of violence. And, finally, the assaults that were based on honor clearly verify impressions of southern violence and volatility.

In South Carolina, the pattern of crime changed little over two centuries. In Massachusetts, however, there was considerable change, suggesting an almost inverse relation between crimes against morality and crimes against property. One recent and widely known interpretation of the historical evolution of crime in Massachusetts is by William E. Nelson. Using criminal prosecutions from 1760 to 1830, Nelson stresses a transition from crime as sin to crime as theft, or from morality to property. From 1760 to 1774, 38 percent of all prosecutions were for violations of sexual morality. Offenses against morality and religion together constituted 51 percent of all prosecutions. Only 13 percent were for crimes against property and 15 percent for crimes of violence. The revolutionary era represented something of a turning point. From 1790 to 1830, by contrast, 41 percent of all prosecutions were for crimes against property and only 7 percent for crimes of morality.[7] Nelson relates this shift to a more general and simultaneous change in the Massachusetts legal system from ethical concerns (that is, morals) in the colonial period to the protection of the bases of the commercial economy in the early nineteenth century (that is, property). The data presented in this study certainly offer some support for Nelson's interpretation. But a more sensitive analysis shows that Nelson's explanation, though not incorrect, is an oversimplification. The nature, timing, and degree of this shift all seem to demand reconsideration when the data are examined in more detail.

First, let us consider crimes against morality. By the second half of the eighteenth century, when Nelson picks up the story, the concern of the legal system in prosecuting sexual offenses had al-

6. *State* v. *Toussaint* (1811), *State* v. *Magee* (1829), *State* v. *Denny* (1817), *State* v. *DeBow* (1816), *State* v. *Timmons* (1832), *State* v. *Thompson* (1810), *State* v. *Mandeville* (1817), *State* v. *Maynon* (1823), *State* v. *Massolon* (1836), *State* v. *Geeldes* (n.d.), *State* v. *Bradley* (1838), *State* v. *Summers* (1812), and many similar prosecutions, ibid.

7. William E. Nelson, *The Americanization of the Common Law*, pp. 37–39, 118.

ready shifted from moral disapproval to economic interest. In the seventeenth century, courts prosecuted even the most minor, unthreatening deviations from moral norms. Of the prosecutions for sexual crimes in seventeenth-century Essex County, for example, 37.9 percent involved married couples with an early birth. Only 12.3 percent were bastardy cases.[8] Thus, in the seventeenth century, control of behavior, not economic interest, was the primary motive for these prosecutions.

By contrast, in late eighteenth-century Middlesex County, all but 10 of 210 fornication prosecutions involved illegitimate births. Since the economic interest of the town was at stake in such proceedings, to interpret them strictly as prosecutions for sin is misleading. Prosecutions for bastardy continued well into the late nineteenth century. In short, the shift away from prosecutions for unambiguous crimes against morality happened earlier than Nelson describes.

Moreover, Nelson tends to divorce behavior from prosecution. That is, he implies that the shift from crime as sin to crime as theft occurred within the legal system, which changed its emphasis as reflected by prosecutions. But in the case of sexual behavior, we have a rare opportunity to observe behavioral changes and their impact on the legal system. Marriage and birth records reveal the percentage of brides who were pregnant at marriage. Such premarital pregnancy ratios are indicative of changes in the relative levels of sexual behavior. By comparing fluctuations in the premarital pregnancy ratios with fluctuations in prosecutions for sexual offenses, we can determine whether prosecution was linked to or separate from behavior. Consistently throughout the colonial period in Massachusetts, peaks in the prosecution of sexual offenses matched peaks in the premarital pregnancy ratios. Unwittingly, Nelson finds high rates of prosecution for sexual misconduct during a period in Massachusetts when nearly half of all brides were pregnant at marriage.[9] When Nelson finds a decline in prosecutions, sexual practices were also changing. The year Nelson begins his research, 1760, is a demographically inopportune time to use for a major interpretation of legal change. In fact, the pattern of prosecutions for sexual offenses in eighteenth-century Middlesex County shows a greater peak in 1731–35 than that observed by Nelson for 1760–74. Moreover, the interim decades show a significant decline in fornication prosecutions. Thus, looking over the entire eighteenth century, it is

8. Daniel Scott Smith and Michael S. Hindus, "Premarital Pregnancy in America, 1640–1971," p. 554.

9. Ibid., pp. 537–39.

difficult to conclude that the period 1760–74 was typical of the colonial pattern.[10] Study of the previous century and a half of legal enforcement of sexual mores shows that Nelson's attempt to link his paradigm to the American Revolution ignores a much more significant long-term trend. Finally, Nelson's paradigm ignores one of the great and ironic consistencies in the history of crime in Massachusetts. By the late eighteenth century, the criminal justice system of Massachusetts was beginning to display certain elements of class control.

Whereas seventeenth-century criminal defendants seem to have been heterogeneous economically, the new pattern—prosecuting mothers of bastard children where child support was uncertain—illustrates something of a double standard. The period marked the beginning of the institutionalization of the poor at the same time that the pace of social stratification was quickening. The transition from morality to property in the criminal law should not mask the development of class control as one object of criminal justice. In the late eighteenth century, mothers of bastards were treated the same way drunks were a century later. In both cases, the criminal sanction was extended to people who had not injured specific individuals but whose nonconforming behavior posed a threat to the social order. They were distinct from the rest of society not by virtue of their actions (for other classes could hide their bastards and their drunkenness) but of their position in society.

One part of Nelson's analysis is clearly true. Offenses against morality were not pursued as vigorously in the nineteenth century as in the seventeenth and eighteenth centuries. The routine, non-threatening offenses were ignored in the nineteenth century, in part because they were now viewed differently by the general society and in part simply because previous efforts at prosecution had failed. Despite rigorous efforts to ferret out all fornicators, premarital pregnancy ratios rose dramatically in the eighteenth century. Continued prosecution of this minor offense would have only served to undermine the law, rather than to control behavior.

There was a gradual shift from crime as sin to crime as theft, but it was quite different from that described by Nelson. First, the shift took two centuries, not a few decades. Second, it was related in part to evolving concerns in the legal system, but also to shifting patterns in behavior and society. Sexual behavior changed, as did the conditions that gave rise to crimes against property.

In a larger sense, crimes against morality never ceased to be a

10. George Elliott Howard, *A History of Matrimonial Institutions,* 2:193.

central concern of the legal system. What changed was the type of morality proscribed and prosecuted. Instead of premarital fornication, in the late eighteenth and nineteenth centuries, only the more serious and threatening sexual offenses were prosecuted, such as bastardy, incest, polygamy, bigamy, adultery, and sodomy. The nature of offenses that were prosecuted shifted from private to public —almost literally from indoor to outdoor. The drunk, vagrant, prostitute, or purveyor of spirits became far more important than the unwed parent or pregnant bride. These new "crimes" were certainly crimes against morality as much as they were crimes against the public order. Commitments for drunkenness and violations of the license law climbed steeply with the passage of restrictive liquor legislation; in effect, such legislation criminalized a common habit of a major segment of the population.[11] The object of punishment for such crimes was not so much to cure behavior as to rid the streets of the offensive presence of those who committed it. Long-term confinement for such convictions was both unjust and prohibitively expensive. As an expedient compromise, drunks were arrested, released after paying a small fine and perhaps spending a night or two in jail, and then picked up again. Multiple arrests for drunkenness became the expectation.[12] One set of victimless crimes simply replaced another; morality prosecutions did not decline, but their focus and emphasis shifted.

If the moral vigilance of Massachusetts represented one extreme, the apparently libertine inaction of South Carolina represented another. South Carolina prosecuted no sexual offenses except bastardy where child support was the main concern. Church courts were much weaker in South Carolina than in either England or the other American colonies. In this instance, however, the South Carolina experience was not typical of the region. Both Maryland and Virginia vigorously prosecuted violators of sexual standards.[13]

By the nineteenth century in Massachusetts, crimes against property—particularly theft-related offenses—sharply increased as a per-

---

11. There are some indications that people were aware of this; see the discussion in Chapter 9.

12. The *Annual Reports* of the Massachusetts Board of State Charities were filled with stories of people arrested dozens of times for drunkenness. See especially the *Sixth Annual Report*, 1870, pp. 20–25. Note also that convictions and cases in trial courts for liquor-related offenses were dominated by violations of the license law, while commitments to jails and correction houses were dominated by arrests for drunkenness. The difference, of course, is that drunkenness was tried summarily.

13. David Flaherty, "Law and the Enforcement of Morals in Early America"; see also Arthur P. Scott, *Criminal Law in Colonial Virginia*, pp. 239–92, and Raphael Semmes, *Crime and Punishment in Early Maryland*, pp. 174–206.

centage of all prosecutions. This was in part the result of increasing social stratification and population concentration. Although geographic segregation by economic class was beginning to occur, cities and towns were still sufficiently compact so that criminal and victim lived or worked in some proximity. Many places experienced geographic specialization by economic function. Thus, large areas of port cities were predominantly commercial and provided opportunity for thefts.[14] Certain crimes, as nineteenth-century observers realized, were associated with advances in technology and with an increasingly complex commercial economy.[15] These were the white collar crimes—forgery, counterfeiting, extortion, embezzlement, and fraud. In contrast with Massachusetts and indicative of the relative status of economic development, white collar crimes were virtually insignificant in nineteenth-century South Carolina.

What about the incidence of crime itself? Although one historian contends that crime declined in Massachusetts from the mid-nineteenth century on, the only consistent figures show the decline occurring after 1880.[16] What about the previous half century? The total commitment rate to Massachusetts penal institutions fluctuated throughout the period with a peak in the mid-1850s (Figure 3.1). If only offenses against persons and property are measured, however, there was a substantial increase between 1837 and 1855, with no significant trend thereafter.[17] Therefore, there is no evidence of a decline in serious crime before 1880, but some evidence for a decline in minor crime.

From these data, one can see that the crime wave that followed the Mexican War was only part of a long-term upward swing that peaked well after the "crime wave" itself was recognized. Similarly, the celebrated post–Civil War crime wave was serious only in relation to the abnormally low rates during the war itself, when many

14. Sam Bass Warner, Jr., describes Boston as a "walking city" in this period (Streetcar Suburbs, pp. 16–21).

15. See the articles by Roger Lane and Richard D. Brown. Lane points out that the simultaneous growth of cities and industry was unique to America ("Crime and the Industrial Revolution"). Brown discusses urbanization in Massachusetts outside of Boston during this crucial period ("The Emergence of Urban Society in Rural Massachusetts, 1760–1820"). See also Francis Lieber, Remarks on the Relation between Education and Crime in a Letter to the Rev. William White D.D., p. 5.

16. Lane, "Crime and Criminal Statistics"; Theodore N. Ferdinand, "The Criminal Patterns of Boston since 1849," p. 87. Ferdinand uses police arrest records.

17. Commitments were not affected in any way that can be determined by the capacity of the institutions or by economic fluctuations. Correlations between commitment rates for property crimes and the Pearson-Warren Price Series and correlations between actual commitments and several different variables related to capacity yielded nothing of significance.

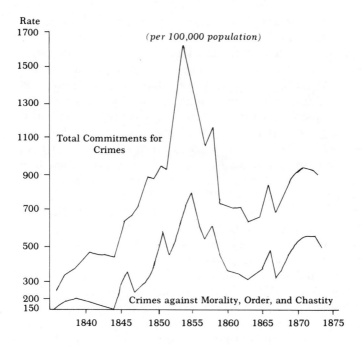

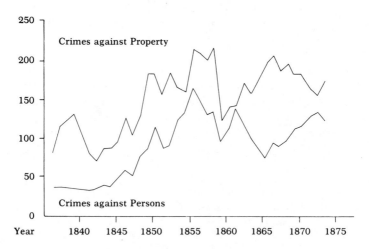

Figure 3.1. Commitments in Massachusetts, 1836–1873

Sources: Computed from the annual *Abstracts of Returns of the Keepers of the Jails and Overseers of the Houses of Correction, 1833–1863,* Massachusetts Legislative Documents (none published for 1840). Data for 1869–71 are from the *Annual Report of the Massachusetts Board of State Charities, 1869–71.*

men were away at war and others were given a choice between prison and the army.[18] This crime wave sorely strained the capacity of penal facilities, caused substantial changes in pardoning and sentencing policies, and inspired the construction of a new state penitentiary. Therefore, it is noteworthy that it did not represent a substantial change in observed criminal behavior, particularly when one considers only commitments for serious crimes against persons and property.

A durable stereotype that predates and survives the nineteenth century is the connection between cities and crime. Cities have been seen as centers of crime and vice in contrast to the peaceful countryside.[19] But how much crime was urban? And was urban crime different in nature from that of other areas?

Urban crime in Massachusetts was distinctive in both its pattern and its incidence. Suffolk County, which consisted solely of the cities of Boston and Chelsea, had from 13.0 to 18.2 percent of the state's population throughout this period. But from 24.9 to 51.4 percent of the commitments to the state's jails and houses of correction were in Suffolk County and from 31.4 to 43.7 percent of the verdicts in criminal cases were in Suffolk. Commitment rates were from 2.2 to 3.7 times as high as for the state as a whole. Of course, these rates do not reflect the fact that the number of people in a city at any given time exceeds its resident population. But these figures do predate extensive daily commuting from "streetcar suburbs." To see urban crimes simply as the result of such factors as high-density housing, high levels of transiency, and ethnic heterogeneity is tautological since these features characterized life in nineteenth-century cities.

Both the commitment rates and the distribution of verdicts (Tables 3.3 and 3.4) for Suffolk County point to a distinctive urban pattern of crime. Suffolk County had a disproportionate amount of theft; the rate in 1849–51 was eight and one-half times the state rate. Consistent with Boston's position as a major financial center, frauds, forgery, and counterfeiting proliferated. Ethnic tensions and street brawls account for the high proportion of assault and battery cases. On the other hand, crimes of public order were not a uniquely urban concern, although the rate of commitments was extremely high. The most salient fact about urban crime—and one that calls

18. As is shown in Figure 3.2, female commitment rates rose during the Civil War as women were forced to support families. The increase in the commitment rate for females did not, however, offset the overall decline.

19. Beattie, "Pattern of Crime," p. 81; Lodhi and Tilly, "Urbanization, Crime, and Collective Violence," p. 306.

Table 3.3. Suffolk County Commitment Rates, 1839–1870
(commitments per 100,000 population)

Crime	1839– 1841	1849– 1851	1859– 1861	1869– 1870
Crimes against Persons				
Murder	2.1	3.4	3.1	7.0
Assault	78.3	328.7	282.7	292.8
Rape	2.0	6.2	1.7	5.2
Total	82.4	338.3	287.5	305.0
Crimes against Property				
All theft	431.2	691.7	432.5	478.9
White collar	23.0	14.9	3.0	28.8
Total	454.2	706.1	435.5	507.7
All Serious Crimes	536.6	1,044.9	723.0	812.7
Crimes against Morals and Order				
Drunkenness, license law	567.0	1,034.8	701.0	1,046.9
Sexual offenses	128.4	137.5	39.3	49.1
Total	695.4	1,172.3	740.3	1,096.0
Other	614.0	1,236.5	181.5	213.3
Total	1,846.0	3,453.7	1,644.8	2,122.0

Sources: Computed from the annual *Abstracts of Returns of the Keepers of the Jails and Overseers of the Houses of Correction, 1833–1863,* Massachusetts Legislative Documents (none published for 1840). Data for 1869–71 are from the *Annual Report of the Massachusetts Board of State Charities,* 1869–71.

sharply into question any hypothesis about the civilizing effects of cities[20]—is that Suffolk commitment rates were higher than those of the entire state for every crime and for every decade in the period.

This pattern was not universal to major commercial port cities. Charleston experienced a pattern similar to that of the state at large. In fact, the proportion of property convictions was lower than for the state as a whole (Table 3.5). Did Charleston, like Boston, experience an inordinate share of the state's crime? Evidence is scanty,

20. Lane, "Crime and Criminal Statistics"; Monkkonen also finds certain crimes more closely correlated with urbanism (*The Dangerous Class,* pp. 34–37). Crimes of theft are highly correlated, crimes of violence much less so.

Table 3.4. Urban Crime Patterns: Percentage of Massachusetts
Verdicts from Suffolk County, 1833–1859

Crime	1833–1839	1849–1859*
Total	31.4	43.7
Above Average		
Assault	39.1	46.1
Theft	33.4	49.5
Brothels, sexual misconduct	34.4	53.5
Forgery, counterfeit, fraud	50.3	51.1
Arson	36.0	
Rape		52.3
About Average		
Murder, manslaughter	27.3	40.9
Below Average		
Rape	0.0	
Arson		5.3
Nuisance, vagrant	11.1	24.2
Drunkenness, license law	26.4	26.5
Number	3,049	7,458

Sources: *Reports* of the Attorney General for the years covered.
*1849–52; 1854–59.

and the criminal court handled cases from the entire Charleston
district (including rural and outlying areas). But for 1859, Charleston's prosecution rate was 1,417 per 100,000, or more than four
times the statewide maximum and very close to Suffolk's commitment rate for the same period (1,645 per 100,000 in 1859–61). Although Charleston did not share Boston's tendency toward higher
rates of crimes against property and white collar crimes, the city did
conform to the urban pattern of increased crime.[21]

The most distinct divergence between the crime pattern in South
Carolina in general and that in Charleston was in the slave-related
offenses. Southern cities faced peculiar problems in slave control, as
the Vesey Rebellion in Charleston had shown over three decades

21. Jack Kenny Williams reaches this conclusion using a slightly different calculation and also found that Charleston had a higher rate of larceny (*Vogues in Villainy*,
p. 2). In all likelihood, the difference involves categorization; I have lumped together
all animal thefts with larcenies. These, of course, are more common in agricultural
and rural districts.

Table 3.5. Urban Crime in South Carolina

Crime	Distribution of cases	
	South Carolina (excl. Charleston)	Charleston
Crimes against Persons		
Murder	2.2	1.2
Assault	55.8	57.1
Rape	.3	.1
Total	58.3	58.3
Crimes against Property		
Theft	12.5	12.3
Arson	.6	.6
Total	13.1	12.9
Crimes against Order and Morals		
License law	4.4	2.2
Sexual offenses	2.7	1.2
Nuisance, vagrant, riot	9.6	2.3
Total	18.0	5.7
White Collar		
Forgery, counterfeit, fraud	.7	.8
Slave-related		
Liquor to slaves		17.0
Slavery-related	9.8	5.3
Total	9.8	22.3
Total Number Above	11,912	1,041
Other	522	41
Total Number of Cases	12,434	1,082

Source: Same as Table 3.2.

earlier. One of the specific justifications for establishing a police force in 1857 was to halt the sale of liquor to slaves, a commerce in which the old city guard was alleged to have had a financial interest. The court records indicate that the new police took this function seriously. Although only 7 of 1,249 surviving indictments from 1800 to 1842 were for selling liquor to slaves, this offense accounted

Table 3.6. Rates of Criminal Prosecutions, Massachusetts and South Carolina (per 100,000 per Year)

Year	Massachusetts	South Carolina*
1801–1810		198
1811–1820		364
1821–1830		293
1831–1840	169	272
1841–1850	277	322
1851–1860	265	333

Source: Same as Table 3.2.
*Rates based on white population only.
   Districts used by decade:
   1801–1810: York, Spartanburg, Richland, Edgefield (1808–1810),
          Laurens (1801–1805)
   1811–1820: York, Spartanburg, Richland, Edgefield (1811–1815;
          1818–1820), Kershaw (1811–1814), Greenville (1817–
          1820), Lexington
   1821–1830: York, Spartanburg, Richland, Lexington (1821–1824),
          Edgefield, Newberry (1822–1830)
   1831–1840: Spartanburg, Edgefield, Greenville (1836–1840),
          Newberry (1831–1834), York (1831–1838), Richland
          (1831–1835)
   1841–1850: Edgefield, Spartanburg, Union, Greenville, Kershaw
   1851–1860: Edgefield, Union, Spartanburg, Greenville, Horry (1855–
          1860), Charleston (1858–1860), Newberry (1858–1860),
          Kershaw (1851–1855)

for almost one-sixth of all bills presented to the grand jury from 1857 to 1859.[22]

Although the crime patterns varied greatly in the two states, South Carolina's rates were consistently higher. Such a measure must be used with extreme caution, given the differences in jurisdictions and the paucity of South Carolina data (which require extrapolation from a single district for two decades). Nevertheless, the consistency with which South Carolina's rates exceeded those of Massachusetts belie any notion of rural tranquility (Table 3.6).

Another important question concerns the relationship between

22. There are two sets of criminal records for Charleston. Both are in the South Carolina Archives. The more reliable of the two is the Sessions Journal for 1857–60 (although 1860 is not complete and is therefore excluded). This is the source used in Tables 3.2 and 3.7. Indictment rolls survive for the earlier period (1800–1842), but they are incomplete. They are used here to indicate changes over time in Charleston (where they are sufficiently indicative of trends), but not for the statewide calculations.

crimes and economic conditions. In the nineteenth century Americans first began to feel themselves at the mercy of impersonal economic forces, represented in their most sinister form by the seemingly immutable business cycle. It is difficult to trust any possible correlation between crime rates and economic conditions. Studies of crime in eighteenth- and nineteenth-century England show a correlation between crime and the economy, but the actual correlation is not clear. One study finds crime rates positively correlated with prices; the other finds crime negatively correlated. Using Boston and Charleston prices, I was unable to find any significant correlation between changes in prices and changes in the crime rate.[23] This perhaps should not be surprising, for dire permanent poverty was not the constant in America that it was in Europe, and crime may have been more influenced by social disruption (such as waves of immigrants) than by prices per se.

Concern about lawlessness in South Carolina was largely a concern about violence. Grand jury presentments, the most reliable source of public sentiment about crime in the state, complained about assaults, dueling, and carrying concealed weapons.[24] Other major problems included violations of race control (such as trading with blacks), violations of morals (which were not indictable because they were not legally proscribed), and attacks on slave property (the wanton killing, beating, and stealing of slaves).

Complaints about crimes against property fell into two categories. The first decried the periodic raids and visits of robber gangs, horsethieves, and swindlers. The second dealt with local theft, viewed almost exclusively as the work of blacks. Thefts by slaves were cited as the rationale for stronger laws against trading with and hiring out slaves. Petty thievery was rarely seen as the work of whites. Because there was a ready pool of slave suspects and thefts rarely occurred in a witness's presence, the cultural stereotype of slave thievery precluded acknowledgment of a white predatory class

23. Correlations between prices and crime rates have been inconclusive. Beattie finds a positive correlation ("Pattern of Crime," pp. 87–92). Gatrell and Hadden find an inverse relationship ("Criminal Statistics"). Whether this is the result of faulty measurement or the difference between the rural eighteenth century and the urban nineteenth is not clear.

24. Presentments are comments to judges and legislatures about the state of legal affairs in the districts. They are distinct from bills, which are indictments for crimes. Grand juries regularly issued presentments at the beginning of each court term. The presentments are in the Legal System Papers, SCA. Each presentment contained from one to several dozen complaints; since they were issued twice annually in every district, the sum total amounts to several thousand comments on law, crime, politics, and social affairs. See also Richard Younger, *The People's Panel.*

and therefore contributed to the low rate of prosecution of whites for property crimes in both urban and rural areas.

Another area in which cultural patterns and crime patterns converge is in the sex of those who were prosecuted. One durable stereotype in southern history has been the idealization of womanhood in the antebellum period. In Charleston, at least, women got off their pedestals to assault both sexes. Women accounted for 10.9 percent of all assault defendants from 1800 to 1842. In 41 percent of the cases, men were the alleged victims. The image of female virtue may have strengthened toward the end of the period. By 1857–59 women figured as defendants in only 8.0 percent of assault cases and only 7.3 percent of all prosecutions. The comparable rate in Massachusetts was nearly twice as high (14.8 percent for 1866–72). To the Charleston court, however, women were still pristine. Few females ever went to trial. Only 6 out of 105 named for assault in the earlier period were tried. From 1857 to 1859, only 20 percent of females named in grand jury bills were tried for any crime, less than half the rate for men (43.7 percent).

The Massachusetts pattern of female crime differed from that of Charleston in three respects. First, obviously, the level of female crime was significantly lower. Second, females were underrepresented in crimes that depended either on participation in the economy or on positions of authority and dominance (Table 3.7). No females were indicted for forgery or retailing liquor without a license. Women were also underrepresented in selling liquor to slaves (frequently a crime committed by small merchants and tavern owners) and in slave-related offenses where the authority of the male as master was frequently at issue. Last, women were underrepresented in crimes against morals and order. In Charleston, however, where crimes against morality were rarely prosecuted, this category was dominated by rioting. The sex-related offenses for which Massachusetts women were regularly committed had no counterpart in Charleston. Seven people were accused of maintaining a disorderly or bawdy house; only one was female, and her case was dropped.

In the Bay State, female defendants were seen primarily as sexual miscreants. Except during the Civil War, female commitment rates generally paralleled the total pattern (Figure 3.2), but at a lower level.[25] The percentage of female commitments for each crime

25. The two lines in Figure 3.2 are not completely comparable. For the sake of consistency, the total commitment rate is the same as in Figure 3.1. The female commitment rate is based on all commitments, not those only for crime. Unfortunately, these are the only data available for females before 1866, when detailed

Table 3.7. Female Crime in Charleston, 1857–1859

	Females	
Crime	Number	Percent
Crimes against Persons		
Murder	3	4.6
Assault	39	60.0
Rape	0	0
Total	42	64.6
Crimes against Property		
Theft	13	20.0
Arson	0	0
Total	13	20.0
Crimes against Order and Morals		
Nuisance, riot, vagrant	0	0
License law	0	0
Sexual offenses	1	1.5
Total	1	1.5
Slave-related Crimes		
Liquor to slaves	6	9.2
Trading with slaves	2	2.1
Other slave-related	1	1.5
Total	9	12.8
White collar (forgery)	0	0
Total of Above	65	100.0
Other	0	
Grand Total	65	

Source: Charleston District Court of General Sessions Journal, 1857–59, S

(Table 3.8) does reveal a pattern. Since only 14.8 percent of all commitments were female, one may consider any crime for which at least 25 percent of those committed were female a significant offense for women. This was the case for twenty-four crimes in this period. With only two exceptions, female crimes were crimes of

breakdowns by offense are possible. The only difference is that the data used in Figure 3.1 include commitments for debt and examination, a negligible amount compared to commitments for crime. Nevertheless, the female rates are slightly inflated.

| All | | Percent |
Number	Percent	Female
9	1.1	33.3
487	57.1	8.0
1	1.1	0
497	58.3	8.5
105	12.3	12.4
5	.6	0
110	12.9	11.8
20	2.3	0
19	2.2	0
10	1.2	10.0
49	5.7	2.0
145	17.0	4.1
17	2.0	11.8
28	3.3	3.6
190	22.3	4.7
7	.8	0
853	100.0	7.6
32		0
885		7.3

sexual misconduct.[26] Thus, in each state, female criminality had a pattern distinct from that of the state as a whole, but conforming to regional cultural stereotypes about women.

26. Vagrancy was the charge for which prostitutes were arrested. For another discussion of this aspect of female criminality, see Freedman, "Their Sisters' Keepers," pp. 5, 34–36. The proportion of female criminality in eighteenth-century England was similar to that in nineteenth-century Massachusetts. See John M. Beattie, "The Criminality of Women in Eighteenth-Century England." The pattern cannot easily

Table 3.8. Female Commitments to Jails and Houses of Correction as Percent of All Commitments, Massachusetts, 1866–1873

Crime	1866	1867	1868	1869	1870	1871	1872	1873
Murder	7.4	27.6	15.2	11.1	14.0	8.1	5.9	5.9
Manslaughter	0	22.2	30.0	16.7	0	6.7	0	0
Assault	12.3	12.5	9.6	9.5	9.2	7.5	8.2	7.3
Vagrancy, nuisance	26.0	23.8	28.1	27.1	24.2	21.4	25.4	24.4
Drunkenness	11.5	18.6	15.1	13.1	11.9	11.8	10.1	13.0
Larceny	23.8	20.2	21.1	18.4	16.5	14.6	15.2	13.2
Lewdness	18.3	31.3	27.3	21.2	21.2	15.6	23.0	31.8
Arson	7.1	8.3	15.5	4.3	22.6	23.7	19.0	9.7
Burglary	0	3.6	1.7	2.0	1.8	0	1.7	0
Forgery, counterfeit	7.2	3.3	8.3	2.8	7.9	0	2.6	0
Brothel	67.9	72.3	72.3	77.5	20.8	77.4	32.0	75.8
License law violation	19.7	19.0	23.4	18.9	13.5	12.6	9.8	8.8
Robbery	4.1	7.8	1.0	1.6	1.7	0	1.9	2.4
Fraud	4.7	4.5	8.7	12.5	9.4	10.1	4.3	8.5
Adultery	26.7	33.0	29.8	33.3	27.4	24.7	34.0	35.0
Breaking and entering	3.1	4.0	1.8	3.4	.9	1.7	.5	1.0
Other	28.0	29.3	27.3	32.7	29.9	18.8	19.7	21.6
Total	25.7	26.7	16.7	24.2	23.3	21.4	19.5	19.3

Source: Annual Reports of the Massachusetts Board of State Charities, 1865–73.

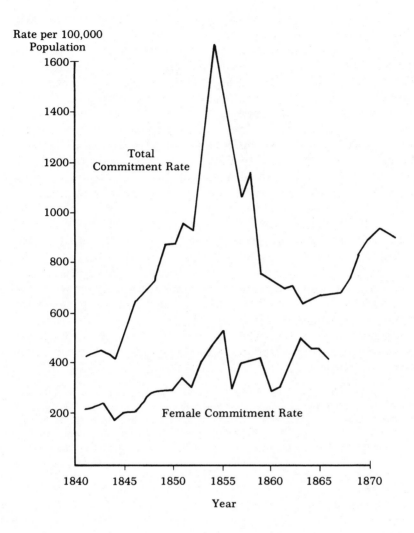

Figure 3.2. Female Commitment Rates in Massachusetts, 1840–1865

Sources: Computed from the annual *Abstracts of Returns of the Keepers of the Jails and Overseers of the Houses of Correction, 1833–1863,* Massachusetts Legislative Documents (none published for 1840). Data for 1869–71 are from the *Annual Report of the Massachusetts Board of State Charities,* 1869–71.

We can see, therefore, that the patterns of prosecutions in each state are closely correlated with economic and social factors. Although crime varied over the period studied, although cities contributed a variation on the pattern and incidence of crime, and although sex was also a factor, the most important aspect of prosecution patterns was the virtually reciprocal frequency distributions in the two states. From these contrasts the rest of the picture falls into place. Given the apparent threat to property relationships and to order generally posed by crime in Massachusetts, we can understand the massive commitment to crime control. On the other hand, given the apparently personal nature of much of South Carolina's crime, we can perhaps understand the state's more restrained response. And, as we shall see when discussing ideology, class, and reform, the character of each state's crime (as well as the character of the offenders) did not go unnoticed in planning the social response to crime and disorder.

To determine these trends, I had to cast the widest possible net —to identify people and offenses at their earliest contact with law enforcement and justice. Not only were many of the people who appear as numbers in this analysis not guilty of any crime, but their experiences in the criminal justice system varied greatly. Now we turn to what happened to people who were caught up in the criminal justice system.

---

be compared with the data here, since Beattie used serious offenses only. Monkkonen finds an increase in the proportion of female defendants during the Civil War in Columbus, Ohio, but the postwar levels are about half those observed here (*The Dangerous Class*, p. 62). The 14.8 percent figure for female commitments cited in the text is the overall average during the period for commitments for crimes only.

Chapter 4.
Trial by Jury

Arrest of a defendant was the first step in the criminal justice process. How a suspect was treated before trial, when or whether that trial occurred, and its outcome were all matters of discretion and uncertainty. Yet the assumptions underlying the criminal justice system did not admit such discretion. The ideal model, one that would protect both personal liberty and societal values, could be termed the automatic justice machine. In such a model, defendants would be arrested only after probable cause was established, the grand jury would weed out the marginal prosecutions, and cases that reached a jury usually would result in conviction. The trial would resolve legal questions, such as whether all elements of specific charges were sufficiently proved, and would resolve contradictory evidence, but little more.

As imperfect as this model appears, it is nevertheless the goal of any criminal justice system that does not purport to try defendants capriciously. In actual practice, of course, the criminal justice system does not function this way at all, primarily because of discretion. Discretion exists at all stages of the process—from the discretion of arresting officer or prosecutor to that of the judge. Discretion rests on inchoate claims of expertise, inchoate because in the nineteenth century it was rarely tested, although frequently challenged. And, not surprisingly, elements of discretion varied widely in the two states.

Before looking at the outcome of criminal trials in the two states it is useful to consider the implications of discretion. Discretion amounts to nonrandom deviation from the automatic justice model. Discretion assumes informed choices, but not necessarily impartial, rational, or equitable ones. To arresting officers, discretion is the choice to arrest for certain offenses while overlooking others—as well as the choice to arrest certain offenders. To the prosecutor, it is the choice whether to proceed. To the judge, discretion is a part of sentencing. Finally, the executive who possesses the pardon power exercises the last and most unchecked form of discretion. At a functional level, discretion represents the practical realization that resources are not available to deal with all crimes, that choices must be made, and that priorities must be identified.

What does discretion reveal about a society's criminal justice system? It is almost a cliché to associate predictability and certainty with the commercial-industrial order of the modern world, yet these were, nevertheless, paramount values. Large-scale enterprise of every sort required some form of guarantee of stability, some assurance that certain basic entitlements—such as the sanctity of private property—would not be upset. Promoters of such enterprises frequently turned to the legal system for protection. Discretion is a measure of the degree of certainty and predictability in the criminal justice area.

Since certainty was a value in private law, it is not surprising that it was also sought in the administration of criminal law. For the criminal law to have legitimacy, it must steer a relatively middle path, avoiding both the wholesale railroading of innocent persons and the unjustified release of the guilty. This was particularly true in the nineteenth century, when most prosecutions were victim-initiated, rather than police-initiated. An inefficient criminal justice system in which too many suspects are not tried or not convicted may encourage extralegal action to curb crime and will further erode the role of formal law and authority.

When we look at the operation of criminal justice in the two states, we find both contrasts and similarities. Conviction rates were high in both states for cases that went to trial, but in South Carolina far fewer cases reached the jury than in Massachusetts. Certainty of conviction appeared to be a goal in Massachusetts, but it is by no means clear that this was true of South Carolina. Instead, the act of initiating a prosecution in many cases seemed far more important than seeing it to completion. The Massachusetts pattern was indicative of the centrality of law, the need for the law to be the final arbiter of a conflict. In South Carolina, by contrast, the criminal justice system was a malleable adjunct to the other, traditional forms of authority that felt free to manipulate the legal system for personal ends, depriving it of the force of legitimacy.

Now we can turn to the trial level to see how these themes were played out. Both states had different courts and jurisdictions for different types of offenses. In Massachusetts, suspects arraigned for all but the most serious felonies and most trivial misdemeanors could be tried either in Common Pleas (Superior Court after 1859) by a jury or summarily by a police court or justice of the peace. Those accused of capital offenses were tried by the Supreme Judicial

Table 4.1. Suffolk County Convictions in Municipal Court and Police Court, 1839

Crime	Municipal Court	Police Court	Convictions Total	Percent, Municipal Court
Crimes against Persons				
Murder	0	0	0	0
Assault	20	176	196	10.2
Rape	1	0	1	100.0
Total	21	176	197	10.7
Crimes against Property				
Theft	143	155	298	48.0
White collar	19	0	19	100.0
Total	162	155	317	51.1
Crimes against Morals and Order				
Nuisance, riot, vagrant	0	69	69	0
License law	2	11	13	15.4
Drunkenness	0	538	538	0
Sexual offenses	26	69	95	27.4
Total	28	687	715	3.9
Other	29	127	156	18.6
Total	240	1,145	1,385	17.3

Source: *Report of the Attorney General* (1839).

Court presiding over a jury. Only a small fraction of the total number of criminal cases were heard by a jury. In 1839, for example, only 17.3 percent of convictions in Suffolk County were by a jury in Municipal Court (Table 4.1). From 1860 to 1862, the Superior Court handled 14.4 percent of all cases (Table 4.2). Not surprisingly, this percentage was much higher for certain crimes and categories of offenses. White collar crimes and felonious assault were most likely to be heard before a jury, with crimes against property and violations of the license law following behind. Crimes of public order and morals, such as fornication and drunkenness, were rarely tried by a jury. Adultery was an exception because conviction could lead to a sentence in the state prison.

In addition to trial justices, police courts, and various jury trial

Table 4.2. Prosecutions by Jurisdiction and Category,
Massachusetts, 1860–1862

Category	Cases Settled in the Superior Court	All Cases	Percent, Superior Court
Against the person			
Feloniously	435	1,066	40.8
Not feloniously	1,735	16,806	10.3
Against property	2,523	13,704	18.4
Against the currency and criminal frauds	497	1,250	39.8
Against public justice	153	488	31.4
Against the public peace	120	2,494	4.8
Against chastity, morality, and decency	2,553	23,715	10.8
Against public policy (mostly license law)	1,006	5,463	18.4
Total, Morals and Order	3,679	31,672	11.6
Total of above	9,022	64,986	13.9
Other	1,006	4,796	21.0
Grand Total	10,028	69,782	14.4

Source: Report of the Attorney General, 1860–62 (categories are those used in the reports).

courts, Massachusetts had justices of the peace who could handle minor offenses. They served in areas where access to any other form of justice was inconvenient or impossible. In 1839, justices of the peace convicted 243 people, or only 8.3 percent of the total convictions in the state. Almost half (102) were for drunkenness. Other crimes included assault (38) and larceny (50). The other 40 convictions were scattered among diverse offenses such as profane swearing or fraud. Only the least serious of assaults and larcenies were heard in this manner.

South Carolina had a similar hierarchy of courts, peace justices, and magistrates. Charleston had a mayor's court that heard cases summarily. A city court had concurrent jurisdiction with the district Court of General Sessions to try cases of misdemeanor, grand

and petty larceny, and assault and battery.[1] Town councils could also hear cases involving minor violations of state and municipal ordinances. The upcountry town of Anderson heard cases of disturbing the peace, assault, drunkenness, affray, and similar offenses. In 1849, for example, the council, responding to citizens' complaints, arrested Temperance Patterson for running a brothel.[2]

The significance of summary jurisdiction in South Carolina is difficult to determine. In Charleston, which had the state's only standing court of summary process, the mayor's court handled far more cases than the district court. In 1838, the court handled 831 cases. All but 143 of the defendants were discharged on the spot, usually having spent the preceding night in jail. Only 8 people were held for trial and 47 forced to give bail.[3] Two decades later the Charleston district court handled about 400 cases a year—or less than half the mayor's court's caseload—for a white population considerably larger than that of the city alone.

In Massachusetts and, in all likelihood, in South Carolina as well, the vast majority of criminal business was dispatched by such summary means. But the most serious offenses—those that had the most impact on penology and reform—were handled by the trial courts. In addition, the trial courts contained one other extremely critical ingredient: the jury. The significance of the jury must not be minimized. The jury trial is the only stage from arrest to punishment in which popular opinion is directly involved. As a result, grand jury indictments and petty jury verdicts are significant indicators of attitudes about crime, criminals, and punishment. Although there is no sanction in law for such behavior, juries will acquit if they feel the law is unfair or the punishment too severe for the offense. Personal prejudices against the criminal's class, race, ethnicity, age, or sex may also influence the verdict. To understand more fully the complex interaction of laws, values, and behavior, we must, therefore, study not only who was arrested and for what acts, but also the way the legal and criminal justice systems responded from arraignment and indictment to trial and punishment. The historian can hardly use these fragmentary records to second-guess nineteenth-century jurors. Conviction rates tell us little about the actual behavior of defendants. But as an

1. 7 *Statutes at Large* 319, 338; H. L. Pinckney, *Report containing a Review of the Proceedings of the City Authorities of Charleston*, p. 35.

2. Anderson, South Carolina, "Journal of the Proceedings of the Town Council," 9 April 1845, 4 June 1846, 13 Feb. 1847, 16 Dec. 1847, 29 March 1849, typescript in SCA,

3. Pinckney, *Report of the Mayor*, p. 35.

average measure, they do reveal how the criminal justice system functioned.

Interpreting verdicts without retrying cases from the hindsight of at least a century requires the acceptance of certain assumptions. First, one must believe that prosecutors desired convictions and that prosecutions were in fact initiated for probable cause. One most also assume that wholesale railroading of innocent defendants did not take place. Even so, only a substantial variation in jury treatment of criminal cases—such as that presented here—constitutes convincing evidence that differences were not the result of either ruthless or incompetent prosecutors.

In contemporary America, the simple conviction rate (the ratio of convictions to the total number of verdicts) is one of the most significant single measures of the effectiveness of the criminal justice system and of the extent to which the various elements within it—law, police, juries, and judges—are in consonance. But a more reliable measure would take into account the reason why many cases never reached the trial stage. Such a measure would not only reflect petty jury behavior, but would also consider grand juries, prosecutors, and plaintiffs whose actions before trial determined whether there would be a trial. A measure that reflects these factors can be termed the effective conviction rate. This is the ratio of convictions to all cases that reached grand or petty juries. It takes into account both the "no bill," a finding by a grand jury that insufficient evidence existed to indict, and *nolle prosequi,* the decision by the prosecutor or plaintiff not to proceed.[4]

A comparison of both types of conviction ratios in the two states is revealing. The simple conviction ratios were surprisingly similar —86 percent for Massachusetts and 72 percent for South Carolina (Table 4.3). In both states, well over two-thirds of all those tried were convicted. The Massachusetts figure shows a striking degree of certainty, but in both states conviction upon trial was the norm.

When we look at the far more sensitive effective conviction rates, however, an entirely different picture emerges. In South Carolina, only about a third of all cases presented to the grand jury resulted in conviction, slightly less than half the Massachusetts rate. The low effective conviction rate in South Carolina was not simply a function of assaults; when assaults are excluded, the results are similar.[5]

4. The method of reporting by several South Carolina districts showed an awareness that all impediments to conviction were part of one phenomenon. Such reports had only two categories—cases presented to the grand jury and convictions.

5. The same pattern held true in eighteenth-century Virginia; see Arthur Scott, *Criminal Law in Colonial Virginia,* pp. 319–21. When Scott's figures are recalculated

Table 4.3. Simple and Effective Conviction Ratios, Massachusetts (1833–1859) and South Carolina (1800–1860)

Crime	Effective Conviction Ratio		Simple Conviction Ratio	
	Mass.	*S.C.*	*Mass.*	*S.C.*
Murder	51.7	37.5	72.6	50.5
Assault	60.6	35.3	82.5	79.6
Rape	43.2	18.9	59.4	63.6
Nuisance, vagrancy, riot	50.3	25.4	86.6	69.0
Drunkenness, license law	60.2	26.4	84.4	71.7
Theft	74.4	21.9	88.0	54.0
Arson	54.7	9.6	70.8	24.1
Sexual offenses	64.7	44.0	89.7	82.2
Forgery, white collar	47.7	18.5	76.4	35.4
Slave-related		32.2		68.3
Other	31.2	22.9	69.6	56.8
Total	65.8	30.9	85.9	71.5
Number of Cases	33,520	13,516		

Sources: Same as Table 3.2.

There are two issues involved in the difference between the two states in their simple and effective conviction rates. The first includes all pretrial factors, such as arrest without sufficient cause, frivolous prosecution, and overcharging. The second includes factors that show up in the course of trial and deliberation. These include, in addition to guilt or innocence, severity of the penalty, justness of the law, and attitudes of the jurors toward the defendant's race, class, sex, or ethnicity. We can partition the effective conviction rate to reflect pretrial and trial factors. The total effect of the pretrial factors can be measured by subtracting the effective conviction rate from the simple conviction rate. The result can be termed the pretrial component of the conviction rate (Table 4.4). This component was over twice as important in South Carolina as in Massachusetts.

---

to fit the categories used here, they show a low effective conviction rate (52.4 percent) and a low simple conviction rate (70.3 percent) despite the deliberate exclusion of assault cases in prerevolutionary Virginia.

Table 4.4. Components of Conviction Rates

Crime	Pre-Trial Component		Trial Component (Simple Acquittal Rate)	
	Mass.	S.C.	Mass.	S.C.
Murder	19.9	13.0	27.4	49.5
Assault	21.9	44.3	17.5	20.4
Rape	16.2	44.7	40.6	36.4
Nuisance, riot, etc.	36.3	43.6	13.4	31.0
Drunkenness, license	24.2	45.3	15.6	28.3
Theft	13.6	32.1	12.0	46.0
Arson	16.1	14.5	29.2	75.9
Sexual offenses	25.0	38.2	10.3	17.8
White collar	28.7	16.9	23.6	64.6
Slave-related		36.1		31.7
Other	38.4	33.9	30.4	43.2
Total	20.1	40.6	14.1	28.5

Source: Same as Table 4.3.

In practice, the difference between the two states is in their use of the no bill and *nolle prosequi*. These elements involve the grand jury and prosecutor; it is clear that their functions were radically different in the two states. In Massachusetts, where no bills were returned in only 16.5 percent of all cases, grand juries limited themselves simply to ruling on probable cause for trial, without reaching any final verdict on the merits of the case. This is the classic role of the grand jury in Anglo-American law. But in South Carolina, the high rate of no bills among many juries and over a long period of time is a strong indication that grand juries were using the no bill as a preliminary acquittal. Solicitors and grand juries screened out the weaker cases, perhaps to alleviate the perennially crowded dockets.

The no bill as a form of preliminary acquittal is particularly obvious in the case of assault prosecutions; 34.8 percent of all cases ended in this manner. That the grand juries thought these were frivolous cases is obvious from the presentments. Since grand juries handled bills and presentments at the same time, their complaints in the latter about frivolous prosecutions for assault followed their own rejection of most of them.

The second major influence on conviction rates is what can be called the trial component. This is the simple acquittal ratio (of acquittals to all verdicts), which includes all the impediments to conviction—excessive punishment, popular approval of criminal behavior, and, of course, innocence. Since cases that went to trial in South Carolina had already been screened by a grand jury and solicitor, one might expect the acquittal ratio to be relatively low. Instead it is two and one half times that of Massachusetts. The most important reason for this disparity is the harshness of the South Carolina criminal code.

In Massachusetts, punishments for most crimes were altered at regular intervals—and usually were lowered. The number of capital offenses dropped gradually until only murder remained in 1852; later, murder was divided into degrees, so that the death penalty was not automatic. South Carolina, by contrast, adopted an unusually harsh English penal code in its entirety in 1712 and made no substantial revisions until Reconstruction. When Massachusetts had only one capital offense, South Carolina had twenty.[6] For the most part, Massachusetts juries could feel that even if punishments were not always commensurate with the offense, at least juries were spared deciding on life or death. South Carolina juries, on the other hand, had to determine not simply guilt or innocence, but also whether offenses such as burglary, grand larceny, horse stealing, or forgery were worth condemning a prisoner to hang.

It is impossible to determine the extent to which juries were reluctant to convict because of excessive penalties. Nineteenth-century jurors cannot be polled, and such capital offenses as murder and rape had the strictest standards of proof for conviction, even discounting the effect of the death penalty on jurors. Nevertheless, some patterns are clear. In Massachusetts, the simple conviction rate for capital offenses was well below that for all crimes (Table 4.5). In South Carolina, the situation was similar. When Benjamin F. Perry polled local districts in 1838 and 1839, he found that in fifty capital trials there had been only three convictions. In fifty-one trials of capital crimes in Chester District from 1806 to 1835 there were only six convictions. Murder trials in nine South Carolina districts show similarly low simple (26.1) and effective (17.5) con-

6. John M. Beattie points out that many crimes were made capital in the late seventeenth and early eighteenth centuries ("The Pattern of Crime in England, 1600–1800," p. 48). South Carolina adopted a penal code that was not only not tried and tested, but was unusually harsh by English standards. This quirk of fate was not changed until Reconstruction. A high number of capital crimes was part of a southern regional pattern. In 1849, the five states with the highest number of capital crimes were all southern (*Prisoner's Friend* 3 [1850]: 391).

Table 4.5. Verdicts, Sentences, and Dispositions in Capital Trials in Massachusetts, 1832–1851 (excluding 1843–1844)

Crime	Number Persons Tried	Convictions	Partial Convictions	Acquittals	Executions	Disagreements*	Effective Conviction Rate	Simple Conviction Rate†
Murder	50	12	18	17	7	6	22.6	63.8
Arson	16	4	1	11	2	2	22.2	31.3
Rape	14	2	7	5	0	3	11.8	64.3
Robbery	0	0	0	0	0	2	2	2
Burglary	1	0	1	0	0	0	0	0
Total	81	18	27	33	9	13	19.8	67.7
All crimes (from Table 4.3)							69.6	87.6

Source: Report of the Special Joint Committee to Whom was Referred an Order of February 11, 1852 to consider the Expediency of Abolishing the Punishment of Death (Massachusetts Senate Document 102, 1852), pp. 10–11.
*Hung juries, new trials, and others (not included in total number tried).
†Includes all convictions, full or partial.

viction rates.[7] In both states, then, convictions in capital cases were difficult to obtain, although, consistent with what we have already seen, South Carolina's rates were lower than those of Massachusetts.

Another way to determine whether the death penalty inhibited conviction is to examine the conviction rates for an offense before and after it ceased to be capital. Unfortunately, official records listed crimes by generic categories; for arson, robbery, and burglary in Massachusetts, it is impossible to tell which cases might have resulted in the death penalty and which could not. The only offense that was capital in every case and later removed from the list of capital crimes was rape. Two cases out of sixteen resulted in full conviction during the two decades prior to the elimination of the death penalty for rape in 1852, but there were nine convictions in sixteen cases in just four years after the 1852 modification.[8]

These figures suggest that the death penalty had an inhibiting effect in two ways: prosecutors were reluctant to press charges and juries were reluctant to convict. Not only were district attorneys undoubtedly disinclined to proceed with what must have seemed a futile effort, but the prosecutrix was probably unwilling to risk embarrassment, shame, and possible character assassination to the same end. In South Carolina, this reluctance to convict was a much more significant factor in the workings of the criminal justice system than it was in Massachusetts.

Another major reason for the disparity in conviction rates between the two states is the different conception of the role of state authority in Massachusetts and South Carolina. In Massachusetts, the security of property and person and the maintenance of order were social values incorporated into law. To protect these principles, professional police forces were established, and the costs of prosecution, formerly borne by the victim or offended party, were

7. Chester District, Record of Convictions, SCL; Benjamin F. Perry, *Report of the Special Committee Appointed at the Session of 1838 on the Subject of the Penitentiary System*, p. 7; because of the ambiguity of the laws and the operation of benefit of clergy, it is difficult to determine in many cases what was capital; presumably Perry could distinguish such cases. The clerk of the Chester court noted when a case was capital. The other districts included Richland (1800–1835), Grand Jury Findings, SCA; Spartanburg (1800–1860), Sessions Journal, SCA; Charleston (1857–59), Sessions Journal, SCA; Horry (1800–1835), Laurens (1806–35), York (1800–1839), Lexington (1800–1826), miscellaneous manuscripts, SCL; Edgefield (1844–58), Jack Kenny Williams, *Vogues in Villainy*, p. 38.

8. *Reports of the Attorney General* and Table 4.5. Many of those charged with rape when it was a capital crime were convicted of lesser crimes (such as assault with intent to rape or ravish). Seven of the sixteen tried in the earlier period were convicted of crimes other than rape.

paid by the state. In sum, state power was exercised for general ends. Conviction and punishment were the ends of the criminal justice system; barriers such as penalties in excess of popular values had to be and were removed.

In South Carolina, however, general principles were often less important than private and personal considerations. Prosecutions for assaults were initiated by the injured or presumed injured party, who used the tools, power, and prestige of the state to satisfy personal grievances. The code of honor was no myth—duels were common—but what is more striking is the extent to which citizens used the official authority of the state to achieve what the duelist would term satisfaction.

Assault prosecutions in nineteenth-century South Carolina resembled those of eighteenth-century England, which Blackstone decried for their private nature:

> It is not uncommon, when a person is convicted of a misdemeanor, which principally . . . affects some individuals . . . as a battery . . . for the court to permit the defendant to *speak with the prosecutor,* before any judgment is pronounced; and if the prosecutor declares himself satisfied, to inflict but a trivial punishment. This is done to reimburse the prosecutor his expenses, and to make some private amends. . . . [P]rosecutions for assaults are by this means too frequently commenced, rather for private lucre than for . . . justice.[9]

Admittedly, Blackstone was referring to postconviction procedures, but the essentially private nature of assault and battery prosecutions was a feature common to South Carolina as well as to Blackstone's England.

Understanding the procedure involved in such a prosecution in South Carolina will make this clear. The injured party swore out a complaint to a magistrate in which the assault was described. This testimony was sufficient to cause the arrest and arraignment of the accused party, who then had to give a bond for good behavior toward the plaintiff, or prosecutor, as he was called. Up until this point the prosecutor risked nothing and could continue the case through indictment and possible trial. If a conviction resulted, the prosecutor could rest secure in the knowledge that thanks to his or her efforts, the state treasury was enriched by a fine of perhaps ten dollars. In

9. William Blackstone, *Commentaries on the Laws of England* 4:430–31 (363–64 in the original pagination).

any event, the maximum satisfaction for the prosecutor was the bond for good behavior.

Not surprisingly, many (20.4 percent) assault prosecutions were dropped at this point on the condition that the defendant pay costs. It was a compromise, in a sense, but one much to the advantage of the prosecutor. If the case reached a grand jury, a no bill was returned in 66.3 percent of the remaining cases, or 52.8 percent of the total cases.[10] The no bill rate was indicative of a high level of frivolous prosecutions, but even in such cases the prosecutor lost nothing—the bond for good behavior came at an earlier stage, and court costs were not required unless a case went to trial and the plaintiff lost. Either way, the state became the unwitting accomplice in this proceeding. In fact, the high rate of no bills returned suggests that South Carolina grand juries did not even regard these personal grievances as crimes. The high (by South Carolina standards) simple conviction rate for the assault cases for which true bills were returned indicates that only the most unambiguous cases went to trial.

Part of the problem was simply a function of the offense itself. There were relatively few unambiguous cases of one person striking another without provocation. Most prosecutions resulted from insults. In a simple street brawl, it was frequently impossible to determine the blame, or even who instigated the affray. In such cases, the defendant in a resulting assault case may simply have been the adversary who was slower in getting to the courthouse. Many of the cases dropped before trial were cross-prosecutions in which each party charged the other; these were frequently compromised by having all charges dropped. Obviously, in such cases the official verdict was irrelevant to the real point of the indictment—harassment, revenge, or perhaps guarantee of relief from future misconduct.

That these cases were prosecuted at all shows that not all affronts to honor were taken to the dueling grounds. On the other hand, this exercise shows the limits of the criminal justice system in handling what were essentially private disputes. By dropping cases before verdicts, South Carolinians may have shown a certain skepticism about the ability of jury trials to give them satisfaction. Although some serious conflicts were relegated to the field of honor, in Charleston, at least, citizens showed no hesitation whatsoever in manipulating the legal system to their own advantage, stopping precisely at the point at which that advantage could be placed in jeopardy. At the same time that this practice illustrated a reliance on

10. These data come from indictments (1800–1842) and Sessions Journal (1857–59), both in the South Carolina Archives.

judicial institutions, it also weakened them. A system so easily manipulated, in which a decision was frequently to be avoided, was not a system to turn to when decisive action was necessary nor one to trust to protect life, rights, and property.

The low effective conviction rate was characteristic of the uncertainty that undermined the South Carolina criminal justice and legal systems.[11] South Carolina juries implicitly expressed sentiments on everything from the crowded dockets (hence no bills as preliminary acquittals) to excessive and archaic penalties (acquittals because of punishments). Of course, conviction is not intended to follow automatically from arrest; if such were the case, indictment and trial would hardly be necessary. But in South Carolina, people were subjected to arrest and trial for insufficient grounds and jurors were forced to evaluate the legal system as well as the evidence.

The distinction between public and private ends in the prosecution and punishment of crime operates on several levels to explain the differences between the two states. First, the types of offenses prosecuted were different. The most common form of prosecution in South Carolina was assault, the result of an affray between two or more individuals. Such affrays, arising from disputes over honor, insult, or property, grew out of private concerns. Furthermore, initiation of the prosecution was by a private party. The result in South Carolina was a criminal justice apparatus that apparently responded to privatism, to particularistic concerns. Universal standards of justice, to the extent that they existed, were far less important than these private goals.

In Massachusetts, by contrast, the most common forms of prosecution were public ones—drunkenness. Not the result of private initiative, they were a function of the establishment of a preventive police force. Society had a general interest in prosecution and conviction, whereas in South Carolina, private parties could decide whether to pursue the prosecution further. Since in Massachusetts prosecution was less dependent on private whim, Massachusetts more closely resembled the automatic justice model than did South Carolina.

Arrest and trial reveal the contrasting conceptions of law in the two states. Both processes invoked state or private action, and the outcome seemed to depend on which type of authority was invoked. Our final stage in this analysis is to look at punishment—the bottom line both of certainty and of discretion.

11. Francis Lieber complained about this in his introduction to Gustave de Beaumont and Alexis de Tocqueville's *On the Penitentiary System in the United States and Its Application in France*, p. xxiv.

Chapter 5.
Making the Punishment Fit

We have already seen significant contrasts in the types of offenses for which people were arrested in the two states and the likely results of such arrests. Now we will look at the last phases of the criminal justice process—sentencing and punishment. These are two distinct steps, because what the judge decrees to be the sentence may well not be the actual punishment suffered by the convict. Both the types of punishments and the means of mitigating punishment varied in the two states, but one feature was common. In South Carolina and Massachusetts, judges were accorded considerable latitude in sentencing, and executive discretion often seemed necessary to adjust some of the inequities that resulted.

The need for and existence of these various types of discretion muted the obvious differences in the patterns of punishment practiced in the two states. To understand these differences it is necessary to look at the available forms of punishment, the actual sentencing patterns, and the ways in which sentences were ameliorated after the defendant left the jurisdiction of the court. Despite contrasting punishment systems in South Carolina and Massachusetts, the problems created by sentencing discretion were similar. Although both states relied on various executive prerogatives to relieve the problems caused by judicial discretion, in Massachusetts there was a special twist because prison officials asserted bureaucratic expertise in a successful attempt to outflank the governor.

During the colonial period, punishments in Massachusetts and South Carolina were similar. Serious crimes were felonies and, under the harsh common law as well as colonial statute law, were capital. In South Carolina, where the English penal code had been adopted wholesale in 1712, there were as many as 165 capital offenses. In Massachusetts, where statute law controlled, there were 12. In practice, because of the operation of benefit of clergy in South Carolina, the differences, though significant, were not of the enormous magnitude suggested by the numbers. Pecuniary punishments were the most common for nonfelonies, coupled with a variety of shaming and corporal punishments. These included stocks, the pillory, whipping, branding, and sitting on the gallows with a rope around one's neck.

Shaming and corporal punishments are significantly different from other forms of retribution. Unlike later punishment systems, they offered no pretense of reforming the offender.[1] Rather, they were aimed strictly at deterrence through pain or shame. Whipping and branding were corporal punishments, but because of the manner in which they were applied, they form a subcategory of shaming punishments. Branding and whipping were painful, to be sure, but much of that pain was derived from present and future shame. The brand was the most literal way a society had of labeling a person as a deviant, thus combining present pain with permanent shame. And whipping was invariably a public event.

Although both South Carolina and Massachusetts used shaming punishments during the colonial period, Massachusetts quickly abandoned them after the Revolution. South Carolina continued to whip white offenders until the Civil War. The abolition of shaming punishments in Massachusetts was more than a response to the development of alternatives such as incarceration. It reflected changes in both the culture and social structure of the state. With the new Enlightenment era emphasis on individual dignity, shaming punishments came to be seen as inhumane and degrading, unsuitable for miscreants who were expected to reenter society. But, in addition, Massachusetts itself had changed in some significant ways, and this, too, affected the manner of punishment. Shaming punishments were most effective in relatively close-knit, stable communities. Although sitting in the pillory is a mild discomfort, the punishment comes from the ridicule of friends, neighbors, and kin who in the course of daily business pass the town common and see the person so seated. Shaming punishments succeeded—if indeed they did—because the culprit was subject to scorn and ridicule. In the increasingly anonymous and transient world of Federalist Massachusetts, this type of punishment was less effective than it had been in the relatively closed colonial communities. Accordingly, Massachusetts abolished whipping, branding, the stock, and the pillory in the 1804–5 legislative session, or roughly simultaneously with the opening of the Massachusetts State Prison in 1805.[2]

It is necessary to distinguish between punishments that deliberately shame and humiliate the offender and the stigma attached to

1. For a penetrating and provocative discussion of this point, see Michel Foucault, *Discipline and Punish.*

2. Massachusetts *Acts*, 1804, chaps. 120, 123, 131, 143.

punishment itself. Although the first form of shame may be easily abolished, the second may be almost impossible to eradicate. In Massachusetts, for example, eliminating some of the less subtle forms of stigmatization took a long time. The tattooing of recidivists in prison, a less painful but equally permanent form of branding, continued until 1829. Elimination of the visitors' fee, which put prisoners on display as if in a zoo, came in 1853. But other forms of shame and stigma could not be erased by policy, law, or fiat, as evidenced by the countless complaints of discharged convicts unable to find employment because of their prison records.[3]

In Massachusetts, shaming punishments were eliminated because they were seen as less effective (as well as less humane) than the new reformatory modes of punishment. South Carolina, on the other hand, retained many of these same punishments throughout the antebellum era. Several factors account for this. The most obvious, perhaps, was the state's extraordinary reluctance to tamper with the penal code. Moreover, South Carolina did not build a penitentiary, thus making long-term incarceration all but impossible. But the existence of shaming punishments is clearly more than a matter of neglect or intransigence in the face of trends in other jurisdictions. In South Carolina, at least, these punishments seemed entirely compatible with the state's concern for honor. All the reasons that made these punishments less attractive in Massachusetts simply were not operative in South Carolina, a relatively stable rural state where face-to-face contact remained important and where honor was accorded great protection.

Shaming punishments were not universally endorsed in South Carolina. But whipping was not objected to because it was inhumane or ineffective, the arguments used in Massachusetts. Rather, whipping put into conflict two fundamental principles of South Carolina society—honor and race control. Whipping was suspect because it was the characteristic punishment for slaves. As such, it was *too* effective; it shamed whites not only in the eyes of other whites, but in the eyes of blacks as well. The problem, in the words of a Charleston grand jury, was "the crowd of our colored population usually attendant upon such exhibitions who can be activated by . . . self-gratulation in the degradation of the white by the same punishment." Maintaining that "a Southern state could not afford to humiliate a white man," Governor Whitemarsh Seabrook suggested hard labor instead. Governor John H. Means, citing pressure to commute such punishment, wanted whipping either eliminated or done

3. See a discussion of these points in Chapter 7.

in private.[4] Despite this widespread sentiment, no change occurred. Although it has been assumed that whipping fell out of fashion, that sentence can be found for larceny up to the eve of the Civil War.[5]

South Carolina also maintained the punishment of branding until 1833. When Michael Toohey was branded for manslaughter, "an immense concourse of persons thronged the court and all the avenues leading to it."[6] Every person punished for manslaughter in the several South Carolina districts selected for detailed analysis was branded with the letter "M" prior to 1830; of fifty-five punished for larceny, five were branded with the letters "T" or "S." A Charleston grand jury condemned shaming punishments as "barbarous, disgusting, and unworthy of a free people." But the legislature did not agree. A committee considering the abolition of whipping in 1843 deemed it "inexpedient to discard shame and disgrace" as punishments.[7]

In sum, Massachusetts moved away from shaming punishments, while South Carolina preferred to keep them. This contrast, divorced from our presentist notions of the relative humanity of certain punishments, was very logical. In Massachusetts, changes in both culture and society argued for an end to shaming punishments. But in South Carolina, shaming punishments conformed both to the state's social structure and its ideology. Aside from Charleston (which had a large jail and workhouse) most South Carolinians lived in relatively stable rural communities. Thus, public punishments would indeed shame the convict in front of people whom he would encounter again. Similarly, such a punishment meant a loss of honor in a society in which honor was a highly valued commodity. Shame itself, therefore, was a deterrent.

Another form of punishment that initially also had a dual function was hanging. Well into the nineteenth century, public hangings provided proof of the state's magisterial authority and confirmation of religious faith for those hoping for a last-minute confession. We have already seen what the prospect of a death sentence could do to conviction rates. Similarly, the sentence itself was by no means tantamount to execution. In Massachusetts, 61 persons were exe-

4. Charleston Grand Jury, 1846, Presentments, Legal System Papers, SCA; Governor's Messages, 1850 (Seabrook), 1852 (Means), SCA.
5. Newberry *Rising Sun*, 28 April 1858; the judge was O'Neall. The claim that whipping was falling out of favor on the eve of the war is made in Jack Kenny Williams, *Vogues in Villainy*, p. 110, and Ira Berlin, *Slaves without Masters*, p. 334.
6. Martin Strobel, *A Report of the Trial of Michael and Martin Toohey*, p. 160; 6 *Statutes at Large*, p. 481.
7. Charleston Grand Jury, Fall 1825, Presentments, Legal System Papers; Report, Committee to Consider Abolishing Whipping, 1843, Reports, Penal System Papers, 1831–59, SCA.

cuted between 1780 and 1845 (Table 5.1). Over half (33) took place in the turbulent decades at the end of the eighteenth century. Equally significant, nearly two-fifths of those sentenced to die (38 out of 99 at risk) had their sentences ameliorated by pardon or commutation. It is impossible to determine how many whites were executed in South Carolina, although that state hanged at least 296 blacks from 1800 to 1855. Throughout the first half of the nine-

Table 5.1. *Disposition of Capital Sentences in Massachusetts by Crime and Decade, 1780–1845*

Crimes	Exe-cuted	Com-muted	Par-doned	Died in Prison	Total
From 1780 to 1790					
Treason	0	2	14	0	16
Murder	4	0	0	0	4
Arson	1	0	0	0	1
Burglary	15	1	2	0	18
Robbery	8	0	0	0	8
Piracy	1	0	0	0	1
Total, 10 years	29	3	16	0	48
From 1791 to 1800					
Murder	3	0	0	0	3
Burglary	1	1	0	0	2
Total, 10 years	4	1	0	0	5
From 1801 to 1810					
Murder	6	0	1	0	7
Rape	2	0	1	0	3
Burglary	0	1	0	0	1
Total, 10 years	8	1	2	0	11
From 1811 to 1820					
Murder	2	2	0	1	5
Rape	3	0	0	0	3
Total, 10 years	5	2	0	1	8
From 1821 to 1830					
Murder	6	2	0	1	9
Arson	1	0	0	0	1
Rape	1	0	0	0	1
Robbery	3	1	0	0	4
Total, 10 years	11	3	0	1	15

Table 5.1. (continued)

Crime	Exe-cuted	Com-muted	Par-doned	Died in Prison	Total
From 1831 to 1845					
Murder	2	7	0	0	9
Arson	2	2	0	0	4
Rape	0	1	0	0	1
Total, 15 years	4	10	0	0	14
From 1780–1845					
Treason	0	2	14	0	16
Murder	23	11	1	2	37
Arson	4	2	0	0	6
Burglary	16	3	2	0	21
Robbery	11	1	0	0	12
Rape	6	1	1	0	8
Piracy	1	0	0	0	1
Total in 66 years	61	20	18	2	101

Source: *Prisoner's Friend* 3 (1851): 396–97.

teenth century, South Carolina defendants were sentenced to die for forgery, horsestealing, slavestealing, rape, and murder. If court records are any guide (and their accuracy for postconviction matters may be questioned), a much smaller percentage were pardoned in South Carolina than in Massachusetts. As we shall see, the pardon was a key issue in both states.

In most cases, conviction for a capital offense automatically mandated the death penalty; for all practical purposes, this meant that the ultimate determination of punishment was transferred from the trial judge to the executive, who possessed the pardoning power. But for almost every noncapital offense, the trial judge determined the sentence in accordance with statutory preferences and limits. The result was an arbitrary pattern of caprice and whim that dashed the Beccarian hopes for certainty of punishment. For noncapital cases in Massachusetts, moreover, sentencing discretion resulted in a battle between trial judges, prison wardens, and governors for the ultimate determination of sentence length. In order to see how this battle evolved, we must first look at actual sentencing patterns.

Statutes define the permissible punishments, except for capital offenses, but they rarely mandate specific punishments. In both South Carolina and Massachusetts, judges had considerable latitude in sentencing. Lacking both the details of specific cases and the proper set of critical standards by which to reach conclusions, we cannot determine whether judicial discretion was abused, but we can measure the extent of that discretion. In South Carolina, the pecuniary punishment for assault and battery ranged from one cent to five hundred dollars. Judges could also sentence people to short-term confinement in local jails. Although this confinement was usually of less than one month's duration, sentences of one year for assault were not unknown. Finally, judges could order both confinement and a fine.[8]

Sentencing trends in South Carolina show a tendency toward increased severity of both fines and confinement and a greater tendency to employ confinement. Although incarceration by itself remained a small part of the punishment scene, some kind of confinement was involved in half of all assault punishments by the 1850s. Fines were still important; indeed, when confinement reached 50 percent, fines were still given to 87 percent of the convicted population.[9] The fine, though certainly not unknown to other jurisdictions, played an uncommonly large role in the South Carolina punishment scheme. It seems likely that those who could afford to pay the fine avoided a term in jail, adding a clear class bias to the criminal justice system. Francis Lieber warned that "the state must never appear to be the pecuniary gainer by crime"; but as was so often the case, his advice went unheeded.[10] The fine continued to be the most common form of punishment for South Carolina whites, even when short-term incarceration became increasingly frequent.

Massachusetts judges had to balance a complex set of factors in their sentencing determinations. Incarceration was the most common form of punishment in nineteenth-century Massachusetts. Judges could determine not only the length of the sentence, but also the institution in which it would be served. The statutes reflected the belief in Massachusetts that only those convicts in greatest need of reformation should be sent to the state prison. Since rehabilitation took time, sentences to the state prison had to be long. By contrast, sentences to the houses of correction were much shorter and frequently included a fine. Grand larceny, for example, was

8. Drawn from practices in the District Courts of General Sessions of South Carolina in the nineteenth century, WPA typescripts, SCA. Districts used were Edgefield, York, Spartanburg, Greenville, Union, Newberry, and Richland.
9. Ibid.
10. Francis Lieber, *Letter to His Excellency Patrick Noble, Governor of South Carolina, on the Penitentiary System*, p. 43.

punishable by up to five years in the state prison, or by a maximum of only two years in a house of correction coupled by a fine of no more than $600. This disparity in terms between the prison and other institutions was much greater for some crimes. Manslaughter, for example, was punishable by up to twenty years in the prison, but only three years in a house of correction.

Sentencing policy is significant because in every year studied, a minority of those convicted of "penitentiary" crimes were sentenced to prison (Table 5.2). A similar pattern is evident in the sentences for larceny in Suffolk County in 1850 (Table 5.3). Even sentences to the same institution for the same offense varied considerably (Table 5.4). Sentencing policy is of critical importance in the history of penal institutions. The "crime wave" of 1848–49, blamed on Irish immigration and the return of veterans from the Mexican War, was, as we have seen, only a small part of a much longer upward swing in the commitment rates. Since penal institutions have fixed capacities, the growth of the Massachusetts population alone would have strained the capacity of prisons, even had the rate remained steady. But the overcrowding of 1848–50 that prompted the first—albeit overdue—expansion of the Massachusetts State Prison in 1851 resulted not only from an increase in convictions, but also from an abnormally high percentage of eligible convicts sent to the prison in 1840 (34.6), compared to the ratio before (31.8) and after (27.4) that year. Therefore, the overcrowding that led to the expansion of the prison was due as much to a sentencing wave as to a crime wave.

Without the facts of each case at hand, it is hazardous to second-guess nineteenth-century judges. Nevertheless, it is clear that discrepancies in punishments may in fact indicate capriciousness and abuse in the exercise of judicial discretion. This situation led to demands for pardons in order to equalize sentences and to attempts to alter the laws to eliminate such judicial discretion.

The final part of this analysis will look at the evolution of the pardoning problem and its partial resolution. Massachusetts adopted a bureaucratic method of dealing with sentencing discretion, whereas South Carolina preferred its more personal, particularistic approach. In Massachusetts, moreover, the pardoning issue became intertwined with the governance of the state prison itself, as wardens, in an attempt to gain greater control over their inmate population, sought to wrest the traditional authority from the executive.

In both states, pardons provided an indispensable safety valve to guard against indiscriminate slaughter. But just as judicial discre-

Table 5.2. *Percent Sentenced to Massachusetts State Prison of Those Convicted of Crimes Punishable in Massachusetts State Prison, 1833–1858*

C = number of convictions   P = number sent to Massachusetts State Prison

Crime	1833		1834		1835		1836		1837		1838		1833–1838, % to Mass. State Prison
	C	P	C	P	C	P	C	P	C	P	C	P	
Murder, manslaughter	1	0	3	2	3	2	4	3	3	3	2	3*	62.5
Felonious assault	12	8	11	4	8	4	8	2	4	0	6	2	40.8
Total, against persons	13	8	14	6	11	6	12	5	7	0	8	5	46.2
Arson	0	0	1	0	3	2	6	1	2	1	1	1	38.5
Burglary	4	7*	0	4*	2	3*	2	3	6	1	12	2	76.9
Larceny	200	83	264	87	247	77	241	65	206	66	269	65	31.0
Robbery	0	0	7	0	2	1	0	1*	0	0	4	2	30.8
Fraud, cheating	0	2*	0	0	8	2	25	0	22	0	6	5	14.8
Total, against property	204	92	272	91	262	85	274	70	236	68	292	75	31.2
Forgery, counterfeit	29	0	23	10	12	11	19	6	21	12	37	7	32.6
Adultery	6	2	12	6	10	2	5	1	15	4	15	2	27.0
Sexual misconduct	9	2	7	0	5	0	3	0	4	1	10	1	10.5
Total	261	114	328	113	300	104	313	82	283	85	362	90	31.8
Percent to Massachusetts State Prison	43.7		34.5		34.7		26.2		30.0		24.7		

Table 5.2. (continued)

Crime	1849 C	1849 P	1851 C	1851 P	1852 C	1852 P	1858 C	1858 P	Total 1848–1858 C	Total 1848–1858 P	1849–1858 % to Mass. State Prison
Murder, manslaughter	2	5*	0	1*	6	1	10	8	18	15	83.3
Felonious assault	13	10	20	5	28	14	22	6	83	35	42.2
Rape	0	0	1	1	2	0	3	4*	6	5	83.3
Total, against persons	15	15	21	7	36	15	35	18	107	55	51.4
Arson	12	4	4	3	11	9	8	9*	35	25	71.4
Burglary	25	15	22	5	46	21	40	7	133	48	36.1
Larceny	367	91	349	72	325	69	292	55	1333	287	21.5
Robbery	3	2	5	3	16	3	21	12	45	21	46.7
Breaking and entering	39	43*	111	49	86	40	156	46	392	178	45.4
Total, against property	446	155	491	132	484	142	517	130	1938	559	28.8
Forgery, counterfeit	23	8	38	11	7	9*	53	24	121	52	34.4
Adultery	24	4	17	3	20	2	33	4	94	13	13.8
Sexual misconduct	29	4	9	5	11	2	23	4	72	15	20.8
Total, against morals	53	8	26	8	31	4	56	8	166	28	16.9
Total	537	186	576	158	558	170	661	180	2332	694	29.8
Percent to Massachusetts State Prison	34.6		27.4		30.5		27.2				

Sources: *Reports of the Attorney General; State Prison Reports.*

*The total sent to the prison exceeds the convictions. This is the result of incomplete data in the attorney general's reports and the fact that the same person may appear twice for a fact, once for the prison and the attorney general. There is no reason to think that those

Table 5.3. Sentences for Larceny in Suffolk County, 1839 (Supreme Judicial Court and Municipal Court only)

| | Place | | |
| | House of | | |
Term	Correction	State Prison	Total
Less than one year	5	0	5
1 year to less than 2	16	5	21
2 years to less than 3	8	19	27
3 years to less than 4	3	6	9
4 years or more*	2	5	7
Total	34	35	69

Source: *Report of the Attorney General* (1839).

*The longest sentence was five years; one person received that sentence to the house of correction, another to the state prison. Police court commitments do not give sentences (these are presumably quite short, reflecting the summary nature of this jurisdiction). The police court sentenced 81 offenders to the house of correction for larceny; 50 people convicted were fined (47 in police court); 17 juveniles were sent to the house of reformation from police court, nine from municipal court.

tion did not guarantee justice in any particular individual case, neither did the pardon. The judge did not need to offer any justification for a sentence; neither did the governor in ameliorating one. Just as defendants were likely to be singled out for harsh treatment during a crime wave, the executive might refuse to pardon for the same reason. And, like so many other aspects of discretionary justice, this phenomenon was not confined to one state. In 1838, two men were hanged in Massachusetts for setting fire to a tenement filled with Irish families. The governor decided to make an example of them to stem an outbreak of incendiarism. In Charleston, Martin Toohey was sentenced to be executed for murder because of the recent "multiplication of crimes." One observer called this a policy of "hanging a murderer today and pardoning one tomorrow, and hanging the next lest two successive pardons be dangerous and pardoning the next lest so many executions seem sanguinary." [11]

As we have seen, graduated punishments did exist in South Carolina for noncapital offenses, but the range of available options was narrowly compressed compared to those in Massachusetts. The

11. *Prisoner's Friend* 4 (1851): 74; Strobel, *Trial of Michael and Martin Toohey*, p. 159; E. B. Hall, "Punishment of Death," p. 52.

Table 5.4. Distribution of Sentences to Massachusetts State Prison by Crime, 1839–1840

Crime	Sentences (in years)						
	0–2	2+–4	4+–6	6+–10	10+	Life	Total
Larceny	97	46	9	5	0	0	157
Larceny and arson	0	0	0	1	1	0	2
Arson	0	0	1	0	0	0	1
Robbery	0	0	1	3	0	0	4
Breaking and entering	1	2	0	2	1	0	6
Burglary	2	1	2	1	0	0	6
Felonious assault	2	2	3	2	0	1	10
Manslaughter	1	0	0	1	0	0	2
Attempted rape	0	0	0	1	0	0	1
Forgery, counterfeit	6	1	6	1	0	0	14
Cheat, fraud	4	1	1	0	0	0	6
Adultery	9	3	0	0	0	0	12
Sexual misconduct	3	1	0	0	1*	0	5
Other	3	3	1	1	0	0	8
Total	128	60	24	18	3	1	234

Source: *Report of the Attorney General (1839–40)* (published 1840–41).
*Incest (20-year sentence).

focus of punishment amelioration in South Carolina, not surprisingly, was on the death penalty. Two safety-valve measures helped ensure that the bloodbath prescribed by statute would not occur. The first was benefit of clergy. Originally a medieval practice that exempted the clergy from civil trial on the assumption that they would be tried by an ecclesiastical court, benefit of clergy went through several permutations over the centuries. In the New World it became a pardon for first-time felons, granted automatically, although often accompanied by branding or banishment.

In South Carolina, this privilege did not extend to the most serious felonies, such as murder, rape, arson, and slavestealing. Yet it would be misleading to view only the exempted offenses as capital crimes, since the other felonies were capital on the second conviction. Benefit of clergy was not unique to South Carolina; the accused in the Boston Massacre trial pleaded their clergy in 1770.[12] In

12. John Adams, *The Legal Papers of John Adams*, 3:31; for a general discussion of this practice, see George W. Dalzell, *Benefit of Clergy in America*.

South Carolina this practice persisted until after the Civil War. Massachusetts abolished it in 1785 claiming that it "operates very inadequately and disproportionately."[13] At a time when many jurisdictions were trying to rationalize their legal systems, South Carolina retained this relic and released many convicted felons with little or no punishment for the first offense. Benefit of clergy, for all its inequities, was at least automatic. Those convicted of a clergyable felony for the first time knew that they would be spared the gallows but that they were put on notice for the consequences of future crimes. If not ideal, it provided an element of predictability frequently missing in the South Carolina penal system.

The second safety valve was the pardon. As in Massachusetts, the pardon came under attack in South Carolina for its capriciousness. But in the Palmetto State, the pardon was a much more appropriate device. Like many other elements of South Carolina justice, it was an exercise of personal discretion and was therefore compatible with other particularistic elements in the state's penal system. It is impossible to determine what percentage of condemned convicts were spared in South Carolina. Impressionistic evidence indicates that the pardon was far from uncommon. One governor twice ran out of pardon forms for white convicts. This form of discretionary justice was sufficiently pervasive that the governor also ran out of pardon forms for blacks![14]

South Carolina's governors, who had the power of life and death in their hands, exercised it in an arbitrary fashion. Some relied on the traditional criteria of character or a jury's recommendations for mercy; others decreed that they would either pardon or not pardon all. Jurors, who frequently knew of the governor's position on this issue, occasionally followed the English practice of bringing in false verdicts in order to avoid a capital conviction. In 1815, for example, a jury found a defendant guilty of petty larceny (not capital) despite the fact that witnesses under oath testified the value of the goods to be far in excess of the requirement for the capital crime of grand larceny. Other juries, confident that the governor would exercise clemency, could consider a case on its merits, freed from the dilemma of condemning a prisoner to death. William Blanding, after sitting on a jury that had convicted a person of a capital crime, told his wife, "no doubt he will be pardoned."[15]

13. *Massachusetts Perpetual Laws,* law of 4 March 1785.
14. Governor Patrick Noble to Secretary of State Max Laborde, 10 Feb. 1839, 11 Feb. 1840, Governor John Richardson to Laborde, 24 June 1842, Governor's Correspondence, SCA.
15. Lawrence M. Friedman, *A History of American Law,* p. 252; such verdicts

Several governors complained, publicly and privately, about the constant demands for pardons, which they saw as a consequence of the antiquated criminal code. Although F. W. Allston publicly attached firm conditions for pardons, Oscar Lieber noted that he "pardoned every single one," whereas his successor, William Gist, "has made up his mind not to pardon."[16] Realizing that both excessive penalties and frequent pardons were disruptive to the legal system, proponents of change accompanied their proposed reduction in the number of capital offenses with a commensurate reduction in the governor's discretionary powers. Benjamin F. Perry, for example, sought to eliminate pardons except where innocence was later proved.[17]

Pardoning was an issue in South Carolina because of the absence of an intermediate mode of punishment between short jail sentences and hangings. In Massachusetts, capital sentences produced similar demands for executive clemency, demands that were satisfied in almost two-fifths of all cases. But the pardon question was not confined to capital cases alone. With the advent of long-term incarceration in Massachusetts, pardons took on many auxiliary functions, including equalizing sentences and acknowledging the reformatory effects of imprisonment in the new-style penitentiary.

But as pardons became the primary form of early release in the decades before the introduction of the indeterminate sentence in 1882, the pardon took on an additional critical function. The new prison bureaucrats sought and received input into the pardon process, a move that would give the warden a powerful tool with which to control inmate behavior. At the same time, the historic power of the judge to set sentences was significantly undermined; the mysterious and arbitrary process by which judges set prison terms was replaced in part by the extrajudicial factor of behavior within the prison itself. The history of the pardon in Massachusetts is more than the history of the response to real and potential abuses of judicial discretion; it represents an attempt to substitute a new form of professional expertise for this traditional judicial prerogative.

---

were common in eighteenth-century England as well; see John M. Beattie, "The Decline of Capital Punishment in Eighteenth-Century England," p. 12. The similarities to conditions in nineteenth-century England are disarming, but hardly coincidental. William Blanding to Rachel Blanding, 27 March 1834, William Blanding Papers, SCL.

16. Oscar Lieber to Matilda Lieber, 18 March 1859, Francis Lieber Papers, SCL.

17. Benjamin F. Perry, *Report of the Special Committee Appointed at the Session of 1838 on the Subject of the Penitentiary System*, p. 32; Isaac W. Hayne, *Report to His Excellency the Governor on Prisons, Prison Discipline, and the Criminal Law*, p. 8.

The sentencing and pardoning dilemmas go to the heart of the purpose of a prison sentence. If intended for punishment, sentences to the prison should be graduated according to the severity of the offense. But if for reformation, sentences should be related to that goal; once rehabilitated, prisoners should be released. Throughout the period under study, the graduation principle was embodied in law, although the compelling logic of the second maxim attracted many converts. Judicial discretion in sentencing was a continual issue throughout the nineteenth century because this was a far more important—and unpredictable—determinant of the size and character of the prison population than was the mere number of offenders apprehended. Samuel Sewall and Nathan Dane, authors of the 1805 revision of the penal code in Massachusetts, proposed restricting the prison to those sentenced by the Supreme Judicial Court. This sytem was not enacted, although by 1818 judges could order sentences of three years or less to be served in either the prison or a house of correction. This was a crude attempt at specialization that in reality added to the confusion inherent in the sentencing process. Various acts over the ensuing sixty years attempted to reduce this duplication and uncertainty, but the first effective measure did not come until 1878, when a three-year minimum sentence to the Massachusetts State Prison was enacted.[18]

The data clearly show that judges enjoyed and exploited their sentencing authority. Judicial discretion in sentencing survived all frontal assaults, although it was clear to many observers that such discretion was undermining the certainty these devotees of Beccaria were trying so hard to achieve. One warden complained that "[e]ach of our judges seems to have a standard of his own by which he is guided." Another critic charged that sentence apparently depended on "the time of the day, the state of the judge's stomach, the number of culprits to be disposed of in a given day, or the importunity of friends."[19] Unequal sentences for the same offense were seen as having a demoralizing influence on convicts, who might view themselves (with justification) as the victims of judicial caprice.

The ideal was a more or less automatic system of criminal justice under which, if a person was found guilty, the location and duration of the punishment would follow as a matter of course. Convicts would not have to pay the additional price of satisfying public hysteria. The conditions—if any—for early release would also be known. But this goal, conflicting as it did with compelling legal

18. Massachusetts *Acts*, 1880, ch. 15.

19. Gideon Haynes, *Pictures from Prison Life*, p. 253; "Inequalities in Penal Legislation," p. 166.

precedent, was not easily realized. In 1826, a legislative committee declined to tamper with judicial discretion in sentencing.[20] Despite the frequent complaints of wardens and reformers, this prerogative actually widened over time.[21] Only in the post–Civil War years, when prison administrators successfully prosecuted their claim of greater expertise and secured the indeterminate sentence, was this power in any way abrogated.

The problems created by unequal and excessive sentences were so severe that some form of safety valve had to exist. From the beginning, the pardon served this purpose. As Warden Gideon Haynes put it, "If our . . . judges [were] infallible, there would be no necessity for pardons."[22] Historically, the pardon power was intended to free prisoners who had been wrongly convicted or who had been convicted for political reasons. But, in addition, the executive always had the authority to pardon for whatever extenuating circumstances struck his fancy. It was this residuum of power which the governor utilized in Massachusetts to ameliorate long sentences.

In every period, the longer the sentence to the state prison, the greater was the chance of a pardon (Table 5.5). But pardoning as a corrective to judicial discretion could be just as inherently capricious. Those sentenced to life imprisonment not only had a greater chance of being pardoned; they served on the average less time than those sentenced for ten years or more. No wonder penologists Enoch C. Wines and Theodore Dwight called them a "privileged class."[23]

Pardons did more than alleviate sentences; they could reduce the prison population. In 1842, the warden proposed shorter sentences in order to relieve overcrowding and reduce the applications for pardons. In 1867, conditional pardons were proposed explicitly for this purpose. Warden Haynes estimated that up to one hundred convicts might be released in this manner.[24] But pardons were not used systematically to relieve overcrowding.[25] Pardons apparently

20. Senate Document 6, 1826, p. 16.

21. In 1871, judges were given the added power to sentence to either life or a term of years those convicted of first-degree rape, arson, or burglary. Previously, life was mandatory. This law was changed when it became obvious that those sentenced to life were actually serving shorter terms than those sentenced to ten years. See *Eighth Annual Report MBSC*, 1871, pp. 182–83.

22. Haynes, *Pictures*, p. 293.

23. Enoch C. Wines and Theodore Dwight, *Report on the Prisons and Reformatories of the United States and Canada Made to the Legislature of New York, January 1867*, p. 302. See also *State Prison Report*, 1863, pp. 10–11.

24. *State Prison Report*, 1842, p. 26; *Third Annual Report MBSC*, 1866, p. 100; *Fourth Annual Report MBSC*, 1867, p. 49.

25. There were no significant correlations between pardons and a variety of variables concerning capacity and total admissions for the entire period.

Table 5.5 Pardons from the Massachusetts State Prison, 1807–1865

Term (Years)	Number Pardoned	Average Percent of Sentence Served
A. 1807–1829		
up to 2	58	64
2+–4	85	66
4+–6	73	63
6+–10	36	61
10+–19	25	67
20+	2	39
Life	87	5.1 years
Total (except life)	279	64
Total	366	

	Number Sentenced	Number Pardoned	Percent Pardoned	Average Percent of Sentence Served
B. 1836–1845				
up to 2	551	19	3.4	67
2+–4	275	42	15.3	62
4+–6	110	39	35.5	67
6+–10	64	22	34.4	75
10+–19	11	6	54.5	64
20+	0	1*		34
Life	14	16*		7.5 years
Total (except life)	1,011	129	12.8	64
Total	1,025	145	12.6	
C. 1833–1865				
10 years	108	31	28.7	68
15 years	26	12	46.2	53
20 years	16	7	43.8	45
Life	95	44	46.3	6.3 years
Total	245	94	38.4	

Sources: *State Prison Convicts* (House Document No. 63, 1846); *State Prison Report* (Public Document No. 19, 1863), p. 11.

*This percentage is meaningless because some (obviously) of those pardoned were sentenced in the earlier period. This error affects most of the calculations to some extent.

were increased when the prison was full, perhaps in an attempt to relieve the worst of the overcrowding in the hope that whatever "crime wave" (or "sentencing wave") produced the situation would soon subside. This occurred in 1819–20 and 1841. If that crime wave was prolonged, however, high levels of pardoning were not sustained. Pardons did have a substantial impact on the size of the prison population at any given time. In 1875, for example, a change in policy that substantially reduced the number of pardons was blamed for some of the worst overcrowding in the history of the prison.[26]

Some alternative obviously was needed to correct the inequities and abuses of the sentencing process, but the pardon posed serious problems as well. The governor had sole power in this area (although in practice this was delegated to a committee of the governor's council), and it was totally up to him to decide what information was relevant to the determination. Furthermore, the governor and council did not have to give any justification for their decision either to reject or to grant a pardon.

Just as the pardon did not decisively solve the problems created by discretionary sentencing, it eventually came under the same type of criticism. Lieber, for example, believed that the pardon limited the effectiveness of the penitentiary. He and Dorothea Dix both thought that it vested too much power in one man.[27] In the absence of clear guidelines, standards, or policies, the pardon undermined the certainty of punishment without providing a rational basis on which to make individual determinations. Because pardons raised the hopes of many convicts—which were often later dashed—discipline within the institution also suffered.[28]

As was the case with sentencing, the crux of the pardoning dilemma was in the split between reformation and punishment. Only a small number of prisoners would ever be pardoned for reasons of health, trial irregularities, or new evidence of innocence, but to pardon on proof of reformation was risky. There was widespread

26. *Papers Relating to the New State Prison*, House Document 120, 1875, p. 67. From 1869 to 1871, 128 were pardoned from the state prison. From 1872 to 1874, however, only 45 were pardoned, a very significant difference of 83 prisoners. The figures for 1869–71, however, were abnormally high.

27. Gustave de Beaumont and Alexis de Toqueville, *On the Penitentiary System in the United States and Its Application in France*, p. xxix (this is part of Lieber's "preface" as translator; typically, Lieber could not resist the temptation to turn that into a minor treatise on penology); Dorothea L. Dix, *Remarks on Prisons and Prison Discipline in the United States*, p. 32.

28. *State Prison Report*, 1868, p. 11. Haynes complained that it was impossible to maintain discipline in such a situation.

fear that convicts would easily feign reformation until they were pardoned.[29] Since the pardon meant a complete severance from the penal system for that offense, there was no legal way of rectifying an error in this admittedly unscientific area. The solution to this dilemma came from two directions. Within the prison, the warden won greater power over sentence length; outside the prison, the state gained greater control over pardoned convicts.

From the start the pardon promised a reward for good behavior in prison. Convicts were told in 1815, "If . . . any of you flatter yourselves with the hope of receiving clemency from the government, . . . your success will depend upon the correctness of your conduct while confined here." Information on convicts' behavior was solicited by the governor. The connection between the pardon and inmate behavior was well known; pardons were justified as having "greatly tended . . . to produce a spirit of order, submission, and tranquility, which . . . has produced reformation."[30]

During a severe wave of overcrowding in the state prison in 1849–51, the warden suggested that he be given the power to reduce sentences by one or two days a month for good behavior. This proposal was not adopted. In the next decade, however, the warden was granted the power to commute sentences for good behavior according to a fixed formula.[31] This was part of a major increase in the warden's power; at almost the same time, the warden was given full discretion to order whipping as a punishment within the prison. Thus the warden had both the carrot and the stick.

Despite the promise of the commutation power, it did not replace the executive pardon, nor did it solve the pardon problem. The commutation formula required the convict to serve at least 83.5 percent of his sentence; at no time did the average time served until pardon exceed 75 percent, and most often it was much less. For prisoners with longer sentences, this difference was considerable. A convict

29. William Tudor, "On the Penitentiary System," p. 418; see also *Seventh Annual Report MBSC*, 1870, p. 32: "Prison life furnishes no test . . . of the reformation of a convict."

30. James Pierce, *An Address Delivered in the Chapel of the State Prison in Charlestown . . . to the Convicts*, pp. 14–15; *Rules and Regulations for the Government of the Massachusetts State Prison*, 1823, p. 22.

31. *State Prison Report*, 1843, p. 5. Because of some arithmetic bungling, which enabled a convict with a ten-year sentence to serve a shorter time than one with a nine-year sentence, the plan was slightly revised in 1859. All calculations based on the commutation system use the revised figures. The plan provided that a convict could have one day remitted per month for a sentence less than three years, two days for a sentence from three to seven years, four days for seven to nine years, and five days for ten or more years.

with a fifteen-year sentence, for example, had to serve twelve years and three months under commutation; the average sentence served if pardoned was eight years. The commutation system routinized for the first time the warden's input in the final determination of sentence length. But the governor also possessed this power through his pardoning authority, a situation that contained the potential for conflict.

The attitude of one particularly important and articulate warden, Gideon Haynes, is illustrative. From his first report in office in 1858 to the conditional pardon act of 1867, Haynes annually protested not only the liberal use of the pardon power, but, more specifically, his exclusion from the process. "No pardon should be granted," Haynes asserted, "except upon the recommendation of the authorities of the prison."[32] Since the pardon was an exclusive power of the executive, Haynes had no legal basis for exerting any influence. Undaunted, he complained about pardons being granted without his knowledge on the grounds that they interfered with such minor administrative matters as work schedules. A trivial basis for a grievance, this nevertheless indicated Haynes's claim to professional status. As an administrator, he implied, he had a right to be so informed. His proposed alternative was a variation on the English "mark" system, in which time served was almost totally dependent upon conduct within prison walls. Haynes wanted the authority not only to reduce time for good behavior, but also to add time for bad conduct. Answering the objections that this was too great a grant of power, Haynes responded: "But is it not as safe to intrust one man with power as another if the party can be selected and held responsible? Can not a man be found who may be trusted with these, as well as a judge who is intrusted with still greater powers? . . . It is never intimated that a judge's authority is too great, or that it is ever abused."[33] The warden had a short memory; he had been a constant critic of judicial discretion. But Haynes had found a new approach; instead of challenging a jurist's professional competence in this area, he offered his own and claimed it was superior.

Haynes's plan was not adopted, but the conditional pardon of 1867 represented an interim solution to the problem. The essence of the conditional pardon was that if the conditions were not met, the pardon could be revoked and the offender returned to prison. Attaching conditions to the pardon was one method of lessening the "reformation risks," since the convict was still under some form of

32. Haynes, *Pictures*, p. 260.
33. For Haynes's complaints, see the prison reports for these years. The quote is from *Pictures*, pp. 260–61.

official jurisdiction. This was hardly a conceptual milestone in 1867, but it was a very significant administrative one. In 1808, the Massachusetts General Court had passed a bill granting the governor the right to issue conditional pardons,[34] but this innovation was vetoed as a violation of the bill of rights because of the potential for punishment without a new trial. On Governor Edward Everett's prodding in 1836, penal reformer Robert Rantoul pushed through a law providing for a trial to determine whether the condition of the pardon had been violated. If so, the convict would return to prison. But because of the inconvenience of this feature, the law became a dead letter.

In the mid-1860s, proponents of the conditional pardon cited this existing statute as a precedent to the requisite change. In 1867, under the pressure of prison overcrowding caused by the conviction of hundreds of Civil War veterans, the law was altered. The governor and council now determined whether a condition of a pardon had been violated. If so, the convict would return to prison to serve the remainder of his sentence.[35] This was very close to the modern parole system, in which convicts can be returned to prison without a trial and without necessarily having committed a crime. Judicial discretion and executive authority remained intact, but administrative and bureaucratic encroachments on the sentencing power finally triumphed.

The conditional pardon and the commutation system were efforts at rationalizing sentencing within as well as beyond the prison. But even these measures were seen as inadequate by some critics. The final attack on sentencing and release procedures had as its object placing full control over time served in the hands of penal professionals. The first hint of this new direction came in 1867. Following a traditional attack on sentencing policies, Enoch C. Wines and Theodore Dwight endorsed the "reformation sentence" then being publicized in England by Frederick and Matthew Davenport Hill. Using the mental hospital as their analogy, the Hills proposed that prisoners be confined until reformed (that is, "cured").[36] Three years later, the Massachusetts Board of State Charities—using the same analogy—concluded that "this view is worthy of serious reflection."

34. Massachusetts General Court, *House Journal*, 1808, pp. 275–77.

35. Governor Edward Everett, *Address*, January 15, 1836, p. 12; *Third Annual Report MBSC*, 1866, p. 97; the law is in *Acts*, 1867, ch. 301.

36. Wines and Dwight, *Report*, pp. 276–580. Not surprisingly, this idea had surfaced much earlier in America. In a letter published in the *Prisoner's Friend* 2 (1849): 247–48 and dated 1 October 1849, Samuel May stated that prisoners should be confined until reformed. Furthermore, he did not think that judges should have any say whatsoever in determining the length of sentences.

Concern for civil liberties as well as a sense that reformation could not be determined by behavior in prison led the board to reject this concept.[37] Nevertheless, it was clear that the conditional pardon of 1867 had not settled the matter.

The context in which the Board of State Charities first considered the indeterminate sentence is extremely illuminating. Rather than employing such a scheme for dangerous felons, the board proposed indeterminate sentences for habitual drunkards. In no other single document are the class-control implications of nineteenth-century penal policy so evident. The problem of habitual drunkenness, admittedly, cannot be easily solved by short "drying out" stints in a local jail or correction house. But, on the other hand, had massive penitentiaries been built to rid the streets of the offending presence of drunkards? Did the silent system and the separate system contend for their souls? This document reveals the convergence of several strands of penal and social thought at a time when eugenic notions were finally coming to the surface and influencing penal policy in a nefarious way.

While exploring analogies between their proposal, use of court-appointed guardians for the incompetent, and the practice of institutionalizing the insane until pronounced cured, the board opted for a definite sentence—with a minimum of one year and a maximum of three or four years. Prison trades, it seemed, could not be learned in less time. Indeed, contractors refused to accept convicts who had served short sentences, and thus they had been forced into idleness. Drunkards were the refuse of society not simply because of their drinking habits, but rather due to their working habits, or lack of same. That alcoholism was increasingly considered to be a disease was of little solace to the chronic drunk; the disease analogy simply reminded the board that the length of hospital and asylum commitments depended upon the wisdom of the physician. As an index to the concerns of proper society, which, after all, was well represented on the charities board, it is of great significance that the first discussion of the indeterminate sentence was focused not on hard-core or violent felons, but on concededly ill people. And if the cure was odious, the board seemed to imply, it was the only way to avoid inconveniencing prison labor contractors.[38]

Ironically, the board next considered the pardon, having suggested precisely the sort of capricious and disproportionate sentencing policy that helped make pardons necessary. Only subsequent changes

37. *Seventh Annual Report MBSC,* 1870, pp. 30–32.
38. Ibid., p. 28.

in the law, improper conviction, or new proof of innocence justified a pardon. Among the factors that should not be considered were the conduct, age, or health of a convict. Moreover, pardons should not be granted without a distinct reason, nor to equalize sentences or to effect a practical repeal of a law. Promising to leave the state was not sufficient grounds. Finally, pardons were not justified because they were requested by petitions from honorable citizens (nor even with the consent or desire of the injured party).[39] The board's recommendations tried to limit the use of the pardon to its historic functions of correcting errors and providing a final appeal. Changes in confinement and sentencing policies, it implied, should be independent of the pardon system. But the suggestions were almost totally ignored. From 1873 to 1878, 109 prisoners were pardoned by the governor for a total of 226 different reasons (Table 5.6). Virtually all the canons of 1870 were violated.[40]

What was heralded as the final resolution of the pardoning and sentencing dilemma came about in 1884 with the passage in Massachusetts of the nation's first indeterminate sentence law. This was a variant on the Hills's reformation sentence. Prisoners receiving a sentence of less than five years would be released upon recommendation of the prison commissioners after reformation had been adequately demonstrated. This attempt at individualizing justice, reform, and punishment, with its clear recognition of the emerging profession of penology, did little to stem dissatisfaction with the procedures for determining sentence length. Whereas judges and governors had once been accused of being arbitrary and capricious, these complaints were now hurled at wardens and parole boards. The indeterminate sentence did nothing to eliminate arbitrary and capricious sentences. It only shifted the blame for them. And rather than make the warden's job easier, the indeterminate sentence may well have had the opposite effect. The uncertainty of the length of the sentence proved to be a destabilizing influence on the convict population.

In their sentencing and pardoning policies, both states were influenced by Beccaria's maxim that the certainty rather than the severity of the punishment determined its effectiveness. And yet, neither

39. Ibid., pp. 49–62. Ironically, this issue is treated entirely separately from the indeterminate sentence. This article is on "Executive Pardons"; the one cited just above is on "Habitual Offenders."

40. Actually, one more person was pardoned, but this was strictly a technicality so that a person who had been released from prison in the 1840s could testify in a criminal case. Although no convict was ordered to leave the state (which was a common condition of pardon earlier in the century), two promised to leave the country—one going to Canada, another to Turkey.

Table 5.6. Pardons from the Massachusetts State Prison by Crime and Reason, 1873–1878

			Reason or Factor				
Crime	Per-cent	Number of Cases	Petition (Victim)	Warden's Request	Char-acter	Re-formed	Ill (Died)
Murder	2.8	3	1	2		2	1(1)
Burglary	3.7	4	2(1)	1		1	
Rape, attempted rape	15.6	17	13(2)	2	1	6	1(1)
Arson	11.9	13	7(2)	1	1	2	1
Larceny, common thief	12.4	14	9(2)		4		6(4)
Breaking and entering	17.4	19	7(1)		3	4	7(4)
Sodomy, adultery	2.8	3	1		1		
Felonious assault	2.8	3	2	1		1	1
Cheating	2.8	3		1		1	2(1)
Manslaughter	6.4	7	5(1)	1	1	1	3(1)
Robbery	14.7	16	7(1)	2	1	5	8(6)
Forgery, counterfeiting	4.6	5	3(1)		1	2	1
Other	1.8	2					
Total		109	57(11)	11	13	25	31(18)
Percent			25.2	4.9	5.8	11.1	13.7

						Reason or Factor			
Law Change	Sentence Excessive	Old	Young	Feeble-minded	Drunk	Innocent, Guilt in Doubt	Mistakes at Trial	Other	Total Number of Reasons
								1	7
						1	1	1	7
7	1		2	1	5	2	4	1	46
1	2		3	1		1	1	3	24
			1			2	2	1	25
	5				1	1		4	34
	1					2	2		7
1		1				2	1		10
								1	5
	1			1	1		2	1	17
	2					3		2	30
	2	1			1			1	12
							1	1	2
9	14	2	6	3	8	16	14	17	226
4.0	6.2	.9	2.7	1.3	3.5	7.1	6.2	7.5	

state was able to implement innovations that would help institutionalize this principle. Ironically, the pardon then took on a new vitality as an arbitrary and capricious corrective of arbitrary and capricious judges. In South Carolina, the pardon was necessary because of the legislature's refusal to change the criminal code. Massachusetts, on the other hand, was pulled by several forces. On the one hand was the traditional prerogative of judges in a state that revered judicial discretion and activism. On the other hand was a penitentiary system promising reformation. At this crucial time, then, Massachusetts penal laws reflected an uncertainty as to whether punishment should fit the offense or the offender. Despite their remarkably different penal codes, despite the different types of penalties available, both states relied heavily on pardons to ensure some measure of flexibility.

In every stage of the criminal justice process, from indictment to the ultimate determination of sentence length, South Carolina and Massachusetts appear to be quite different. The types of crimes prosecuted, the outcome of indictments, the options for punishment, and the forms of sentence modification all demonstrate the contrast between bureaucratic efficiency and highly personalized, *ad hominem* justice. Assembly-line justice, with its tendency not simply toward efficiency, but to ruthlessness and railroading as well, was appropriate to the class-control function of many criminal prosecutions in Massachusetts. To the extent that defendants were seen as members of a deviant or dangerous class, they lost their individuality. For the offenses that characterized class-control types of prosecutions—drunkenness, riot, petty theft—error was permissible; value inculcation was the objective. Defendants seemed almost interchangeable. But in South Carolina, crime, prosecution, punishment, and even pardons were all far more personal. White South Carolina deviants were not seen as members of a dangerous class. Individual honor and prestige, rather than threats to property and propriety, lay behind much of the crime the courts were called upon to handle; questions of personal character were admissible evidence for determination of sentence and pardon.

So far we have seen these themes played out in determining the boundaries of authority and in following the criminal justice process. The next step is to look at the most characteristic and symbolic institutions in each state—the prison and the plantation.

Part III
Two Peculiar Institutions

In looking at courts, criminal trials, and punishments, it is evident that the legal and criminal justice systems of the two states were different in many ways. Yet, when we look beneath the surface, at the underlying causes of assaults in South Carolina, at the class-control forms of criminal prosecutions, and at the means for mitigating punishments, we find similarities that are not obvious only from statutes and dockets. These substantive similarities coexist with the contrasting modes of exercising authority and handling deviance and criminality, as exemplified by the workings of formal and informal authority, the pattern of criminal prosecution, and the response of components within the criminal justice system.

Now we will turn to two more vital parts of the system of crime and punishment, the prison and the plantation. Again, we will explore both the critical contrasts and subtle similarities between the two institutions. Outwardly, South Carolina slavery and the Massachusetts State Prison hardly seem to be subjects for comparison. Neither had a clear counterpart in the other state; one was a penal institution, tangential to the social system, and the other was a labor system, central to the nature of society. But having conceded these fundamental contrasts, we can explore the realm of less obvious similarities.

Both prison and plantation confronted the most critical problems of crime and control in each state. Both institutions reflected the most important features of each state's demographic history: immigrants in Massachusetts, blacks in South Carolina. And both institutions confined those people seen to be the most threatening to the social order. The Massachusetts State Prison housed (and for long terms) only the most serious and incorrigible of the state's offenders. Reformation may have been the goal, but incarceration was the means, and incapacitation (that is, the inability to commit additional crimes while confined) was always a result. Similarly, in South Carolina, slavery was a method of confining the most threatening element of that state's population. White crime, as noted earlier, was seen primarily as the result of personal animosities. With the exception of murder, white crime was not considered a vital social problem. Punishments were insubstantial, and few resources were devoted to improving courts or jails.

Yet control of the slave population—and particularly of slave criminality—was just the opposite. Slaves were not simply the state's labor source and most valued investment. The entire way of life in South Carolina depended upon the maintenance of race control, and that principle could not be allowed to be threatened. Unlike white offenders, whose crimes of violence were largely attributable to unchecked passions, slave criminals posed a threat not only to property, but also (in its extreme forms of insurrection and resistance to authority) to white hegemony. Prison and plantation, therefore, were where both states became serious about controlling their troublesome populations.

The absence of slavery was not the motive for building a penitentiary in Massachusetts, but it is not an exaggeration to argue that the presence of slavery prevented South Carolina from building one. In this sense the Palmetto State was not unique. Although some slave states did build penitentiaries, all the states that did not were southern. And almost nowhere in the South did prisons resemble the northern penitentiary. Southern prisons were like centralized state jails; secure confinement was the goal, not programmed reformation or disciplined labor. These institutions paid little more than lip service to the purposes of their northern counterparts, and public disillusionment with them was rampant. The Georgia state prison was abolished for a time, and Louisiana displayed similar skepticism.[1] Because of slavery, the penitentiary never gained a strong foothold in the South before the Civil War.

Despite their obvious dissimilarities, then, the prison and the plantation had much in common. Obviously, this was not the intent of these institutions. Slavery was not primarily a penal institution, though that was one of its results. In addition to its role in the southern labor and social system, the plantation kept under confinement and control the one class that was most threatening to the social order. Similarly, the prison was not primarily a labor system, but it mandated labor for rehabilitation, profit, and internal order. The prison adopted many features of the factory system and justified forced labor of convicts because of the moral uplift it provided.

Despite the obvious and significant differences between the prison and the plantation, there are some similarities that reflect

1. James C. Bonner, "The Georgia Penitentiary at Milledgeville, 1817–1874," p. 309; Mark T. Carleton, *Politics and Punishment*, pp. 8–11; in general see Hilda J. Zimmerman, "Penal Systems and Penal Reform in the South since the Civil War."

the salient features of each state's criminal justice systems.[2] Prison and plantation confined at forced, unpaid, large-scale labor those people in society seen as threatening. Both inmates and slaves were deprived of basic political, civil, and human rights by a legal system sworn to uphold those rights for others. Both institutions relied on corporal and shaming punishments for discipline. In both states the internal workings of the institutions were shielded from external scrutiny. Finally, both institutions were linked to the productive systems of the states. The Massachusetts State Prison, with its labor and discipline, was a distorted model of the factory; the South Carolina plantation was the main productive unit in the state. Thus, without forcing these similarities to become an imprecise and misleading analogy, we can begin to see why an analysis of prison and plantation is essential to understanding crime, justice, and authority in these two states.

2. The analogy between prison and plantation was suggested by George Frederickson and Christopher Lasch in "Resistance to Slavery," pp. 315–29. This article did not come to my attention until after this study was conceived and the title determined. Frederickson and Lasch are not concerned with crime or justice, but rather with trying to recast slavery as a total institution using an alternative model to Elkins's concentration camp. Their prison analogy comes from works in the sociology of asylums, notably Erving Goffman, *Asylums,* and Gresham Sykes, *The Society of Captives.* Sykes and Goffman analyzed contemporary prisons and mental institutions. The Frederickson-Lasch analogy is based on a comparison between slavery and twentieth-century prisons and is not concerned, as this study is, with the role of prison and plantation in the criminal justice and legal systems of two contrasting social orders. Another work completed while this one was in progress makes a similar argument on a world historical scale, J. Thorsten Sellin, *Slavery and the Penal System.* There is a chapter on the antebellum South, but it is based almost exclusively on impressionistic and secondary sources.

Chapter 6.
Black Justice under White Law: Criminal Prosecutions of Blacks in Antebellum South Carolina

> On our estates we dispense with the whole machinery of
> public police and public courts of justice. Thus we try, decide,
> and execute the sentences, in thousands of cases, which in
> other countries would go into the courts. . . . If there is any
> fault in our criminal code, it is that of excessive mildness.
> —James Henry Hammond[1]

> Of all the evils to which the slave is exposed . . . the most
> pestilent in its effects, is the practical outlawry to which he is
> subjected by the refusal of his evidence in the courts of
> justice. . . . For him the court of law is no sanctuary.
> —James Stirling[2]

These two observers of antebellum South Carolina society held
sharply contrasting views of the position of blacks accused of
crimes. Hammond's position was that of the planter aristocracy,
satisfied with nothing less than total dominance over the servile
class, confident that fairness and compassion resided more in the
slaveowner than in the judiciary. Stirling trusted the emotionless
rigidity of law and lamented its unequal application. In this chapter,
I will investigate the relationship of the slave and free black to the
criminal law, the protection blacks received from it, the uneasy
coexistence of plantation justice and slave trials, and the fate that
awaited the black defendant who ended up in court.

The position of the black defendant in South Carolina cannot be
understood apart from the state's entire legal system. Justice for

1. James H. Hammond, "Hammond's Letter on Slavery," in *The Proslavery Argument*, pp. 130–31.
2. James Stirling, *Letters from the Slave States*, pp. 291–92.

whites was a mixed lot at best. But the combination of archaic laws, penalties far in excess of popular values, and lack of facilities for long-term confinement could easily be turned to a defendant's benefit. Cases ending in conviction were a small minority of those brought by district solicitors. Convicted defendants stood a good chance of being pardoned. The uncertainty and ambiguities of the South Carolina criminal justice system saved white lives and hides, even if they did not always serve the ends of justice. White justice, as we have seen, was largely a private affair, and one not taken too seriously. Black justice also served private ends, most obviously the need for certain slaveholders for certification, for the legitimacy the legal system provides, without the necessary fairness and impartiality that system frequently imposes as the price exacted from those who wish its cloak of legitimacy. Blacks were accorded few procedural rights in the courts, could be convicted without regard to legal charges, and were punished with substantial severity. Because the system of trying slaves for crimes coexisted with a form of extralegal authority—namely, plantation justice—planters were able to make use of this dual system to settle their own private feuds with neighboring slaveholders. Ultimately, the formal system of trying slaves shows that despite plantation justice, formal law and authority reached the plantation to a considerable extent, even if in an imperfect and unfair form.[3]

3. Views of the slave codes have followed the historiography of slavery. Ulrich B. Phillips minimized the impact of admittedly harsh codes: "It became a fixed custom in most states to legislate in prevention of possible emergencies, with a consciousness that if the law should prove inconvenient to the community, it would be allowed to lie unenforced until the occurrence of the contemplated emergency should call it to life. In fact, most provisions of the repressive legislation were dead letters at all times . . . each slave was under a paternalistic despotism, in the majority of cases benevolent but in some cases harsh and oppressive" (*The South in the Building of the Nation,* 4:200). The major revisionist answer to Phillips, Kenneth M. Stampp's *The Peculiar Institution,* argues that "probably most minor offenses . . . were disposed of without resort to the courts" (p. 224). Regardless of the manner of trial, Stampp concludes, it was "difficult to get a fair trial" (p. 226). Robert W. Fogel and Stanley Engerman, in an uncharacteristically nonquantitative assertion, hold that slaves convicted of capital crimes were more likely to be banished than executed, since banishment represented no loss of capital (*Time on the Cross,* 1:55, 129). Recently, scholars using appellate cases involving slaves convicted of crimes and whites convicted of abusing slaves have stressed the liberality of southern judges in searching for technicalities to spare black lives. A political scientist, A. E. Keir Nash, has written four articles in this vein: "A More Equitable Past?"; "Fairness and Formalism in the Trials of Blacks in the State Supreme Courts of the Old South"; "Negro Rights, Unionism, and Greatness on the South Carolina Court of Appeals"; and "The Texas Supreme Court and the Trial Rights of Blacks, 1845–1860." See also Daniel J. Flanigan, "Criminal Procedure in Slave Trials in the Antebellum South," which, in its use

Despite their obvious limitations in describing actual practice, statutes are the best source to determine the legal status of blacks. The basic slave law of South Carolina was written in 1740 after the Stono Rebellion.[4] The crimes, penalties, and procedures for trial defined at that time remained the penal code for blacks until the end of the Civil War and were typical of such legislation in the South. These laws bear out Beaumont and Tocqueville's observation, "In every place where one-half of the community is cruelly oppressed by the other, we must expect to find in the law of the oppressor, a weapon always ready to strike nature which revolts or humanity that complains."[5]

In criminal cases, as in all trials, blacks were not permitted to give sworn testimony, nor could they initiate prosecutions except through a guardian. All crimes for which whites could be arraigned were criminal when committed by blacks, but blacks were liable to be prosecuted for a great many additional offenses. If a black man wounded a white man, he could be executed; the third conviction for striking a white man was also capital. Eighteenth-century fears and experiences contributed to making poisoning, attempted poisoning, burning crops, and insurrection all capital. In addition, slaves were subject to special penalties for buying and selling goods, harboring runaways, and assembling without white permission. Some crimes were considered more serious when committed by blacks. In 1843, for example, assault with intent to rape a white woman was made capital.[6]

The 1740 law also established the basic mode for trying slaves and free blacks. Local magistrates assembled juries from among neighborhood freeholders. The precise composition of the tribunal changed over time, but a unanimous vote was never necessary for conviction. There was no random or impartial jury selection, and no officials higher than magistrates presided. Certain procedural changes were instituted in the nineteenth century. In 1833, appeals were permitted in capital cases; accordingly, written records of the trials became mandatory. In 1838, conviction required the agree-

---

of appellate court records and its emphasis on procedural matters, fits into the Nash mold. Eugene D. Genovese uses these same records for somewhat different ends in *Roll, Jordan, Roll,* pp. 25–49.

4. The basic slave law is 7 *Statutes at Large* 397. For the legal status of the slave prior to 1740, see M. Eugene Sirmans, "The Legal Status of the Slave in South Carolina, 1670–1740." For an excellent study of slavery in South Carolina prior to Stono, see Peter Wood, *Black Majority.*

5. Gustave de Beaumont and Alexis de Tocqueville, *On the Penitentiary System in the United States and Its Application in France,* p. 15.

6. 9 *Statutes at Large* 279.

ment of at least four freeholders, and in 1839, the defense was allowed three preemptory challenges.[7] The two parishes comprising the city of Charleston required a unanimous vote for conviction in capital cases only.

The slave as victim of crime received some protection from the 1740 law. Anyone convicted of killing a slave was subject to a £700 fine; cruelty to slaves was also prohibited. In 1821, after decades of agitation from grand juries complaining of wanton killing of slaves, the legislature made slave murdering a capital offense.[8] The significance of this law should not be underestimated. According to Justice John Belton O'Neall, it "elevated slaves from chattels personal to human beings."[9] The law also provided that if the killing occurred "in heat and passion," the penalty would be a $500 fine and six months in jail.

Contrary to the charges of abolitionists, the "heat and passion" clause was not a device to reduce the penalty for slave murder to a slap on the wrist. Instead, this clause permitted prosecution for a lesser degree of homicide, manslaughter. Since slaves were not under the protection of the common law in South Carolina, every possible crime committed against them had to be spelled out. This provision made possible prosecution and punishment in cases that did not meet the stiff test of murder.[10] Finally, in 1841, cruelty to a slave was made a misdemeanor punishable by a $500 fine and up to six months in jail.[11] Because of the inadmissibility of black testimony, if a white was accused of cruelty to a slave and there were no other white witnesses the defendant could exculpate himself by maintaining his innocence under oath. O'Neall called this feature an "invitation to perjury,"[12] but it was a logical consequence of the state's twin ideals of gentleman's honor and white dominance. If a

7. John Belton O'Neall, *The Negro Law of South Carolina*, pp. 33–36; 6 *Statutes at Large* 489; 11 *Statutes at Large* 26.

8. 6 *Statutes at Large* 158; presentments from Barnwell (1818, 1812), Kershaw (1808, 1818, 1819), Charleston (1792, 1820), Richland (1819), Newberry (1814). The passage of the law hardly stemmed the complaints (see Richland presentment, 1830). All presentments (with one exception) are in Presentments, Legal System Papers, SCA. The 1792 Charleston presentment is in Presentments, 1792, SCA.

9. *State* v. *Jonathan Maner*, 2 Hill (Law) 453 at 455 (1834).

10. In *State* v. *Raines*, 3 McCord 533 (1826), it was ruled that prosecutions for manslaughter were illegal under the 1821 law; they had to take the form of murder "in sudden heat and passion." This was overruled in *State* v. *Fleming*, 2 Strobhart 464 (1847), which held that "in sudden heat and passion" was equivalent to manslaughter.

11. 11 *Statutes at Large* 169.

12. O'Neall, *Negro Law*, p. 20.

slave was found off the plantation and refused to submit to investigation, any white had the right to kill him summarily.[13]

Of all the legal restrictions on blacks the most severe was prohibition of sworn testimony. Blacks did testify—both in trials of other blacks and on their own behalf against whites—but they were unable to contradict any statement of a white witness or prosecutor. Whites assumed a black proclivity for lying and believed the oath provided insufficient sanction. O'Neall hoped that this prohibition would be lifted. Blacks "will feel the sanction of an oath," he argued, "with as much force as any of the ignorant classes of white people." Such suggestions were not widely discussed; Governor Whitemarsh Seabrook requested that the legislature print O'Neall's digest, but without the comments of the author.[14]

Statute law did not fully encompass the black's legal impotence. Denied the protection of the common law, he was nevertheless subject to another form of unwritten law—common custom. In 1847, South Carolina higher courts held that slaves could be punished for simple insolence to whites, even though such behavior was never specifically proscribed. It was understood, ruled Judge David Wardlaw, that all statutes relating to slavery in South Carolina "contemplate throughout the subordination of the servile class to every free white person."[15]

Laws could be passed restraining whites in their behavior toward and treatment of blacks, but to prosecute and convict them was another matter. In fact, South Carolina's record of prosecuting whites for slave murder was mixed. On the one hand, 71 whites were prosecuted in eighteen of the state's forty-six districts. This compares favorably with the 191 whites accused of murdering other whites in thirteen districts.[16] Only 16 whites were convicted, for an

---

13. Ibid., p. 36.

14. Governor Whitemarsh Seabrook's Message No. 2, *South Carolina House Journal*, 1849, p. 82.

15. *Ex parte Boylston* (in the matter of slave Jim), 2 Strobhart (Law) 41 at 43–44 (1847).

16. This figure was drawn from the records of the following districts (years covered in parenthesis): Laurens (1801–60); Marion (1800–1838); Darlington (1812–61); Spartanburg (1800–1860); Williamsburg (1813–60); York (1800–1835); Chester (1800–1835); Richland (1800–1835); Sumter (1827–54); Newberry (1840–60); Kershaw (1789–1860); Marlborough (1800–1860); Union (1804–60); Lexington (1806–35); Horry (1800–1835); Fairfield (1785–1817); Charleston (1800–1817); Greenville (1806–60). Sources: Spartanburg, Horry, Charleston, Fairfield, York, Richland, Williamsburg (part), Marion: Penal System Papers, SCA; Lexington, Laurens, Chester: Miscellaneous manuscripts, SCL; Greenville, Darlington, Williamsburg (part), Sum-

effective conviction ratio of 22.5 percent.[17] The comparable figure for murders of whites by whites was 45.5 percent, suggesting that South Carolinians were at least half as concerned about the murder of slaves as they were about murders of whites. Most of the convictions were for less than first-degree murder, but the punishments were far from negligible. Furthermore, the high number of prosecutions and the fact that the conviction rate was not inordinately low by South Carolina standards indicate that black life was far from disregarded.

Only one of those convictions definitely carried the death penalty, and there is no proof that the sentence was carried out. In a separate case, not included in the above figures, Governor Pierce M. Butler flatly refused to pardon Nazareth Allen for slave murder despite petitions demanding that he do so. Allen was a young man, and the jury had apparently recommended him to mercy, but Butler argued that the fact that the victim was a slave "is a reason for being especially cautious of intercepting the just severity of the law. This class of our population are subjected to us, as well for their protection as our advantage."[18]

Appellate records contain seventeen cases of defendants convicted of murdering slaves in antebellum South Carolina. These records suggest that only the most atrocious or public murders, frequently committed by men of low standing, resulted in conviction. In one case the victim was a young boy killed while being punished;[19] in another, an innocent bystander was shot during some horseplay among whites.[20] One master was convicted of shooting his slave in cold blood.[21] Martin Posey forced his slave Appling to kill Posey's wife; Posey rewarded Appling's obedience by killing him.[22] One man had been gambling with blacks, lost, and shot the winner. Conviction seemed to rest on the extreme disdain the jury

---

ter, Newberry, Kershaw, Marlborough, Union: Howell M. Henry, *The Police Control of the Slave in South Carolina*, pp. 71–74.

17. Includes sources in note 16 except Marion, Darlington, Sumter, Williamsburg, Marlborough, and Fairfield districts, but includes Edgefield (1807–15, 1818–60), Sessions Records, WPA typescript, SCL.

18. Pierce M. Butler to Sheriff of Richland District, Governor's Correspondence, 3 Oct. 1838, SCA.

19. *State* v. *Bradley*, 9 Richardson 168 (1855).

20. *State* v. *Moses Smith*, 2 Strobhart 77 (1847). Of the seventeen defendants who appealed, at least seven had been convicted of manslaughter or its equivalent.

21. *State* v. *Taylor*, 2 McCord 483 (1823).

22. *State* v. *Posey*, 4 Strobhart 103, 142 (1849); slaves were also used as an instrument of murder in *State* v. *Crank*, 2 Bailey 66 (1831), and *State* v. *Sims*, 2 Bailey 29 (1830).

had for any white man who would gamble with blacks.[23] One slave was slowly tortured before at least three witnesses; the judge appeared to use the conviction, ironically, as proof that slavery was not the brutal institution portrayed by northern publicists. "However such disclosures [of the details of the murder] may awaken the bitter calumny of ignorant and deluded opposers of our institutions," commented Judge J. H. Whitner, "*such* means . . . will never find vindication nor excuse among ourselves."[24] Even the one conviction that was overturned was in this same brutal mode. A slave had been killed trying to prevent his owner's oxen from being stolen. Although the reversal was technically correct, O'Neall fumed in dissent that the defendants were "plainly guilty of the most atrocious murder ever committed in this state."[25]

In South Carolina, only one of the eighteen appeals for slave murder was overturned; convictions at the local level, then, showed considerable concern for black lives. But given the fact situation in these appellate cases, and given the overwhelming percentage of whites who were not convicted, it is difficult to share the enthusiasm recently expressed by three scholars for the protection afforded blacks by the appellate courts.[26] What looms as more significant is the behavior of General Sessions juries where whites were tried. The statement by a South Carolina jury foreman that "he would not convict the defendant, or any other white person of murdering a slave" is well known.[27] Less familiar is the outcome of the case. The remark was made after the closing arguments, before the jury began its deliberations. The judge refused a mistrial and denied a prosecution motion to submit a *nolle prosequi* and retry the case. True to the foreman's word, the jury acquitted. This was exactly the type of case that rarely reached the appellate court.

That such cases were prosecuted at all is a tribute to the diligence of certain solicitors and other individuals willing to act as prosecutors; the fact that so many of them were dropped before trial indicates how rarely those qualities were found in holders of a relatively minor post. In the above case, the judge cited the "laudable motives" of the prosecutor. In another case, Judge Elihu Bay praised the prosecuting witness for his "great merit in carrying on this prose-

---

23. *State* v. *Cheatwood*, 2 Hill (Law) 459 (1834); Henry, *Police Control*, p. 70n.

24. *State* v. *Winningham*, 10 Richardson 257 (1857) at 270.

25. *State* v. *Motley*, 7 Richardson 327 (1854) at 336. The defendant had not been furnished with a copy of the indictment, nor had he asked for one.

26. These scholars are Nash, Flanigan, and Genovese, cited in note 3.

27. *State* v. *M'Kee*, 1 Bailey 651 (1830); Stampp quotes this in *Peculiar Institution*, p. 22.

cution in the cause of humanity."[28] The commendation—in a formal written opinion—is further indication of the rarity of such actions.

Prosecutions for cruelty to slaves show a similar pattern to those for slave murder.[29] A fairly high number of whites were prosecuted (eighty-three for the districts mentioned for slave murder), conviction rates were low (37.3 percent, higher, though, than for slave murder), and appellate cases again demonstrate the extreme behavior that warranted conviction. One man convicted had given a slave three hundred lashes for violating curfew even though the bondsman had a pass. Cropping a slave's ear was ruled an acceptable punishment; pistol-whipping was not, even when performed by a patrol. One man convicted of ill-treatment had fed his slaves nothing but cornmeal.[30] Judge Edward Frost upheld this conviction, but in so doing also expressed a sentiment indicative of the South Carolina attitude toward law.

Frost hoped that such prosecutions would rarely come to court. "Public opinion derives its force from its sanction," he ruled, "and the rapaciousness of the owner is checked by fear of its active interference."[31] Frost admitted that in such extreme cases as the one before him, legal intervention was necessary. But he placed the burden of enforcement on public opinion, an informal, potentially unreliable means of enforcing norms and values, especially on behalf of a legally powerless class. The quest for alternatives to the exercise of formal law and authority was a common theme in South Carolina's legal history, but one would hardly expect to find this notion so explicitly outlined by a judge.

Frost's position was characteristic of the state's attitude toward its legal obligations to protect the slave. Laws were necessary, but principled gentlemen should not have to be coaxed. The impact of public opinion was not Frost's creation. Many slaveowners were careful to avoid the appearance of mistreatment.[32] When two allegedly insubordinate blacks died on Langdon Cheves's plantation after repeated, severe beatings, Cheves held an informal inquest to deter-

28. *State* v. *Taylor*, 2 McCord 483 (1823) at 484. In all, twenty-one of the seventy-one prosecutions were dropped before trial.

29. The districts, years, and sources are the same as in note 16.

30. *Solomon Owens* v. *Jesse Ford*, Harper (Law) 25 (1823); *Daniel Caldwell et al. ads. James Langford*, 1 McMillan 275 (1841); *State* v. *Zachariah Bowen*, 3 Strobhart (Law) 573 (1849); *Martha Tennant* v. *Charles Dendy*, 1 Dudley (Law) 83 (1837); *Rowe* v. *State*, 2 Bay 565 (1804).

31. *State* v. *Bowen*, 3 Strobhart (Law) 573 (1849) at 575.

32. Genovese makes this point quite cogently in *Roll, Jordan, Roll*, pp. 30–32, 40–43.

mine the cause of death.[33] But as these cases indicate, public opinion and gentleman's honor were often uncertain guarantors of the life and limb of a majority of the state's population.

If slaves and free blacks could expect little protection from the law, what sort of treatment awaited them as defendants? It has been a cliché over the years to refer to plantation justice, those secret mock trials held by slaveowners subject to no law other than their own. This seemed to be the feudal or seigneurial side of slavery in its most blatant form. In fact, as many plantation records reveal, such informal methods of justice were employed, reducing even further the utility of the formal legal system and constricting the influence of that system in southern society.

But plantation justice was not the only mode of handling slave criminality, although in the lowcountry it may well have been the way plantation-centered crimes were disposed of. There was a legally constituted apparatus for trying slaves accused of crimes, as has been mentioned. Through an investigation of 1,076 trials of slaves in two upcountry districts, Spartanburg and Anderson, we can determine what form of justice awaited slaves tried by these bodies.[34] Admittedly, evidence from the lowcountry, where the above-the-law mentality of the large planters was deeply ingrained, would have been more revealing. But the surviving records of these inland districts illustrate far more than could be anticipated from plantation folklore alone.

Where plantation justice and "regular" slave justice coexisted, it is virtually impossible to determine their relative importance. It simply cannot be determined how many criminal offenses were thought to have been committed by slaves. Furthermore, plantation records do not recount every instance of punishment for an offense and make little attempt to differentiate punishment seemingly required for the maintenance of race control from the formal crimes in the admittedly imperfect and vague South Carolina slave code. A comparison of trial rates for both races in Spartanburg District shows that whites were slightly more likely to be tried than were blacks (Table 6.1). But only if we assume that blacks committed crimes at the same or greater rates than did whites and that similar

33. Landgon Cheves to Judge Huger, General Hamilton, and Robert Habersham, 6 April 1834; James Hamilton to Langdon Cheves, 22 April 1834, Langdon Cheves Papers, SCHS.

34. These records are in the South Carolina Archives. Their completeness after 1833 reflects the law of that year requiring written records of the proceedings. I am grateful to Michael Mullin and Martha Mullin for bringing these records to my attention.

Table 6.1. Trial Rates for Whites and Blacks, Spartanburg District, 1830–1860

Year	White Population	Black Population	White Cases (preceding decade)	Black Cases (preceding decade)	White Rate (per 1,000 per year)	Black Rate (per 1,000 per year)
1830	16,144	4,904				
1840	17,924	5,609	306	25	1.7	.5
1850	18,311	7,608	399	152	2.2	2.3
1860	18,537	8,567	511	144	2.8	1.8

Sources: Spartanburg Court of Magistrates and Freeholders, Index to Spartanburg Court of General Sessions, 1800–1910, SCA.

percentages of total offenses were discovered and prosecuted can we assume that plantation justice explains the difference. The figures are too close and the legal system too elusive for us to conclude much from these data. What they do indicate is that if formal trials were not the dominant mode of dealing with slave criminality, they were certainly not unimportant. These records allow us to see that certain types of offenses were less suited to plantation justice than others.

Plantation justice was used to settle thefts on the plantation, fights between slaves of the same owner, and many (but not all) altercations between an owner and his slave. But in any capital case, the owner was required to submit his slave for trial.[35] Furthermore, any case that crossed plantation boundaries or involved race control (such as gambling or illegal assembly) was likely to turn up in the magistrates' courts. Plantation justice may well have served Hammond's view of the private relationship between master and slave, but the majority of cases that came before the magistrates and freeholders courts involved relations between nearby slaveowners, relations that were not always very neighborly.

The records of the magistrates and freeholders courts indicate what cases came under the purview of this formal, if imperfect, system. Obviously, much of the most intimate forms of criminality remained hidden on the plantation. Yet, despite this fact and despite the irregularities and severities of the justice dispensed by these courts, it is obvious that in upcountry districts, at least, the penetration of the formal legal system into the master-slave relationship was far more significant than contemporaries, Hammond, or historians have allowed.

What do these records reveal about black criminality and white justice? The overwhelming majority of defendants were slaves— only 7.2 percent were free blacks—but, in proportion to their population, free blacks were prosecuted at about six times the rate of slaves. Plantation justice—for better or worse, inapplicable to free blacks—probably accounts for part of this difference. But much of it probably represented simple harassment. One couple in Spartanburg, Jesse and Catherine Hughey, found themselves defendants a total of thirteen times in nineteen years! On the three occasions when Jesse Hughey was accused of a serious crime—larceny or receiving stolen goods—he was acquitted. The other ten times the couple ran afoul of the statute preventing return of free blacks into the state once they had left. They were never convicted, though the

35. *State* v. *Gabriel South*, 5 Richardson (Law) 489 (1852).

prosecutions lasted over six years. The continuing prosecution of this one couple was hardly trivial; it accounted for most of the district's criminal prosecutions of free blacks. Similar harassment prompted one free black to petition the legislature for a return to slavery, complaining that he was accused of every crime that occurred in his district.[36]

By far the most common crime was theft. Simple stealing and larceny accounted for 27.5 percent of all prosecutions; all theft-related categories accounted for 34.6 percent. Assaults on whites accounted for 11.5 percent of all prosecutions. Arson, assumed to be a common slave crime, was only the tenth most frequent in these two counties.[37] In all, crimes against property were the largest category of offenses for which slaves were tried (Table 6.2).

This pattern was exactly the opposite of that for white criminals in South Carolina, where assaults dominated the dockets. There are several reasons for this mirror image. First, the old folklore about slave thievery was not completely inaccurate. In the early eighteenth century, in response to increasing restrictions on their freedom, South Carolina blacks developed the practice of taking what they were denied and using it in trade.[38] Much later a member of one of the most prominent lowcountry plantation families complained that her slaves "*think it right* to steal from us." O'Neall admitted that "occasional thefts . . . may be expected."[39] But planters did not simply resign themselves to this situation, as the number of prosecutions for theft indicates. They recognized that such thievery represented more than simple loss, for slaves could use their booty to trade with unscrupulous whites for liquor. Any unsanctioned commercial activity, of course, increased the slave's autonomy at the expense of the master's control.

In addition, thefts were prosecuted because they were frequently committed by groups. Altogether, over three-fourths of those prosecuted for theft in the two districts were charged with other defendants (Table 6.3). Most theft that resulted in trials, therefore, was part of the elusive subculture of upcountry slave life which these trials occasionally illuminate. Although slaves could trade the

36. Petition of William Bass, 14 Dec. 1859, in Ulrich B. Phillips, ed., *Plantation and Frontier Documents*, 1:163. Ira Berlin notes that extralegal terror was part of the system of disciplining free blacks in the South (*Slaves without Masters*, p. 338).

37. Stampp, *Peculiar Institution*, p. 127.

38. Wood, *Black Majority*, p. 212–17.

39. Quoted in Robert F. W. Allston, *The South Carolina Rice Plantation as Revealed in the Papers of Robert F. W. Allston*, p. 213; *Johnson v. Wideman*, Rice 325 (1839) at 342; for an excellent discussion of this issue in general, see Genovese, *Roll, Jordan, Roll*, pp. 599–612.

Table 6.2. Crimes of Blacks Tried in Anderson and Spartanburg Districts, 1818–1860

Crime	Number Tried	Percent
Crimes against Property		
Larceny	296	28.4
Animal stealing	15	1.4
Grand larceny	9	.9
Petty larceny	22	2.1
Receiving stolen goods	14	1.3
Breaking and entering	34	3.2
Burglary	15	1.4
Arson	26	2.5
Other	22	2.1
Total	453	43.3
Crimes against Persons		
Assault	106	10.1
Murder	9	.9
Poisoning	8	.8
Other	5	.5
Total	128	12.3
Verbal Crimes	47	4.5
Crimes against Morals		
Gambling	55	5.2
Sabbath violation	44	4.2
Drinking	6	.6
Total	105	10.0
Sexual Offenses		
Rape	2	.2
Attempted rape	3	.3
Attempted seduction of white female	2	.2
Other	4	.4
Total	11	1.1
Undefined, discretionary	85	8.1
Crimes against Order		
Riot	38	3.6
Fighting	10	1.0
Total	48	4.6

Table 6.2 (continued)

Crimes of Slave Status		
Harboring runaway	63	6.0
Entering state	7	.7
Other	52	5.0
Total	122	11.7
Crimes Threatening White Authority		
Impudence	7	.7
Insolence	6	.6
Runaway	15	1.4
Insurrection	3	.3
Firearms	3	.3
Other	11	1.0
Total	45	4.3
Total	1,044	100.0
Unknown	32	
Grand Total	1,076	

Source: Anderson and Spartanburg District Courts of Magistrates and Freeholders Records, SCA.

items that were stolen, for the most part the thefts involved staples, tools, or supplies—all things that could be used in the slave quarters. Only a small fraction of the total number of thefts for which the contraband is identifiable were items that might be termed plunder.[40] Technically, a slave could own no personal property. Although this restriction was frequently ignored, it did mean that the burden of proof of ownership rested with the slave. Given this fact, it is not surprising that whites, having lost goods, would be quick to try any slave who seemed to possess them.[41]

Relative to crimes against property, the number of prosecutions involving personal violence was exceedingly small. Violence among slaves was slightly regarded; there were only ten cases of fighting in

40. Of the 106 cases in which the item stolen can be identified, 41.7 percent involved food, 33.3 percent clothes, 7.1 percent tools, 4.7 percent firearms, and 13.1 percent plunder (money, wallets, pocketbooks, and the like)

41. In one Spartanburg case, however, a search warrant was required to enter the slave quarters in search of stolen property (*State* v. *Jerry*, Spartanburg Court of Magistrates and Freeholders, 1847, SCA).

Table 6.3. Group Prosecutions

| Crime | Same Owner | | Different Owners | | Total Number of Defendants | Percent of all Defendants in Category |
	Number of Cases	Number of Defendants	Number of Cases	Number of Defendants		
All theft-related offenses	17	49	72	258	307	76.2
Gambling	2	4	6	51	55	100
Riot, disorderly conduct	1	3	9	49	52	91.2
Assault and battery	2	4	10	33	37	30.6
Harboring slaves	0	0	6	56	56	88.9
Sabbath violations	0	0	7	44	44	100
Other	13	31	34	104	135	100
Total	35	91	144	595	686	65.7

Source: Spartanburg and Anderson District Courts of Magistrates and Freeholders, SCA.

the two districts. Given the notoriously free sexual access of white men to black women and the denial of legal recognition to slave marriages, whites, not surprisingly, could not conceptualize the rape of a slave by a fellow slave. Thus, with few exceptions, slaves were prosecuted only for crimes of violence that were committed against the white minority of the population. The number of cases that involved sexual assaults and advances was remarkably small, given the hysteria over such incidents. There were only eleven in the entire period; two involved rape and six attempted rape.

The trial records portray the underside of slave life—the gambling, carousing, fighting, and stealing that whites periodically and unsuccessfully tried to suppress. The large number of cases involving slaves from more than one plantation shows the high level of mobility and fluidity in slave life rarely acknowledged in plantation lore. The trials not only attempted to discourage theft and punish assaults and insolence, but also tried to suppress or at least control this side of slave life. This motive for the trials can be inferred from the prosecutions of fourteen slaves of ten owners for rioting, sixteen slaves of twelve owners for harboring a runaway, twelve slaves of ten owners for drinking and playing cards on the Sabbath, and ten similar prosecutions.

We have already seen that only a small minority of white suspects were convicted; slaves were convicted at approximately double the ratio for whites. Of course, blacks did not have the opportunity for a preliminary acquittal provided by the grand jury; still, the conviction ratio of nearly 70 percent indicates that South Carolina meant business when trying blacks. The low conviction ratios that characterized the prosecutions of whites simply could not be tolerated for slaves because they were perceived as far more threatening to the social order than were petty white criminals.[42]

Conviction rates varied according to the type of offense (Table 6.4). Conviction rates for assault, where the inadmissibility of black testimony often precluded an effective defense, were high. Rates were lower for crimes where convictions usually depended on locating an eyewitness. Since arson was highly feared, some prosecution was likely to follow all but the most innocuous of fires, even though witnesses were rare and evidence seemed inconclusive. Breaking and entering and burglary also had high acquittal rates; anything stronger than theft required more evidence than the mere possession of clandestine goods.

42. The comparable measure is the percent convicted of all cases originally presented to the grand jury. This rate was 34.3 percent in South Carolina and 69.6 in Massachusetts.

The pattern of crime and conviction varied by sex. Seven-eighths of the defendants were men, but the percentage of female defendants was higher among slaves than among whites in South Carolina. Women were involved in crime that did not involve an economic motive, such as crimes of violence and crimes of speech. Furthermore, women were disproportionately represented in prosecutions for harboring fugitives and runaways. This was a domestic crime; its success depended on the woman's relative autonomy in the slave household and living quarters. No women were prosecuted for violations of morality. Men were convicted in 67.7 percent of all cases that reached a verdict, women, in 60.2 percent.

The most common punishment was whipping; 94.7 percent of those convicted felt the lash. Recommending the scriptural limit of thirty-nine lashes, John Belton O'Neall complained that those whippings were "most enormous—utterly disproportionate to offenses, and should be prevented."[43] Was O'Neall exaggerating? Severity of punishment depended not only on crime, but also on sex and status (Table 6.5). In almost every category, women and free blacks received lighter sentences than male slaves, the one significant exception being female slaves convicted of crimes against the person.[44] The average number of lashes inflicted was only slightly beyond O'Neall's recommendation of thirty-nine. But punishments in the South Carolina slave courts could be extreme; one out of twelve (8.4 percent) received one hundred or more lashes.[45]

Only 10.4 percent of those convicted received any other punishment. Thirty-six were jailed, mostly for short terms. This was an unpopular sentence because it deprived an owner of his slave's value even more thoroughly than death (for which the owner might be compensated) and forced owners to endanger the health of their slaves in the notorious, overcrowded, and decrepit local jails. Other sentences included death (seven cases) and banishment from the state (nine cases). There are no instances in these districts of the

43. O'Neall, *Negro Law*, p. 35.
44. Many prosecutions in this category were alleged to have been committed by female house slaves against the master's children. Thus, the harsher punishment should not be unexpected.
45. Fogel and Engerman emphasize that whipping was not exclusively a phenomenon of the slave South (*Time on the Cross*, 2:116). But southern whites were whipped less frequently after 1830 and rarely given more than thirty-nine lashes. Prisoners in the Massachusetts State Prison rarely received more than ten lashes for a single offense. Francis Gray mentions that the maximum punishment in the Massachusetts prison was fifty lashes (*Prison Discipline in America*, p. 49). Some slaves received both a whipping and a term in jail (which is why there is a slight overlapping in the text).

Table 6.4. Prosecutions and Convictions by Crime and Sex

	Crimes against Property	Crimes against the Person	Verbal Crimes	Crimes against Morality
Males prosecuted	381	104	33	103
% Male	87.6	83.9	71.7	100
Acquitted	121	28	8	17
Convicted	195	50	24	54
Conviction rate*	61.7	64.1	75.0	76.1
Females prosecuted	54	20	13	0
% Female	12.4	16.1	28.3	0
Acquitted	18	4	5	0
Convicted	17	14	5	0
Conviction rate	48.6	77.8	50.0	0
Total prosecuted†	435	124	46	103
Total convicted	230	66	30	54
Conviction rate	60.3	66.0	69.8	76.1

*All conviction rates are ratios of convictions to total verdicts; number prosecuted in each category, therefore, does not necessarily equal sum of verdicts (verdicts unknown in 19.5 percent of total number of cases).

†Included in this figure are cases for which verdict and/or sex are unknown.

more bizarre forms of punishment for which South Carolina attained notoriety, such as burning a slave alive.[46]

Finally, these courts responded to South Carolina's racial crises. Conviction rates, which had been declining, underwent a reversal in the troubled 1850s (Table 6.6). Punishments became more severe for crimes against property, crimes threatening white authority, crimes against morality, and verbal crimes (Table 6.7). Except for crimes against property, these were the categories that most tended to undermine white authority and control. Furthermore, the average whipping upon conviction rose from thirty-three lashes in the 1830s to fifty-six lashes in the 1850s.

Another form of punishment inflicted on slaves in Charleston that became infamous through abolitionist lore was the Charleston workhouse, immortalized by the Grimké sisters in Theodore

46. For an example, see Petition of Thomas Goodman, Accounts, 1825, Penal System Papers, SCA.

Sexual Offenses	Unde-fined; Discretionary	Crimes of Status	Crimes against the Public Order	Threats to White Authority	Total
11	80	95	41	36	884
100	94.1	79.2	87.2	83.7	87.2
3	22	19	12	3	233
6	45	59	26	30	489
66.7	67.2	75.6	68.4	90.9	67.7
0	5	25	6	7	130
0	5.9	20.8	12.8	16.3	12.8
0	1	7	1	1	37
0	2	10	3	5	56
0	66.7	58.8	75.0	83.3	60.2
11	85	120	47	43	1014
6	48	69	29	37	569
66.7	66.7	71.9	67.4	90.2	66.7

Dwight Weld's *American Slavery as It Is.* Although the Charleston institution was best known, other coastal cities had similar establishments.[47] The workhouse was thoroughly compatible with many of the contradictions of the peculiar institution. Owners of difficult slaves could send them to the workhouse to have a specific punishment applied. For a fee, the master of this municipal institution administered the desired punishment, regardless of its justice or severity. The master of the workhouse functioned as the paid agent of the slavemaster; just as there were few limits on the master's authority to correct or punish on the plantation, the workhouse existed primarily to promulgate the master's will. The building also served as a jail for slaves and free blacks arrested by the city guard or police and as a holding tank for slaves awaiting sale.

Although in many ways the brutal chamber decried by Weld, the workhouse was also, in some significant ways, a rational modern institution, alone in that respect in the state's legal and penal appa-

47. Theodore Dwight Weld, *American Slavery as It Is,* pp. 22, 53–54. Savannah slaveowners could send their slaves to the city jail to have punishment administered. A workhouse was authorized in 1857 but never built (Richard H. Haunton, "Law and Order in Savannah, 1850–1860," pp. 17–18).

Table 6.5. Punishment according to Crime, Sex, and Status (in percentages)

	Crimes against Property	Crimes against the Person	Verbal Crimes	Crimes against Morality
Slave				
Male	54.6	44.9	31.9	26.7
Female	42.0	65.0	16.3	
Total	53.5	48.3	29.5	26.7
Number of cases	97	54	26	51
Free				
Male	35.0	32.0	50.0	26.3
Female		36.0	5.0	
Total	35.0	34.2	27.5	26.3
Number of cases	10	9	2	3
Total				
Male	52.6	43.8	32.7	26.7
Female	42.0	54.6	14.0	
Total	51.8	46.2	29.4	26.7
Number of Cases	107	63	28	54

Source: Anderson and Spartanburg Courts of Magistrates and Freeholders, SCA.

ratus. Physical conditions of confinement to the workhouse were actually praised by numerous visitors who were hardly apologists for slavery. Boston reformer Samuel Gridley Howe singled out the workhouse for commendation: "The only clean, well-organized, and thoroughly administered institutions which I have seen in the South are the Slave Depositories. . . . That in Charleston is a large airy building, with ample courtyards and well-ventilated rooms. Every part is kept scrupulously clean; everything is well adapted for its purpose; every officer is active and energetic; its treadmill and its whipping post are the *ne plus ultra* of their kind."[48] In contrast to the state's notorious jails, the physical environment of the workhouse was not a source of complaint.

48. Samuel Gridley Howe to Horace Mann, 23–26 Dec. 1841, Samuel Gridley Howe Papers, Houghton Library, Harvard University; F. C. Adams, *Manuel Pereira*, p. 129; Karl Bernhard, *Travels through North America during the Years 1825 and 1826*, 2:9. Howe was describing the old workhouse, replaced in 1851 after the inmates' escape of 1849.

Sexual Crimes	Discre- tionary Prosecu- tions	Crimes of Status	Crimes against Order	Threaten- ing White Authority	Total
127.3	34.2	42.1	14.1	156.2	47.4
	12.5	25.5	15.0	35.4	33.4
127.3	33.2	39.9	14.1	148.5	46.5
6	46	60	29	21	39.0
		20.6		21.6	28.6
		7.1			27.4
		19.9		21.6	28.6
		9		4	37
127.3	34.2	39.2	14.1	133.6	
	12.5	23.5	15.0	35.4	
127.3	33.2	37.2	14.1	129.8	
6	46	69	29	25	

Ironically, what abolitionists objected to most—the unfailing obedience of a municipal institution to the whim and authority of the master—was precisely the feature that set it apart as rational. Modern penal systems are characterized by professionalism and specialization. The workhouse embodied both by separating the act of punishment from emotional considerations. Owners, because of their emotional ties to the slaves, were often ill-suited by temperament to punish them. Extreme anger could result in serious injury or death to the slave, depriving the owner of labor or capital. Court records and planter diaries offer testimony on the consequences of unintended severity.

The workhouse, on the other hand, as a specialized institution that separated actual correction from vengeance, was, in fact, a far more rational institution than usually found in the South Carolina criminal justice system—or that its critics gave it credit for being. The workhouse led one critic of slavery to comment that the law became a science in South Carolina when it came to managing

Table 6.6. Verdicts in Trials of Blacks, 1818–1860

	1818– 1830	1831– 1840	1841– 1850	1851– 1860	Total
Acquitted					
Number	10	29	139	104	282
Percent	19.2	22.8	41.0	31.7	33.3
Convicted					
Number	42	98	200	224	564
Percent	80.8	77.2	59.0	68.3	66.7
Total	52	127	339	328	846
Verdict Unknown	28	55	66	76	225
Grand Total	80	182	405	404	1,071

Source: Anderson and Spartanburg District Court of Magistrates and Freeholders, SCA.

blacks.[49] Ironically, in every other area of law, science was defiantly eschewed.

Whether whipping, hanging, jailing, or a visit to the workhouse, punishments of slaves were likely to be harsh. But were they unjustly determined? Exactly what kind of justice did these courts provide? Condemnation from the North was to be expected; one northern jurist decried these proceedings as "acts of unlawful assemblies." Apparently, many South Carolinians agreed; the most severe criticism came from within the state. O'Neall called the courts "the worst system which could be devised" and complained that "no jurisdiction did exist which is liable to more abuse." Governor James H. Adams believed that "their decisions are rarely in conformity with justice or humanity." Several grand juries demanded reform.[50]

Ignorance of the law, overreaction during times of racial panic, admission of questionable evidence, illegal composition of the courts, punishment for behavior not defined as criminal, and inbred jury selection were some of the factors that inspired little confi-

49. Adams, *Manuel Pereira*, p. 129.
50. John Codman Hurd, *The Law of Freedom and Bondage in the United States*, p. 305n; O'Neall, *Negro Law*, p. 35; James H. Adams, *Address*, in *South Carolina Legislative Times*, p. 323; Presentments from Laurens (1838), Newberry (1814), Pendleton (1827), Kershaw (1828), and Sumter (1829) in Presentments, Legal System Papers; Charleston *Courier* 25 Sept. 1849.

dence in the judgments of these courts. So antiquated was the state's legal system that the blame could hardly rest on the presiding magistrates alone. In one case, for example, conviction was overturned because the magistrate's court was ignorant of the law—but the relevant statute had been omitted from John F. Grimké's presumably authoritative compilation.[51] Magistrates were often criticized for their general ignorance of the law, regardless of the race of the defendant, as well as for a tendency to initiate frivolous prosecutions to bolster their own fees.[52] The lives and limbs of whites, of course, did not ordinarily rest upon magistrates' jurisdiction. But the exclusion of the slave from common law protection invited ambiguities too subtle for a magistrate, poorly trained in law, to perceive.[53] An appellate decision was needed to rule that slaves could not be tried twice for the same offense. That ruling was not sufficient to prevent a slave from being executed for a crime for which he had already been whipped, a decision that caused O'Neall to complain in dissent, "If the prisoner was a *white man and not a Negro* could such a course receive the countenance of anyone?"[54]

Although the criteria for assembling a magistrate's and freeholder's court were not rigorous, they were not always followed. One conviction was overturned because the court included men fraudulently posing as magistrates; another was set aside because one freeholder was not a resident of the district.[55] One slave's life was spared because the trial was held in the wrong district. One scholar sees this case as a further example of the liberality of the appeals court, reaching ·for technicalities in order to save black lives.[56] But since the trial should have been held in Charleston, the only part of the state that had stronger statutory requirements for conviction in capital cases, it is hard to credit the court with much generosity. This difference in rules was a life-or-death matter.

In these cases, appellate courts were called upon to remedy procedural irregularities. But appeals were costly and infrequent; they were hardly representative of cases at the local level. But the Spartanburg District records show procedural irregularities that are too

51. *State* v. *Nicholas*, 2 Strobhart 278 (1848); Nicholas was the slave who led the escape from Charleston workhouse in 1849.

52. Charleston *Courier*, 1 April 1835, 25 Sept. 1849.

53. *State* v. *Maner*, 2 Hill 453 (1834); *Ex parte Boylston*, 2 Strobhart 32 (1847).

54. *State* v. *Nathan, slave of Gabriel South*, 5 Richardson 219 (1851) at 232–33; the double jeopardy ruling was *State* v. *Jesse Brown*, 2 Bailey 323 (1831).

55. *Ex parte Richardson*, Harper 308 (1824); *State* v. *John Hudnall, et al.*, 2 Nott and McCord 419 (1820).

56. Nash, "Negro Rights," pp. 169–70; *State ex rel. Matthews* v. *Toomer*, 1 Cheves 106 (1840).

Table 6.7. Whippings according to Type of Crime and Time Period

Years	Crimes against Property	Crimes against the Person	Verbal Crimes	Crimes against Morality
1818–1830				
Mean number of lashes	26.2	11.4	12.0	
Number of cases	9	14	5	
1831–1840				
Mean number of lashes	44.1	22.1	28.5	21.7
Number of cases	27	11	6	15
1841–1850				
Mean number of lashes	43.7	71.3	26.6	21.2
Number of cases	74	20	5	25
1851–1860				
Mean number of lashes	62.1	58.0	38.4	39.7
Number of cases	109	20	13	13
Total				
Mean number of lashes	52.7	45.9	28.9	28.4
Number of cases	219	65	29	53

obvious to have been the result of chance or inattentiveness. In sexual matters, for example, normally accepted standards of evidence seem to have been disregarded. One slave was convicted of rape despite the fact that the court described the alleged victim as an imbecile incapable of reasoning. Her testimony would not have been admitted had the defendant been white. Another slave was convicted of the same crime even though the alleged victim did not know her age, the meaning of a sworn oath, or "what the Bible taught would become of anyone who spoke falsely." A third defendant was prosecuted for rape even though testimony revealed that he never touched the prosecutrix or her dress.[57] These were the only

57. *State* v. *Harry*, 5 Nov. 1851; *State* v. *Daniel*, 15 Jan. 1859; *State* v. *Reuben*, 2 Aug. 1850, all in SCMF.

Sexual Crimes	Discretionary Prosecutions	Crimes of Slavery	Crimes against Order	Threatening White Authority	Total
	23.8	8.0			16.7
	4	2			34
	37.8	32.4	29.3	31.7	33.2
	13	18	3	4	97
71.3	35.9	48.3	31.9	78.6	44.6
3	18	27	13	10	195
275.0	31.8	30.5	22.6	84.4	56.1
3	10	22	13	12	215
127.3	34.4	37.3	27.4	72.8	45.4
6	45	69	29	26	541

urce: Anderson and Spartanburg District Courts of Magistrates and Freeholders, SCA.

detailed rape cases in Spartanburg, and all of the prosecutions seem of questionable validity.

Two other aspects of slave justice cast further doubt on its fairness. First, magistrates' courts punished behavior of which they did not approve, even if the evidence in a particular case did not warrant conviction. One slave was ordered whipped "because under no circumstances a Negro ought to raise a stick at a white person." Admittedly, the mere act of raising a stick could constitute assault in the common law sense. But what is intriguing about the order for punishment was that the court had explicitly declared the charge "not proven," yet had ordered the whipping anyway! Another slave was acquitted of theft, then given eighteen lashes for taking "a liberty a Negro ought not to take."[58] It is clear from such cases that the court was more concerned with preserving white dominance and control than with justice.

The second revealing aspect of slave justice was its tendency to border on lynch law in times of panic. Psychological terror was used as a punishment for a defendant in the Camden insurrection of 1816. He was ordered to be hanged, but part of the sentence not read to him called for his being pardoned after watching his fellow slaves hang. Supreme Court Justice William Johnson recalled an innocent slave who was killed to satisfy local hysteria.[59] In such cases, the line between formal justice and vigilantism became fine indeed.

The hastily assembled court that tried the suspects in the Denmark Vesey revolt of 1822 itself was suspect. Johnson's brother-in-law, Governor Thomas Bennett, wrote to Attorney General Robert W. Hayne, questioning the legality of Charleston's establishing a court to try slaves in secret, but explicitly denying that he was seeking to reopen the case against the Vesey defendants, six of whom were to hang the next day. Hayne took no chances: noting that Bennett was not referring to the Vesey defendants, he pleaded ill health and claimed he would issue a ruling in the following week.[60] In such exceptional times, justice was a rare commodity. Judge Elihu Bay actually defended the right of magistrates' courts to bend the law in certain circumstances: "When the dreadful . . . consequences of the insurrection of slaves . . . are taken into consideration, it appears to me that the judges . . . ought to be extremely cautious in interfering with the magistrates and freeholders . . . they ought not to be eagleeyed in viewing their proceedings."[61]

As we have seen, these courts did not always conform to the standards traditionally associated with Anglo-American justice. But in addition to the procedural irregularities, even the composition of the panels was not necessarily conducive to an impartial judgment based on the evidence. Most South Carolina districts had a relatively small and homogeneous white population. But even so, men were not expected to serve on Sessions and Common Pleas juries more than once very few years.[62] These juries were chosen from panels randomly selected. In trials of blacks, a magistrate could

58. *State* v. *Lease,* 21 July 1841; *State* v. *Green,* 8 Sept. 1849, SCMF.

59. Kershaw County, miscellaneous trial record, 3–17 July 1816, Miscellaneous manuscripts, SCL; Robert S. Starobin, ed., *Denmark Vesey,* pp. 68–70.

60. Thomas Bennett to Robert Hayne, 1 July 1822; Hayne to Bennett 1 July 1822, Legal System Papers Letters; half of the slaves sentenced to hang belonged to Bennett.

61. *Kinloch* v. *Harvey,* Harper 508 (1830) at 517.

62. *Legislative Times,* p. 245.

summon any eight freeholders, from whom the defense could pick five. Since jurors in such trials were not paid, one might expect that this was an odious task and a burden to be widely shared. Instead, one finds in Spartanburg a small cluster of men who kept reappearing as jurors.

The composition of the juries suggests that not only were these trials neighborhood events, but were frequently family affairs as well. Of 174 trials in Spartanburg County for which the jury could be identified, over a third involved juries consisting of more than one person of the same last name.[63] Magistrates seem simply to have gone to the most convenient farms and plantations and summoned fathers, sons, and other relatives to sit. This practice may not have necessarily affected verdicts, but it does indicate the informal organization of these courts and the extent to which these trials were local and private.

At times the trials became procedurally incestuous. In nine cases, one or more jurors had the same last name as the magistrate. In five cases, the owner of the slave being tried and one member of the jury had the same name. In other cases, the person from whom property was alleged to have been stolen had the same last name as two jurors, a juror was a prosecution witness, and the presiding magistrate owned the defendant. Finally, one trial took place at the home of the owner whose slave allegedly murdered another slave of the same household. Justice for whites in the nineteenth century was hardly perfect, but trials were at least held in courthouses, presumably neutral sites. Moderate proposals to move only capital trials of slaves to courthouses were roundly condemned.

The irregularities in this system were frequently a matter of life or death. South Carolina consistently had more capital crimes than other states, but whites stood a good chance of avoiding the gallows. Juries frequently recommended mercy, benefit of clergy was available for many felonies, and pardons were liberally distributed. But what of blacks convicted of capital crimes? Could they rely on the idiosyncrasies of the South Carolina legal system to spare them? Could they rely on the economics of slaveholding to save them from the gallows?[64]

63. Spartanburg had the second largest white population of any district in the state. Therefore, this pattern is not simply the result of inbreeding in a small county. The total number of juries in which two or more men shared a surname was 63. Research in progress by Jane Pease indicates that this pattern of jury selection and service was common in trials of whites as well.

64. Fogel and Engerman, *Time on the Cross* 1:55, 144–45. Blacks, of course, could not receive benefit of clergy, still available for whites.

To some extent they could. One governor ran out of pardon forms for blacks as well as for whites. Governor James Adams, a severe critic of the magistrates' courts, proclaimed that even though he no longer pardoned whites, in the case of blacks, he "felt constrained in a majority of cases brought to his notice either to modify the sentence or set it aside altogether."[65]

Even though execution did not automatically follow a death sentence, blacks were still executed in antebellum South Carolina at a high rate. The number of executions can be determined from the attempts of owners to receive compensation for executed slaves. Such reimbursement had been instituted to prevent owners from concealing slaves accused of capital crimes. A compilation on this basis understates the actual level of executions because payments were sufficiently low that not all owners may have sought compensation. Because slave crime was in part ascribed to owner mismanagement, the state balked at full compensation.[66] Moreover, the two most common offenses for which slaves were executed, murder and insurrection, were excluded from the compensation scheme before 1843. Nevertheless, compensation records indicate how many slave executions can be firmly documented, even though this figure no doubt understates the actual number.

During the five and one-half decades for which records are available, at least 296 slaves were executed for criminal offenses in South Carolina (Table 6.8). Only 5.5 percent of those for whom the sex is known were female. Despite the restrictions on compensation for murder before 1843, this was still the crime for which slaves were most frequently executed. The crimes most feared by whites—rape, arson, poisoning, and insurrection—each resulted in proportionately fewer executions. Taken together, however, these crimes that created terror for whites accounted for 34.1 percent of all executions and 45.1 percent of all executions for which the crime was known. Times of racial crisis were particularly fatal for black defendants.

65. Patrick Noble to Max Laborde, 20 Feb. 1839, 11 Feb. 1840, Richardson to Laborde, 24 June 1842, Governor's Correspondence, Legal System Papers; Adams in *Legislative Times*, p. 323. Out of seven slaves sentenced to hang in Anderson and Spartanburg districts, only two met the criteria to be traced (convicted of a crime other than murder or insurrection if before 1843 and sentenced before 1855). Of these two, one was executed. Three of the convictions were for murder prior to 1843 and two were after 1855.

66. 11 *Statutes at Large* 285; Hammond proposed in 1855 that owners be compensated at full value (*Legislative Times*, p. 48); for the debate on this proposal, indicating the extent to which owners were held partially responsible for slave misbehavior, see Report of the Committee on Ways and Means (n.d., but probably 1855), Slavery Papers, Petitions, SCA.

Table 6.8. Executions of Slaves in South Carolina, 1800–1855

	Mur-der	Insurrec-tion	Bur-glary	Assault	Arson	Poison	Rape	Unknown	Total
1800–1804	4	1	4	5	0	1	1	1	17
1805–1809	4	2	4	1	4	0	3	2	20
1810–1814	1	1	5	2	1	0	2	0	12
1815–1819	3	5	6	2	2	1	2	2	23
1820–1824	5	36	5	4	0	5	1	4	60
1825–1829	3	0	4	2	4	5	5	4	27
1830–1834	8	1	1	5	2	3	0	7	27
1835–1839	7	0	0	1	2	0	3	2	15
1840–1844	11	0	1	3	2	1	1	4	23
1845–1849	10	0	0	2	0	1	2	21	36
1850–1854	8	0	1	1	0	0	1	16	27
1855								6	6
No date								3	3
Total	64	46	31	28	17	17	21	72	296
Percent	28.6	20.5	13.8	12.5	7.6	7.6	9.4		100.0

Sources: Slavery Petitions, Reports and Resolutions of the General Assembly, 1837–1855, South Carolina Treasury Ledgers, South Carolina Treasury Journals, SCA. Four executions were discovered in one appellate court case (State v. Sims, 2 Bailey 29, 1830) and three from newspaper reports.

Excluding the extraordinary year of 1822, two of the three years with the highest number of executions (eleven) were 1823, the year following the Vesey scare, and 1851, the year of the first secession crisis. The decade after 1822 had sixty-two executions, compared with thirty-four in the decade previous, even though the latter figure included the Camden insurrection. The total number of executions averaged six per year.[67]

Given the economic advantages of not executing and the increasing hostility to capital punishment in nineteenth-century America, this figure is startling. By 1850, the black population of South Carolina was 412,320. In Massachusetts, which had a population of 994,514 by 1850, only twenty-eight executions occurred between 1801 and 1845. This large number of executions calls into question economic self-interest as an ultimate guarantor of slaves' well-being;[68] banishment was clearly not a complete substitute for execution.

When looking at the entire system of trying, executing, and protecting blacks in South Carolina courts, the restriction on black testimony becomes merely the most obvious symbol of the black's legal impotence. Blacks in court could almost literally do nothing on their own. They were at the mercy of high-minded and courageous men who would undertake the thankless task of prosecuting their fellow whites. This was a risky business. After indicting a prominent owner for slavebeating, Benjamin F. Perry lost the next election.[69]

If convicted of a capital offense, slaves were at the mercy of their owners to appeal. Costly and difficult, appeals were not even permitted until 1833. Nevertheless, many owners did seek appellate review of their slave's conviction. Gabriel South, for example, doggedly pursued all legal remedies and even risked jail to save his slave from a patently unfair conviction. Another owner successfully convinced the Spartanburg court that it had exceeded its jurisdiction in handing down a particularly severe sentence, and a Charleston man petitioned the governor to reduce a harsh penalty which he claimed his slave could not survive.[70] Yet even John Belton O'Neall, whose dissent in South's case is widely quoted and who opposed

67. Henry, *Police Control*, p. 57, claimed that the usual number was two or three, but that for many years there were none and that the maximum number was seven.

68. Fogel and Engerman, *Time on the Cross*, 1:55, 144–45.

69. Elizabeth Perry to Benjamin F. Perry, 8 March 1847, Benjamin F. Perry Papers, SCL.

70. *State* v. *Nathan*, 5 Richardson 219 (1851); *State* v. *South*, 5 Richardson 489 (1852); *State* v. *Lotty and Jerry*, 23 Sept. 1844, SCMF; Petition of Edward Carew, 3 July 1834, Slavery Petitions.

capital punishment, did not stall the execution of his own slave.[71] And if not O'Neall, then who in South Carolina? Owners also determined the nature of the defense. Slaves were allowed an attorney and the right to call witnesses, but both were expensive. Lowcountry planters claimed that slaves always had the best lawyers and that convictions were hard to obtain.[72] One planter's diary shows that although the former was sometimes the case, the latter did not necessarily follow. John Grimball engaged B. C. Pressley, author of the *Law of Magistrates*, and Thomas S. Grimké, a leading Charleston attorney, on two separate occasions to defend his slaves for murder. Both slaves were convicted, although not executed.[73]

Not everyone in South Carolina was pleased with this situation. And yet, despite the pleas of judges, governors, and grand juries, only slight procedural changes were enacted.[74] Ironically, lowcountry planters, who claimed to have little need for such a court system, defended it most vigorously against the proponents of change. Every grand jury presentment calling for reform came from the extreme upcountry; conversely, the votes in the assembly that defeated a general overhaul in the courts came from the lowcountry.[75]

What did lowcountry planters have to gain from this system that caused them to defend it against even the most innocuous-appearing changes? First, owners were not absolutely free to chastise another person's slave, even for a crime; the owner of the injured slave could sue for damages. Therefore, these courts were necessary to resolve disputes that crossed plantation lines. Second, no compensation was available to owners of slaves executed as a result of summary plantation justice. And finally, these trials may have been in part the result of local tensions and neighborhood feuds. In effect, a slave-owner might have brought criminal charges against his neighbor's slave in part as a surrogate for civil litigation. Such trials may rep-

71. Slavery Petitions; O'Neall's slave was executed for murder (*South Carolina Reports and Resolutions*, 1844, p. 90). The petition was filed after the law was changed making indemnification for murder possible; one must assume that the execution preceded the four-year grace period because O'Neall's claim was denied.

72. *Legislative Times*, pp. 138–39.

73. John B. Grimball Diary, 5–11 May 1840, 25 Nov. 1858, 30 Dec. 1858, 12, 18 Jan., 28 Feb. 1859, 11 Jan. 1860, Charleston Library Society. Grimball actually preferred to get James L. Petigru, but feared that "men of his practice would . . . be unwilling to go into . . . a magistrates' case."

74. The governors were James H. Adams, John P. Richardson, John L. Wilson, and Robert Y. Hayne (Governor's Messages, SCA). The grand jury presentments are in note 50.

75. For an analysis of the roll call, see Robert Nicholas Olsberg, "A Government of Class and Race," p. 55.

resent another manifestation of a phenomenon we have already encountered: the use of the criminal justice system for private ends. One Spartanburg slaveowner successfully appealed a conviction in part because "the presiding magistrate is, . . . was, . . . and for a long time before on unfriendly relations with the owner of the slave."[76]

Why, then, the opposition to reform? Like most South Carolinians, planters had a complex attitude toward legally constituted authority. When it suited them, they required and appreciated the formal imprimatur. But as wielders of another sort of authority—based on social standing, prestige, and honor—they jealously resisted any intrusion. They ridiculed the charge that secret trials of slaves were held in secluded locations; they, after all, knew where the trials were and why they should be secluded and private. Complaints that local passions and prejudices influenced the course of justice did not bother them as long as they could direct those emotions. And the thought that a slave of a rich or well-liked man could get off scot-free while that of a poor or unpopular man could be hanged was hardly objectionable.[77]

In a debate in 1855 on reform of the slave trial system, Franklin Moses, a leading upcountry lawyer, charged, "We know that Negroes are tried in the hidden corners of our districts, and the prosecutor, in every instance, has the right to select his own magistrate, and to whisper in his ear who the freeholders are to be upon the jury." In response, Senator John Townsend, one of the largest Sea Island cotton planters in the state, sneered, "The gentleman does not speak as a planter."[78] The cry of noninterference with domestic institutions in South Carolina was taken very literally. The existence of slavery, particularly in the predominantly black lowcountry, depended upon a variety of informal arrangements that could not be subject to public scrutiny. And the survival of these arrangements was far more important than justice for a legally inferior caste.

These trials demonstrate why the notion of justice for slaves may be self-contradictory. On the one hand, the trials show that the master's authority was indeed limited. Slaveowners could not exercise unfettered dominion over their own or anyone else's slaves. On the other hand, the function of the law was to circumscribe permissible behavior and ostracize and penalize the unacceptable. It was to

76. *State* v. *Hamp*, 1857, SCMF.

77. These criticisms are in the Charleston *Mercury*, 1 Dec. 1841; see also Edgefield *Advertiser*, 6 Dec. 1838.

78. *Legislative Times*, pp. 136–39; identifications from the *Biographical Directory of the Senate of the State of South Carolina*, pp. 278, 323.

regulate, but not supersede or even interfere with the relationship between master and slave.

As we have seen, these courts were hardly a rubber stamp—the difference between a conviction rate of 100 percent and the actual rate of 67 percent is not trivial. But it is also clear that these trials existed not simply to deter criminality, but also to support white dominance.

In retrospect, those who did not realize that the term "black justice" was inherently contradictory did not appreciate the function of law and authority in South Carolina. The system of trying, convicting, and punishing blacks may have seemed informal and capricious, but that is to judge it by the standards of Anglo-American criminal law, where the fundamental presumption of the adversary system was that both prosecution and defense enter the courtroom on terms of equality. But this presumption, sorely tried and rarely realized for whites in either the North or the South, was simply "inadmissible" for blacks. Black justice may have served some bureaucratic need for certification while at the same time soothing some slaveholders' consciences, but its primary purpose was not to be just.

On the surface, black justice was permeated with the same laxness and incompetence we have already seen for whites. But with the security of property and social order at stake, substantive justice was another matter. Vigorous prosecution of slaves for crimes against property and authority reflect this concern. The low conviction rates for white brawlers could not be tolerated for slaves, when any breach of law or authority was seen as incipient rebellion. Thus, despite the ignorant and unscrupulous magistrates, ineffectual patrol laws, and irregular courts, acquittal rates were low. When dealing with slaves, South Carolina justice got down to business. And in the types of offenses prosecuted, the frequency of conviction, and the relative severity of punishment, South Carolina black justice suddenly and strikingly resembled that of Massachusetts. Even though hampered by crude forms and poor officials, the ends of criminal justice suddenly became very clear. Punishments for slaves were as harsh as were economically feasible, conviction rates were high, and reprimands to whites who abrogated the slave's few legally protected rights were rare. In its own way, justice in South Carolina was as rational and utilitarian as that in Massachusetts when the state's vital interests were at stake.

Chapter 7.
"A Great Manual Labor School": The Massachusetts State Prison, 1805–1878

In the nineteenth century, the state prison replaced the city on a hill as the embodiment of many of Massachusetts's ideals and as the model for the rest of the civilized world to follow. Although the prison was the repository for only a small percentage of the state's convicts, its significance cannot be overestimated. As a model institution, the prison influenced the course of corrections. It was also the focus of much of the discussion over the prospects of penitence and reformation. As a substantial capital investment, the prison was visible proof of the seriousness with which the state took both crime and its elusive cure. And, by its quest for profit, the prison revealed the ultimate softness of that commitment while also reflecting in a ludicrously precise manner the entrepreneurial spirit of the age that produced the edifice.

Because of the professed goal of reformation and because of its position at the top of the state's penal hierarchy, the Massachusetts State Prison is a compelling barometer of changes in the history of criminal justice. Throughout the nineteenth century, the prison was a center of attention. Inspectors and prison officials issued annual reports; governors and legislators lavished attention on the facility. An influential reform society, the Prison Discipline Society of Boston, assumed informal guardianship of the institution. Finally, the prison was a mandatory stop for American and foreign visitors interested in the new science of penology.

As a result of this interest, historians know more about the daily workings of the prison (albeit through the not always unprejudiced eyes of wardens, politicians, and reformers) than about any other aspect of the criminal justice system. We know not only what the prison was, but also what various people hoped it would be. The optimistic hope of reformation represented some of the most admirable features of human nature, but the prison also brought to the surface the darker side of vengeance and punishment. The history of the internal management of the prison shows the interplay of professionalism, bureaucracy, and control. The prison, in sum, was a catalyst for a multitude of significant and conflicting ideas.[1]

This discussion will focus on the evolving purposes and practices of the institution, tracing what changed over three-quarters of a century, but, more important, what did not. To do so, it is useful to divide the history of the prison into three phases. The first phase covers the years 1805 to 1829. Opened in 1805 at Charlestown, the prison at first resembled a large county jail, with congregate living arrangements and individual piecework labor. By 1829, the prison had been completely remodeled. The new prison was built on the Auburn plan of congregate labor by day and cellular separation at night. During this period, which might be termed the reform era, the fiercest ideological struggles occurred over the nature and operation of this institution. The third phase, which began with the expansion of the prison in 1851 and ended with its move to Concord in 1878, may be termed the bureaucratic phase. Ideology was replaced by professional élan as the warden and his staff acquired considerable autonomy.

The essence of this institution, opened in 1805 with the seemingly contradictory goals of both punishment and reformation, can best be understood by looking at the labor system within the prison, the rights accorded the prisoner, and the ultimate replacement of reformist ideology by pragmatism and bureaucratic discretion. Although one may find many examples of evolution and adjustment, in many ways the basic nature of the institution was fixed from the start.

The concept of hard labor is an appropriate starting point, for the early prison had little in common with its successors other than the requirement of labor within the walls. Hard labor was not unknown in Massachusetts: it was first authorized in 1767. Penal servitude, of course, was well known in the colonies. Utilizing the labor

1. Many of the issues in this chapter were influenced by David J. Rothman's *The Discovery of the Asylum*. The interpretation presented here differs from Rothman's in its assessment of the fundamental nature of penal institutions, the timing of significant shifts in penal policy, and the motives and ultimate influence of reformers. In addition, I tend to be skeptical of an interpretation based on uniquely American factors of events that were occurring simultaneously on both sides of the Atlantic. Although I do not mean to minimize these differences, I do not wish in any way to detract from Rothman's impressive (and essentially correct) reinterpretation of a significant cultural trend in nineteenth-century social history. Obviously, my own view of these events was shaped to no small extent by Rothman's conceptualization. Having sketched out this position, I will refrain from citing in the text every point of disagreement or agreement.

within the institution was attractive because it promoted discipline by occupying convicts' time. This was particularly important because of the potential for disruption inherent in the congregate living arrangements of the prison's first decades. Moreover, the proceeds from the labor defrayed part of the prison's expense. Finally, forced labor—even with the potential promise of a small wage —was seen as punishment because crimes were assumed to be committed by those who did not believe in honest work.

In the early years, there were few illusions about the prison actually producing a profit. In 1815, Warden Gamaliel Bradford called it a "fond, though false expectation" that the proceeds from the convicts' labor would be sufficient to pay expenses. Indeed, Bradford termed the prison a "benevolent institution" that deserved state support. Two years later, a legislative committee affirmed: "It is not to be expected that a Penitentiary will support itself."[2] Nevertheless, financial returns were a high priority; only six years after the prison opened, prison labor was contracted to private concerns (although performed within the confines of the institution) in order to yield a high return. In 1821, eleven different trades were represented, but already the trend was clear; over one-third of those employed productively were stonecutters.[3] Much of the other labor in these prefactory decades was simple piecework carried on individually in cells. Labor was both a means to a financial return and a way to keep prisoners busy; it had not yet become a means for ordering the prisoners or a virtue in itself. The use of the "overstint," or incentive bonus for work performed beyond a specified quota, was an indication that during this period, the prisoner retained some personal value in his labor.

The early prison was a scene of riot. Blame, like disorder, was rampant. The overstint, it was charged, encouraged gambling and endless appeals.[4] Neither the living arrangements nor the work situation was conducive to order. Against this chaotic backdrop, the system of prison discipline popular in New York had particular appeal. This was the Auburn system of congregate, but silent, labor by day, and solitary confinement at night.

The Auburn system involved large-scale convict labor during the

2. Gamaliel Bradford, *Description and Historical Sketch of the Massachusetts State Prison,* p. 10; Commissioners of the State Prison, *Report,* p. 15.

3. Gamaliel Bradford, *State Prisons and the Penitentiary System Vindicated,* p. 55.

4. *Committee of Both Houses Report,* 1818, p. 2. Governor Lincoln used this phrase in 1826 (*Governor's Message,* Levi Lincoln, p. 16); *Annual Report of the BPDS,* 1828, p. 33.

day, essential for the prison to produce the financial surplus explicitly promised by its backers. But profit was hardly the sole virtue. Labor itself became a way to redeem the criminal class. Because many convicts were believed to have been idle before committing a crime, and because idleness was seen as promoting vice and crime, the discipline of honest labor would itself be an important step on the road to reformation. "It is much more difficult to prevent human beings from doing mischief when they have nothing else to do, than when they are busily and usefully employed," reported the Boston Prison Discipline Society. "The busy hum of industry" in the Auburn-style prison "is a striking contrast to the oaths and imprecations, the obscenity and pollution, the schemes of villainy, and malignant soliloquies which may be heard . . . in many prisons."[5] Reformer Francis Gray boasted that the prison was "a great manual labor school," comparable to the new factory system at Lowell.[6]

It is important to understand that some form of hard labor in the prison preceded the development of the factory system. The reform era did not change the essential structure or operation of the prison, but infused both with an ideology influenced by developments in the outside world. Thus, the prison was a mix of Enlightenment humanist views on the nature of crime and the industrial-era solution to the problem of human weakness. The prison had always been a place of labor; the Auburn-era reformers copied features of production and profit explicitly from the new industrial order. The reform group that closely monitored the Massachusetts State Prison was the Prison *Discipline* Society. The similarities to the factory in both practice and theory were ironic; the advent of the industrial order itself, of course, had been blamed for much of the era's crime. Because teaching the prisoners the value of honest labor was seen as a reward, administrators during the Auburn decades never spoke of restoring the overstint. The prison actually removed all monetary incentives for meritorious labor. Ironically, during the period when the most value was placed on labor, nothing was paid for it.

With the demise of the Auburn system and the concurrent attack on convict labor, the profit motive lost its central place. The remaining justification for hard labor was simply practical—as a way of ordering daily prison life. When, after the Civil War, fires, overcrowding, and fiscal reverses kept many prisoners idle, wardens complained that this undermined the discipline of the institution.

5. *Annual Report BPDS*, 1827, p. 36.
6. Francis Gray, *Prison Discipline in America*, p. 47; Warden Frederick Robinson used that same figure of speech in his annual report, *State Prison Report*, 1847, p. 22.

Only in this last period was prison work seen for what it actually was—a means of keeping the prison population reasonably under control by occupying prisoners' time in a structured fashion during the day.[7]

Order and submission were always among the highest priorities of the prison. From the early decades of the century, prisoners were made to understand that obedience to the rules "constitute[d] their sole claim to favor and indulgence of privilege." On the other hand, "all obstinate . . . behavior will subject the offender inevitably to punishment, till subdued or reclaimed."[8] The convict's mind, it was believed, "ought to be reduced to a state of humiliation and discipline." In short, convicts were to be like "clay in the hands of the potter."[9]

These early statements of policy and intent indicate that the Auburn system did not invent a new concept of order for Jacksonian America; the value of discipline and submission was established in the prison from the beginning. The Auburn system simply attempted to provide the methods by which these objectives could be achieved. To Tocqueville and other observers, the very essence of the Auburn system was its emphasis on order.[10] The directors of the Massachusetts State Prison wanted the inmates to "move and act like machines," an appropriately factorylike metaphor. After one full year of operation, the warden boasted that all movements in the prison were "conducted in the most perfect military order."[11]

The image of the Auburn prisoner marching lockstep, working, and eating in total silence became a staple of nineteenth-century travel and reform literature. The benefits seemed widespread. Regimented labor made the management of the prisoner easier; the prisoner learned the merits of discipline and labor; and the scale of enterprise possible under such an arrangement guaranteed a good return to the state. It can hardly be a coincidence that the years in which the Auburn system was most rigorously applied in Massachusetts were also the years that, according to the prison's own

7. The importance of prison labor as a daily diversion should not be overlooked. In one twentieth-century maximum security prison, officials had only one effective means of coercing prisoners to work—prisoners unwilling to work must remain idle for at least six months (Gresham M. Sykes, *The Society of Captives*).

8. *An Account of the Massachusetts State Prison* . . . , p. 32.

9. Gideon Haynes, *Pictures From Prison Life*, p. 233 (quoting from a report of the directors, 1815).

10. Gustave de Beaumont and Alexis de Tocqueville, *On the Penitentiary System in the United States and Its Application in France*, pp. 22, 25.

11. *Rules and Regulations for the Government of the Massachusetts State Prison*, 1829, p. 102; *State Prison Report*, 1830, p. 3.

accounting, produced the greatest profit.[12] The Auburn system, then, can claim credit for an ideological integration or order, labor, and profit, but order and labor were always central to the prison's existence, and the balance sheet was never ignored.

Just as order and labor had different connotations in the three periods, so did the concept of prisoners' rights. Such a term must be used in a relative sense. Prison always meant a loss of freedom, but it did not always mean a loss of self-dignity or demolition of individual will.

At no time in the nineteenth century was the life of the prisoner to be envied. Although Americans never explicitly adopted the policy of "less eligibility," under which life inside custodial and penal institutions was intentionally designed to be less attractive than life outside, so that people would not be tempted to devise schemes for entrance, this concept, which so infamously characterized English workhouses and almshouses, nevertheless flourished in America on an informal basis. During the first decades, prison officials felt compelled to prove that life in prisons was less desirable than life on the outside and pointed out that prisoners, by their constant escape attempts and frequent applications for pardons, made their own preferences clear.[13] Even as late as 1855, the inspectors felt compelled to dispel the notion that some men deliberately tried to enter prison because of the allegedly soft life inside.[14] Yet, clear differences in the treatment of prisoners existed in all three periods.

When the prison opened, convicts did not lose all their rights upon entering. Most significantly, they retained the right to some proceeds from their labor, although the overstint was never given to them without conditions. Only convicts eligible for a good conduct certificate upon discharge could receive that payment. In 1818, the percentage of the overstint available was made dependent upon the class in which the convict was placed.[15] Nevertheless, these measures demonstrated recognition of the prisoner's own will. Normal incentives were seen as effective means of ordering both the prison and the convict's behavior. There were other subtle acknowledgments of this fact. In 1806, a rule on the precise length of sentences to hard labor was clarified in response to a petition by the convicts. In later years, such assertiveness would be suppressed, not rewarded. Moreover, although the early institution confined convicts at forced labor, it did not prohibit all contact with the outside. The

12. *Fifteenth Annual Report MBSC,* 1878, Appendix p. 62.
13. Bradford, *State Prisons,* pp. 14–15.
14. *State Prison Report,* 1855, p. 7.
15. *Rules and Regulations,* 1823, p. 58.

rule that letters had to be approved by the chaplain shows that correspondence was permitted.[16]

Despite these policies, this was by no means an idyllic period for prisoners. Iron collars and leg irons were used to prevent escapes. After the disorders of 1816, a number of repressive measures were passed. Recidivists were tattooed with the letters "MSP," an early illustration of labeling theory. In addition, time spent in solitary confinement as punishment no longer counted as part of time served.[17] But some basic rights were not forfeited by conviction.

Under the Auburn system, most of these rights disappeared. The prisoner was seen as a child—a willful being whose spirit had to be crushed. "It is with convicts as it is with children," wrote Dorothea Dix in 1845.[18] The same year, Chaplain Jared Curtis lauded the warden's efforts to make the government of the prison a *"paternal one."*[19] The most significant privileges that were eliminated related to communication, both within the prison and with the outside world. Prisoners were not only forbidden to speak to one another, but letters and visitors were absolutely prohibited.

One of the ironies of the prison reform movement was that it asserted that prisoners should be treated like human beings but denied them certain basic human rights. Prisoners were expected to learn the value of hard labor, yet the overstint was taken away. The silence rule was admittedly at odds with human social requirements, yet was justified as preventing convicts from scheming. It was generally recognized that imprisonment posed a special problem for prisoners with families, yet all contact with one's family, written or personal, was proscribed.

Although certain rights and privileges were curtailed in the reform period, the lives and prospects of prisoners were improved in one major respect. Reformers attempted to eliminate the stigma attached to the prison sentence. One of the first acts of the new prison administration was to abolish the tattoo for recidivists. This was a symbolic affirmation of their belief in human perfectibility. During this period, the first primitive efforts were inaugurated on behalf of discharged convicts.

But beginning in the 1850s, with no apparent design, prisoners began to enjoy some rights and privileges resulting from the decline of the reform movement, with its immpossibly inflexible ideology,

16. *An Account of the Massachusetts State Prison*, p. 39.

17. Ibid., p. 26; Bradford, *State Prisons*, p. 47; *Rules and Regulations*, 1823, p. 38.

18. Dorothea Lynde Dix, *Remarks on Prisons and Prison Discipline in the United States*, p. 22.

19. *State Prison Report*, 1845, p. 24.

and the increased power of the warden. The warden acted, or chose not to act, out of simple common sense and a concern for the smooth functioning of the institution. Ideology was replaced by pragmatism.

There are two vivid examples of this new flexibility. The first was the abrogation of the silence rule that clearly demonstrates that the demise of the Auburn system penitentiary was more a pragmatic bureaucratic adjustment than a self-conscious shift in ideology. There were two reasons for the end of the silence rule. First, by the 1840s, much of the prison production was in the hands of subcontractors, who were more interested in profit than in enforcing a seemingly unreasonable measure. Second, the assumption that conversation was corrupting was yielding to the realization that the cost of preserving silence probably exceeded its benefits.

By the mid-1840s, conversation had come to be regarded as not injurious and perhaps even beneficial. in 1846, the warden argued, "I have not experienced so much evil from the illicit conversation which convicts can have in the prison" to warrant the trouble of preventing it. Furthermore, "the few words which a convict can steal the opportunity to say is . . . as likely to be good and encouraging as evil and debasing."[20] Less than a decade later, a warden condemned total silence as a "living death," and boasted, "Happily, such isolation is as impossible as it would be injurious."[21]

Other changes in life at the prison helped undermine this basic tenet of the silent system. For example, under the not so subtle stimulation of Warden Frederick Robinson and Chaplain Jared Curtis, the Massachusetts State Prison Society for Moral Improvement and Mutual Aid was formed in 1847.[22] When a former inspector of the prison, Francis Gray, published his defense of the Massachusetts institution, he declared, "But this . . . it will be said, is not the Auburn system." To those ideologues Gray replied simply, "So be it. No matter for the name."[23]

Another sign of this changing attitude toward the prisoner was the abolition of the twenty-five-cent visitors' fee, paid by anyone who wished to view the prison. This charge had been in effect for over three decades and was staunchly defended as an easy source of income during a time when the final ledger line, no matter how spuriously determined, was regarded as crucial to the success of the

20. Ibid., 1846, p. 19.
21. Ibid., 1854, pp. 8–9.
22. The constitution of this rather remarkable society is reprinted in ibid., 1847, pp. 18–21.
23. Gray, *Prison Discipline*.

institution.[24] Proud of their prison, reformers at first had no quarrel with the fee. The prisons of America were, after all, magnets for foreign dignitaries, the most prominent of whom came to America especially to view them. It was only logical—and perhaps democratic—to allow the general public to see this splendid institution. Because the reformers, while proclaiming faith in the humanity of the prisoners, did not always treat prisoners as human beings, this humiliating practice continued for some time. In the mid-1840s, the visitors' fee came under attack from Dix and Howe.[25] But not until 1863 did prison officials look beyond the financial interest of the institution and abolish the practice of unlimited admission for a small fee, a custom that, despite bringing in over $1,500 per year, exposed convicts to shame. No longer did the prison provide an afternoon's diversion for all who could afford it.

Other subtle changes can be detected after the 1851 expansion. In 1853, prisoners were allowed to purchase their own reading matter. By 1855, contractors were forbidden to "inflict any punishment, in any manner, upon any convict whatever."[26] In 1864, the Board of State Charities, with its customary realistic view of life outside the walls, but continual naiveté about what the state was willing to or could do within the prison walls, urged that convicts learn only trades that could be useful upon their release. Prisoners were permitted to send one letter every three months. In the 1870s, it was proposed without success that prisoners or their families on the outside should receive some return for their labor. In 1875, after a bitter controversy that led to the firing of the chaplain, Catholic services were held for the first time in the prison. Over half the prison population attended,[27] hardly surprising given the ethnic makeup of the convict population. Three years later, the "gag," a device placed in the prisoner's mouth to prevent speech, was outlawed as a punishment within the prison, and the prisoners were

24. The charge first appears in the 1823 *Rules and Regulations*, p. 61. The $1,500 realized annually was no small sum for such a cost-conscious operation. The prison —by its own accounting—showed a profit in only six of the ten years from 1838 to 1847. In only one of those years (1839) was the stated profit larger than the income from the visitors' fee. Conversely, an average gain of $1,500 per year meant that about twenty people per weekday came through the prison to eye the prisoners. Although abolition of the fee was no small sacrifice, it was made at a time when perhaps in fact—although certainly not in theory—this method of calculation was assuming less importance. From 1853 (when the fee was abolished) until 1866, the prison showed a profit only once (1860).

25. Dix, *Remarks*, p. 10; Samuel Gridley Howe, *An Essay on the Separate and Congregate System of Prison Discipline*, p. 46.

26. *State Prison Report*, 1853, p. 29; *Rules and Regulations* 1855, p. 13.

27. *Report of the Committee on Prisons*, 1877, p. 6.

provided with locked boxes for private communication with the warden.[28]

Even the prison uniforms reflected this subtle shift in attitude. The old-style multicolored outfit was discarded in 1865 because it was "calculated to drive [the prisoner's] manhood from [him]," and that was the "thing we want him most to maintain." Every article of clothing bore the prisoner's name, "so that he has a kind of property in his clothes."[29] In all, the "rights" granted to the prisoners certainly did not amount to much. But they did indicate a recognition that prisoners would lead a life in the outside world as well and that it was not sound policy to set aside all values of the larger society, such as incentive, pride, and will, while ostensibly aiding prisoners to return to that world.

The issues of order within the prison and the rights of convicts became fused in the question of the punishment of the convict within the prison. Again, at first, policies were not articulated very clearly. Guards were forbidden to speak insolently to prisoners, and the warden was instructed to "carefully guard himself against every impulse of personal resentment."[30] But disorders in 1816 resulted in a change in policy and attitude. Guards were held guiltless if a convict was wounded or killed while resisting their command.[31] Corporal and shaming punishments, along with solitary confinement, were used for minor infractions.

As hard labor became the dominant mode of punishment in the early nineteenth century, many of the old penalties at first glance appeared to have been discarded. No longer could a court sentence a person to the stock or pillory, order a person to sit on the gallows with a noose around his head, or have first-time felons branded. But, ironically, these punishments were not abolished, but rather were transferred to the prison itself. All of the above punishments were used in the early years to maintain internal order.

By midcentury, corporal punishment in the prison was a source of considerable controversy. In New York's Auburn prison, prototype for the silent system, the lash was frequently and proudly used to maintain order and silence. Massachusetts adopted this mode of

28. The bills passed were in 1878, ch. 276 (guaranteed communication) and 1879, ch. 181 (gag forbidden).

29. *State Prison Report*, 1864, p. 8; Enoch C. Wines and Theodore Dwight, *Report on the Prisons and Reformatories of the United States and Canada made to the Legislature of New York, January 1867*, p. 182.

30. *An Account of the Massachusetts State Prison*, p. 28.

31. In a riot in 1821, in which a prisoner was killed, it was later proved that he had been shot in the back. The killing was done pursuant to an order from the warden (James T. Austin, *Reply to the Centinel Review*, p. 3).

discipline along with the other tenets of the silent system. In 1841, again following New York's lead, Massachusetts introduced the shower bath, in which victims spent hours under a steady stream of water. This brutal punishment had been a mixed success in New York, and the warden of the Massachusetts State Prison was not optimistic about its utility.[32] His doubts soon proved warranted. In 1843, convict Abner Rogers, after two successive days under the shower bath for talking in his cell, murdered warden Charles Lincoln, a tragedy that terminated the brief tenure of that device.

Frederick Robinson, Lincoln's replacement, steadfastly opposed all corporal punishment. Robinson believed that preserving the prisoners' manhood and humanity would itself assure the internal harmony of the institution. His views seemed so heretical that the usually benevolent Dorothea Dix charged that he did not believe in punishment. Robinson replied that without the lash, convicts were "as orderly, as industrious, and obedient as heretofore, and more contented, docile, and happy."[33]

In 1849, whipping was abolished by statute, outraging all the officers of the prison except Robinson. The inspectors compared this to a school announcing that it had abolished corporal punishment, even though another prison reformer, Horace Mann, was trying to prove that schools could be so run. Chaplain Curtis likened this measure to the spirit of anarchy that was ruining schools and families and predicted that the next step would be to set all prisoners free. As a crowning touch, he reprinted a decade-old interview with Louis Dwight on this issue. Dwight had argued that the lash was an indispensable part of prison discipline. Under such pressure, the legislature promptly repealed the act and granted the warden discretion to whip, subject to the concurrence of one inspector.[34]

With the passage of the new law, whipping again became an important tool for discipline. At first, the punishment was used sparingly. Only 2 were whipped in 1851; 7 in 1853. But over the next four years, 110 convicts were whipped, 45 (40.9 percent) for infractions relating to the authority of the officers and the general order of the prison. Punishments for these offenses were the most severe

32. *State Prison Report*, 1841, p. 12. An official of New York's Auburn prison told Lieber that the shower bath did not affect its victims equally; some were not bothered by it, and others seemed to fall apart, not to recover for hours (Blanchard Fosgate to Francis Lieber, 6 April 1846, Francis Lieber Papers, Huntington Library).

33. Dix, *Remarks*, p. 19; Hon. Frederick Robinson, "Treatment of Prisoners," *Prisoner's Friend* 2 (1850): 490.

34. *State Prison Report*, 1849, pp. 4–7, 32–39; *Prisoner's Friend* 2 (1850): 374; *State Prison Report*, 1850, p. 30.

by a substantial margin. Of the 18 convicts who received six or more lashes for misconduct, 14 were punished for such infractions.[35]

Perhaps because they were being called to approve this measure so frequently, in 1856 the inspectors delegated all authority for whipping to the warden. This action prompted a legislative investigation into the possibility of abolishing stripes, although no alteration resulted.[36] Yet the die was cast; the warden had the authority, but he could choose not to exercise it. In 1858, Gideon Haynes became warden and ended the practice. Pragmatism and bureaucratic power had become more important than ideology in determining how the prison was to be run.

The maintenance of order, labor, and discipline was crucial to the daily operation of the prison. While policies in this area affected life within prison walls, policies in a related area not only helped determine (if any such factor could be considered determinative) a convict's chances upon release, but also indicated the confidence people had—or lacked—in the institution. This issue was the fate or treatment of convicts upon release. To test the effectiveness of the prison's rehabilitative program, the recidivism rate was closely monitored.

The recidivist was living proof of the prison's failure, but proper treatment of the discharged convict posed a subtle dilemma for those who wished to utilize aftercare to reduce that telltale rate. A substantively strong commitment to the discharged convict was a tacit admission of the failure of the prison to prepare inmates for life beyond the walls. But, on the other hand, few were confident that discharged convicts were destined for success in the outside world.

Concern for the fate of the newly released prisoner surfaced with the adoption of the Auburn system. High rates of recidivism in the past could be easily attributed to the lack of facilities for reformation. As one legislative committee noted of discharged convicts: "The unwillingness to employ them is the natural consequence of their crime and conviction, and is increased, no doubt, by the belief (*which formerly, at least was just*) that a State Prison is a seminary of corruption. . . . This difficulty must exist . . . till our prisons shall become places of reformation *and be so considered.*"[37] The committee initially proposed an asylum for discharged convicts. Fearing

35. *State Prison Reports,* 1853–56.
36. This report is House Document 227, 1857.
37. *Report of the Inspectors of the State Prison . . . on Discharged Convicts,* pp. 4–5. Emphasis added.

that this, too, might be a place of corruption, the committee proposed labor by day and solitary confinement at night. Since this was a closed community, no money would be needed—and thus would not be allowed. Eventually, the legislators realized that they proposed creating an institution very much like the one the prisoners had just left. "Whether any discharged convict," the committee concluded, "would voluntarily enter such an Establishment may well be doubted."[38] Were they so confident in the prison that it automatically served as a model? Or were they cynically assuming that recidivism rates could not be reduced by institutions that promised reform? Whatever people's real thoughts, some attention was paid to the plight of the discharged convicts.

In 1845, Massachusetts established an agent to provide food, shelter, clothes, and employment for discharged convicts. Two years later, the warden of the state prison reported that the agent had never "failed to find, for everyone who asked for it, employment at the work he wished."[39] This modest start was noteworthy for its somewhat realistic appraisal of the needs of such men. In addition to basic, immediate necessities, the agent loaned money, financed the purchase of necessary tools, helped find lodging, and even tried to locate the prisoner's family.

With the state agent came the inevitable Boston Society for Aiding Discharged Convicts. The society and the state produced an incestuous alliance of the sort that frequently characterized reform. The society's agent and the state's agent were the same person. The society thus had official representation in the prison and could talk to inmates and negotiate for job help on the outside. The Boston society jubilantly spoke of making "all society one great society for aiding discharged convicts." Samuel Gridley Howe was the president and kept it going almost single-handedly for many years.[40] Nevertheless, these efforts did not appreciably reduce the recidivism rate, and former convicts seeking employment found that the public was not convinced of the prison's success in anything short of incarceration.

When evaluating policy changes in the prison's history, it is useful to keep in mind the possible effects of changes in the characteristics of the prison population. Attitudes toward corrections were

38. Ibid., pp. 8–9.

39. *State Prison Report*, 1848, p. 16.

40. *Second Annual Report of the Boston Society for Aiding Discharged Convicts*, 1848, p. 28; see Howe's plea for funds in the 1857 *Annual Report*. In the 1870s the society was called the Massachusetts Society for Aiding Discharged Convicts; Howe was President; see *Ninth Annual Report MBSC*, 1872, p. 136.

influenced by prejudices against certain racial, national, or age groups, particularly when those groups appeared to comprise inordinate proportions of the penitentiary's population. When the prison was filled with people seen as marginal, innately inferior by reaons of race or nativity, and therefore not reclaimable, idealistic plans yielded to a frank desire to keep such misfits out of sight. The prison management was aware at all times of the social characteristics of the prisoners, although changes in the prison population itself in part reflected demographic trends in the larger society.

From the opening of the prison in 1805, statistics were kept on the age, race, and nativity of the inmates. This fact alone shows that prison officials suspected (and perhaps expected) that certain demographic groups were overrepresented in the convict population. In fact, the implicit suspicions proved correct. Immigrants, migrants, blacks, and youths were sentenced to the prison in disproportionate numbers until the 1870s.[41] The percentage of foreign-born increased dramatically (Table 7.1, Figure 7.1). The increase in foreign-born after 1846 can be explained by the striking rise in immigration, particularly from Ireland, beginning in that year. From 1837 to 1844, the number of immigrants arriving at the port of Boston never exceeded 5,500. In 1845, there were 8,550; in the following year that figure had nearly doubled, and by the next year the number was 24,245. The number of immigrants did not return to the earlier range until 1858, and by then, the demographic composition of the state had been measurably altered. From 1848 to 1854, immigrants from Ireland accounted for almost three-quarters of the total.[42] Since the pre-1845 figures already showed an overrepresentation of Irish-born convicts, it is not surprising that the changes in the prison population reflected the later immigration trend.

The overrepresentation of native-born migrants reflects the well-known mobility of nineteenth-century Americans. In 1850, for ex-

41. This refers to the population at large. Another question, which concerns sentencing bias, is the proportion sent to the state prison compared to the total arrested. Using total commitments to jails and correction houses as a crude substitute for total arrests, we find that less than 1 percent of all immigrants committed were sent to the prison, compared to 2.35 percent for Massachusetts natives and 3.4 percent for other U.S. natives. Since this figure is not controlled for crime, however, it is difficult to know whether this indicates that sentencing bias was not present or whether (as is more likely) immigrants were sent to jails and correction houses in large number for minor offenses. The comparable figure by race is 2.6 percent for blacks, 1.18 percent for whites.

42. These figures all come from *Fifteenth Annual Report MBSC,* 1878, pp. 32–35. Eric Monkkonen also finds migrants and immigrants overrepresented in the criminal courts of Columbus, Ohio (*The Dangerous Class,* p. 85).

Table 7.1. Age, Race, and Nativity of Convicts Committed to the Massachusetts State Prison, 1833–1860

	1833–1835	1836–1840	1841–1845	1846–1850	1851–1855*	1856–1860
Nativity						
Massachusetts	165 (39.5)	203 (39.1)	194 (38.3)	243 (33.6)	211 (34.0)	264 (32.8)
Other U.S.	152 (36.4)	194 (37.4)	210 (41.4)	247 (34.2)	187 (30.2)	237 (29.5)
Foreign	101 (24.2)	122 (23.5)	103 (20.3)	233 (32.2)	222 (35.8)	303 (37.7)
Total	418	519	507	723	792	804
Blacks	33 (7.9)	32 (6.2)	50 (9.9)	62 (8.6)	60 (7.6)	n.a.
Age						
Under 20		52 (10.1)	45 (14.4)	142 (20.2)	163 (26.3)	133 (16.5)
21–30		245 (47.4)	139 (44.6)	361 (51.3)	294 (47.4)	444 (55.2)
31–40		140 (27.1)	74 (23.7)	99 (14.1)	97 (15.6)	141 (17.5)
41–50		53 (10.3)	36 (11.5)	66 (9.4)	47 (7.6)	55 (6.8)
51–60		14 (2.7)	15 (4.8)	29 (4.1)	14 (2.3)	24 (3.0)
Over 60		13 (2.5)	3 (1.0)	7 (1.0)	5 (.8)	7 (.9)

Source: *State Prison Reports*, 1833–60.

*Nativity and ages omitted from report on prisoners entering in 1852. Percentages (except for number of blacks) based on 620, the numbers admitted during the period, excluding 1852.

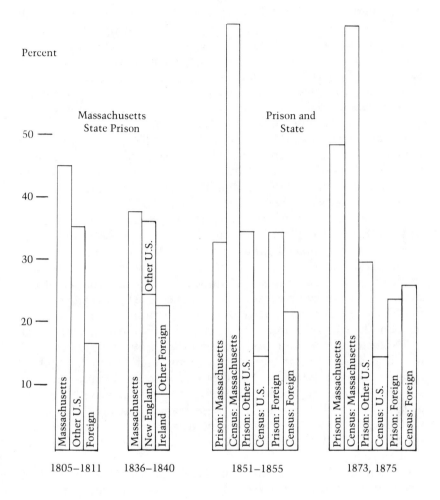

Figure 7.1. Nativity of Convicts and Population in Massachusetts, 1805–1875

ample, natives of Massachusetts comprised a third of the prison population, less than half of their percentage in the state. Those born in other New England states were overrepresented in prison (11.4 percent of state population, 17.6 percent of prison population), as were the Irish (11.7 percent to 17.7 percent), all foreign-born (16.2 percent to 33.2 percent), and blacks (.9 to 8.6 percent). Such figures were widely cited as confirmation of both the depravity of the newcomers and the innate virtue of the natives.

The demography of the convict population led to the complacent view that the state's population was not depraved and to a search for simplistic exclusionary solutions. In 1822, for example, it was suggested that black convicts should be returned to Africa and that foreign-born convicts should be repatriated.[43]

Interstate and transatlantic mobility was a favorite scapegoat of prison officials. Chaplain Curtis attributed the increase in convicts in 1834 to "an unusual influx into our state of unprincipled foreigners and natives from other states." The next year he termed them the "very refuse of the poorhouses and penitentiaries of Europe." In the following decade, they had become "a floating population who seek their fortune wherever inclination may lead them."[44] In 1849, the warden blamed the increase in commitments on "want and starvation in Britain and Ireland" that drove "to this country multitudes of the most destitute, ignorant, and criminal." And, of course, just as such facts and perceptions were not invented in Jacksonian America, they did not die there. In 1878, when commitments of the natives of Massachusetts were higher than ever, and when the foreign-born were underrepresented in the prison population for the first time, crime was still blamed on a "large floating element" coming to Boston.[45]

Prison officials resisted the demographically induced temptation to justify recidivism and internal disorder as symtomatic of innate inmate depravity. Well into the 1860s, faith in reformability was unshaken. Even after the insidious notion of stock began to appear in the reform literature, the prison remained committed to reformation. But penal reformers still were not always able to make the goal of reformation compatible with principles of justice and equality.

In the decade of the Civil War, the Massachusetts State Prison

43. *Report on the State Prison* (legislative report *re* the governor's message), 1822, p. 14.
44. *State Prison Reports*, 1834, p. 23; 1835, p. 6; 1845, p. 25.
45. Ibid., 1849, p. 19; *Fifteenth Annual Report MBSC*, 1878, p. xlix.

was a mixture of the ancient and the new. It was still located on the same site in Charlestown as when it opened in 1805, but many additions had changed the exterior, and ideology had transformed the interior. Decades of experimentation had created an entirely different institution, albeit one technically still committed to the Auburn system. As a result of such factors as partial control over sentence length and influence in pardoning decisions, the warden was no longer a caretaker, but a powerful figure who had many institutional sanctions with which to order the inmates.

But though the internal affairs of the prison seemed well under control, the role of the prison within the larger society and within the criminal justice apparatus was under attack. Decades of experience with the bucolic descriptions of wardens, decades of promises quickly dashed, had fed a new skepticism outside the walls. Even the annual reports, those widely distributed, glowing pronouncements of faith, were no longer to be believed. One legislative committee complained:

> In concluding this review of our state institutions, your committee cannot refrain from attesting to the unsatisfactory character of the reports annually submitted. . . . Their forms are copied from year to year. . . . We are sure to learn one fact, viz., that all superintendents, matrons, chaplains, physicians, and other officials perform herculean labors, to the entire satisfaction of the Inspectors, while the latter, under this stereotyped mutual admiration system comes in for a full share of the plums distributed by the former in their various sub-reports. The whole forms a vast undigested mass of matters for which only the printers can feel grateful.[46]

By the 1870s, criticism of the prison came from a new source. The Massachusetts Board of State Charities, created in 1864, replaced the inspectors as outside overseers of the prison. Composed of men prominent in the formation of the state's social policies, the board had little tolerance for the prison bureaucracy, causing a final split between humanitarian reform and prison management. Throughout the 1870s, the board decried the prison—praised so highly in 1867 by Enoch Wines and Theodore Dwight—as a place where no reformation could occur. A secretary of the board, Franklin Sanborn, severely criticized the management of the prison and printed the

46. *Report on the Various Charitable, Reformatory, and Penal Institutions . . . by a Committee Appointed by the Governor,* undated but probably first half of 1862.

inmates' complaints against the institution.[47] Annual reports were frequently criticized.[48]

During these years, faith in the institutions that had once been so promising was profoundly shaken. In 1871, masters of houses of correction declared that they had no illusions about reform.[49] Samuel Gridley Howe, secretary of the charities board and a veteran reformer, wondered whether hanging might be preferable to a term in prison. The condemned man, he argued, "is safe from being further demoralized by a short term in prison or emasculated by a long one." The need for huge penitentiaries was no longer taken for granted. Howe observed, "We are beginning to find out that a considerable proportion of our lunatics may be left at large. . . . We shall find out by and by, that a considerable proportion of our convicts can serve out a large part of their sentence without being confined by day and by night within the walls of a prison."[50]

Howe's successor on the board, continuing this implicit reevaluation of the prison, declared that the war against vice and crime would never be won in prisons and reformatories.[51] Despite these doubts and frustrations, the basic nature of the prison remained unchanged. When the Massachusetts Board of State Charities criticized the warden of the prison for being hostile to reform, it was an ironic complaint.[52] The warden remained; the board was soon demoted. One astute legislator recognized what was happening: "The tendency of the present system or want thereof is to perpetuate itself and . . . institutions once established will be regarded as fixed facts, to be conducted and managed but not tested."[53]

In 1878, the state prison, rechristened a reformatory, moved to that center of contemplation, Concord. But the new name and new site were misleading. Reformation was still nominally the goal, but incarceration was still the function. Very little, in retrospect, had changed since the opening of the first prison in 1805. But illusion had been shattered; the reformatory was not the institution that would single-handedly reshape society and solve the problem of crime. Prison management was now in the hands of bureaucratic

---

47. Franklin Sanborn and John Ayres, "A Preliminary Report by a Subcommittee of the Department," pp. 357–74. Almost every report of the Massachusetts State Board of Charities was highly critical of the prison, particularly after 1867.

48. Franklin Sanborn, "North American Prisons," p. 384.

49. *Report of the Committee on Prisons*, 1871.

50. Howe, "Treatment of Prisoners," MS. in Samuel Gridley Howe Papers, Houghton Library, Harvard University, undated (but marked by a previous scholar as 187–).

51. *Seventh Annual Report MBSC*, 1870, p. 207.

52. *Tenth Annual Report MBSC*, 1873, p. 102.

53. *Report on the Various Charitable Institutions.*

professionals, not evangelical reformers, and members of this new occupation would have been by temperament, as well as by training and inclination, incapable of proclaiming unattainable fantasies. But one lesson had been learned: if the prison could not reform the most incorrigible members of the criminal class, at least it could contain them. The fortresslike walls that in the early nineteenth century had ostensibly protected inmates from the corrupting world outside shed their symbolic facade, and, as Howe astutely predicted, they would "not be so easily gotten rid of."

Part IV
The Making of the
Criminal Class: Reform
and Retreat

Up to now we have examined differences in almost every aspect of crime and justice in each state. Patterns of formal and extralegal authority, prosecutions, and punishment all point to different conceptions of the role of law and crime in each society. These differences have been related to contrasts in the economy and society of one prototypical industrial, urbanizing state and the most aristocratic rural slave state. But correlation is no substitute for explanation. To try to understand many of the differences between the legal and criminal justice systems of these two components of the same country, we need to look at one more piece of the puzzle, namely, the efforts made in each state to reform and perhaps to improve the system of law and justice.

This is an appropriate final topic for many reasons. First, efforts for change tell us what people at the time thought were the most serious flaws in their legal apparatus. They offer a vision—flawed though it may be by its necessary atypicality—of the ideal societal solutions to the dilemma posed by crime and an imperfect system of justice. Many of the insights available to the legal historian through the use of statistics were not cognizable to those wrestling with the consequences of crime and class. The significance of reform is the glimpse it gives us into attitudes toward crime, punishment, and the role of society generally in securing order and enforcing behavioral norms through the legal system.

This look at reform consists of two parts. First, I will scrutinize efforts for change in three areas so critical to nineteenth-century law and penology that they might serve as reference points—codification, capital punishment, and penal reform. Here we will see contrasts more of degree than of kind, as both states took similar ideological positions. Differences in achieving desired ends were more significant. Then I will try to account for the differential success of reform efforts and will concentrate not only on the role of reformers in society, but also on the world view of those seeking to change or defend present conditions and the amount of support generated by each. The result is what the statistics can hint at, but never explicitly relate—the role of class in American intellectual life as a force for blocking social change and social reform. We will see that when crime control becomes contaminated by class control (as it inevitably must) the success of social reform becomes limited. Class—and, in the South, the association of class with race—becomes a crucial explanatory vehicle.

Chapter 8.
Reforming Law and Justice

Whether it was the high acquittal rates in the Carolina courts or the absence of a prison, whether it was the high recidivism rates in the Massachusetts State Prison or the increase in crime, one did not have to look far in the nineteenth century to find widespread dissatisfaction with the system of justice. And the first half of the nineteenth century was not a time when people were particularly complacent about the social problems they identified. Not surprisingly, then, concerted efforts were made during these years to try to correct the faults in the criminal justice system. Although the problems in the two states were very different, reform efforts fell into the same general categories. The most important of these were codification, capital punishment, and incarceration. Despite these similarities, the conditions that spurred demands for change, the means to achieve the necessary goals, and the results of such efforts all were quite different in the two states.

Codification was an effort to correct the law itself. Codification in America was a many-sided movement, forcing a strange and often strained alliance between legal populism and legal rationalization. Even though the proponents of codification did not have the criminal law specifically in mind, the links between codification and penal reform are substantial. The aim of codification was to extend to all areas of law the great Beccarian notion of certainty. The codifiers' complaint that the law was unknown was particularly damning in the case of criminal law, where the specter of conviction without a statute was especially rankling. One of the earliest decisions that reflected the spirit of codification was *U.S.* v. *Hudson and Goodwin*,[1] which refused to recognize the existence of federal common law crimes. Many of the leading proponents of codification were also active in penal reform—particularly such men as Thomas Grimké and Robert Rantoul. They understood perhaps better than did their successors the need for civil and criminal law to be consistent with each other. Indeed, the only serious attempt at codifica-

1. 7 Cranch 32 (1812).

tion in either of the two states resulted in the drafting of a penal code. Codification was the broadest manifestation of the desire for certainty and rationality, a desire central to understanding much of the impetus for criminal justice reform.

The aim of codification was to combine the entire body of statute law with both the common law and relevant court decisions in an organized fashion to produce a permanent, definitive code available to all who sought it. Because all the various interpretations and ramifications of the law were to be written down, some of its advocates claimed that codification would reduce the need for legislation and litigation and would enable every person to know the law. Others simply wanted to bring up to date and in one place the current state of the law—to provide a basis from which future legislation and court decisions could begin.

Key to understanding the relationship between codification and criminal justice is a concept I will call legal rationalization. Legal rationalization is both an attitude and a process. As society becomes more complex and impersonal, the sphere of law intrudes into more areas of human life. Legal transactions, being more frequent, become more routinized. Legal rationalization includes the measures taken to accommodate elaborate and rigorous legal formalities to daily, ordinary applications. In the criminal law, for example, one manifestation was the use of printed indictment forms. Because indictments had to follow a precise form and the slightest error was sufficient to quash an indictment, printed forms routinized what had been a hazardous and uncertain proceeding. In general, legal rationalization attempted to place all aspects of the law on a more precise and regularized footing. The appearance of digests, treatises, and printed state reports in the early nineteenth century was a significant step in this direction. Such measures illustrated the new spirit of logic and utility essential to legal rationalization in this period.

When seen in this context, criminal law and codification are not merely distant cousins. Criminal law and procedure cannot be easily separated from the legal system at large. Problems of organization and efficiency that impaired the functioning of courts in their civil capacity marred the efficacy of criminal justice as well. Thus, problems with antiquated statutes and procedures were not limited to one sphere, whether it be civil or criminal, but affected the operation of the entire legal system. For that reason, the codification movement had a potential impact on criminal justice in each state, even though the primary substantive focus was on the civil law. In South Carolina, the condition of the criminal justice system mirrored that of the legal system as a whole, with its ancient statutes, dual system of courts, and lack of a final authority. In Massachusetts, the desire to reduce capriciousness and discretion in trial and punishment of criminal suspects paralleled the attempts in the commercial arena to employ the law as the guarantor of predictability and certainty.

In both states, codification had a dual nature. On the one hand, it sought to limit the discretion of the common law, to make law both more responsive and more accessible. This form of argument was structural and procedural. But underlying these arguments was a substantive suggestion. It must be only a suggestion, for in neither state did any proponent openly declare that the purpose of codification would be to change the substance of the laws. But one need only look at context to appreciate the power of this hidden agenda. In South Carolina, for example, codification was clearly seen as an opportunity to deal with the state's antiquated criminal code; grand juries called for penal reform and codification in the same sentence. Furthermore, when a statutory scheme was eventually drafted—the clear legacy of the codification effort—it was attacked and rejected precisely because it tampered with substantive law in a critical area: the rights of slaves and the law of race relations. In Massachusetts, the context of codification cannot be ignored. The dictum in *Commonwealth* v. *Hunt* (that the common law of criminal conspiracy was in effect in Massachusetts), though not the holding, irked Rantoul and his followers. Since the codifiers would have to resolve conflicting lines of common law holdings, some of the skirmishes over the issue were probably related to the hopes and fears about who would serve as code commissioners.

The specific motives for codification were quite different in each state. In South Carolina, there was a perceived need to revise and reform completely the statute law. Indeed, both the most populist-inclined upcountry bar and the aristocratic, commercially oriented Charleston bar supported codification as a means of overhauling the statutes. In Massachusetts, however, codification was intertwined with the politics of the Jacksonian era. The most articulate proponent of codification in Massachusetts was Robert Rantoul, Jr., a radical Jacksonian attorney and politician. Rantoul objected to the ease with which aristocratic judges could invoke the unwritten common law to decide a case against what he determined was the public interest.[2] Worse, these decisions became precedents that had the

2. Robert Rantoul, Jr., "Oration at Scituate (1826)," in *Memoirs, Speeches and Writings of Robert Rantoul, Jr.*, pp. 278–83; Leonard W. Levy, *The Law of the Commonwealth and Chief Justice Shaw*, p. 197.

force of law. Such judge-made law had to be eliminated. Rantoul denounced the common law as having originated "in folly, barbarism, and feudality." Nor could it even function as law. "No man can tell what the common law is," Rantoul reasoned, "therefore it is not law: for law is a rule of action; but a rule which is unknown can govern no man's conduct."[3]

Proponents of codification charged that judge-made law was insidious in a democracy for two reasons. First, since the common law could be discovered and interpreted only by judges, other people had no way of knowing what the law was, a system that seemed unsuitable for a self-governing people. Second, the substantive content of the common law seemed frequently at odds with the popular will; thus the common law, unless checked, could subvert democratic principles. Proponents of codification sought to check judicial discretion and replace the common law with their codes, so that all laws would emanate from the decisions of popularly elected legislators. Proclaiming that "statutes speak the public voice," Rantoul demanded, "all American law must be statute law."[4] Codification was also part of the general antilawyer sentiment that surfaced in the Jacksonian years. By demystifying the law, by making it accessible in a compact and convenient form, codification promised to free nascent entrepreneurs from exploitation by unscrupulous attorneys. It is not surprising that Rantoul also supported the efforts of libertarian Lysander Spooner to open the bar to all comers.[5]

Opponents of codification, who included most of the legal and judicial hierarchy, claimed that the common law had too many nuances to be put into words, that the sort of code Rantoul demanded would be too bulky to be of practical use and too inflexible to respond to changing conditions, and that law was a specialty that could not be mastered by a layman.[6] Although the codifiers did not prevail in Massachusetts, the principle of legal rationalization (which propelled much of the reform effort) did prevail in revising the statutes.

The relationship between codification and legal rationalization can be seen in the 1835 *Revised Statutes* and in Joseph Story's 1837

3. Rantoul, "Oration at Scituate," p. 279.

4. Ibid., p. 280.

5. Lysander Spooner to Robert Rantoul, Jr., 15 July 1835, Robert Rantoul Papers, Beverly Historical Society; Robert DeGroff Bulkley, Jr., "Robert Rantoul, Jr., 1805–1852," pp. 166–67.

6. These arguments are summarized by Joseph Story in *Report of the Commissioners Appointed to Consider and Report upon the Practicability and Expediency of Reducing in a Written and Systematic Code the Common Law of Massachusetts*; see also Levy, *Law of the Commonwealth*, pp. 196–202.

report on the issue. Prior to 1835, the laws of Massachusetts had been collected only in a chronological format. There was no way, short of relying on a slim subject index, to determine at a glance all the legislation in a given area. Cross-references were scanty, and it was impossible to tell what was obsolete. In 1832, a three-member commission was established by the legislature to "revise, collate, and arrange the Colonial . . . Provincial . . . and General Statutes." This commission was charged with remedying "such contradictions, omissions, or imperfections as may appear" and producing a volume that would be "concise, plain, and intelligible."[7] The result was the *Revised Statutes* of 1835, topically arranged with obsolete material omitted. The volume—and all the statutes fit into one— was thoroughly cross-indexed and included citations to relevant court decisions.

This was not a code, of course, because it did not enact court decisions and did not incorporate common law. It was a thorough reorganization of the statute law that set an important precedent for periodic arrangement of the state's laws. The *Revised Statutes* were an example of legal rationalization, and contemporaries lauded the effort. In 1836, Governor Edward Everett claimed that the volume would make the laws more accessible to the people, thus preempting one of the primary goals of codification. Even Rantoul termed them "excellent . . . contrasted with the chaos for which they are substituted."[8]

If the publication of the *Revised Statutes* in 1835 undercut the practical force of the codification movement, then Joseph Story's report in 1837 sounded its death knell. Story was a bellwether, having previously supported the concept of codification and prepared one of the early chronological arrangements of the statutes. In his report to the General Court, Story sharply opposed codification, protesting privately, "We have not yet become votaries to the notions of Jeremy Bentham."[9]

Story dismissed the notion that all statute and common law should or could be reduced to a code. He reiterated as fallacies the claims that a code could obviate the need for amendment or could be devised in a way that would be both complete and of use to the layman. In other words, he made short work of the "legal populist" side of the movement. But Story did consider what part of the com-

7. Resolve of 24 Feb. 1832; *Address of His Excellency Levi Lincoln,* Massachusetts Legislative Documents, 1833; *Governor's Message* (1835), p. 30.

8. Edward Everett, *Governor's Message,* 1836, p. 10; Rantoul, "Oration at Scituate," p. 278.

9. Quoted in Levy, *Law of the Commonwealth,* p. 197.

mon law could be reduced to a code. One such area was the penal law. But another area touched Rantoul's Jacksonian entrepreneur in his daily life—commercial law.[10] Thus, Story presaged *Swift* v. *Tyson* while rejecting the overall thrust of codification. Like the proponents of the *Revised Statutes*, but in sharp contrast to Rantoul, Story was able to distinguish between the practical needs codification was addressing and the implied underlying values, which Story opposed. Thus, the dual nature of codification was its eventual undoing in Massachusetts.

Of the areas Story suggested for codification, the only one on which action was taken was the criminal law. The penal code was finished under the pressure of time in 1844 (seven years after Story's report), corroborating Story's claim that full codification would take decades. It was a true code, with common law references, judicial clarifications, and statutory precedents. By the time the work was finished, however, the legislators had lost interest in the issue, and the code was never enacted.[11] Thus the codification movement in Massachusetts suffered an anticlimactic demise.

When Rantoul complained that the law was unknown and inaccessible, he was referring to judge-made common law in appellate decisions. But in South Carolina, when similar charges were made, they applied primarily to the patchwork of legislation and adoption that comprised—or would to anyone with the patience and perspicacity to find out—the statute law of that state. The codification movement in South Carolina espoused the same two lines of argument as in Massachusetts: a practical effort at legal rationalization through statute reorganization and an ideological opposition to judge-made law. Whereas in Massachusetts, the second feature was the major rallying point, in South Carolina, conditions were such that the first issue was the major priority. Lack of a judicial system in the latter state that created law with the flair and controversy of the Massachusetts Supreme Judicial Court in the heyday of Chief Justice Lemuel Shaw meant that the common law issue was secondary to the critical need for legal rationalization.

The problem of South Carolina's statutes had its origins in the eighteenth century. In 1712, South Carolina became the first colony to declare specific English statutes to be in force.[12] This was, perhaps, the last "first" in the state's legal history. Most of the penal

10. Story, *Report*, pp. 706–31.

11. *Report of the Penal Code of Massachusetts*, pp. iv–v; Story, *Report*, pp. 710, 732; Levy, *Law of the Commonwealth*, p. 201.

12. Elizabeth Gaspar Brown, *British Statutes in American Law, 1776–1836*, p. 17.

laws were included in this wholesale adoption, although the English criminal code at the time was unusually harsh. The statutes became part of South Carolina law with no change in wording and no acknowledgment that conditions in this New World colony were different from those of Elizabethan and Restoration England, the source of many of these laws. The penal statutes remained the basic criminal code for South Carolina whites until after Reconstruction.

Having adopted these laws, the colony resisted any attempt to revise them. In 1753, for example, the Lords Justices of England asked the governor, council, and assembly to consider, revise, and digest all the province's laws. The assembly rejected this request, citing "insuperable obstacles" and arguing that the volume of both new legislation and amendments proved the impossibility of "making a Body of Laws that would in all respects be beneficial to the Province for so short a term as Twenty years," much less for perpetuity.[13]

Many colonies seized upon the Revolution as an opportunity for long overdue legal reform; South Carolina's constitution of 1778 committed the state to revising its penal code. But that constitution was superseded before the provision could be carried out. In the 1770s and 1790s, grand juries complained that the laws were unpublished and unknown. In 1785, Judge John F. Grimké and two other jurists were appointed to prepare a digest of South Carolina law. This digest was not adopted, but Grimké on his own published another version in 1790.[14] An improvement and an aid, Grimké's work was no substitute for a complete edition or revision of the statutes. Grimké published the titles of all the statutes, but only some of the laws. Compilations of postrevolutionary statutes were published, but obviously were of limited value. Unlike Massachusetts, which had reenacted significant English laws and totally revised its penal code, South Carolina still relied on the adoption of 1712, and these statutes were excluded from the compilations. Thus, even though both states published their statutes in chronological fashion, the utility of these collections varied substantially.

South Carolina's mixture of common law, ancient English statutes, and state laws confounded laymen and lawyers alike. Grand juries constantly complained about their inability to determine

13. South Carolina Commons Journal, 19 April 1753, SCA; I am indebted to R. Nicholas Olsberg for bringing this item to my attention.

14. James W. Ely, Jr., "American Independence and the Law," p. 939n; John F. Grimké, *The Public Laws of South Carolina*; the commission proposal appears as a title in the Evans Collection (number 21867), but no extant copies have been found.

what the laws were, much less have them arranged in an accessible and orderly fashion.[15] Adamus Burke, appointed to a commission to digest the law, complained, "The laws ... now lie concealed ... mingled in a confused chaos ... past all possibility of being known." A grand jury complained in 1829 that "even judges are lost in mystery." Three decades later, grand juries were still not reconciled to this situation. "Confusion and obscurity ought not to exist in an enlightened community," one complained in 1857. The following year, another protested that the laws were "undigested ... and unintelligible."[16]

One ground for complaint concerned the form of the laws. The other major area concerned substance. In Massachusetts, the question of substantive content to codification was in the background. Rantoul's positions were well known, and the specific context of codification, Jacksonian politics and *Commonwealth v. Hunt*, were strongly suggestive. In South Carolina, on the other hand, certain substantive issues, particularly involving the criminal law, were intimately linked to codification. Codification in South Carolina was seen as a chance for badly needed revision, most obviously in the criminal code. Governors and grand juries agreed that the penal law needed immediate alteration and that codification provided the opportunity. Many appreciated—and deplored—the irony that South Carolina was left with a barbaric penal code that had long been abandoned by the country that had spawned it.[17]

Codification in South Carolina was the product neither of nationalism nor of Jacksonianism. Rather, it was an attempt, in one jump, to take the laws out of their confused, ambiguous, and antiquated state and put them in line with the needs and values of a different world. This is most obvious when Rantoul's orations are contrasted with those of South Carolina's best-known codifier, Thomas S. Grimké. None of Rantoul's legal populism is found in Grimké. Rantoul denounced the common law; Grimké embraced it, wanting only to transmute it into a more useful form. Unlike Rantoul,

15. Charleston Grand Jury Presentment, October 1774, Charleston Sessions Journal, SCA; Pinckney Grand Jury, 1796; Chesterfield, 1790, Camden, 1796, Presentments (eighteenth century), SCA.

16. Quoted in John Belton O'Neall, *Biographical Sketches of the Bench and Bar of South Carolina*, 1:35; Fairfield Grand Jury, November 1829, Barnwell, 1857, Barnwell Sessions Journal, SCA; Spartanburg, 1858, Presentments, Legal System Papers.

17. See the messages of the following governors (found in the House and Senate Journals and reprinted in the Charleston newspapers) Bennett (1822), Allston (1857), Seabrook (1850); Barnwell Grand Jury, Barnwell Sessions Journal, 1857, SCA; Charleston Grand Jury, 1856; Fairfield, 1857, Horry, 1858, Presentments, Legal System Papers.

Grimké did not attack judge-made law. Rantoul wanted to break the monopoly of the professional bar; Grimké readily conceded that even a compact code would be of little use to the layman, neither ending litigation nor enabling every man to be his own lawyer.[18]

Grimké's goal in promoting codification was considerably different from Rantoul's. Fully accepting and recognizing the importance of law in a modern society, Rantoul wanted to ensure that the knowledge and benefits of law would be widely distributed. But in South Carolina, the role of the legal system was implicitly less clear, hampered as it was by obsolete statutes, unreliable courts, incompetent officials, and extralegal accommodations.

Grimké was primarily concerned with elevating the role of law in South Carolina in the broadest possible sense. He did not believe that a code would attain the utopian goals envisioned by Rantoul, but he felt that it would improve popular intelligence and appreciation of the law. Grimké also believed that legal rationalization would attract more able people to bench and bar, people dissuaded by the chaos then confronting them. Even the quality of legislation would improve. In the most general sense, proclaimed Grimké, the code would substitute "*method . . .* for *confusion. . . .* A state of order, as contrasted with chaos, is justly esteemed." In short, Grimké believed that in order for law to fulfill its expected role "for the regulation of the various and complex affairs of a changeable state of society," legal rationalization was a necessity.[19]

Although Grimké's orations represent the state's most sophisticated arguments for codification, he was hardly a lone voice in the wilderness. In the 1820s, codification had relatively broad support in South Carolina. Its advocates included Thomas Cooper, president of South Carolina College, Governor John Lyde Wilson (himself "codifier" of the rule of dueling), and Benjamin F. Perry, lawyer, editor, and politician. Grand juries and governors also advocated a code. Grimké confidently predicted that codification was inevitable, but the South Carolina legislature adamantly rejected all appeals.[20]

18. Thomas S. Grimké, *Anniversary Oration Delivered before the South Carolina Bar Association,* pp. 10–11, 15–16.

19. Thomas S. Grimké, *Report on the Practicability and Expediency of a Code;* Grimké, *Anniversary Oration,* pp. 24, 22.

20. Thomas Cooper, "Letter to Chancellor Sampson"; Cooper, "Bentham's Judicial Evidence," pp. 381–426; Grimké, *Anniversary Oration,* p. 21; Lillian Kibler, *Benjamin F. Perry, South Carolina Unionist,* pp. 54–55; see also Perry Miller, *The Life of the Mind in America,* pp. 246–49. Miller's interpretation is different from the one here. First, Grimké was hardly a lone voice in South Carolina; he was simply the only one who discoursed on codification in such classical, easily quoted orations. Second, codification did not cause his premature death. The actual cause was an

Recognizing that the existent situation was intolerable, it approved in 1834 the publication of all the statutes of South Carolina. Cooper, by then hounded out of office, was chosen to edit them. Cooper had to be content with much less than his professed goal, but he believed that his compilation would lead to codification and hoped that his annotated index might serve as the basis for a code.[21]

On the surface, then, it would appear that the codification movement suffered a similar fate in each state. Noble efforts to systematize the law and to make it accessible ended up with a revision of the statutes. But, as is the case with so much of South Carolina's legal history, the first impression is misleading. Cooper was permitted to do far less than his Massachusetts counterparts who assembled the *Revised Statutes*. The *Revised Statutes* were a topical reorganization of the statute law with new material added and obsolete provisions deleted; Cooper's *Statutes at Large of South Carolina*, with the interesting exceptions of laws relating to slavery, the militia, Charleston, courts, and rivers, were actually a chronological compilation. Tellingly, nothing remained of the first two statutes but their titles. Furthermore, Cooper was not permitted to eliminate any obsolete provisions. The legislature reasoned that such was too subtle a task to be left to one person's judgment, even to a man of Cooper's intellect.[22]

The publication of the ten-volume *Statutes at Large* did not end the controversy. After more complaints by grand juries and other officials, and during what appears to be almost a legal housekeeping prior to the final sectional crisis, the legislature in 1859 appointed James L. Petigru as code commissioner. This title was a misnomer. Petigru's mission was to edit obsolete material and reorganize the statutes into topical categories, rather than produce a full code. In short, Petigru was asked to produce—a quarter century later—a volume similar to the *Revised Statutes* of Massachusetts.

The reaction to Petigru's draft compilations shows why the legislature had previously forbidden Cooper from exercising any editorial judgment other than collecting and copying. Judge David Wardlaw, in a long private communiqué, criticized the result both for its un-

---

infectious disease, but a much greater strain in his life was yet to come—Nullification. Finally, little of Miller's legal nationalism (pp. 255–56) can be found in either state. Only Cooper in South Carolina was explicitly concerned with replacing English law with a national American code. Grimké and Rantoul both addressed themselves to specific needs and perceptions in their own states, although their conclusions were reached in quite different ways.

21. 1 *Statutes at Large* xi.
22. *South Carolina Reports and Resolutions*, 1839, p. 92.

warranted modifications of existing law and for its timidity in revising other areas of law. Wardlaw strongly disapproved of Petigru's changes in laws affecting race relations; fully half his comments concern this small fraction of Petigru's total work.[23] The legislative committee passing on Petigru's posthumous draft in 1864 rejected it for having made too much new law.[24]

In South Carolina, then, in contrast to Massachusetts, codification was clearly entwined with substantive legal change and was thus unacceptable to the defenders of the chaotic status quo. A cumbersome, ten-volume chronological compilation of the statutes was all that survived the committee's sharp scrutiny. Only after the defeat of South Carolina in the Civil War was the principle of legal rationalization eventually to triumph there. Perry, as military governor, secured the adoption of a code based on Petigru's draft.[25]

Codification did not succeed in either state, but there the similarities end. Statute reform, clarity of organization, and rationalization all were incorporated into the Massachusetts legal system as further manifestations of that state's commitment to predictability and utility. In South Carolina, the defeat of any similar efforts is further evidence of the different conception of law and authority in the Palmetto State. The next significant issue, capital punishment, took a similar course.

Capital punishment is an extremely complex subject. This discussion will focus on the interplay between humanitarian concerns about the sanctity of human life and the allegedly degrading impact of capital punishment on the legal and criminal justice system. The issue of capital punishment represented a continuation of the debate over the nature of criminal justice. It was attacked as undermining the certainty of punishment and degrading the law inasmuch as juries would sometimes return false verdicts because they felt the penalty was excessive. From a practical perspective, the persistence of capital punishment required liberal use of pardons and commutations and encouraged juries to evaluate the offender as well as the offense in reaching a verdict. The issue, once again, was drawn between certainty and predictability and a more personalistic, discre-

23. David L. Wardlaw to Samuel McGowan, 10 Dec. 1860, Samuel McGowan Papers, SCL.
24. James L. Petigru, *Portion of the Code of Statute Law of South Carolina Submitted to the General Assembly as Required;* Report of the Commission of the Code of the Statute Law of the State, Legal System Papers, 1861–65, Report, SCA; Report of the Commission on the Code, 2 Dec. 1864, ibid.; *Report of Certain Members of the Commission on Petigru's Code of the Statute Law of South Carolina.*
25. Benjamin F. Perry, Speech, 24 Oct. 1865, in Scrapbook, Benjamin F. Perry Papers, SCL.

tionary system. Not surprisingly, once more Massachusetts and South Carolina chose different courses in dealing with this dilemma.

To the extent that capital punishment was the culmination of a trend away from shaming and corporal punishments, differences between the two states on this score are already apparent. But, in fact, the arguments against the death penalty in each state were very similar—they were both humanitarian and practical. Not only was the infliction of death a cruel and unusual punishment, but the executions—particularly public ones—brutalized society. Moreover, the opponents' arguments ran, the death penalty exceeded the limits of state power. Equally telling was the impact of capital punishment on the criminal justice system itself. In defiance of the procedural safeguards of criminal appeals, the death penalty was irreversible; innocence could be revealed too late. Finally, the death penalty was so severe that juries frequently acquitted because of the punishment, not the evidence. Thus the penalty actually undermined justice. All these arguments were made in both states, although the emphasis varied.

One simple difference was in the number of capital offenses and therefore in the relative frequency and importance of the punishment in each state's criminal justice system. By 1828, when the drive to end capital punishment began, Massachusetts had six capital crimes. South Carolina, by contrast, had dozens. In 1813, there were 165 capital crimes; Perry listed 32 in 1838, and Governor Seabrook claimed 22 in 1850.[26] The persistence of portions of the old English penal code made it impossible to determine with any degree of finality the exact number of capital offenses. Accordingly, changes in the operation of capital punishment in South Carolina were part of various proposals to overhaul the entire criminal justice system; pragmatic objections to the death penalty were paramount. In Massachusetts, the situation was quite different. Reformers pressed their philosophical and humanitarian objections, reserving the pragmatic ones as the trump card.

The movement to abolish the death penalty in Massachusetts was persistent, well-financed, and broadly based. The first efforts began in the legislature, with Robert Rantoul, Jr., initially in his father's footsteps, moving to the forefront in the 1830s. Rantoul's argu-

26. David D. Wallace, *History of South Carolina*, 2:467; Message of the Governor, 1849 (Seabrook); Benjamin F. Perry, *Report of the Special Committee Appointed at the Session of 1838 on the Subject of the Penitentiary System*, pp. 24–25. It is telling that when northern opponents of capital punishment compared the number of capital crimes in the various states, they were at a loss for South Carolina's figure.

ments, climaxed by his legislative report of 1836, blended Enlightenment thought with practical and humanitarian concerns.
Believing that the state had no right to take a life, Rantoul claimed
that capital punishment violated God's law, as well as man's, and
that it brutalized society. Using statistics collected from all over the
Western world, Rantoul demonstrated the capriciousness of the actual application of the death penalty, its failure as a deterrent, the
possibility of error, the problems of conviction, and the promise of
pardon or commutation. After over a decade of annual agitation,
reports, and bills, the Massachusetts General Court removed robbery and burglary from the list of capital crimes in 1839.[27]

In the 1840s, a second attempt was begun to abolish the death
penalty. This one differed from the earlier effort both structurally
and substantively. Whereas the earlier move was largely confined to
members of the legislature, this one was led by the reform-minded
religious and intellectual elite of Boston. Rantoul's arguments were
based on Enlightenment and Utilitarian thought; this movement
was less intellectual, more religious and sentimental. Rantoul was
part of this new effort and in fact was one of its heroes. But the key
figures included abolitionist Wendell Phillips, founder of the Massachusetts Society to Abolish Capital Punishment, and Charles
Spear, a Unitarian minister and publisher of the *Hangman* and the
Prisoner's Friend, two journals devoted to ending capital punishment. Spear's writings stressed the pain and suffering of condemned
men, not the pragmatic problems caused by penalties in excess of
popular values.

The *Prisoner's Friend* was an eclectic collection of sermons, dog-
gerel, and statistics. Dedicated to the abolition of the death penalty,
it branched out into prison reform, abolitionism, phrenology, and
the water cure. Jolted into action every time a capital sentence was
handed down, it monitored all executions. The case of Washington
Goode, a black man convicted of murdering his common-law wife
in 1849, was typical. Goode's trial was reviewed in great detail. His
race increased the reformers' concern; since the laws of Massachusetts rarely protected blacks, the *Prisoner's Friend* reasoned, they
should not be used to execute them.

The magazine, in millennialistic fashion, believed that the total

27. Rantoul's best-known report can be found in Rantoul, *Memoirs*, pp. 436–92;
see also his letters to Governor Briggs, ibid., pp. 492–517. Bulkley summarizes this
phase of Rantoul's career in "Rantoul," pp. 245–59; see also *Prisoner's Friend* 6
(1854): 197–202, and Massachusetts *Acts*, 1839, ch. 127. Rantoul was not in the
legislature at the time, having been defeated because of his support of restrictive
liquor legislation.

abolition of capital punishment was just around the corner. Fully expecting that Goode's execution would be the last one in the state, it prayed that the last person executed in Massachusetts would not be a black man. Spear conducted a massive petition campaign to stay Goode's execution and, as on other occasions, pleaded personally with the governor for a pardon. When that effort failed, Spear interviewed Goode in his cell to determine the condemned man's state of mind, degree of repentance, and preparation for death. The *Prisoner's Friend* reported every detail of the execution—and of Goode's suicide attempt the night before.[28] This was the type of case Spear relished; Goode's suicide attempt provided another opportunity to discourse on the cruelties of a punishment that drove men to self-destruction in the mere contemplation of it.

The wish that Goode would not be the last man executed in Massachusetts was fulfilled the following year, when John White Webster, professor of chemistry at Harvard, was hanged for the murder of George Parkman.[29] The Webster case dominated the *Prisoner's Friend* for most of a year. The frontispiece of the May 1850 issue, usually reserved for a woodcut of an idyllic scene, was a diagram of Webster's lab where he had presumably butchered his victim. To reformers, Webster's execution showed the absolute folly of that penalty: In South Carolina, Lieber was transfixed by that case; not quarreling with the verdict, he demanded that his friends send him all information on the entire affair and confidently told Dix that Webster's death would speed the end of capital punishment.[30]

Two years after Webster's execution, Massachusetts removed arson, rape, and treason from the list of capital offenses and adopted the "Maine law" requiring a one-year delay between sentence and execution.[31] Naively assuming that the delay would enable the governor to make a rational decision on execution without the emotional encumbrances of a recent murder and sensational trial, reformers jubilantly proclaimed the end of capital punishment in Massachusetts. Their celebration was premature. Hostile to such a ban, the governor successfully sued to have the provision annulled

28. *Prisoner's Friend* 1 (1849): 368–69, 381–82, 391–401, 410–11, 415–17, 485, 502–7.

29. The details of the Webster case are too well known to be summarized here; see Levy, *Law of the Commonwealth,* pp. 218–28; also Robert Sullivan, *The Disappearance of Dr. Parkman,* and the trial record itself, George Bemis, ed., *Report of the Case of John W. Webster.*

30. Francis Lieber to George Hilliard, 6 April 1850; Lieber to Dix, 11 Sept. 1850, Francis Lieber Papers, Huntington Library; he also included it in his list of fifteen great trials.

31. *Acts,* 1852, ch. 274; *Prisoner's Friend* 6 (1854): 201.

as an infringement of his power. In 1856, after a condemned prisoner killed two deputy officers of the Massachusetts State Prison, the one-year delay was repealed. Murder, the last remaining capital offense, was partially "decapitalized" in 1858 (by being divided into degrees), four years after the *Prisoner's Friend* ceased publication. The reform movement undoubtedly stimulated a climate of opposition to the death penalty, but was unsuccessful in achieving its final goal.[32]

The failure to abolish capital punishment demonstrated the power of the pragmatic arguments. The capital offenses that caused the most trouble for juries were eliminated, but the principle of capital punishment remained. Massachusetts accepted the charge that capital punishment could wreak havoc with its criminal justice system and thus reduced its application, but rejected humanitarian objections to the practice. That the strides taken by Massachusetts to reduce the number of capital offenses were still viewed with disappointment by reformers attests to their belief in the philosophical foundations of their arguments and their tactical use of the pragmatic ones.

In South Carolina, capital punishment was also opposed on both philosophical-humanitarian and pragmatic grounds. But there were very few in the former camp; those opposed because of the difficulty of conviction were not committed to the abolition of capital punishment, but simply to a reduction in the number of capital offenses. The conviction problem in South Carolina was correctly thought to be sufficiently serious to undermine the entire penal system.

The pragmatic base of opposition to capital punishment, therefore, came from those who wanted to keep laws in line with popular values. Acquittals generated by a desire to avoid harsh punishment were seen as undermining respect for law. The source of sentiment for reduction in the number of capital crimes was the same as that for the erection of a penitentiary and revision of the criminal code —governors and local grand juries. Proponents of change were less concerned about humanitarian considerations than about chaos produced by the number of capital offenses. One grand jury specifically denied any interest in abolishing the death penalty, but complained that the present law permitted "criminals to pass, unwhipped of justice."[33] Others complained that the law was "stripped of its sanction" and that the "courts and juries are so slack in not bringing to justice persons charged with murder" that resort to lynch law was

32. Gideon Haynes, *Pictures from Prison Life*, pp. 72–73; David Brion Davis, "The Movement to Abolish Capital Punishment in America," p. 45.
33. Presentment, Fall 1858, Barnwell Sessions Journal, SCA.

likely.[34] Such criticism by grand juries is highly significant. These were the same bodies that determined whether to indict and thus saw firsthand the confusion introduced by the high number of capital offenses. Their complaints are not simply normative, but empirical. Despite evidence for abolition, all attempts to revise this "bloody code" were defeated.

The reluctance-to-convict argument is found in almost every major document on capital punishment in both states. But in Massachusetts it was secondary to questions of principle and humanity and was retained primarily to counter the deterrence argument of the death penalty's supporters. In South Carolina, such philosophical arguments were rare. Governors and grand juries who employed humanitarian terminology were primarily interested in reducing the number of capital crimes; even Lieber thought it could be retained for murder.[35] An itinerant minister reported that a college debate on capital punishment found professors and students united in its defense. Only three voices were raised in South Carolina for outright abolition. Thomas Smith Grimké, arguing as a pacifist, compared capital punishment with defensive wars—and attacked both. These writings were not addressed to South Carolinians and made no mention of peculiar conditions in that state. Only John Blake White, the Charleston physician and amateur dramatist, discussed the issue on philosophical grounds; Perry sought complete abolition for pragmatic reasons.[36] Neither state ended the death penalty, but Massachusetts went farther than South Carolina in reducing its incidence and impact on the legal system.

A secondary goal of the opponents of capital punishment was an end to public executions. Like capital punishment, itself, public executions were seen as brutalizing society. Public hangings originally had three purposes: to deter by example, to engender a swell of loyalty to the king by showing the awesome power of his law, and to elevate the crowd if, as expected, a last-minute profession of faith was extracted by the officiating clergy. By the late colonial period, these affairs had turned into circuses. By the nineteenth century, the republic obviated the second reason, and public professions of faith were less significant. The sole justification remained

34. Lancaster 1858; Chester, Fall 1830; Presentments, Legal System Papers.

35. Perry, *Report*, pp. 25–32; Francis Lieber, *Letter to His Excellency Patrick Noble, Governor of South Carolina, on the Penitentiary System*, pp. 46–48.

36. Rev. John McLees, Diary (12 vols.) vol. 2, 20 Dec. 1842, Miscellaneous manuscripts, SCL; Thomas S. Grimké, "Defensive War," pp. 140–51; see also Peter Brock, *Radical Pacifists in Antebellum America*, pp. 56–60; John Blake White, "Essay on Capital Punishment," 14 Feb. 1834, ms. in John Blake White Papers, SCHS.

deterrence. But the carnival atmosphere seemed inappropriate to such a solemn event and in reality helped elevate the condemned man to something of a folk hero. Its value as a deterrent was sharply questioned. Rantoul methodically showed that capital crimes increased in the vicinity of a public execution.[37] Thus many reformers believed that if executions could not be eliminated, they should at least be put out of sight.

In 1832, a Massachusetts legislative committee recommended that all executions be private with a black flag over the gallows to mark the occasion. This bill was not enacted, but the *Revised Statutes* three years later provided for executions in the jailyard. When Webster was executed in 1850, however, public curiosity was so intense that hundreds jammed the tenements overlooking the Boston city jail to get a glimpse of the morbid event.[38] Nevertheless, executions were not generally public.

In South Carolina, two attempts in the early 1840s to end public executions were rebuffed. Characteristically, opponents of change argued against "any alteration in the immemorial usages of this state and of our ancestors from whom we derive our Common Law." Having dispensed with the inevitable ancestor worship, the investigating legislative committee took an interesting line. Public executions should be retained, they argued, because "the public authority should do nothing which we people dare not look upon." Ironically, the committee feared that a despot might use "the secrecy of Private punishment" to inflict death for "crimes of the slightest enormity."[39] This was exactly what opponents of capital punishment feared would happen but for the intervention of juries and governors! As late as 1859, an execution could attract a huge crowd in Charleston.[40]

Public executions were abolished during the Reconstruction legal housekeeping, only to reemerge in a far more tragic form.[41] Lynch

37. Robert Rantoul, Jr., "Letters on the Death Penalty" (1846), reprinted in Rantoul, *Memoirs*, pp. 504–8; "Remarks on Capital Punishment," ibid., p. 431; a fascinating discussion of the symbolic function of capital punishment can be found in Michel Foucault, *Discipline and Punish*, pp. 32–69.

38. *Report on the Punishment of Death* (House Document 2, 1832); *Revised Statutes*, ch. 139, sec. 13 (nearest citation is to a 1777 law that makes no mention of location of execution; therefore section must be new); *Prisoner's Friend* 4 (1851): 72.

39. Report of the Committee on the Judiciary on a Resolution as to Executing White Criminals in Private, 1843, Reports, Penal System Papers, 1831–59, SCA.

40. For a description of a public execution in Charleston on the eve of the Civil War, see Percy Nagle to his mother, 26 March 1859, Miscellaneous manuscripts, SCL.

41. Albert D. Oliphant, *The Evolution of the Penal System of South Carolina from 1866–1916*, p. 6.

law, which replaced formal race control and criminal law for much of the post–Civil War era, resurrected the public execution; indeed, the "strange fruit" were allowed to rot on the branch to serve as a deterrent to those who would challenge white hegemony in much the same manner as the formal public execution was intended to serve as a deterrent.

Neither Massachusetts nor South Carolina embraced codification or abolished capital punishment. In the third major area of activity, penal reform, the results were quite dissimilar. Conditions in the two states were, of course, different from the outset. Massachusetts established a prison in the early years of the nineteenth century, and much energy was channeled into trying to improve that institution. In this discussion, however, we will focus on alternative forms of incarceration and release and on efforts to improve the criminal justice process. In South Carolina, erecting a penitentiary was a precondition for any other attempt at penal reform. A state without a prison need not consider whether women, children, debtors, and the insane belonged in one. In Massachusetts, then, the focus was on efforts to fine tune the penal system; in South Carolina, the basis for discussion is the foundation of reform efforts—establishing a state prison.

In addition to being one of the great crusades in the North in the antebellum years, penal reform was one of the few areas of "freedom's ferment" that made any headway in the South. There were special reasons to expect it to succeed in South Carolina. Francis Lieber, who coined the term "penology" and was one of the most influential leaders in this field, lived in South Carolina for two decades. On his first visit to Charleston, Lieber visited the "prisons and the work houses"—and regarded South Carolina's backwardness as a great challenge. "This is a glorious field," he told one of his European correspondents, "which attracted me at once when I resolved to go South."[42] Although Lieber's efforts in his adopted state led only to frustration and isolation, this was hardly a foregone conclusion.

Both states had in common one penal institution, the local county jail. Although prisons represent the pinnacle of the corrections hierarchy, the majority of suspects and convicts were confined to local jails and houses of correction. In both states, jails were used for debtors, witnesses, suspects awaiting trial, and vagrants, drunks, or

42. Francis Lieber to Councillor Mittermaier, 13 June 1835; Lieber Journal, 21 March 1835, both in Lieber Papers; Clement C. Eaton, *The Growth of Southern Civilization*, pp. 272–73.

vagabonds committed by local peace justices. In South Carolina, runaway slaves and convicts confined for noncapital crimes were also committed. In Massachusetts, convicts not sent to the state prison were sent to a local house of correction. Conditions in prison were controversial, but no disagreement existed concerning conditions in local penal institutions. In both states they were wretched.

The institutions themselves were appalling. In South Carolina, well over one hundred grand juries expressed concern about the conditions of the jails, making this the single most common complaint. In many districts, escapes were common. Ventilation, of great importance in the languid South, was a particular problem. A Lexington grand jury termed the air "deleterious." Prisoners in Laurens were "obliged to breath impure and unwholesome air, which renders the place extremely unhealthy and disagreeable, so much so that it is a place of torture and punishment." One grand jury calling attention to a sick prisoner noted that "to be sick in a jail need not be remarked upon."[43] William Grayson humorously recalled conditions in the Coosawatchie jail: "It was unnecessary to try a criminal there charged with a capital offense. All that was required was to put him in jail. . . . The State paid for a coffin, and saved the expenses of trial and execution. At night the jailer thought it unnecessary to remain in jail. He locked his doors and went away to some healthier place . . . confident that his prisoners had neither strength nor spirit to escape."[44]

Conditions in Massachusetts were similar. Lice and bugs were common to many jails. Investigators in 1827 described rooms at the Ipswich House of Correction as "very miserable, dirty, and squalid."[45] As late as 1834, three facilities had dungeons, dark, airless cells left over from colonial times. Inspectors found taverns and inns connected to jails and were "forcibly struck by the impropriety" of this practice.[46] In both states, jailkeepers and sheriffs were paid on a fee basis, determined by multiplying a maintenance allowance by the number of prisoners. In South Carolina, for example, prisoners were to be supported on 37.5¢ a day.[47] This amount was

43. Presentments from Edgefield (Fall 1824), Charleston (Fall 1812), Lexington (Fall 1829; Fall 1818), Laurens (Spring 1815) Legal System Papers; Jack Kenny Williams, *Vogues in Villainy*, p. 116, and, in general, pp. 113–18. There were literally hundreds of presentments complaining about the jails.

44. William J. Grayson, *James Louis Petigru*, pp. 69–70.

45. *History of the Gaols in This State*, p. xxvii (and the document in general for conditions in jails throughout the state).

46. *Ninth Annual Report BPDS*, 1834, p. 20; *History of the Gaols*, p. 18.

47. Sheriff's Accounts, Penal System Papers; Williams, *Vogues in Villainy*, p. 117. The fee was reduced in the 1830s to thirty cents.

barely adequate, but reimbursement at a fixed rate regardless of actual expenses accrued gave jailers a personal incentive to stretch the stipend even further. Massachusetts inspectors recommended in 1827 that salaries of sheriffs and jailkeepers not be dependent on the number of commitments, but six years later a legislative committee noted that "obviously money is made in proportion to the neglect and hunger and cold from which the prisoners suffer."[48]

Houses of correction, though similar in function to penitentiaries, were generally built like jails. In 1819, the Massachusetts legislature required counties to build correction houses with individual cells, facilities for rehabilitative labor, and programs for education; the law was repealed after four months. Three years later, Josiah Quincy complained that sentences to solitary confinement and hard labor were "never executed" because the facilities did not exist. In 1827, such laws were described as a "dead letter."[49] As pressure from an increased convict population forced the erection of additional local penal institutions in Massachusetts, convicted criminals were eventually separated from the other categories of unfortunates. By 1852, six correction houses had facilities for some form of labor.[50] But immigration, with its attendant increase in convictions—not attention to humanitarian principles—was responsible for such changes. In all, attempts to improve conditions in the local institutions were not very successful, leading a British investigator to conclude, "More injury results from the county prisons of America than benefit from her penitentiaries."[51]

Since so little improvement was made in these institutions, Massachusetts reformers tried to remove as many people as possible from them. The first category included those who, it was increasingly believed, never belonged in the first place: the insane, the debtors, and the young. The second category included those who were there primarily because of inadequate arrangements elsewhere: female convicts confined in correction houses because after 1825 the penitentiary accepted only males and serious offenders confined because the overlapping jurisdiction between the penitentiary and correction house had never been clarified.

48. *Report on Gaols and Houses of Correction*, p. 56; *History of the Gaols*, p. 18.
49. Quincy, *Remarks*, p. 17; *History of the Gaols*, p. 7.
50. *Twenty-Seventh Annual Report BPDS*, 1852, p. 25.
51. *Review of Crawford's Report on the American Penitentiaries*, p. 6; *Ninth Annual Report BPDS*, 1834, pp. 8–29; Robert Waterston, *Thoughts on Prison Discipline*, p. 25; *Prisoner's Friend* 2 (1850): 208–9; Franklin B. Sanborn, "North American Prisons," p. 389; *History of the Gaols*; *Report on Gaols and Houses of Correction in the Commonwealth of Massachusetts*.

Because of the consensus of outrage at the injustice those in the first category suffered, removing them proved relatively easy. In the 1830s, Horace Mann helped establish a hospital for the insane, but there was no general policy of removing destitute lunatics from jails. In 1842, the same year that Samuel Gridley Howe entered the legislature intending to remove the insane from the jails, Dorothea Dix toured the penal facilities in the state and wrote her landmark *Memorial to the Legislature of Massachusetts*. Dix charged that the insane were "confined in this Commonwealth in *cages, closets, cellars, stalls, pens, chained, naked, beaten with rods*, and *lashed into obedience*." This situation also did "injustice . . . to the convicts," who were "doomed day after day and night after night to listen to the ravings of a madman."[52] Thanks to the efforts of Dix, Charles Sumner (her companion on some of those visits), and Howe, Massachusetts took steps to reduce the number of insane in local jails. Young offenders were removed to other institutions with the opening of the State Reformatory School for Boys in 1848 and the establishment of a similar school for girls six years later. In all these instances, the sole question seemed to be finding the proper institution; few seriously challenged institutionalizing the young or the insane.

The abolition of imprisonment for debt was another matter. Although indebtedness carried some of the moral stigma associated with criminality, the punishment was counterproductive in that the honest debtor was deprived of the opportunity to work to pay off the obligation. The practice was hardly uncommon. When Governor Levi Lincoln began his campaign in 1830 to abolish this "punishment for poverty," Massachusetts confined over three thousand debtors annually; in the Worcester County jail, debtors outnumbered convicts by a ratio of three to one.[53]

Reformers hailed an 1834 law entitled "An Act to Abolish Imprisonment for Debt," but their enthusiasm was premature because the statute included a glaring loophole. In cases of ten dollars or more in which the plaintiff believed that the defendant might leave

52. Dorothea L. Dix, *Memorial to the Legislature of Massachusetts*, pp. 2, 30; Dix to Sheriffs and Several Official Persons in the State of Massachusetts, 1843; John W. Proctor to Dix, 10, 14 July 1843; Anson Hooker to Dix, 12 Jan. 1843, all in Dorothea Lynde Dix Papers, Houghton Library, Harvard University; Harold Schwartz, *Samuel Gridley Howe, Social Reformer, 1801–1876*, p. 121; Jonathan Messerli, *Horace Mann*, pp. 122–29.

53. *Speech of His Excellency Levi Lincoln Delivered to the Two Branches of the Legislature in Convention, May 29, 1839; Message of Governor Lincoln; Sixth Annual Report BPDS*, 1831, p. 17; *Fifth Annual Report BPDS*, 1830, pp. 32–39.

Table 8.1. Imprisonment for Debt in Massachusetts, 1825–1874

A. Imprisonment for Debt in Boston, 1825–1834

Year	Committed for Debt	All Commitments	Percent Committed for Debt
1825	699	1,784	39.2
1826	822	1,689	48.7
1827	1,180	2,124	55.6
1828	1,057	1,889	56.0
1829	1,027	2,002	51.3
1830	1,253	2,249	55.7
1831	1,128	2,144	52.6
1832	738	1,442	51.2
1833	674	1,716	39.3
1834	722	2,197	32.9
Total	9,300	19,236	48.3

Source: *Plain Facts, Showing the Amount, Expense, and Principle Cause of Delinquency, Vice, Crime, and Pauperism in the City of Boston, for Ten Years,* pp. 9–10.

the jurisdiction before trial, he could have the debtor confined. In a state in which a high proportion of likely debtors were mariners, this loophole gutted the act.[54] For the next two decades, up to a quarter of all annual commitments were still for debt, amounting to up to nearly fifteen hundred persons (Table 8.1). Finally, an 1855 act declared that "imprisonment for debt is hereby forever abolished in Massachusetts." The only exceptions this time were for clear cases of fraud involving debts exceeding twenty dollars.[55] Nevertheless, in the two decades after this act, an average of over one hundred persons a year were imprisoned for the new "crime" of debt.

Women were the last to receive the attention of reformers. In the 1840s, the Boston Prisoner's Friend Association was formed to help female convicts upon their release. In 1854, a legislative committee produced a scathing indictment of conditions for women, focusing primarily on the lack of reformatory facilities (such as useful labor)

54. Massachusetts *Acts,* 1834, ch. 167; *Twelfth Annual Report BPDS,* 1837, p. 75.
55. *Prisoner's Friend* 7 (1855): 206; 6 (1854): 165; 6 (1853): 13; *Thirteenth Annual Report BPDS,* 1838, p. 79; Massachusetts *Acts,* 1855, ch. 444, sec. 1.

B. Imprisonment for Debt in Massachusetts
Compared with Commitments to Jails, 1837–1874

Year	Committed for Debt	All Commitments to Jails	Percent Committed for Debt
1837	982	4,107	23.7
1841	792	3,096	25.6
1842	742	2,987	24.8
1843	669	3,102	21.6
1844	548	2,825	19.4
1845	752	3,254	23.1
1846	953	4,552	20.9
1847	1,060	4,917	21.6
1848	1,177	5,770	20.4
1849	1,434	6,944	20.7
1850	1,461	7,463	19.6
1851	1,363	8,394	17.5
1852	1,126	7,688	17.7
1853	1,126	10,343	10.9
1854	1,091	11,526	9.5
1855	1,035	12,858	8.0
1856	138	9,419	1.5
1857	161	7,903	2.0
1858	138	8,603	1.6
1859	143	8,286	1.7
1860	133	6,752	2.0
1861	106	5,693	1.9
1862	109	5,211	2.1
1863	79	5,568	1.4
1865	16	3,075	.5
1866	59	6,759	.9
1867	91	5,770	1.6
1868	80	6,199	1.3
1869	104	7,200	1.4
1870	101	7,850	1.3
1871	112	8,018	1.4
1872	120	7,728	1.6
1873	169	6,734	2.5
1874	163	6,965	2.3

Source: *Abstracts of Returns of the Keepers of the Jails and Houses of·Correction,* 1837–63; Massachusetts Board of State Charities, *Annual Reports,* 1865–74.

and of matrons.[56] Only in the 1870s, after the increase in female commitments during the Civil War had made the plight of women more visible and after the establishment of the private Dedham Asylum for Discharged Female Convicts, was agitation for a separate female institution effective. In 1874, former Governor Emory Washburn published an impressive case for a woman's prison. The local institutions, Washburn complained, had "more than equal capacity to harden and degrade," and they put women under the control of "rough, coarse men." Calling this treatment "inequality in the administration of justice," Washburn urged the establishment of a reformatory under the control of women. Three years later, such an institution opened in Sherborn.[57]

By midcentury, Massachusetts had erected the scaffolds of a modern criminal justice system. An assortment of institutions had been established, and the most severe features of the penal code had been eliminated. But, in a way, the criminal justice process seemed to have fallen victim to the talismanic goals of certainty and predictability. The entire system seemed geared to producing the maximum amount of confinement with minimal concern for the fate of any individual defendant. What was intended to be an even-handed adversary system now seemed to be a ruthless, if efficient, monster. In response to this situation, some people began paying attention to pretrial and presentencing stages with an eye to improving both procedure and substance.

One of the most celebrated and interesting of these efforts was made by a Boston bootmaker, John Augustus, whose shop was adjacent to Boston's courts. Appalled by the ordeal faced by youngsters caught in minor scrapes with the law, Augustus began to serve as a surety in 1841 for people arrested for minor offenses. Believing that many drunkards, first offenders, and juveniles could be "reclaimed" if saved from the stigma of conviction and the contamination of confinement, Augustus annually posted bond for hundreds of drunkards, prostitutes, young thieves, and liquor sellers. He also boarded dozens of youths while they searched for jobs. Priding himself on his high success rate, he claimed that less than 10 percent defaulted. In seventeen years, he stood as surety for almost two thousand persons at a liability of almost a quarter of a million dollars.[58]

56. Boston Prisoner's Friend Association, *Circular*, 1849; C. R. Bellows, *Commissioner's Report on the Subject of Matrons and Labor in the Common Jails.*

57. Emory Washburn, *Reasons for a Separate State Prison for Women;* see also Estelle Brenda Freedman, "Their Sisters' Keepers."

58. John Augustus, *A Report of the Labors of John Augustus for the Last Ten Years*

The significance of his efforts lies mostly in his understanding that the search for certainty and uniformity had produced a court system that was not sufficiently flexible to be the proper repository for his charges. Whatever advances the prisons had promised for the more serious offenders, local jails and houses of correction—where the long arm of reform had not yet reached—were inappropriate for his impressionable youths. His experience also illustrates the hostility faced by anyone wishing to work outside of the formal criminal justice process. Augustus was barred from the courtroom by court officials, in part because his efforts cost them the *mittimus* fees for transporting convicts to correction houses and in part because of their hostility to his mission.[59]

Augustus entered the scene after conviction; other reformers found fault in earlier stages of the criminal justice process where they felt the cards were clearly stacked against the defendant. The power of the state was marshaled against him in every way possible: police arrested, the state prosecuted, but protection of the presumption of innocence was a private matter. Many felt justice was nearly impossible under these circumstances. One of the earliest and most consistent proposals was for a system of state-paid defense attorneys. In 1786, Benjamin Austin, in his classic attack on the legal profession, called for public defenders. But such an office was far in the future, and not until *Gideon v. Wainwright* (1963) would this principle be as broadly applied as Austin and others had wanted.[60]

Even with legal representation, the suspect was at a tremendous disadvantage before trial. In the 1850s, efforts were made to clarify suspects' rights in the crucial pretrial period, which was just being recognized as an important determinant of the ultimate disposition of the case. Bail discriminated against poor defendants in two ways. First, a person not yet convicted was forced to languish in jail for lack of bail. But, more insidious—because of the likelihood that it confounded the ends of justice—being in jail demoralized a suspect and made him less able to prepare an adequate defense. Feeling that this situation was hopeless, the innocent defendant might confess. Under these circumstances, it is hardly surprising that the first indications of plea-bargaining appear in this period.[61]

in the *Aid of the Unfortunate*, pp. 4, 15, 27, 33; *Letter Concerning the Labors of Mr. John Augustus, the Well-Known Philanthropist from One Who Knows Him*, p. 9.

59. Augustus, *Report*, pp. 15–16, 19, 22–23, 37–38.

60. Benjamin Austin, *Observations on the Pernicious Practice of Law by Honestus; Prisoner's Friend* 1 (1848): 32; *Second Annual Report of the Massachusetts Society for Aiding Discharged Convicts*, p. 24; *Prisoner's Friend* 2 (1850): 324.

61. Haynes, *Pictures*, pp. 218–20; *Twenty-Eighth Annual Report BPDS*, 1853, pp. 5–8; Enoch C. Wines and Theodore W. Dwight, *Report on the Prisons and Reforma-*

Eventually, the problem was taken back one more step and even police conduct was questioned. In 1853, the Prison Discipline Society demanded that police be fair-minded and free of prejudice to ensure that suspects were arrested solely for good cause. One governor thought most policemen were corrupt. There were hints throughout these decades that stationhouse justice was practiced—arrestees beaten and otherwise punished and abused by the police either to extort a confession or because police feared that the verdict and sentence would not be to their own liking.[62]

An entirely new set of expectations from the criminal justice system was emerging. In the early nineteenth century, the prison was the focal point—through its own efforts and by example, the prison was expected to help reduce crime. But the criminal justice process itself was regarded as sound. By midcentury, much had changed, in part because of the failure of the original expectations and in part because of changed circumstances in the state. Crime had become a mass phenomenon, closely associated with certain groups at the bottom of society. Few convicts saw the inside of the penitentiary, which now held only the most hardened offenders. Moreover, the careful guarantees of the adversary system seemed to dissolve into assembly-line justice. As order replaced rehabilitation, as class control replaced crime control in the administration of justice, accuracy replaced reformation as the primary end of justice. Though a much less lofty goal, accuracy was not only more attainable, but in many ways more desirable.

While Massachusetts confronted the complex interrelationship between key elements of the criminal justice process, penal reform efforts in South Carolina were far simpler. All those interested in reforming the criminal justice system in South Carolina regarded establishing a penitentiary as the necessary first step. Revision of the penal code—replacing hanging and branding with hard labor and confinement—was dependent upon the creation of such an institution. Conversely, the state's failure to build a prison hindered all attempts to overhaul the statutes.

The prison was an issue in the Palmetto State for almost an entire century. South Carolina's rejection of a penitentiary is striking because it was a proposal that commanded substantial support from the Revolution to the Civil War. Indeed, writings on this subject by

tories of the United States and Canada Made to the Legislature of New York, January 1867, p. 505.

62. Wines and Dwight, Report, pp. 524–25; for the history of the Boston police during these years, see Roger Lane, Policing the City, pp. 142–79; Twenty-Eighth Annual Report BPDS, 1853, pp. 5–6.

both native and adopted South Carolinians were standard works throughout the United States, even though they failed to have the slightest impact in the state in which they were written. The nearly unanimous support for a prison from South Carolina's governors and jurists only proved how weak such men were in a state where power was too established to be wielded through office alone. The first call appeared in a 1797 Charleston presentment demanding a "bettering house . . . for punishing and reclaiming." That year Governor Arnoldus Vanderhorst asked the legislature to consider the penitentiary question. In response, Robert James Turnbull wrote *A Visit to the Philadelphia Prison.* Replete with Enlightenment and Quaker views of crime and punishment, it became a classic of the prison reform movement. Inspired by revolutionary optimism and influenced by Benjamin Rush, Turnbull was out of touch with the intellectual, social, and political realities of South Carolina. While discussing black convicts, for example, he termed it shocking that his state had not yet abolished slavery. Turnbull did see, however, that the penitentiary question was part of the larger issue of codification and law reform, and he called for progress in those areas.[63]

In the following year, in a wide-ranging message on legal reform, Governor Charles Pinckney recommended a penitentiary. Less than a decade later, Governor Paul Hamilton commissioned Robert Mills to design a penitentiary on the Philadelphia system, but the plans were never implemented. In 1811, a penitentiary bill was defeated by the legislature, the first of many to meet that fate. The impetus for such an institution came readily from governors and grand juries, but all bills died in the legislature.[64]

Interest was revived in the 1830s as the general obsession with prisons and penology reached South Carolina, fueled by Francis Lieber, an internationally renowned penologist, who was by then a professor in the state. In 1835, Phillip Tidyman, lowcountry physician and gentleman planter, published his correspondence with Samuel Wood, warden of the Philadelphia prison, and Henry W.

63. Robert James Turnbull, *A Visit to the Philadelphia Prison,* pp. 55, 79–81, 29, 50; Charleston Grand Jury, 1797, Presentments, SCA. Turnbull's use of medical analogies (p. 55) suggests that he may have been influenced by Benjamin Rush.

64. Charles Pinckney, *Message* (1797; printed copy, but not listed in Evans or Turnbull bibliographies; only known printed copy is at Charleston Library Society. SCA has a manuscript copy); Robert Mills to Paul Hamilton, 7 July, 6, 24 Nov. 1806, Public Improvements, Legislative System Papers, 1800–1830, SCA; South Carolina House Journal, 1810, pp. 85, 87; ibid., 1811, pp. 47, 52, 92, SCA; Lists of Convictions, Penal System Papers; the following grand juries: Abbeville (1817), Barnwell (1812, 1815, 1816), Chester (1810, 1816), Charleston (1817), Presentments, Legal System Papers, 1831–59.

DeSaussure, revered chancellor of South Carolina.[65] Tidyman's Quaker argument for solitary confinement was ignored. By 1839, however, the outlook appeared more favorable because of an alliance between Lieber, upcountry lawyer and legislator Benjamin F. Perry, and Governor Patrick Noble. Perry, whose interest in codification and penal reform predated Lieber's arrival by nearly a decade, was the key figure. He convinced Noble to take an interest in this issue; Noble, in turn, solicited Lieber's advice.

Lieber's extended response stressed both theoretical and practical reasons for a total reorganization of the criminal justice system, based on the establishment of a solitary system penitentiary. Stressing the interdependence of criminal justice components, Lieber hoped that the prison would solve the problems caused by the excessive use of both capital punishment and pardoning. Admonishing that "the state must never appear to be the pecuniary gainer by crime," Lieber hoped that the penitentiary would reduce the role of fines as punishment.[66] Lieber noted that fines represented a double standard of justice based on wealth, but did not discuss the probability that such distinctions were as much a part of the state's political and legal order as of the social structure.

Simultaneously, Perry prepared a legislative report buttressed by evidence collected from states that had penitentiaries. While cataloging all the objections to the current system in South Carolina, he also tried, for the first time in twenty years, to collect statistics on convictions. These were essential for determining the size of the proposed institution. Perry was in a quandary. He first had to convince a skeptical legislature that South Carolina had a sufficient number of serious crimes to warrant building an institution. Statistics could counter the glowing, impressionistic accounts of the state's domestic tranquillity. But if he overestimated the necessary number of cells, the cost would seal the project's doom. As it turned out, even his reasonable figure of 140 cells did not convince the hostile minority of his committee. Perry's report and Lieber's letter generated great interest, but in the end, the measured died in the senate.[67]

65. Phillip Tidyman, *Letters on the Pennsylvania System of Solitary Imprisonment;* grand juries: Chester (1830), Charleston (1825), Kershaw (1828), Pendleton (1827), Spartanburg (1825), Colleton (1837, 1838), Lancaster (1839), Presentments, Legal System Papers, 1800–1830, 1831–59; Governor's Message: 1833 (Hayne), 1837 (Butler).

66. Patrick Noble to Benjamin F. Perry, 11 March 1839, Governor's Correspondence, SCA; Lieber, *Letter,* p. 43.

67. Perry, *Report,* pp. 18, 21.

For the next two decades, the appeal for penal reform remained the litany of the governors and grand juries. Bills were introduced or considered annually; at least eighty-two grand juries from 1846 to 1859 demanded changes. In 1849, presentments from twenty-five grand juries prompted another fruitless inquiry into the desirability, feasibility, necessity, and cost of a penitentiary. In 1852, Attorney General Isaac W. Hayne, at the governor's request, wrote a strong argument for complete penal reform. Hayne culled data from northern institutions and reform societies, but he was very careful to dissociate himself from them. Conceding that he had "no sympathy with the spirit of indiscriminate and sweeping innovation . . . which absolutely runs riot in many states," Hayne hoped that the state would not be "palsied by . . . conservatism." Instead of the controversial and costly Philadelphia plan, he shrewdly recommended the Auburn system. Like the opponents of capital punishment in Massachusetts, Hayne stressed that amelioration of the criminal code, far from representing a retreat in the state's hard line against crime, would significantly increase punishment by reducing the tendency toward acquittal. But Hayne's caution was to no avail. A similar flurry of presentments, messages, and bills accompanied the legal housekeeping of the late 1850s, but the result was the same.[68]

Decades of pamphlets, presentments, messages, bills, acquittals, and pardons produced no substantive change in the South Carolina criminal justice system. Not until Reconstruction—after the social and political system maintained so effectively by the legal structure had been demolished—did South Carolina reform the criminal code and establish a penitentiary.

In both states, legal and penal reform were issues of great interest. And, in both states, the ultimate objectives of those who sought change were not achieved. In Massachusetts, publication of the *Revised Statutes* and a reduction in the number of capital offenses represented pragmatic concessions to reality rather than any wholesale capitulation to the tide of reform. Efforts to fine tune pretrial procedures and to improve incarceration through specialization

---

68. The presentments are in the Legal System Papers, 1831–59; Isaac W. Hayne, *Report to His Excellency the Governor on Prisons, Prison Discipline, and the Criminal Law*, p. 3; Governor's Messages: Richardson (1841), Seabrook (1849), Means (1852), Aiken (1846), Allston (1857–59). Bills were introduced in 1846, 1847, 1849, 1851, Reports, Penal System Papers, 1831–59; presentments: see Table 8.1 and Presentments, Legal System Papers, 1831–59; *South Carolina Legislative Times*, pp. 292–93; Reports (1856), Penal System Papers; *South Carolina House Journal*, 1858, pp. 66, 176.

were of similar magnitude. In Massachusetts, at least, there was accommodation. In South Carolina, where the need was greater at the outset, there was total resistance. In part, inaction was a pragmatic accommodation to the fact that the highly personalistic system of justice created by legislative and judicial inaction seemed to satisfy some needs and avoid the bureaucratic-certainty model that in turn had created so many problems in the North. Ultimately, of course, the fate of such measures reflects contrasting views on the role of law and authority in society and on the nature of crime and the criminal.

Chapter 9.
Social Change and Social Class: An Evaluation of Penal and Legal Reform

The legal and criminal justice systems had sharply different roles in Massachusetts and in South Carolina, but a continuous and logical thread runs throughout each state's legal order. In South Carolina, where formal authority was constrained, the penal system prosecuted less serious offenses, convicted only a small fraction of the defendants, and accorded them punishments that, if not mild, were of short duration. Any major capital or structural investment was shunned; courts remained overcrowded to the point of being inaccessible, confinement was primitive, and even revision of the statutes—an investment in the legitimacy of the legal order—was delayed. The public sector was peripheral, and private enforcement of behaviorial norms was encouraged, if not sanctioned. In Massachusetts, offenders were convicted at high rates for more serious offenses and punished accordingly. Jails, houses of correction, and the state penitentiary stood as granite embodiments of the commonwealth's commitment to the authority of its laws. These are differences in both degree and kind.

Given these two patterns, it is not surprising that efforts to alter, perhaps even to improve, the criminal justice system met with varying degrees of success. But was the receptivity of Massachusetts to reformist notions part of the state's more activist stance, was it simply that the state as an entity was more enterprising, and thus there was more opportunity to affect social policy? Conversely, was there no opportunity in South Carolina for innovation or experimentation simply because the state government was committed to doing as little as possible in every area?

Not surprisingly, in light of the manner in which these questions were framed, the answer involves both structure and substance. The structure of both reform activity and reform objectives explains to no small degree why reformers received a greater hearing in Massachusetts than in South Carolina. To some extent, this reflects the higher degree of organization of all types of enterprise in Massachusetts. From reform groups to political parties, from charity to church, from corporation to labor union, Massachusetts was an early hotbed of pluralism, of interest-group pressure politics. South Carolina remained more individualistic; authority was person-based, not organization-based. This contrast had an impact on reform in two ways: the structure of the effort and the substance of the message.

In the preceding chapter, we saw that at times there was reason to believe that through the efforts of governors, grand juries, and individuals, reform could succeed in South Carolina. There are four possible explanations for intransigence: cost (specifically, of a penitentiary), the association of reform with abolitionism and Unionism, the all-consuming nature of the sectional crisis, and the general conservatism of the South Carolina population. All of these explanations are true to some degree, but they do not explain the summary rejection of most proposals for change.

Cost was a constant concern. When proposing a penitentiary in 1806, architect Robert Mills dwelled on its expense.[1] In 1839, the minority of the Perry committee complained that the state lacked the means to carry out such an expensive "experiment in Criminal Law Reform."[2] In 1849, Governor Whitemarsh Seabrook asserted that finances precluded building a penitentiary, even though one might be "wise and salutory."[3]

While undoubtedly a deterrent, cost alone would not have precluded a prison. The decentralized system of local jails was itself expensive;[4] a penitentiary would reduce, but not eliminate, this expense. In addition, a penitentiary promised some return to the state, even if an actual profit was chimerical. Cost was a factor in a state that kept both taxes and social services low,[5] but it does not explain the rejection of proposals that required relatively little expense, such as court reform and statute revision.

The association of reform with abolitionism and Unionism was also blamed for South Carolina's recalcitrance.[6] Penal and legal reform were linked with Unionists Francis Lieber, Benjamin F. Perry,

1. Robert Mills to Paul Hamilton, 7 July, 6, 24 Nov. 1806, Public Improvements 1800–1830, Buildings (Letters), Legislative Papers, SCA.
2. *Counter Report of a Portion of the Members of the Special Committee on the Penitentiary System*, p. 4.
3. *Message of the Governor* (1849) [Whitemarsh Seabrook] in *South Carolina House Journal* (1849), p. 28.
4. Jack Kenny Williams, *Vogues in Villainy*, p. 74.
5. Bertram Wyatt-Brown, "Southern History Upside Down," p. 461.
6. Frank Friedel, *Francis Lieber*, p. 260; Williams, *Vogues in Villainy*, p. 130.

James L. Petigru, Thomas S. Grimké, and John Belton O'Neall. Lieber was a known friend of abolitionists and was suspected of being soft on the slavery issue. Grimké sympathized with the American Colonization Society. O'Neall outraged the legislature with his appeal for greater legal protection for blacks, and Petigru had an uncanny knack for gaining the acquittal of those suspected of unlawfully passing for white or free.

But these men were not ostracized, nor were all proponents of penal or legal reform connected with other unpopular notions. In 1859, with the sectional crisis coming to a head, Petigru and O'Neall were given the two most influential positions in the state's legal hierarchy—Petigru as code commissioner and O'Neall was chief justice of the new supreme court. This was precisely the time when ideological objections, had they been voiced, would have been paramount.

The correlation between Unionism, softness on slavery, and reform cannot be sustained once one has passed the obvious names. John Lyde Wilson favored codification, court reorganization, and reform of the slave trial system, yet he was a fire-eater who led the raid on the Charleston mails. Robert James Turnbull, who, in 1796, advocated the Philadelphia prison system and declared it shameful that South Carolina had not abolished slavery, served on the court that condemned the Vesey defendants and, as *Caroliniensis,* attacked unpopular court decisions on the Negro Seaman's Acts and propounded early Nullification doctrines. Phillip Tidyman, the cosmopolitan planter who published letters on the Philadelphia prison system, served as a Nullifying delegate. Isaac W. Hayne, author of the last major publication in antebellum South Carolina in support of penal reform, was a leading secessionist.[7] Few of the state's many governors who called for legal reform could be accused of unorthodox views on slavery.

Finally, this explanation clashes with chronology. Attempts to overhaul South Carolina's legal system began in the mid-eighteenth century; attempts at court reorganization date from the 1760s, penal reform from the 1790s. The period between the Revolution and the Vesey Rebellion, which predates concern about abolitionism or Unionism, was a time of agitation for social and political change. At least four attempts were made to establish a penitentiary in the first two decades of the nineteenth century, yet these were rejected out of hand in the zenith of Jeffersonian liberalism in the South.

7. *Dictionary of American Biography* 19:55–56; George C. Rogers, Jr., *History of Georgetown County,* pp. 240–43.

A third explanation was that the sectional crisis precluded consideration of such mundane issues. Lieber called the failure of reform "a striking feature of South Carolina," the result "of her eternal warfare with the general government which absorbs her whole attention."[8] Perry noted that "our quarrel with the general government . . . has absorbed all our thoughts and energies until we are . . . behind our sister states."[9] Seabrook admitted that the "absolute requirement of all funds at command, to put the state in a proper condition of defense" precluded the establishment of a penitentiary.[10]

Like the previous suggestions, this explanation fails to consider the earlier decades. Moreover, the period of greatest sectional tension was also the one in which presentments, governors' messages, and bills for reform appear most frequently, as indicated in the one surviving record of legislative debates, the *South Carolina Legislative Times* for 1855.[11] This was a critical year in the sectional dispute, midway between the state's two secessionist conventions. Moreover, Governor James Adams had raised one of the issues most crucial to the state's autonomy—revision of the Negro Seaman's Acts. Nevertheless, the legislature spent most of its time on state matters unrelated to national issues. These included court reorganization, electoral reform, creation of a new district, and reform of the system for trying slave crimes. The legislature was quite capable of considering such domestic issues; its inability to legislate was hardly a product of the sectional dispute.

The most common and fundamental explanation for inaction is that South Carolina was ubiquitously conservative. One legislator asserted that "the conservative spirit . . . has met with the almost Universal approval of our constituents."[12] Edward Pringle wrote that "the legislature of South Carolina is one of the most conservative in the Union. . . . The very idea of change revolts [the legislators] and they recoil from tampering with the existing state of things."[13] Even the most minor alterations were considered assaults on "landmarks" of law; to describe a practice as deriving from "im-

8. Francis Lieber to Dorothea Dix, 12 Nov. 1851, Francis Lieber Papers, Huntington Library. Lieber also complained that he had not been able to interest a "solitary minister" in the cause of penal reform. This claim was overstated. Lieber had greatly influenced both Governor Patrick Noble and Benjamin F. Perry in the 1839 study of the issue and contributed his own lengthy letter in its support.

9. Greenville *Mountaineer*, 14 Dec. 1849.

10. *Message of the Governor* (1849) [Whitemarsh Seabrook].

11. *South Carolina Legislative Times.*

12. Ibid., p. 29.

13. Edward J. Pringle, "The Judiciary System of South Carolina," pp. 469–70.

memorial usage" was not to suggest stagnation or obsolescence but to endow it with the highest praise.[14]

There is little doubt that South Carolina was a conservative state. But conservatism *as an explanation* is unsatisfying. Such political moves as Nullification and secession were hardly conservative. Similarly, the state displayed little veneration for established principles when it came to legislating slave control after a rebellion or panic. Conservatism as an explanation, then, demands its own explanation.

What has traditionally been ascribed to conservatism—and, accordingly, blamed for South Carolina's immobility—was actually a certain view of society and the groups that comprise it. This view excised from reality those groups that were most likely to benefit from, stimulate, or require social legislation, an attitude that, as will be demonstrated, was rooted in the state's conception of class. This conception, in addition to the lethargy and insensitivity often associated with the state's conservatism, were the real bars to change in South Carolina. A contrasting conception of the social order explains much of Massachusetts's receptivity to efforts for social change and penal reform. It is not sufficient to state that reform succeeded in Massachusetts, but not in South Carolina. Success, like failure, demands an explanation and can also shed light on the contrasting pattern. There are four major areas of explanation that account for the response of each state. Two are structural: the existence or absence of a culture of reform and the relationship of this culture to a more or less responsive and open political system. The other two explanations are substantive: the demands for change in relationship to the existing institutions, laws, and policies and the general world view embodied in the reformist ideology and the compatibility of this ideology with each state's social perceptions.

A Culture of Reform

Antebellum Massachusetts fostered a culture of reform. Almost every social issue spawned one or more organizations, complete with journals and annual reports. Some of the most visible of these organizations were the Boston Prison Discipline Society, the Massachusetts Society for Abolishing Capital Punishment, the Pris-

14. *Message of the Governor* (1847); the governor was David Johnson. Other examples of South Carolina's self-proclaimed conservatism are legion. See the "Report of the Committee on the Judiciary on the Resolutions as to Executing White Criminals in Private" (1844), Penal System Papers, 1831–59, SCA; *Legislative Times*, p. 83.

oner's Friend Society, and the Boston Society for Aiding Discharged Convicts. These organizations structured efforts to change public policy; they established channels of communication among like-minded individuals; and they provided the continuity necessary to any sustained effort. The reports of such organizations were distributed far beyond the membership. The *Annual Reports* of the Prison Discipline Society of Boston were subsidized by the state of Massachusetts[15] and went through many editions and printings. The organ of the movement against capital punishment, the *Hangman*, superseded in 1849 by the *Prisoner's Friend*, was published on a regular basis for over a decade.

The culture of reform was not limited to organizations. Samuel Gridley Howe, Charles Sumner, and Horace Mann were close friends. Others who worked independently were eventually drawn into this circle. John Augustus, whose volunteer probation efforts were funded initially from his own earnings, eventually attracted philanthropic support and published his own report.[16] Dorothea Lynde Dix worked on her own, but had an extremely wide range of contacts.[17] In addition, reformers befriended and corresponded with leading European penal reformers, many of whom they had met as the latter rushed to America to see the prisons. Americans such as Howe, Sumner, and Mann reciprocated these visits.[18]

Americans used their international connections to further their own goals. Most Europeans favored the separate system of prison discipline, perfected in Philadelphia but otherwise ignored in America, except by New Jersey and an impassioned group in Massachusetts. In the 1840s, when Boston was considering a design for a new city jail, Sumner's brother George wrote a tract from Paris in which

15. The printing history is in the Publisher's Note to the Patterson Smith reprint edition of *Reports of the Prison Discipline Society of Boston,* 1:v. One of Howe's first moves as a Massachusetts legislator was to end the state subsidy for printing the society's reports (Howe to Lieber, 19 March 1843, Lieber Papers, Huntington Library).

16. *Prisoner's Friend* 4 (1852): 396–97; John Augustus, *A Report on the Labors of John Augustus for the Last Ten Years in the Aid of the Unfortunate.*

17. Sumner cited her in his attacks on Dwight, claiming she accomplished "*infinitely*" more on her budget of $1,200 than the society did on $3,000 (Charles Sumner to Francis Wayland, 30 May 1846, Francis Wayland Papers, Brown University). On Dix in general see the very rich Dorothea Lynde Dix Papers, Houghton Library, Harvard University.

18. On Mann, see Jonathan Messerli, *Horace Mann,* p. 397; on Howe, Harold Schwartz, *Samuel Gridley Howe, Social Reformer, 1801–1867;* on Sumner see David Donald, *Charles Sumner and the Coming of the Civil War,* pp. 43–69. These men's papers also describe their journeys. Howe accompanied Mann and his second bride on their European honeymoon.

he cited French endorsements to bolster his case for the separate system.[19] Americans used their European allies in their attempt to unseat Louis Dwight, staunch defender of the silent system, as secretary of the Boston Prison Discipline Society.[20]

This network in Massachusetts gave reform efforts an important degree of strength and continuity. In South Carolina there was nothing similar. Except for an occasional antidueling society, no organization dedicated to penal or legal reform surfaced in this period. On the other hand, South Carolina did have permanently organized vigilante societies—a realistic reaction to the perennial ineffectiveness of formal authority in that state. South Carolina's experience was by no means inevitable.[21] Charleston was to the South what Boston was to New England—not merely a commercial center, but also a hub of intellectual life. As a center of southern civilization, Charleston boasted a full complement of cultural, charitable, and philanthropic enterprises. Virtually every ethnic and racial group, including free blacks, had its social and benevolent society.

Reform-minded people in South Carolina were either already serving in a public capacity (such as governors or grand jurors) or were mavericks. In the second category was Robert James Turnbull, who wrote an impassioned defense of the Philadelphia prison and then did not appear in public life for over a quarter of a century. Another maverick was Phillip Tidyman, a prosperous Georgetown planter and physician and the first American to graduate from Göttingen.[22] Since many of the European guests Tidyman entertained in his stylish Charleston townhouse probably included the virtually obligatory visit to American prisons on their itinerary, this social contact may have inspired Tidyman's interest in penal matters.

In South Carolina, only Thomas Grimké and Benjamin Perry were consistently involved in a variety of reform efforts over a sustained period of time. In combining ambitious political careers with an interest in social reform, Grimké and Perry closely resembled Robert Rantoul of Massachusetts. But Rantoul was a backer of the *Pris-*

19. George Sumner, *Mr. Sumner's Letter;* George Sumner to Howe, 16 April 1846, Samuel Gridley Howe Papers, Houghton Library, Harvard University.

20. Joseph Adshead to Samuel Gridley Howe, 12 June 1846, 17 July 1847, Howe Papers; Joseph Adshead, *Prisons and Prisoners,* pp. 123–49. Fearing that Dwight would misrepresent the dissenters, and perhaps hoping to embarrass him on his forthcoming European trip, Howe enlisted the aid of Joseph Adshead, English penal reformer. In *Prisons and Prisoners,* Adshead denounced the evils of the silent system and attributed its persistence to the nefarious actions of Dwight.

21. James Banner, Jr., "The Problem of South Carolina," p. 75.

22. Rogers, *Georgetown County,* pp. 298, 311.

oner's Friend, president of the Massachusetts Society for Abolishing Capital Punishment, and a life member of the Boston Prison Discipline Society; Grimké and Perry worked almost alone.[23]

There was no reform ideology in South Carolina, much less an orthodoxy. Turnbull and Tidyman wrote on prisons, but said nothing about capital punishment or dueling. John Lyde Wilson, on the other hand, wrote informed pamphlets on court reform and codification, but was an active proponent of the code of honor.

Part of the success of reform efforts in Massachusetts, in contrast to South Carolina, is attributable to politics. Reformers ran for public office on their proposals. Samuel Gridley Howe entered the General Court specifically to get the insane out of Massachusetts jails.[24] Sumner began his political career only after years of working for reform.[25] Mann and Rantoul became reformers after their entrance into politics. A public position was useful as a rostrum. Both Mann and Howe wrote their major policy statements in an official capacity, Mann as secretary of the Board of Education, Howe as director of the Perkins School and as secretary of the Board of State Charities.

With people such as Sumner, Mann, Howe, and Rantoul active in politics, reformers could expect a hearing in Massachusetts, and support could be fairly widespread.[26] The ease with which reform efforts became affiliated with the public sphere had its drawbacks. Some organizations became too dependent on such a tie. The Boston Society for Aiding Discharged Convicts withered after it lost the power to appoint the state agent for discharged convicts as well as its right to visit prisoners before their release. Similarly, within months after the editors of the *Prisoner's Friend* lost their visiting rights in the Massachusetts State Prison, the periodical folded.[27]

In South Carolina, structural obstacles blocked public efforts to influence the state's political system in any meaningful way. The

23. *Prisoner's Friend* 6 (1853): 148; 1 (1849): 316; *Twenty-Fifth Report BPDS*, 1850, p. 103.

24. Schwartz, *Howe*, pp. 100–102; Howe to Lieber, 29 Oct. 1842, 17 Jan. 1843, Lieber Papers.

25. Donald, *Sumner*, pp. 148, 168–69, 185, 189, and passim.

26. Robert Rantoul, Jr., to Henry Crocker, 5 Dec. 1836, Robert Rantoul, Jr., Papers, Beverly Historical Society. In 1836, Rantoul's legislative program included codification and the abolition of capital punishment, indicating that these issues were expected to attract voters.

27. *Prisoner's Friend* 9 (1857): 202, 235–36, 242; *Annual Report of the Boston Society for Aiding Discharged Convicts*, 1857, pp. 10–12, 14. This organization was kept alive and was revived almost single-handedly by Howe; see the *Annual Report of the Massachusetts Society for Aiding Discharged Convicts*, 1872.

South Carolina House was apportioned according to a formula based on wealth as well as on population; the Senate was based on the colonial parish system with power permanently ensconced in the plantation lowcountry. There were no political parties and few durable factions in the legislature,[28] robbing any reform effort of the momentum and persistence necessary for success. The legislature had an almost total grip on the state government. It appointed most local officials and elected both governor and presidential electors. The executive was the weakest in the nation, lacking a popular mandate, patronage power, and a veto. Governors and grand juries could be summarily repudiated by the legislature with no fear of reprisal. One plaintive class of presentments, reiterated from the Revolution to the Civil War, complained that the legislature had ignored all previous presentments;[29] such complaints fared no better than the preceding ones had.

These were not the only obstacles. The legislature convened in the last week of November and adjourned before Christmas. This ritual, deliberately copied from the British Parliament,[30] precluded serious and sustained examination of issues. "A proposition to sit longer, be the business finished or not," Francis Lieber quipped, "so that the members would not kiss their wives on Christmas day, would certainly be looked upon as treasonable."[31] Grand juries added this to their standing grievances; O'Neall cited the short session in anticipation of yet another defeat of a penitentiary bill.[32] Compounding this obstacle were the rules of the body itself. Unfinished business—bills and resolutions sent to committee but not reported out by adjournment—were completely dead and had to be reintroduced and shepherded through committee procedure in the following session. This was such a tedious process that in 1858 the judiciary committee complained that it had not the time to consider a penitentiary bill.[33]

This situation was reflected in the amount of business accomplished in any given session. From 1839 to 1849, the South Carolina legislature passed a total of 335 bills, or fewer than the number passed in Massachusetts in 1844–45. This record may seem admi-

28. Banner, "South Carolina," pp. 61, 65, 70, 72, 76–80.

29. Presentments, April 1769, April 1770, May 1773, in Charleston Sessions Journal; Charleston Grand Jury, Spring 1859, Presentments, Legal System Papers, SCA.

30. William Henry Trescot, Memorial of the Life of J. Johnston Pettigrew, p. 30.

31. Lieber to Jared Sparks, 1 Jan. 1840, Jared Sparks Papers, Houghton Library, Harvard University.

32. O'Neall in Newberry Rising Sun, 31 March 1858; Darlington Grand Jury, 1850, Presentments, Legal System Papers.

33. Report of the Judiciary Committee, 1858, Reports, Penal System Papers.

rable at a time when people feel burdened by a press of seemingly unnecessary legislation, but it is questionable whether it served the needs of the people of South Carolina. Clearly, members of the legislature saw themselves as caretakers, concerned with making only those slight adjustments necessary to preserve the status quo. In rejecting grand jury presentments in any given area, committees inevitably responded that it was "inexpedient" to legislate. Legislation in South Carolina was, in fact, a matter of expediency; any item that failed to meet that test was doomed.

In South Carolina, there was no opportunity for sustained efforts for change. Although grand juries clamored for improvements throughout the entire period, these were *ad hoc* bodies with rotating memberships meeting for a few days every six months. The only sustained efforts could come from the prolonged public careers of such men as Grimké, O'Neall, and Perry; all had learned that their careers could be cut short through such efforts. Perry's wife, an astute political observer, begged her husband to abandon the penitentiary cause. "You have already done all you can for it," she insisted. "You have given the state an able report; . . . it is such an unpopular subject that you had better drop it for the present[. N]o good can be gained by bringing it forward."[34]

Efforts for change were influenced by each state's legal traditions. These traditions reflected not only the condition of the legal system, but also the attitude toward change and the reverence for experience. The types of innovations urged by penal reformers were often both linked and cumulative. A change in punishment systems, as we have seen, involved both a change in the law and a capital investment (such as a penitentiary, gallows, or pillory). Building on momentum, arguments for change based on progress and evolution struck a responsive note in Massachusetts. In South Carolina, progress for its own sake was far more suspect. Inaction was justified by experience; progress was invoked to show that South Carolina was falling behind its peers. And the success of that argument would depend in large part on the choice of peers.

Of course, the actual degree of innovation in the two states varied considerably. Massachusetts did build upon its record. When the interest in new forms of penitentiary discipline greatly expanded, the state already had a prison. The concepts of incarceration and hard labor did not have to be sold to a suspicious populace. Instead, debate focused on the best mode of discipline and reformation. Even in Massachusetts, however, proposals that represented a break with

34. Elizabeth Perry to Benjamin F. Perry, 22 Nov. 1840, Benjamin F. Perry Papers, SCL.

past practice had difficulty gaining a hearing. Drunkenness was not decriminalized, the state did not establish a public defender's office, and the indeterminate sentence took nearly a century to gain acceptance. Nor was capital punishment abolished or codification enacted. In South Carolina, by contrast, the changes sought to bring the legal system in line with nineteenth-century trends involved an almost total reconstruction of the penal and legal system. The penitentiary issue provides a good illustration. There was no precedent in the state for long-term confinement or hard labor as a punishment. Ironically, South Carolina reformers may have been hampered by being pacesetters. The plan most often proposed for a penitentiary from 1797 to 1839 was the separate system. More costly than the silent system, this controversial design was shunned by all but two states. Yet most of the discussion and bills favored this plan.[35] Establishment of a penitentiary was unlikely in any case in antebellum South Carolina. But the choice of the most costly, most radical, most controversial system was an additional obstacle.

Class and Crime

The organization and structure of reform campaigns, the relationship between reform and the political system, and the historical context of innovation show important contrasts between the two states. But another explanation for the crucial differences in the social perceptions and realities of the two societies has to do with the extent to which the ideology of reform, or, conversely, the resistance to reform, struck responsive chords in each state. And this, in turn, depended on conceptions of society and of the classes within it.

Basically, the world view of Massachusetts reformers reflected, accepted, and welcomed the destabilizing features of nineteenth-century American life. In South Carolina, a more traditional conception of the place of crime and the penal system in the social order, buttressed by slavery, obviated the need for reforms, and, accordingly, for official collective action to secure them.

Penal reformers in Massachusetts were prepared to come to grips with the new social order that was transforming antebellum America. They spoke to the needs and perceptions of a society in flux,

35. Only Henry W. DeSaussure and Isaac Hayne publicly supported the Auburn plan. See Phillip Tidyman, *Letters on the Pennsylvania System of Solitary Imprisonment*, p. 5; Isaac W. Hayne, *Report to His Excellency the Governor on Prisons, Prison Discipline, and the Criminal Law*, p. 14.

encountering new problems. The stoic acceptance of social reality associated with Calvinism was replaced by Enlightenment optimism and Utilitarian pragmatism. Statistics replaced sermons as the most convincing arguments for social change. In short, the reform program, for all its unbridled optimism, unrealistic expectations, and tendencies toward homogenization and social control, was a positive attempt to reassert man's direction of his own destiny in the face of upheaval.

Ironically, Massachusetts became a negative model for South Carolina. Private feuds between the two states, such as the expulsion of Samuel Hoar and the caning of Charles Sumner by Preston Brooks, heightened the sense that each state stood for a set of conflicting values. Riots and fugitive slave rescues in Boston convinced South Carolinians that, by contrast, they were a peaceful, law-abiding people. Even an article that praised education in Massachusetts and suggested that South Carolina adopt its best features ridiculed the Bay State's interest in social inquiry that led to a "dislike" for "old things."[36]

Discarding any nostalgic yearning for simpler times, social reformers in Massachusetts frankly admitted the correlation between the perceived increase in crime and poverty and the progress of urbanization and industrialization. Few attempted to justify the existence of crime and poverty as the product of divine will or as the result of inherent moral defects. Man had built cities and factories; it was within his power to cure the accompanying social ills. This perception, however, did not guarantee that the cures offered would be either effective or appropriate. Secular panaceas, such as education, temperance, and penal reform, replaced religious ones. To the extent that these goals were compatible with the man-centered ideology of the new sects, religion could support these worldly activities.[37]

Although quick to embrace the material prosperity of the fledgling industrial order, reformers were alarmed to see it accompanied by extremes of wealth, unprecedented poverty, and increases in all forms of undesirable behavior, from crime and riots to drunkenness and prostitution. Reformers hoped that Massachusetts could avoid the experience of England and enjoy the prosperity of the machine age with a minimum of social dislocation. Horace Mann was quick to credit industry and commerce for the state's prosperity, but he

36. "Education in Europe," p. 1.
37. In general see Timothy L. Smith, *Revivalism and Social Reform*. Mann explicitly devoted himself to "subvert[ing] Calvinism" (Mann to Howe, 4 June 1846, Horace Mann Papers, MHS).

was not blind to their consequences. "By its industrial condition and its business operations," he explained "[Massachusetts] is exposed, far beyond any other state in the Union, to the fatal extremes of overgrown wealth and desperate poverty."[38] But reformers responded positively to this nascent industrial order in another way. They determined that the same virtues that were prized in this new order—diligence, thrift, and discipline—could be imparted to the less advantaged classes to salvage them from their habits of idleness, sloth, and vice. Industrialists and reformers shared the same values and goals. One penal institution was actually called the House of Industry, combining in its name, and presumably also in its mission, the two special models of nineteenth-century reform—family and factory.

Penitentiaries promised an opportunity to instill these necessary virtues in a captive and probably unreceptive population. In an interesting and ironic way, the profit, production, and discipline goals of the prison were the same as those of the factory. Not surprisingly, many factory owners were also active in prison reform.[39] This is an interesting connection because of the possibility that the new industrialists influenced the direction of the prison, confident of the factory as a model institution of production. It is ironic, moreover, because industrialization was frequently linked with the crime the prisons were built to cure.

Both the prison and the factory were large-scale institutions; both required disciplined labor; both proclaimed in their architecture the pride of their founders. And yet, it would be anachronistic and far-fetched to see in the system of prison production and discipline any sense that the purpose of the prison was, as Mann's biographer inelegantly put it, to "housebreak the masses."[40] The organization of both factory and prison was in part determined by size, in part by success. The connection is important for what it suggests about nineteenth-century enterprise, for the impact of the factory system as a model for society, and for the profits the prison was expected to produce if it acted like a factory.

But the involvement of the Appletons and the Lawrences is also important because of the alleged relationship between industrial-

38. Horace Mann, *Annual Reports on Education*, p. 668 [from the *Twelfth Report*, 1848].

39. Sumner to A. A. Lawrence, 29 June 1846; Louis Dwight to A. A. Lawrence, 20 April 1839; William Bowditch to A. A. Lawrence, 26 Oct. 1844, 27 Oct. 1844, all in Lawrence Papers, MHS; *Dictionary of American Biography*, 2:46–49; Amos Lawrence, *Extracts from the Diary and Correspondence of the Late Amos Lawrence*, pp. 235, 308.

40. Messerli, *Mann*, p. 346.

ization and crime. Industrialization *per se* was not blamed as a cause of crime. But there did seem to be a correlation between crime and industrialization, and in the world of nineteenth-century social theory, a correlation frequently was mistaken for a cause. The correlation was so feared that "no news" quite literally became "good news." One foreign visitor pointed out that the workers of Springfield, Massachusetts, were free from crime and vice. Lieber toured one of Nathan Appleton's mills in Lowell and remarked upon the millgirls' honesty. Occasionally they would steal a bobbin or some cotton, he noted, "but when told that it is theft, they are surprised and frightened."[41] But industrialists were nevertheless held responsible for attendant social dislocations, as exemplified by a revealing exchange between one of the most prominent industrialists and a reformer of equal stature.

In 1841, Dorothea Dix solicited a contribution of books from Nathan Appleton for use in the Middlesex County Jail in East Cambridge. In making the request, she acknowledged his ready support of benevolent causes. But Dix went one step further, arguing that Appleton had a special obligation to aid such causes because he was responsible for the social ills she was trying to correct. She claimed that "many of the male prisoners—and much the largest proportion of female inmates are received from Lowell. . . . [P]erhaps in a population of operatives . . . nothing better . . . could be expected—and allowing for the variety of exciting causes, probably Lowell may possess no greater proportionate amount of immoral residents than other towns." Appleton gave the donation, but defended his operatives. "Industry well-paid has no temptation to vice," he argued, and suggested that those addicted to idleness and crime were outsiders who came to Lowell to prey off industry. A Lowell Police Court justice supported this view, blaming his crowded dockets on those seeking work in the town.[42] But Dix held Appleton accountable for "the variety of exciting causes." Just as reformers were concerned about problems created by industry, millowners had an interest in using the state to help instill and enforce the values needed in a successful work force. In 1868, for example, industrialists protested loosening the liquor laws on the grounds that such

41. Carl David Arfwedson, *The United States and Canada in 1832, 1833, 1834,* 2:120–21; Lieber, "Visit to the Boot Mills at Lowell . . . Statistics, Conduct of the Factory Girls," 16 Aug. 1838 (with subsequent newspaper clippings), MS. in Lieber Papers.

42. Dorothea Lynde Dix to Nathan Appleton, 28 July 1841; Appleton to Dix, 29 Oct. 1841; Appleton Papers, MHS; Michael B. Katz, *The Irony of Early School Reform,* pp. 171–72.

action would impair the productivity of their workers.[43] In Massachusetts, it is clear that there was no inevitable clash of interests between the advocates of social reform in this field and the dominant economic interests in the state. Again, there is no allegation of conspiracy; rather, this observation shows the relationship between the world view of reformers and the world they confronted.

Social critics in South Carolina shared much of this ideology, but employed it to rout efforts for change. Here, as in Massachusetts, crime was blamed on such modern ills as industry and immigrants. The state had been spared these calamities and therefore had little to fear, or so it was claimed, from their deleterious effects. Even in support of a penitentiary, Attorney General Isaac Hayne felt compelled to repeat the litany. "We have no large cities," he conceded, "the population is nowhere dense . . . [we] have been less subjected to the corruption of foreign immigration."[44] As long as South Carolina perceived no predatory attacks on property from whites, there was no need to erect costly edifices. The dissenting members of Perry's committee stated this view explicitly. The penitentiary, they argued, would be "applied to one-half of our population and that is not the part from which crime usually proceeds."[45]

Such statements, coupled with South Carolina's patterns of crimes of violence among whites, might indicate that only when property is threatened does a society willingly allocate resources to a penal system.

South Carolina was not totally unconcerned about crimes of personal violence. Dueling was not universally applauded. Murder was both prosecuted and punished vigorously. In the 1840s and 1850s, grand juries expressed concern about the carrying of concealed weapons, and in 1858, the legislature enacted a penalty for such conduct.[46] By and large, however, crime in South Carolina was associated almost exclusively with either passions or slaves, and since no thought was given to imprisoning convicted slaves and little could be done about the passions, there was no need for a penitentiary. Thus, even while employing the same causal inferences between crime and modern society used in Massachusetts, South Carolina could justify its continued inaction.

43. *Fifth Annual Report, MBSC,* 1868, p. 36.
44. Hayne, *Report,* p. 4.
45. Benjamin F. Perry, *Report of the Special Committee . . . on the Subject of the Penitentiary System, Counter Report,* p. 1.
46. 12 *Statutes at Large* 634–35; Spartanburg Grand Jury, Fall 1837, 1839; Abbeville Grand Jury, 1838, 1849; Anderson Grand Jury, 1839; Barnwell Grand Jury, 1854; Presentments, Legal System Papers.

A second major difference between the two states was in the methods of social analysis. In Massachusetts, reformers were strongly influenced by English Utilitarian philosophy. Many had eagerly devoured the works of Jeremy Bentham, especially his tracts on codification and prison reform. The Utilitarian attitude swept through many areas of American reform. Although Lieber and Rantoul were not doctrinaire Benthamites, there is a strong Utilitarian strain in their attitudes and proposals. At the heart of Bentham's theory of legislation and his desire for codification was the conviction that law could and should be reduced to a science; this was one of Rantoul's goals. Finally, the Utilitarians in England were among the first to examine social phenomena through the use of statistics. Again, people such as Lieber, Rantoul, Howe, and Mann reflect this spirit.

The use of statistics in social analysis had become increasingly important in antebellum America, independent of Bentham. But the particular use men such as Rantoul and Lieber made of statistics reveals their intellectual debts to Utilitarianism. Both men had an insatiable appetite for quantifiable data. Complaining that the United States had no centralized body to gather statistical information, Lieber suggested creation of such a department with himself as head and encouraged expansion of the information collected by the census.[47] Thwarted in his attempt to become official statistician, Lieber pursued that goal vicariously, gathering information on everything from the inevitable commerce and population figures to the cost of intoxicating liquors in Great Britain ($400 million annually), the upkeep of churches (titled by Lieber, "Expense of Civilization"), and the per capita bread consumption in Ohio.[48]

Rantoul lacked such personal ambitions, but his appetite for statistics was as voracious as Lieber's. More than a mere collector, he used his statistics to promote his political positions. His data on capital convictions and executions in Massachusetts from 1780 to 1847 helped prove his case that juries were reluctant to convict when penalties were excessive. He compared the cost of prisons to the losses due to crime, naively assuming that the first expense might reduce the latter. To determine the beneficial effects of free

47. Lieber to Joseph Henry, 22 Oct. 1847, Lieber Papers; Lieber to Nathan Appleton, 21 Jan. 1834, Appleton Papers; Lieber to Jared Sparks, 25 Jan. 1834, Sparks to Lieber, 4 Feb. 1834, Sparks Papers.

48. Francis Lieber, scrapbook entitled "Items of Political Economy," Bancroft Library, University of California, Berkeley; Introduction to Gustave de Beaumont and Alexis de Tocqueville, *On the Penitentiary System in the United States and Its Application in France*, p. xxviii.

trade, Rantoul assiduously assembled trade statistics. Seeking greater accuracy, he (or his father) recomputed population and tax schedules in his native Beverly. Finally, like Mann, he tried to compute the economic productivity of education, complete with an accounting of the total economic output of Massachusetts.[49]

Statistics permeated many areas of social reform. Reports from prisons, state agencies, and local jails regularly touted the virtues of accumulating social statistics. Efforts were constantly made to improve the collection as well as the presentation of such materials. The annual reports on commitments to jails and houses of correction, for example, underwent four major changes in format in forty years; the attorney general's report went through five changes in twenty-three years. But statistics could be abused as well. In the 1870s, the Board of State Charities complained that penal statistics overestimated the extent of reformation.[50]

The Utilitarian philosophy and the accompanying use of statistics are clearly identifiable as modern modes of social analysis, not dissimilar from contemporary empirical social science. By substituting the hedonic calculus for scripture, proponents of this approach encouraged a flexible response to social conditions. The impact of Utilitarians in English social reform, especially in such crucial areas as public health and penology, has long been recognized. Yet many American reformers, often unaware of their debt to Bentham, perceived the world with a similar methodological vision.

In South Carolina, by contrast, Utilitarian ideas and methods barely got a foothold. Lieber's views on statistics and other Utilitarian concerns were rarely publicized in the South. His proposal to become chief statistician was an effort to leave South Carolina. In his orations on science and codification, Thomas S. Grimké was perhaps the most Utilitarian of native South Carolina reformers, but his influence was minimal. Thomas Cooper, who praised Bentham in his own writings on codification, was hounded out of office as president of South Carolina College by militant Presbyterians who objected to the atheism they saw as inherent in the doctrine. Cooper's successor was a leading Presbyterian, James Henly Thornwell, who bitterly denounced Utilitarianism as a godless ideology.[51]

49. Robert Rantoul, "Lecture on Capital Punishment," "Census of Beverly for 1810 and 1820 and for other Years together with a Variety of Statistical Facts Collected by Robert Rantoul," MS. volume, Rantoul Papers; Robert Rantoul, Jr., "The Education of a Free People," [1839] in *Memoirs, Speeches, and Writings of Robert Rantoul, Jr.,* pp. 125, 138–39.

50. *Seventh Annual Report, MBSC,* 1870, p. 207.

51. Thomas Cooper, "Bentham's *Judicial Evidence,*" pp. 381–426; Clement C. Eaton, *The Freedom of Thought Struggle in the Old South,* pp. 304–7; James Henly

Statistics fared little better; most social data were unavailable in South Carolina. No one knew what the probable utilization of a penitentiary would be; no such information had been collected. In 1838, Perry solicited conviction records from local courthouses. But this was a one-time effort, and Perry complained that his committee had "not been able to obtain all the information they could desire." Proposals to study the penitentiary question stressed the importance of gathering such data.[52] Not surprisingly, opponents of a prison were able to rely on impressionistic observations of light dockets and empty jails.

This situation was not confined to penal matters. In the 1850s, South Carolina attempted to establish a statewide system of vital registration. In a rare concession, the system was deliberately modeled on that of Massachusetts, the first and most successful program of its sort in the country. The Massachusetts registration law was reprinted for the South Carolina legislature as the example to follow. But South Carolina was unable to emulate the success of its northern foil. In the first few years, only a minority of all districts yielded any returns. This was not simply a rural phenomenon; the worst returns came from Charleston.[53] The problem was quite revealing. The registration law provided no reimbursement for collecting and reporting the information and stipulated no penalty for failure to comply. In South Carolina, one needed both carrot and stick. The law was amended to provide a small fee for recording and reporting and a fine for failure to do so.

Both in method and in basic outlook, the proponents for change in both states utilized different types of social analysis. In part, this simply reflected social reality. Massachusetts was consciously aware of its factories, cities, immigrants, and crime. Social change, if not welcome, certainly could not be avoided or ignored. But South Carolina lacked even that external spur. Indeed, the fact that South Carolina society had apparently changed so little seemed to mock those who demanded drastic and immediate change. Reform meant potential interference with a social system that seemed to function, if not smoothly, at least with a minimum of formal effort.

Thornwell, Oration to the Clarisophic Society of South Carolina College, 1839, James Henly Thornwell Papers, SCL.

52. Report on the Penitentiary, 6 Dec. 1849, Penal System Papers; Miscellaneous notes in B. F. Perry's handwriting, n.d., Reports and Resolutions, ibid.; Bills, 1854, SCA; *South Carolina House Journal*, 1849, p. 116; Benjamin F. Perry, *Report of the Special Committee Appointed at the Session of 1838 on the Subject of the Penitentiary*, p. 18.

53. *South Carolina Reports and Resolutions*, 1857, pp. 176–80; Registrar's Report Relating to Births, Deaths, and Marriages, 1858, p. 76; *Legislative Times*, p. 80.

This was a key difference between the two states. As a society undergoing rapid change, Massachusetts was constantly reacting to that process and experimenting with ways to meet or manage that transformation. To do so in South Carolina was apparently unnecessary and potentially dangerous. Any tinkering with South Carolina's apparent social and political stability raised the fear of a black revolt for freedom or a white uprising for political participation. The final, most significant difference in the success and orientation of efforts for change in the two states is based on this understanding of actual and perceived change and highlights most clearly the intellectual and social chasms that separated the states. This contrast can be understood most vividly in each state's views of social class and the relationship between class and crime.

No dictionary definition does justice to the connotations suggested by the term "class." For the purpose of this analysis, class implies groups of people in society sharing similar status and values. Class is not simply correlated with income or ethnicity, although strong associations with each are likely. Class lines are not absolutely fixed, but they are distinct and difficult to cross. It is impossible as well as unnecessary to define social classes here; social scientists have struggled with such definitions for generations. For us, what is important is to know what this term meant to those who contemplated the nature of civil society and how to change it. If one believed that class lines were fixed or strong, then social change became far less possible, and the impact of reform was far more marginal. Conversely, if membership in classes was fluid, if classes always existed, but the composition constantly shifted, then social change seemed within reach.

The notion of class itself preceded the industrial era. But new classes were formed by industrialization, urbanization, and (particularly in America) international and internal migration. These classes were formed by disruption, rather than by the previously acceptable means of tradition and gradual evolution. Some of these new classes were seen as sinister, deviant, or threatening; they were scorned and feared by those who believed such distinctions to be both inevitable and inflexible. As Raymond Williams argues, "It is obvious that this . . . new use of class does not indicate the beginning of social division. . . . But it indicates . . . a change in the character of these divisions and it records . . . a change in attitudes toward them."[54]

The meaning of class to social reformers in Massachusetts under-

54. Raymond Williams, *Culture and Society, 1780–1950*, p. xiii.

went many changes in less than half a century. Creeping into the language initially as an optimistic term, by the end of the period, class had acquired the more sinister overtones of rigidity. In South Carolina, by contrast, class terminology seemed to be virtually enlisted in the service of the ruling elite's ideology. Supportive of a system of legitimation, rather than reflective of social reality, this view of social class buttressed the status quo and helped block even the most modest alterations in the legal, penal, and political systems.

The use of class terminology and the perceptions of the classes thus distinguished and described had a profound effect on social policy in the Bay State. The rigidity implied by class conflicted with the commitment of the penal system to reformation and, indeed, with the commitment of society to equality of opportunity, at least for whites. Throughout much of the nineteenth century, reformers in Massachusetts had it both ways, describing the social classes they wanted to salvage. When despair began to replace optimism after the Civil War, social analysis already had the vocabulary, description, and evidence of such classes to draw on in order to prove their persistence.

Reformers in Massachusetts freely accepted the existence of class divisions in society as the inevitable product of modern life. "Poverty, vice, and crime . . . in our day, are, in fact, in some measure the necessary consequences of the social state," wrote Josiah Quincy in his classic report of 1822.[55] Quincy's ideas were reflected in much subsequent reform thought. "The dangerous class," wrote Theodore Parker, "is the unavoidable result of our present civilization."[56] Howe held a similar view. "The congregation of men in great cities and other *necessary places of civilization*," he wrote, "engender a class which is aptly called the criminal or dangerous class."[57]

Having acknowledged such a class, it was necessary to define its membership. Almost all reformers agreed that there were two distinct groups in the dangerous classes—what Parker called the foes of society and the victims. The foes were those who, either by birth or moral deficiency, were beyond reclamation. The victims of soci-

---

55. Josiah Quincy, *Remarks on Some of the Provisions of the Laws of Massachusetts Affecting Poverty, Vice, and Crime,* p. 4; see also Redmond Barnett, "A Viperous Brood of Beggars."

56. Theodore Parker, "The Dangerous Classes," in *Works,* 10:178.

57. Samuel Gridley Howe, *A Letter to J. H. Wilkins, H. B. Rogers, and F. B. Fay, Commissioners of Massachusetts for the State Reform School for Girls,* p. 12. Emphasis added.

ety were those born and reared in poverty, left unschooled and un-skilled.[58] The latter, particularly its younger members, could be saved; it was the duty of the state to rescue them. This second class was by far larger than the first.

The distinction between victims and foes was critical to the formation of social policy. By minimizing the contributions of birth and innate nature, this concept obligated the state to reclaim those who, but for fortune, could be productive members of society. Furthermore, the existence of a smaller class of those beyond redemption saved penal experiments from the charge of failure. Finally, such distinctions encouraged the principle of selection and separation within penal institutions and the distribution of convicts and delinquents according to age, sex, and prior convictions.

In America, with no hereditary peasant class, people first became aware of classes in the urban environment. Cities, as Howe's comments indicate, were blamed for the existence of classes. This association led to a distinctly antiurban bias in much reform sentiment and programs, a jarringly backward-looking feature. The city itself was seen as the source of evil; tenements were described as incubators of crime.[59] Howe and Augustus, among others, believed that young offenders could be reclaimed if they were taken from the city. Augustus bailed out people on the promise of relocating them in stable family settings in the country. Howe proposed this solution as a substitute for costly and corrupting reformatories.[60]

Those who shared this view were motivated less by a nostalgic vision of country life than by their environmentalist view of class. Cities provided the opportunity, in the sheer concentration of population, for classes to form. Holding to a contagion theory of criminality—with all the appropriate and vivid medical analogies—many believed that impressionable youths had to be separated from bad influences. Those who could form a criminal *class* in cities should be dispersed in families throughout the state.

Where institutions were absolutely necessary, the preferred model was complete separation; Howe, Mann, Sumner, and others championed the Pennsylvania system of complete solitary confinement. All other institutions, to use one prevalent metaphor, were nothing but schools for vice. Eventually the resemblance between patterns of congregation in cities and those in prisons would lead some to view the institutions in the same light as the city, but

58. Parker, "Dangerous Classes," pp. 158–59; Howe, Mann, and Rantoul shared a similar view.

59. *Prisoner's Friend* 2 (1850): 202–3; 1 (1848): 68–70; 2 (1849): 129.

60. Howe, *Letter to J. H. Wilkins*, pp. 12–15; Augustus, *Report*, p. 23.

institutions proved no easier to dismantle than the cities that produced the inmates.

This early view of class can be described as an optimistic one. The explicit environmentalism blamed class distinctions on upbringing —on poverty, intemperance, and ignorance. But such stratification needed to be nipped in the bud. "The distance between the two extremes of society is lengthening instead of being abridged," observed Horace Mann. If nothing was done to narrow the gap, the poorer classes would be in a state of servility relative to the richer.[61]

Even though reformers valued and acknowledged (and, of course, supported) private philanthropy, the problems of poverty, crime, and vice were too extreme to be left to voluntarism. Temperance pledges were insufficient; licensing and retail restrictions were necessary. State action could be both promotive, as in the case of education, or coercive, as with temperance. In any event, these reformers held a view of state power that was expansive, inclusive, and activist. Even in areas on the periphery of social reform, they were confident that the state could and should promote their own personal values in order to achieve the general good. It is no coincidence that early in his career, Mann added an antiobscenity clause to the *Revised Statutes* or that Howe initiated the blasphemy prosecution of Abner Kneeland.[62]

A corollary of environmentalism was that no distinct group, ethnic, racial, or religious, was inherently depraved or inclined toward criminality. If certain groups were overrepresented in almshouses and penal institutions—and observers knew immediately which ones were—it was simply because of their condition in society. Thus, in 1826, the Boston Prison Discipline Society called attention to the high proportion of blacks in the Massachusetts State Prison, but attributed it entirely to "the degraded character of the colored population." [63] This did not mean that no relationship was drawn between blacks, immigrants, and crime. Quite the contrary; race and nativity were among the first variables considered by reformers when the Massachusetts State Prison opened in 1805; and in the 1830s and 1840s, prison officials prided themselves on the small number of Massachusetts-born whites who were inmates. After the Civil War, they expected their institutions to be overrun by former

61. Mann, *Annual Reports*, pp. 666–70.

62. Messerli, *Mann*, pp. 119–20, 122, 327; *Revised Statutes of Massachusetts*, ch. 130, sec. 10; Leonard W. Levy, *The Law of the Commonwealth and Chief Justice Shaw*, p. 43.

63. *First Annual Report of the Board of Managers of the Prison Discipline Society*, pp. 12, 23–24.

slaves coming North without skills or capital.[64] Even the environmentalism of 1826 was a bit strained. The Prison Discipline Society advocated racial segregation in penal institutions, allegedly for the blacks' own good, but suggested that if education and other efforts to improve the character of the black population in the North failed, colonization would be the only resort.[65]

Of course, it is obvious that the constant overrepresentation of blacks and foreign-born in all Massachusetts prisons both resulted from and in turn fueled strong suspicions about the innate depravity of these groups. But Massachusetts reformers retained their faith in reformation until the Civil War. This conviction that class lines need not be fixed enabled them to speak and write with candor about the existence of social classes in a democratic republic. Similarly, reformers shunned the strong nativist movement that dominated the state's politics in the mid-1850s.

Because of the conviction that improved social conditions alone could eliminate the source of crime, environmentalism prompted a reliance on simple solutions. Reformers sought miracle cures for society's ailments. Mann maintained that education alone would reduce class antagonisms.[66] Parker argued that the difference between the poor and the criminal and everybody else was the "result of education and circumstance."[67] Others, blaming crime on intemperance, believed that prohibition would solve all social ills. It is this faith in the imposition of one particular set of values and norms that historians have described as social control.[68] It was control, in that this attitude marshaled the resources of the state to support one particular ideology, but it was perhaps less intentional, perhaps even less effective, than has been described. Some types of social control were resisted. After he supported a restrictive liquor bill, Robert Rantoul, Jr., was voted out of office by the workingmen whose cause he championed but whom he poorly understood.[69] A similar group in Rantoul's Beverly closed a high school that it sensed was promoting values in conflict with their own.[70]

Reformers were most vulnerable in their insistence that such panaceas as temperance, education, and prison reform held the cure for society's ills. These simplistic notions were well-intended and

64. *Report of the State Prison,* 1865, p. 22.
65. *First Annual Report BPDS,* p. 12.
66. Mann, *Annual Reports,* pp. 669–70.
67. Theodore Parker, "The Perishing Classes," *Works,* 10:118
68. The historians who have taken this line are Messerli, *Mann;* David J. Rothman, *The Discovery of the Asylum;* and Katz, *Irony.*
69. Robert DeGroff Bulkley, Jr., "Robert Rantoul, Jr., 1805–1852," pp. 229–30.
70. Katz, *Irony,* pp. 19–27.

awakened the state's conscience. But reformers' overriding confidence, bordering on arrogance, inevitably set the stage for disappointment and, with that, reaction.

Ironically, once attuned to distinctions in society based on wealth, race, and ethnicity, some reformers began to view the entire criminal process in a new light. They understood that the criminal law itself was class-based and reflected values that were neither universally shared nor respected. Parker noted that the Irish hardly condemned brawling or drinking, two of the offenses for which they were frequently arrested. Moreover, he believed, they were rarely guilty of the most serious offenses. In 1861, the state's attorney general complained about the delay in punishments for minor offenses and wondered openly "if common assaults, drunkenness, liquor selling, and other kindred offenses deserve the infliction of any penalty."[71] In 1870, the Massachusetts Board of State Charities challenged the repeated arrests of drunks and prostitutes, charging that they served no purpose other than temporary removal of unsavory individuals from city streets.[72]

Moreover, not all serious crime was street crime followed by arrest. A few reformers were openly critical of the class bias in law enforcement. As Parker put it, the poor "commit the crimes *that go punished by law.*"[73] An attorney general, among others, complained about the infrequency of prosecutions for such white collar crimes as fraud.[74] To Samuel May, the poor were of a different class simply because of their poverty. Implying that there were no other fundamental or immutable differences, May claimed, "Let the poor be represented in the legislature and they will enact laws that ensure equality of property."[75] May found few sympathetic followers.

By the 1860s, faith in reform was waning. The first signs of abandonment of the environmentalist perspective and its replacement with a less flexible doctrine had appeared. This came about for two reasons. First, quite simply, the millennialist expectations of antebellum reformers had not been met. Although many parts of the social reform platform had been enacted as public policy, no fundamental change in the nature of society was evident. The problems that had originally inspired so much agitation had not disappeared.

71. *Annual Report of the Attorney General for the Year Ending December 31, 1861.*

72. *Seventh Annual Report MBSC,* 1870, pp. 11–45.

73. Parker, "Poverty," *Works,* 9:265. Emphasis added.

74. Parker, "Crime and Punishment," *Works,* 9:342–43; *Report of the Attorney General* (1842, Senate Document no. 20), p. 6.

75. *Prisoner's Friend* 7 (1855): 347–48.

The distance between the social classes that had caused Mann so much worry had not been narrowed. Crime had not noticeably decreased; rather, in the years following the Civil War, it had substantially increased. Second, the institutions had failed. As the masters of jails and houses of correction admitted in 1871, they were "sufficiently impressed with the dark side of human nature [to] have no overwhelming faith in reformatory measures."[76]

Perhaps no one person better exemplified these shifting views toward crime and the criminal class than Samuel Gridley Howe. In a public career that spanned over half a century, he founded one of the first institutions for the dependent classes, the Perkins School for the deaf, dumb, and blind. As a pioneer of another sort, he sounded the first cautionary notes on the value of prisons, asylums, and reformatories. Like Parker, Mann, and Augustus, Howe blamed cities for congregating people together in classes. But more than the others, Howe realized that the same evil could be created in institutions that also congregated people together. One could do little about the evils of cities except to remove miscreants from them, as Augustus had done and as Howe intended to do. But Howe carried this logic one step further. People had not consciously created cities in order to perpetuate evil, but people and governments had created institutions to prevent and correct it. To Howe, it was incumbent upon the state to reduce class distinctions and tensions and not to do anything that would increase them.

The first inkling of Howe's departure from orthodoxy came in 1847 in his attack on the Boston Prison Discipline Society. Howe championed the separate system, thinking that it would prevent the contagion of crime from spreading within penal institutions. Since the state owed convicts reformation, it had no right to subject them to possible contamination. "The convict is still a man," he wrote, "and like the rest of men, subject to all those influences, for good or evil, which make the rest of us what we are." The prisoner was to forfeit his liberty "but nothing more." His famous convict's prayer began, "In the name of justice do not surround me with bad associates and evil influences . . . remove me from my old companions and surround me with virtuous associates."[77]

Howe believed that the only separate system could avoid the deleterious effects of contagion. When his efforts in support of this system failed, he became disillusioned with all such institutions and over the next two decades gradually abandoned them. Whereas

76. *Report of the Committee on Prisons* (1871).
77. Samuel Gridley Howe, *Report of a Minority of the Special Committee of the Boston Prison Discipline Society*, pp. 40–41.

the prison was once intended to remove the convict from evil external influences, Howe came to believe that prisons segregated the convict "from all the ordinary and wholesome influences of family and society." The same criticisms applied to all similarly segregated institutions. The evils "are merely *intensified* when the persons are of one class, as of convicted criminals."[78]

Howe believed that penal, reformatory, and even rehabilitative institutions could actually create a class out of people who may have shared only certain characteristics. In the 1850s, he opposed the establishment of a reformatory for juvenile girls for precisely this reason, preferring instead to place them with country families. Even the act of imprisonment helped create a class because of the stigma attached to it. The shame, he believed, "will stick to them for life." Howe feared that even his own Perkins school was becoming an asylum.[79]

In 1863, the Massachusetts Board of State Charities was created to oversee most of the charitable and correctional facilities in the state. Howe, as chairman, wrote the preface to the second report. Representing the culmination of all of Howe's experiences, anxieties, and uncertainties, the report contained three startling conclusions. First, institutions should be avoided wherever possible. Second, institutions, once built, are durable and tenacious. Third, the criminal class was created not only by environment, but also by bad stock. All three points would have been considered heresy had they not come from the pen of the man who knew those institutions more intimately than practically anyone else in the state.

In advocating community and family-based care and corrections instead of institutions, Howe merely followed the logic of the direction he had taken in the previous two decades. Confinement, he argued, actually created the criminal class. While not explicitly urging a dismantling of prisons, his intention and dissatisfactions were clear. If he could, he would have closed down nearly every other type of reformatory, asylum, or almshouse. He also recognized the tendency of institutions to take on lives of their own, continuing as "landmarks" long after they had ceased to perform their function properly. "There is still," Howe complained, "a lingering superstition about the virtues of great institutions. . . . So strongly built, so richly endowed . . . [they] cannot be got rid of so easily."[80]

78. Howe, "Treatment of Prisoners" (n.d.), Howe Papers.
79. Schwartz, *Howe*, p. 272; see also Howe, *Letter to J. H. Wilkins*, and in general, Steven L. Schlossman, *Love and the American Delinquent*.
80. *Second Annual Report MBSC*, 1865, p. xli.

Howe also wondered whether the traditional notions of social class were still applicable. He continued to caution against too strict a use of class terminology, warning that this could create classes rather than merely describe them. "It is undesirable," he complained, "to use such terms as the pauper class, the criminal class, and the like; for such is the strength of association of ideas, that giving a name helps to strengthen the characteristics which it is meant to express." But even after such admonitions, Howe conceded, "No sharply defined classes exist *as yet* in our state," though *"there is a tendency to their formation."*[81]

Howe's apparent uncertainty as to the formation of social classes was a product of this reconsideration of the causes of class distinctions. Essentially, he still believed that birth and environment created the criminal class. But did the causes still act in the same proportion? Was it possible, for example, that the innately depraved were increasing, rather than decreasing, in proportion to the impoverished and ignorant majority?

In the second annual Board of State Charities report, Howe revised the distinction between innate depravity and environmental influences and combined them into something he called "stock." Stock was initially created by the environment, but could be passed on.[82] Over several generations, undesirable traits could be expunged—or new ones added—depending upon the quality of life one led. Inevitably, Howe found that the foreign-born provided bad stock, although this was primarily a consequence of their history of degraded living conditions and presumably could be reversed. To demonstrate the frailty of immigrant stock, Howe published mortality findings comparing a Catholic cemetery with Brahmin Mt. Auburn cemetery. Catholic families had significantly higher infant mortality rates.[83] Because stock was an amalgam of heredity and environment, Howe did not conclude or suggest that reformation efforts should be abandoned. Later generations would conclude exactly that. As Howe had feared, descriptions of class would become definitions, and reformatory institutions would simply incarcerate.

Thus, by 1863, reformers in Massachusetts had not only accepted the notion of classes in modern society, but had come to believe that class lines could be fairly rigid and could not be eliminated overnight. This view took reformers off the hook, for their proposals could no longer be blamed for their failure to alter the innate nature

81. Ibid., p. xix. Emphasis added.
82. Ibid., pp. xxiii–xxx.
83. Ibid., p. xxx.

of certain groups. At the same time, it took some of the urgency out of social reform. Crime and poverty could no longer be ended in a single generation, if indeed they could be ended at all.

This view of the social order, therefore, had an ironic touch. Just as it was a starkly realistic description, it led to pragmatic conclusions. The idealism that gave rise to the penitentiary was replaced by the realism that retained it, if not for reformation, then for incarceration. Howe anticipated this result and unsuccessfully opposed it; others saw this same result and welcomed it. The acceptance of class and stock meant that no one need question the failure of penal reform or the need for prisons.

The concept of class was also an essential part of social thought in South Carolina. "No society has ever existed," observed James Henry Hammond, "without a marked variety of classes."[84] But instead of reflecting social conditions or stimulating social reform, the South Carolina notion of class obscured reality and was used to support an ideology and (ironically) a planter class that thrived on the status quo.

South Carolina recognized only two groups in society, black and white, confusing race, power, and economic status. In 1858, Hammond articulated this view most explicitly, and his famous description deserves to be quoted at length:

> In all social systems there must be a class to do the menial duties, to perform the drudgery of life. That is a class requiring but a low order of intellect and but little skill. Its requisites are vigor, docility, fidelity. Such a class you must have or you would not have that other class which leads progress, civilization, and refinement. It constitutes the mud-sill of society. . . . Fortunately, for the South, she found a race adapted to that purpose at hand. . . . We use them for our purpose and call them slaves.[85]

Black slaves served all the functions of the lower, dangerous, and criminal classes. Why was there apparently little crime? Governor Seabrook credited this to the state's "exemption from the evils of foreign immigration." That class was replaced in South Carolina by slaves, who were "rarely guilty of a heinous offense." Attorney General Hayne, who supported a penitentiary, boasted that "more than half our population, and the portion amongst whom, *from their*

84. James Henry Hammond, *Selections from the Letters and Speeches of the Hon. James H. Hammond of South Carolina*, p. 110.
85. Ibid., pp. 318–19.

position, crime would most naturally abound, are slaves who are kept in order without resort to the courts."[86]

The policy implications of this view were clear. With slaves serving as the lower orders, crime was not seen as the result of poverty or ignorance, but rather of race and status. The only problem was that South Carolina's white criminals were lost in the shuffle. A member of Perry's committee who opposed a penitentiary claimed that South Carolinians were not a "numerous and crime committing people whose crimes proceeded from the unhappy condition of the working classes who are in want of their labor and bread."[87] There was an uncanny congruence between reality and perception on this point. The observable pattern of white crime, with its high proportion of prosecutions for personal violence, bore out the contention that crime was a matter of passions, not need.

The association of crime with race meant that for the most part, no important environmentalist thought surfaced in the state. The view that white crime was the result of passions, not of innate defects or bad influences, had three implications. First, it suggested that crime in South Carolina was neither especially serious nor solvable. Second, it assumed that there was no fundamental error in the criminal that could be corrected: vengeance and deterrence were thus acceptable objects of punishment. Third, this view implied that reformation was unnecessary and impossible. As one penitentiary opponent sneered, "We have little faith in the reformation of criminals."[88] This conception of the social order in South Carolina neatly accounts for the state's intransigence on penal reform. No penitentiary was needed if the state had little serious crime except that committed by slaves. In short, the very nature of South Carolina society justified not building a penitentiary.

Penal reform, of course, was not the only area in which this view stifled activity for social welfare. South Carolina, like many other southern states, lacked a free school system supported by general taxation. What little school funds existed were apportioned according to the wealth of the district. This was justified, with no intended

86. Whitemarsh Seabrook, *Message of the Governor* (1850), p. 17; Hayne, *Report*, p. 4; emphasis added. It is interesting to note that free blacks were sent to penitentiaries in some states, but not for reformatory purposes. When the Virginia penitentiary was too crowded in 1822, free blacks convicted of felonies were whipped and sold into slavery. In Delaware and Maryland, at various times free blacks were whipped or sold out of state. This sheds light not merely on the status of free blacks, but also on the southern concept of class (Ira Berlin, *Slaves without Masters*, p. 183).

87. Col. D. F. Jamison to B. F. Perry, n.d., but probably 1839, in *Reports*, Penal System Papers, SCA.

88. "The Penitentiary Question in South Carolina," p. 367.

irony, because the poor districts had fewer scholars. More significantly, South Carolina spent about $30,000 annually on the support of South Carolina College, which required Greek and Latin for admission.[89] The sons of the aristocracy were guaranteed an education; everyone else fought virtually over crumbs.

The school situation reveals both the irony and the hypocrisy of the South Carolina conception of class. For purposes of racial solidarity, it was necessary to deny class differences among whites. When benefits or power were allocated, white solidarity dissipated. The attempt to minimize class distinctions among whites also inhibited electoral reform. Since there were no competing class interests to maintain, there was no need to reapportion the legislature or to permit popular election of governors and presidential electors. The existing system was defended as avoiding the election mobs that plagued northern cities.[90] In fact, South Carolina's politics were exceedingly deferential.[91] The only popular input was through the election of legislators, but, according to Hammond, the right to vote was exercised "very negligently . . . from time immemorial."[92]

The perceived absence of a white lower class explained the absence of social turmoil. South Carolina was spared, Hammond claimed, the mobs that wrecked convents and the strikes that upset the economy;[93] the reference to Boston could hardly have been coincidental. In short, by accepting all the negative attributes of the less advantaged class and imputing them to slaves, South Carolina thought it had solved most of the social problems confounding the North. The South Carolina concept of class obviated state intervention into such areas as public education and penal reform. The only problem with this view was that crime was not negligible in South Carolina. This perception was not an accurate description of the state's social structure, and the ideology did not always serve the best interests of the state.

On the other hand, it is important to understand why South Carolinians chose to equate class and race. Such an equation played a major role in defeating proposals for change in the penal and legal systems, and crime was far less of a concern than was the maintenance of race control. Few, if any, white criminals bemoaned the

89. James Stirling, *Letters from the Slave States,* p. 255; 5 *Statutes at Large* 738; Thomas F. Jones, *The University of South Carolina;* "Education in Europe," pp. 70–71.

90. *The Electoral Question,* p. 16.

91. Steven Channing, *Crisis of Fear,* p. 155.

92. Ibid., pp. 156–57

93. Hammond, *Letters and Speeches,* pp. 32–34.

lack of a penitentiary. But the state's commitment to defend a way of life depended on maximizing the stake people had in slavery and race control. Thus it was necessary to describe a society in which all whites had some status in order to make every white feel that he had a personal stake in the maintenance of the social order.

The dimensions of crime in the Palmetto State have been explored at length in this study. Even given the number of minor assault cases, the incidence of felony prosecutions was not insignificant. Grand juries constantly complained of crowded dockets. For every sweeping statement of an essayist or politician denying the existence of crime, there were local spokesmen claiming the contrary.[94] When Perry tried to prove by surveying conviction records that South Carolina had enough felons to justify a penitentiary, 80 percent of those he thought would have filled such an institution were convicted for the more seriously regarded crimes against property.[95]

How do the realities of the state's social structure compare with the view of men such as Hammond, Hayne, and Seabrook? Although South Carolina had the highest percentage of households owning slaves in the United States, nevertheless only a minority were slaveholders. Moreover, only 18 percent owned ten or more slaves (Table 9.1) and could be counted in the "property and interest of the State," who, in the view of William Trescot, were the only people really represented in the legislature.[96] Meanwhile, the ideology of class precluded white manual labor. Whites avoided any form of labor that was regularly or traditionally performed by blacks. In 1855, it was argued that despite possible contamination from contact with free blacks, slaves had to continue as dockworkers in Charleston because the city lacked the available white labor.[97] This shortage of white labor was more apparent than real; the city's almshouse was usually filled with unemployed white males, suggesting that whites would not condescend to do such work.

The association of class with race also meant that manual labor was viewed with great suspicion by whites. Yet not all types of manual labor were compatible with race control. Proponents of manufacturing confronted this dilemma. Hammond, among others, argued that slaves could not be permitted to be operatives. "When-

---

94. For example, Edgefield *Advertiser*, 6 April 1837: "It is a fact that *crime is on the increase on our borders.*"
95. Perry, *Report*, p. 17.
96. Trescot, *Pettigrew*, p. 32.
97. *Legislative Times*, p. 193.

Table 9.1. Slaveownership by Household, 1850 (percent)

State	Households Owning Slaves	Slaveowning Households Owning Ten or More Slaves	Total, Households Owning Ten or More Slaves
South Carolina	48.4	37.6	18.2
Alabama	37.9	31.0	12.3
Arkansas	20.8	32.1	4.6
Florida	38.7	30.5	11.8
Georgia	42.0	32.4	13.6
Kentucky	28.9	16.3	4.7
Louisiana	38.2	26.4	10.1
Maryland	18.4	15.8	2.9
Mississippi	44.4	32.0	14.2
North Carolina	26.8	32.8	8.8
Tennessee	26.0	21.9	5.7
Texas	27.3	20.5	5.6
Virginia	32.9	27.4	9.0

Source: J. D. B. DeBow, Compendium to the Seventh Census, pp. 95, 99.

ever a slave is made a mechanic," he maintained, "he is more than half-freed."[98] Yet prevailing ideology had hitherto precluded a white industrial labor force. The ideology had to be altered if factories were to exist. Only in this context can one comprehend the remarkable boast, "Young men in our state are commencing to realize that labor is reputable."[99] To demonstrate the viability of industry in South Carolina, Hammond admitted that there were fifty thousand whites unable to support themselves "as every white person in this country is and feels entitled to." This group alone could supply some thirty-five thousand operatives.[100]

The association of blacks with the criminal class was so strong that white South Carolinians, in contrast to many of their northern neighbors, saw immigrants as an asset, not as a threat. They were welcomed in Charleston at a time when aliens comprised 83.5 percent of the commitments to the house of correction. After the Civil War, tax incentives were offered to immigrants for settling in the

98. James H. Hammond, "Progress of Southern Industry," p. 518.
99. James Orr, "Development of Southern Industry," p. 15.
100. Hammond, "Progress," p. 518. Emphasis added.

state.[101] These measures represented attempts to force the class structure to conform to the ideology. As artisans and unskilled laborers, immigrants could replace the urban slave who was so disturbing to the social order but essential to the economy. The ideal view of society in South Carolina was to see it as white and black, master and slave. Poor whites, white criminals, and, of course, free blacks, all were disturbing reminders that reality did not yet conform to this ideal. It is in this context that we can best understand Governor Adams's campaign to reopen the slave trade in 1856. Because the social system rested so strongly on slavery, the only way to ensure its continuance was to widen the ownership of slaves. This would, of course, increase the number of people with a direct interest in maintaining the political and social status quo. Such a move would also offset the emigration of white slaveholders to more attractive states as well as stem the prices of slaves, which caused one planter to worry that "the possession of Negroes . . . is becoming . . . a mere aristocratic privilege." [102]

As long as it best suited the official policy of the state, perceptions of class in South Carolina admitted only black and white. But as soon as attempts were made to modernize that state by establishing manufacturing, South Carolina not only "discovered" its poor white class, but proposed to put it to work alongside immigrants in factories. In other words, having once boasted of its freedom from such social ills of the modern world as immigration and industry, it was now desperately trying to reap the benefits.

By the eve of the Civil War, then, two societies were grappling with views of class, diametrically opposite and yet both troublesome. In South Carolina, what might have been simply a description was turning into an ideal that threatened to thwart other social goals, such as an increase in manufacturing. In Massachusetts, the once dispassionate analysis of social orders threatened to turn into a rigid orthodoxy that would, in turn, impede that state's efforts to prevent that orthodoxy from coming true.

Ironically, there was a curious convergence of views of class in South Carolina and Massachusetts during the Civil War era. When South Carolina found more variety in its class structure in at least beginning to acknowledge its poor whites as a potential laboring

101. John Higham, *Strangers in the Land,* p. 18.
102. Quoted in Channing, *Crisis,* p. 149; on this issue see Ronald T. Takaki, *A Pro-Slavery Crusade.* This issue was hotly debated. See James H. Adams, "Message to the Legislature, 1856," in *Report of the Special Committee of the House of Representatives of South Carolina on . . . Slavery and the Slave Trade* (1857); James Johnston Pettigrew, *Report of the Minority of the Special Committee. . . .*

class, Massachusetts feared more rigidity. With the acceptance of the notion of stock, Massachusetts seemed to adopt South Carolina's standard of class as genetically determined. Policies in Massachusetts that had the goal of reducing crime and disorder frequently turned into repressive actions against those ethnic and racial groups presumed to constitute the criminal class. And though reformation still remained the official goal of penal institutions, they were no longer justified for that purpose. Massachusetts slowly, perhaps at times reluctantly, groped toward what every South Carolinian seemed to know. What had only been *associations* now became causes.

But the story does not end with such ironies. Antebellum South Carolina had accepted three equations: slaves with crime, blacks with slaves, and imprisonment with slavery. After emancipation, the state found new modes of race control. Sharecropping served that purpose for many freedmen and lynching for an unfortunate minority of the rest. The above three equations led naturally to the establishment of a pentientiary in 1868.[103] This institution was overwhelmingly black from the time it opened its doors, confirming for those who would ignore southern racist justice the validity of the antebellum equations. Emancipation created for black prisoners a new type of slavery, more brutal than that which had preceded it because paternalistic trappings were no longer maintained.

The acceptance of class proved to be a valuable analytical tool for Massachusetts reformers; to South Carolina, it was an ironic device. In each state these class perceptions promoted action by the state. In Massachusetts, this meant laws, institutions, and policies aimed at reducing harsh class distinctions and possible tensions, without changing the nature of the society that had produced such problems. Instead, with its emphasis on order and propriety, Massachusetts criminal justice seemed aimed more at controlling the offensive habits of certain groups in society than at reducing the social stratification and alienation that might have contributed to the problem of serious crime.

In South Carolina, by contrast, state policies were contradictory. On the one hand, there was a refusal to legislate for a class that was perceived not to exist. This was expressed most clearly in the absence of free schools, electoral reform, and a penitentiary. On the other hand, there was a distinct attempt to force the state's social structure to conform to the model. This can be seen in the attempt

103. Albert D. Oliphant, *The Evolution of the Penal System of South Carolina from 1866–1916*, pp. 3–7; see also Daniel T. Brailsford, "The Historical Background and Present Status of the County Chain Gang in South Carolina," pp. 53–69.

• to reopen the slave trade and the encouragement of immigration in order to create a white laboring class without a slaveholding ethos so that all native-born whites could eventually own slaves.

Social control, "housebreak[ing] the masses," has been a fashionable and not entirely inappropriate explanation of Massachusetts reform.[104] Ironically, it is a more accurate description of South Carolina politics, where elaborate measures were taken to stifle all popular input and where government action promoted the most crass disruption of social, economic, and demographic trends to maintain the ideology that was the mainstay of the political system. In both states, the result was the imposition of one set of values onto a less powerful group.

In South Carolina, the goal of all opponents to any sort of legal and penal reform was the absolute preservation of existing authority relationships at all costs. This was the essence of the state's notorious conservatism. Massachusetts reformers tellingly employed the rhetoric of social and human progress to justify their proposals; in South Carolina, obsolete and obscure laws, adopted by sheer chance, became "landmarks of legislation." By invoking the legal ideals of an earlier age, South Carolina had hoped to restore a pattern of deference and unchallenged authority, which, of course, may never have existed. But if the appeal to the past failed to legitimate the social reality, it undoubtedly strengthened the ideology.

104. Messerli, *Mann*, p. 346. Katz's conclusion, that Massachusetts reformers failed to distinguish between a relationship and a cause, is much more to the point (*Irony*, p. 210).

Conclusion

There is no doubt that the systems of crime, justice, and authority functioned differently in the two states. One state modified its penal code with regularity, built impressive institutions, if not for the reformation, at least for the incarceration of its miscreants, came close to abolishing the death penalty, and established professional police forces to put society's official imprimatur on the war against disorder and deviance. The other state built no prison, fiercely retained a criminal code that was more a lineal descendant of medieval times than a clear reflection of contemporary thought, and encouraged extralegal means of dispute settlement.

But this is not simply a study in contrasts; it is an attempt to determine how the fundamental sources of social cohesion and authority functioned in two ostensibly different societies. The structural contrasts are dramatic—the presence of slavery or a penitentiary, antiquated statutes or organized laws, high or low conviction rates—but such outward contrasts do not tell the entire story. In many ways more significant (because in many ways less obvious) are the similarities between the two states.

In order to see these similarities, we have to cast a different sort of net. The similarities fall into two categories. The first might be seen as perennial structural dysfunctions. In this category I would include basic problems of the criminal justice system that defied solution in the nineteenth century—and for which no subsequent solution has apparently been found. One example of such a problem is the court systems of the two states. Although Massachusetts seemed to place much more emphasis on improving and rationalizing the operation of its courts, complaints about delay and use of the courts to harass remained common in Massachusetts as well as in South Carolina. Similarly, despite the occasional effectiveness of the antigallows movement in Massachusetts, that state, like South Carolina, wrestled with a reluctance to convict when the death penalty was a possibility. Other similar problem areas include conditions in local jails and the apparent inequities produced by excessive sentencing or pardoning discretion.

The second area of similarity is functional, not institutional. This has to do with the role of authority in each state. Here we see that the extralegal and informal exercise of authority in South Carolina served many of the functions monopolized by the formal system of legally constituted authority in Massachusetts. Despite the caricatures offered by reformers, the choice was not between civilization and anarchy, but between the use of local customary norms to enforce behavior and to punish violations of local standards and norms or the use of the formal legal sanction to accomplish the same end. Vigilante societies, rather than uniformed police forces, helped to keep order in South Carolina. Potential litigants with honor-related claims preferred the dueling ground to the courts. And adulterous spouses found their own accommodations in South Carolina.

Although perhaps an oversimplification, to a great extent the function of law and authority was to channel the behavior of potentially threatening or dangerous segments of the population. But this channeling did not have to occur in a uniform fashion. Where personal relations and honor were important, as in South Carolina, elaborate institutional arrangements were unnecessary. In the increasingly impersonal world of nineteenth-century Massachusetts, routinized structures for the exercise of authority seemed most suitable. In both instances, developments in the legal system neatly paralleled those in the political and economic spheres. Massachusetts boasted well-organized political machines and forged a commercial law based on universalistic principles. South Carolina politics were based on deference, and its large-scale business was often conducted on the basis of a gentleman's honor and a handshake.

Obviously, in order to understand many of the structural arrangements of the South Carolina system of authority, it is necessary to look at race relations. Similarly, in Massachusetts, where the problem of crime was eventually seen as a matter of class, class relations are a key to understanding the nature of crime and authority. And here we see that when the vital interests of each state were at stake, formal guarantees of justice were subserved to what Eugene Genovese termed the hegemonic function of law.[1] Despite the law reform and the considerable capital expenditure in prisons and reformatories, enforcement of the criminal law in Massachusetts was frequently a matter of class control.

It does not take much imagination to see within the operation of the criminal law this class control motive. The largest single category of arrests in Massachusetts was liquor-related offenses. Arrests for vagrancy and the entire area of sex-related crimes also show that a particular value system was being upheld through law, rather than

1. Eugene D. Genovese, *Roll, Jordan, Roll*, p. 25.

simply that limited list of crimes against persons and property, prosecution for which few people would object to. Class control as a motive, of course, is hard to pinpoint. Yet, there are definite indications that large-scale employers were most concerned about the effects of unchecked drunkenness on the working population of the state and only secondarily concerned about the disruptive impact of measures of harassment against honest and dependable laborers raucously enjoying their scarce free time. Furthermore, as no minimal effort was made toward prevention or rehabilitation of drunks and vagrants, it is hard to see in these perennial arrests anything other than a street-cleaning motive.

In South Carolina, the most threatening population—and one identified as the equivalent of the northern criminal class—was the state's slaves. Here the purpose of the legal system was unmistakable. In addition to the high conviction rates, harsh punishments, and procedural irregularities already noted, the legal system formally sanctioned the exercise of police power solely on the basis of race. Thus, again, in South Carolina, both legal and extralegal authority, acting in a complementary fashion, sought to uphold the power of the dominant groups in society.

In South Carolina, there is yet another part to this picture. Although this study has not attempted to determine the social attributes of the defendant class in that state, we can infer that the dominant interests were served in yet another fashion: they were left alone. Although, as we have seen, the notion of honor was widely shared among South Carolina whites, protection of honor took many forms. The gentleman class took the dueling ground, virtually immune from prosecution despite the legal proscription on dueling, and lesser classes responded to slurs and insults in a violent manner. In many cases, criminal prosecutions resulted from such violence, even though the offense itself was in part based on the South Carolina class system. Thus, by prosecuting people for assaults, riots, and brawls, but not duels, the double standard in South Carolina justice was not limited to blacks.

Finally, it is not too farfetched to see in both states a number of safety-valve mechanisms to ensure that the legal system, the legitimacy of which derives to a great extent from its formal autonomy from the political and social systems, did not get out of hand. The most obvious of such devices was the pardon. Again, impressionistic evidence must suffice, but the case for a pardon was strengthened if a person came from a stable family or had influential friends to support the application. Such was not always the case: Harvard professor John White Webster was executed. But pardons in both states served a crucial, double-edged corrective function; on the one hand, victims of the legal system were given a second chance; on the other hand, an opportunity was provided for certain offenders to escape the harshest rigors of the criminal justice system.

Therefore, despite the different economic systems, despite the vast demographic differences, and despite even the cultural traditions that led to the creation of certain different types of legal structures, the criminal justice systems of both states served similar functions.

Once we go beyond the obvious structural contrasts, when we abandon the litmus-test conviction rates and the disputes over courts and the proper posture of authority and populace, we find that somehow things were not as drastically different in the two states as they appeared. Deference and other forms of traditional authority operated to keep planters and patricians in power in both states. In the highly formalized, legalistic Yankee society, control of political power was part and parcel of this accomplishment. In South Carolina, political control was significant but hardly determinative. That state systematically weakened or dismantled potentially competitive sources of power and authority. And so the courts were kept ineffectual, dueling was clandestinely promoted, and slaves were tried either on the plantation or before neighborhood slaveholders, never in courthouses.

As I have indicated, I believe that legal traditions are as important as economic and social evolution in fashioning a society's legal and criminal justice systems. And, to some extent, tradition has influenced the course of each state's legal development from the nineteenth century to today. By the 1870s the Massachusetts State Prison, now home for many displaced members of the new industrial proletariat, was modeled on a factory, with shops and contractors. But the South Carolina penitentiary, almost entirely black, with its chain gangs, field hands, work songs, and white overseers, resembled the plantation. Thus, even after the formal abolition of slavery, the equation of prison and plantation remained valid. The tradition of personal violence proved to be a persistent characteristic of the entire South; homicide and suicide rates in the decades after Reconstruction were higher than in any other region of the country.[2]

The peculiarities of South Carolina law and justice remain. A few years ago, the legacy of South Carolina justice was revealingly described in two totally unrelated segments of a highly rated network

2. Sheldon Hackney, "Southern Violence."

television news show. One story was on Spartanburg, South Carolina, then the gun capital of the country, upholding the tradition of personal violence in the upcountry. The second story concerned part-time local peace justices, blissfully untrained in law, who settle disputes informally in remote lowcountry areas of the South Carolina coast. Like the untrained and ignorant magistrates who were the object of so many nineteenth-century grand jury complaints, these officials served a purpose while revealing the persistence of the state's ambivalence toward formal justice and authority.

Such vignettes point to a reassuring continuity in South Carolina history. The same cannot easily be said for Massachusetts. The Massachusetts of the nineteenth century was divided between Yankee and immigrant. Racial antagonisms surfaced occasionally, as in the 1863 Boston draft riot, and blacks were more overrepresented in the prison population than any other group. But the major social issue in crime and law enforcement concerned immigrants, with their alien values and suspect genetic stock.

Two things happened in Massachusetts to break the sort of continuity we saw in South Carolina. First, the Yankees and the Irish more or less came to terms with each other. Second, twentieth-century Massachusetts to a great extent accepted the same equation of class and race that characterized nineteenth-century South Carolina. Ceding politics and the police to the new immigrants, Yankees perceived no basic threat to their own position. But there was an interesting trade-off, one in sharp but fascinating contrast to the nineteenth-century quest for certainty and efficiency. No longer can the legal system of Massachusetts be seen as efficient. Its courts are among the most overcrowded in the country. Boston's city councillors risked jail in the 1970s rather than replace the Charles Street jail—the same building that Charles Sumner's brother, George, sought to design from Paris in the 1840s. Lack of enforcement of traffic regulations has created a special form of anarchy which the state insurance commissioner once blamed for the state's high automobile insurance rates.

We should recognize some of these themes from nineteenth-century Massachusetts. The people who were in effect the victims of the periodic obsession of the police with minor vice and drunkenness are the ancestors of those in formal control of the law enforcement apparatus. The minor illegalities so tolerated in Massachusetts represent the response to decades of class control.

And, though always class conscious, Massachusetts today is certainly one of the most race conscious of states, north or south. To no small degree, the recent history of race relations in Massachu-

setts shows that the class control measures of the nineteenth century have been applied to achieve race control in the twentieth. The
anarchy in the streets and courts in Massachusetts is as misleading
today as the absence of a penitentiary was in South Carolina. Just as
nineteenth-century planters retained their hegemony without
building legal and political structures to support it, so today in Massachusetts, formal control of the criminal justice system gives those
groups who enjoy that control apparently only a tenuous foothold
on the crucial ladder that leads to security and respectability.

Ironically, what seemed at first a clear study in contrasts must
yield to an understanding of the essentially similar role of the system of authority and law in preserving, albeit in different forms,
order and social cohesion. The purpose of law and authority, not the
structures and institutions, becomes the point of comparison, rather
than of contrast. And thus, if one society chose the prison and the
other the plantation, it was the criteria for confinement and not the
institutional setting with which we must contend. If we understand
that fact, we will also understand that the same social, racial, and
political antagonisms that fuel the sense of threat and danger will
eventually create a prison or a plantation, no matter what institutional (or anti-institutional) form it takes, no matter what we call
it.

Bibliography

Primary Sources

Manuscript Collections

BERKELEY, CALIFORNIA
Bancroft Library, University of California
  Francis Lieber, scrapbook "Items of Political Economy"
BEVERLY, MASSACHUSETTS
Beverly Historical Society
  Robert Rantoul Papers
  Robert Rantoul, Jr., Papers
BOSTON, MASSACHUSETTS
Massachusetts Historical Society
  Appleton Papers
  George Bemis Papers
  R. H. Dana Papers
  Lawrence Papers
  Horace Mann Papers
  Amasa Walker Papers
CAMBRIDGE, MASSACHUSETTS
Houghton Library, Harvard University
  James Freeman Clarke Papers
  Dorothea Lynde Dix Papers
  Samuel Gridley Howe Papers
  Jared Sparks Papers
  Charles Sumner Papers
CHARLESTON, SOUTH CAROLINA
Charleston Library Society
  John B. Grimball Diary (typescript copy)
South Carolina Historical Society
  R. F. W. Allston Papers
  Langdon Cheves Papers
  Good Hope Plantation Records
  Grimké Family Papers
  Miscellaneous papers and collections
  Pineville Association Records
  Jacob Schirmir Diary
  R. W. Seymour Magistrates Book
  O. M. Smith Docket Book
  John Blake White Papers

COLUMBIA, SOUTH CAROLINA
South Carolina Department of Archives and History
 Anderson Town Council Journal (WPA typescript)
 Bills
 Commons Journal
 Governors' Correspondence
 Governors' Messages
 House Journals
 Legal System Papers
 Legislative System Papers
 Miscellaneous Records
 Penal System Papers
 Penitentiary Records
 Senate Journals
 Slavery Papers
 Treasury Journals
 Treasury Ledgers
South Caroliniana Library
 Hugh Kerr Aiken Papers
 William Blanding Papers
 John Ewing Calhoun Papers
 Thomas Cooper Papers
 Cox Family Papers
 DeSaussure Family Papers
 William Fairey Papers
 James Hamilton Papers
 Wade Hampton I Papers
 Wade Hampton II Papers
 Robert Y. Hayne Papers
 William F. B. Haynsworth Papers
 John Jenkins Papers
 Francis Lieber Papers
 George McDuffie Papers
 Samuel McGowan Papers
 McLean Family Papers
 John McLees Papers
 John L. Manning Papers
 Hugh Middleton Papers
 Miscellaneous manuscripts and collections
 Benjamin F. Perry Papers
 James Louis Petigru Papers
 William Preston Papers
 John Smyth Richardson Papers
 Thomas Richardson Papers
 Rutledge Family Papers
 Singleton Family Papers

James Henly Thornwell Papers
Townes Family Papers
Thomas Twiss Papers
Francis Whaley Papers
PROVIDENCE, RHODE ISLAND
  Brown University
  Francis Wayland Papers
SALEM, MASSACHUSETTS
  Essex Institute
  Samuel Johnson Papers
  Robert Rantoul Papers
SAN MARINO, CALIFORNIA
  Huntington Library
  Francis Lieber Papers

Court Records

Massachusetts (in county courthouses)
  Berkshire County Common Pleas Records
  Essex County Common Pleas Records
  Hampshire County Common Pleas Records
  Middlesex County Common Pleas Records
  Supreme Judicial Court Files
South Carolina (all in South Carolina Archives unless otherwise noted)
  Anderson Court of Magistrates and Freeholders Records
  Barnwell Sessions Journal (WPA typescript)
  Charleston District Court of General Sessions Journal, 1769–76; 1857–
    60
  Charleston District Court of General Sessions Indictments, 1800–1842
  Chester, Sessions Clerk Compilations, South Caroliniana Library
  Darlington Sessions Journal (WPA typescript)
  Edgefield Sessions Journal
  Greenville Sessions Journal (WPA typescript)
  Kershaw Sessions Journal (WPA typescript)
  Laurens Sessions Journal (WPA typescript)
  Lexington, Sessions Clerk Compilation, South Caroliniana Library
  Newberry Sessions Journal (WPA typescript)
  Richland Grand Jury Findings, 1800–1835
  Spartanburg Court of Magistrates and Freeholders Records
  Spartanburg Sessions Index, 1800–1910
  Spartanburg Sessions Journal (WPA typescript)
  Sumter Sessions Journal (WPA typescript)
  Union Sessions Journal (WPA typescript)
  York Sessions Journal (WPA typescript)

Public Documents

Massachusetts

Abstracts of Returns of the Keepers of the Jails and Overseers of the Houses of Correction (1833–63).

Acts and Resolves (1796–1885).

An Account of the Massachusetts State Prison Containing a Description and Plan of the Edifice; the Laws, Regulations, Rules, and Orders: With a View of the Present State of the Institution by the Board of Directors (Boston, 1806).

Annual Report of the Massachusetts Board of State Charities (1864–78).

Austin, James T. *Report and Opinion of the Attorney General on the Subject of the Expenses of Criminal Justice* (Massachusetts Senate Document 34, 1839).

Bellows, C. R. *Commissioner's Report on the Subject of Matrons and Labor in the Common Jails* (Boston, 1854).

The By-Laws and Orders of the Town of Boston (Boston, 1818).

Commissioners Appointed by the Legislature March 3, 1826 on the Subject of the . . . State Prison (Senate Document 6, 1826).

Commissioners of the State Prison, *Report.* Boston, 1817.

Committee of Both Houses Report (1818).

Committee on the Judiciary, *Report* (Senate Document No. 18, 1853).

The General Laws of Massachusetts from the Adoption of the Constitution to February 1822 (Boston, 1823).

The General Statutes of the Commonwealth of Massachusetts (Boston, 1860).

Governors' Messages (various years found in *Legislative Documents*).

History of the Gaols in This State with Tables Showing the Commitments for Five Years (Boston, 1827).

House Journal.

The Laws of the Commonwealth of Massachusetts from November 28, 1780, to February 28, 1807 (Boston, 1807).

Legislative Documents (1796–1855).

Letters of the Justices of the Massachusetts Supreme Judicial Court to His Excellency the Governor (1804).

Massachusetts Board of State Charities, *Special Report on Prisons and Prison Discipline* (Boston, 1865).

Public Documents (1858–81).

Report of the Attorney General (1833–43; 1848–63).

Report of the Commission Appointed to Revise the General Statutes of the Commonwealth (Boston, 1834).

Report of the Committee on Judicial Reform (1798).

Report of the Committee on Prisons (Boston, 1871).

Report of the Committee on Prisons (Boston, 1877).

Report of the Committee on the Abolition of Capital Punishment (Senate Document 73, 1836).

Report of the Committee on the Expediency of Abolishing Capital Punishment (Senate Document 69, 1837).

Report of the Committee to Whom was Referred the Consideration of the Laws in Relation to the Punishment of Death (House Document 36, 1835).

Report of the Inspectors of the State Prison . . . on Discharged Convicts (1830).

Report of the Penal Code of Massachusetts (Boston, 1844).

Report of the State Agency for Discharged Convicts (1845–60).

Report of the State Prison (Boston, 1865).

Report on Commitments and Pardons of State Prison Convicts (House Document 63, 1846).

Report on Gaols and Houses of Correction (Boston, 1834).

Report on the Punishment of Death (House Document 15, 1831).

Report on the Punishment of Death (House Document 2, 1832).

Report on the State Prison (Boston, 1822).

Report on the Various Charitable, Reformatory, and Penal Institutions . . . by a Committee Appointed by the Governor (1862?).

Report Related to Capital Punishment (House Document 32, 1836).

Report Relating to the New State Prison (House Document 120, 1875).

Revised Statutes of the Commonwealth of Massachusetts (Boston, 1836).

Rules and Regulations for the Government of the Massachusetts State Prison (1823, 1829, 1855).

Rules and Regulations of the Reformatory Prison for Women (Boston, 1878).

Sewall, Samuel, and Dane, Nathan. *Communication from Hon. Samuel Sewall, Esq. and the Hon. Nathan Dane, Esq. . . . for the Regulation of the State Prison and the Alteration of the Criminal Laws of the Commonwealth* (Boston, 1805).

State Prison Reports (1829–83).

South Carolina

Counter Report of a Portion of the Members of the Special Committee on the Penitentiary System (Columbia, 1839).

A Digest of the Ordinances of the City Council of Charleston from the Year 1783 to October 1844 (Charleston, 1844).

Mayor's Report on City Affairs (Charleston, 1857).

The Mayor's Report Respecting the General Condition of City Affairs with Suggestions for the Improvement of the Different Branches of the Public Service (Charleston, 1839).

Pinckney, H. L. *Report Containing a Review of the Proceedings of the City Authorities of Charleston.* Charleston, 1839.

Registrar's Report Relating to Births, Deaths, Marriages (1854–58).

A Report Containing a Review of the Proceedings of the City Authorities (Charleston, 1838).

Report of Certain Members of the Commission on Petigru's Code of the Statute Law of South Carolina (Columbia, 1864).

Report of the Committee on the Colored Population on the Petition of the South Carolina Mechanics Association. Also the Petition of the Mechanics and Working Men of the City of Charleston, also the Memorial of the Charleston Mechanics Society, also the Presentment of the Charleston Grand Jury . . . All in Reference to the Enactment of Laws Preventing Negroes from Hiring Out Their Own Time (Columbia, 1858).

Report of the Free Colored Poor of the City of Charleston (Charleston, 1843).

Report of the Special Committee of the House of Representatives of South Carolina on . . . Slavery and the Slave Trade (Columbia, 1857).

Rules and Regulations for the General Government of the Police Department of the City of Charleston (Charleston, 1858).

South Carolina House Journal.

South Carolina Legislative Times, Being the Debates and Proceedings in the South Carolina Legislature at the Session Commencing November 1855 (Columbia, 1856).

South Carolina Reports and Resolutions.

South Carolina Senate Journal.

Newspapers, Periodicals, Annual Reports

Boston Prison Discipline Society, *Annual Report* (Boston, 1826–55).

Boston Society for Aiding Discharged Convicts, *Annual Report.*

Carolina Law Journal (1830).

Charleston *Courier*

Charleston *Mercury*

Edgefield *Advertiser*

Greenville *Mountaineer*

Laurensville *Herald*

Massachusetts Society for Aiding Discharged Convicts, *Annual Report.*

Newberry *Rising Sun*

Prisoner's Friend (1848–58).

Books, Articles, Pamphlets

Adams, F. C. *Manuel Pereira; or the Sovereign State of South Carolina with Views of Southern Laws, Life, and Hospitality.* Washington, 1853.

Adams, John. *The Legal Papers of John Adams.* Edited by L. Kinvin Wroth and Hiller B. Zobel. 3 vols. Cambridge, 1965.

Adshead, Joseph. *Prisons and Prisoners.* London, 1845.

Allston, Robert F. W. *The South Carolina Rice Plantation as Revealed in*

the Papers of Robert F. W. Allston. Edited by J. H. Easterby.
Chicago, 1945.

Amory, Thomas C. *Life of James Sullivan with Selections from His Writings.* 2 vols. Boston, 1859.

Arfwedson, Carl David. *The United States and Canada in 1832, 1833, and 1834.* 2 vols. London, 1834.

Augustus, John. *A Report of the Labors of John Augustus for the Last Ten Years in the Aid of the Unfortunate.* Boston, 1852.

Austin, Benjamin. *Observations on the Pernicious Practice of Law by Honestus.* Boston, 1786.

Austin, James T. "Punishment of Crimes." *North American Review* 10 (1820) : 235–59.

———. *Reply to the Centinel Review.* Boston, 1824.

Bartlett, Elisha. *A Vindication of the Character and Condition of the Females Employed in the Lowell Mills against the Charges Contained in the Boston Times and the Boston Quarterly Review.* Lowell, 1841.

Beaumont, Gustave de, and Tocqueville, Alexis de. *On the Penitentiary System in the United States and Its Application in France.* Philadelphia, 1833.

Bemis, George, ed. *Report of the Case of John W. Webster.* Boston, 1850.

Bernhard, Karl. *Travels through North America during the Years 1825 and 1826.* 2 vols. Philadelphia, 1828.

Blackstone, William. *Commentaries on the Laws of England.* 4 vols. Boston, 1962.

Boston Prisoner's Friend Association, *Circular,* Boston, 1849.

Bowen, F. "Gray on Prison Discipline." *North American Review* 66 (1848) : 145–90.

Bowen, Nathaniel. *Duelling under Any Circumstances the Height of Folly.* Charleston, 1823.

Bradford, Gamaliel. *Description and Historical Sketch of the Massachusetts State Prison.* Boston, 1816.

———. *State Prisons and the Penitentiary System Vindicated.* Charlestown, 1821.

Brevard, Joseph. *An Alphabetical Digest of the Public Statute Law of South Carolina.* 3 vols. Charleston, 1814.

Buckingham, James Silk. *The Slave States of America.* 2 vols. London, 1842.

"Capital Punishment." *Southern Quarterly Review* 4 (1843) : 81–97.

Capital Punishment; Reasons for Its Immediate Adoption. Hopedale, Mass., no date.

"Carolina Political Annals." *Southern Quarterly Review* 7 (1845) : 479–526.

Carpenter, S. C. *Report of the Trial of Richard Dennis the Younger for the Murder of James Shaw on the 10th of August 1804.* Charleston, 1805.

Catterall, Helen Tunnicliff, ed. *Judicial Cases Concerning American Slavery and the Negro.* 5 vols. Washington, 1929.

Cooper, Thomas. "Bentham's *Judicial Evidence.*" *Southern Review* 5 (1830) : 381–426.

———. *The Case of Thomas Cooper.* Columbia, 1832.

———. "Colored Marriages." *Carolina Law Journal* 1 (1830) : 92–106.

———. "Letter to Chancellor Sampson." *Statesman,* 21 April 1824.

———, and McCord, David J. *The Statutes at Large of South Carolina.* 10 vols. Columbia, 1836–40.

"Criminal Code of South Carolina." *American Jurist* 20 (1838) : 236.

DeBow, J. D. B. *Compendium to the Seventh Census.* Washington, 1854.

Dickinson, Rodolphus. *A Digest of the . . . Powers and Duties of Justices of the Peace.* Deerfield, 1818.

Dix, Dorothea L. *Memorial to the Legislature of Massachusetts.* Boston, 1843.

———. *Remarks on Prisons and Prison Discipline in the United States.* Boston, 1845.

Dole, Benjamin. *An Address to the People of Massachusetts on the Subject of Human Rights.* Boston, 1838.

———. *A Circular.* Boston, 1846.

———. *An Examination of Mr. Rantoul's Report for Abolishing Capital Punishment in Massachusetts.* Boston, 1837.

———. *A Review of Mr. Rantoul's Report of 1836.* Boston, 1837.

"The Duel." *Russell's Magazine* 1 (1857) : 439–54

"Duelling." *Russell's Magazine* 1 (1857) : 132–42.

Dymond, Jonathan. *An Inquiry into the Accordancy of War with the Principles of Christianity.* Philadelphia, 1834.

"Education in Europe." *Southern Quarterly Review* 7 (1845) : 1–74.

"The Effect of Foreign Divorces on South Carolina Marriages." *Carolina Law Journal* 1 (1830) : 377–83.

The Electoral Question: The Present System of Appointing Presidential Electors in South Carolina Considered. Charleston, 1849.

Faux, William. *Memorable Days in America.* London, 1823.

Flagg, Charles. *Digested Index of the Statute Law of South Carolina, 1837–1857.* Charleston, 1858.

Freeman, Samuel. *The Massachusetts Justice.* Boston, 1795.

Galison, John. "Prevention of Crimes." *North American Review* 4 (1819) : 288–322.

Gray, Francis. *Prison Discipline in America.* Boston, 1847.

Grimké, John F. "Charge to the Grand Jury in Charleston, October 1789." *American Museum* 8 (1790) : 31–35.

———. *The South Carolina Justice of the Peace.* Philadelphia, 1796.

Grimké, Thomas S. *Anniversary Oration Delivered before the South Carolina Bar Association.* Charleston, 1827.

———. "Defensive War." *Calumet* 2 (1835) : 140–51.

———. *Report on the Practicability and Expediency of a Code.* Columbia, 1827.

Hall, E. B. "Punishment of Death." *North American Review* 62 (1846) : 40–70.
Hamilton, James, Jr. *An Account of the Late Intended Insurrection among a Portion of the Blacks of This City.* Charleston, 1822.
Hammond, James H. "Progress of Southern Industry." *DeBow's Review* 8 (1850) : 501–22.
———. *Selections from the Letters and Speeches of the Hon. James H. Hammond of South Carolina.* New York, 1866.
Hayne, Isaac William. *Report to His Excellency the Governor on Prisons, Prison Discipline, and the Criminal Law.* Columbia, 1852.
Haynes, Gideon. *Pictures from Prison Life.* Boston, 1869.
Henry, Robert. *Discourse Occasioned by the Death of Edward P. Simons, Esq. and Archy Mayson, Esq. . . . Delivered in the Representatives Chamber.* Columbia, 1823.
Hillard, George S. "Lieber's *Essay on Penal Law.*" *North American Review* 47 (1838) : 452–64.
Howe, Samuel Gridley. *An Essay on the Separate and Congregate System of Prison Discipline.* Boston, 1846.
———. *A Letter to J. H. Wilkins, H. B. Rogers, and F. B. Fay, Commissioners of Massachusetts for the State Reform School for Girls.* Boston, 1854.
———. *Remarks upon the Education of Deaf Mutes in Defense of the Doctrines of the Second Annual Report of the Massachusetts Board of State Charities.* Boston, 1866.
———. *Report of a Minority of the Special Committee of the Boston Prison Discipline Society.* Boston, 1846.
"Inequalities in Penal Legislation." *Pennsylvania Journal of Prison Discipline and Philanthropy* 5 (1850) : 161–68.
"John Belton O'Neall's Digest of the Negro Law of South Carolina." *Advocate* (January 1849; exact date uncertain; article bound into Lieber's personal copy of O'Neall's *Digest,* University of California, Berkeley, Library).
"The Judicial Tenure." *Southern Quarterly Review* 7 (1845) : 448–55.
Lawrence, Amos. *Extracts from the Diary and Correspondence of the Late Amos Lawrence.* Edited by William R. Lawrence. Boston, 1856.
Legare, Hugh Swinton. "Codification." *Southern Review* 7 (1831) : 391–412.
A Letter Addressed to His Excellency John L. Wilson Governor of the State of South Carolina on the Subject of the Judiciary. Charleston, 1823.
Letter Concerning the Labors of Mr. John Augustus, the Well-Known Philanthropist from One Who Knows Him. Boston, 1858.
Lieber, Francis. *Letter to His Exellency Patrick Noble, Governor of South Carolina, on the Penitentiary System.* Columbia, 1839.
———. *Miscellaneous Writings.* 2 vols. Philadelphia, 1881.
———. *Remarks on the Relation between Education and Crime in a Letter to the Rev. William White D.D.* Philadelphia, 1835.

———. *Slavery, Plantations, and the Yeomanry.* New York, 1865.

Lowell, Charles. *A Sermon Preached at the State Prison in Massachusetts, November 29, 1812.* Boston, 1812.

Mann, Horace. *Annual Reports on Education.* Boston, 1868.

"Marriage and Divorce." *Southern Quarterly Review* 17 (1854) : 332–55.

O'Neall, John Belton. *The Negro Law of South Carolina.* Columbia, 1848.

Orr, James. "Development of Southern Industry." *DeBow's Review* 19 (1855) : 1–22.

Parker, Theodore. *Works.* 15 vols. Boston, 1907.

Parsons, Theophilus. *Memoir of Theophilus Parsons.* Boston, 1858.

Patterson, Giles J. *Journal of a Southern Student, 1846–1848.* Nashville, 1944.

"The Penitentiary Question in South Carolina." *Southern Quarterly Review* 18 (1850) : 357–74.

Perry, Benjamin F. *Report of the Special Committee Appointed at the Session of 1838 on the Subject of the Penitentiary System.* Columbia, 1839.

Perry, Elizabeth, comp. *In Memoriam: Benjamin Franklin Perry, Ex-Governor of South Carolina.* Greenville, 1887.

Perry, Hext, ed. *Letters of My Father to My Mother.* Philadelphia, 1889.

Petigru, James Louis. *Life, Letters, and Speeches of James Louis Petigru, the Union Man of South Carolina.* Edited by James Petigru Carson. Washington, 1920.

———. "Oration Delivered on the Third Anniversary of the South Carolina Historical Society." *South Carolina Historical Society Collections* 2 (1858) : 9–21.

———. *Portion of the Code of Statute Law of South Carolina Submitted to the Assembly as Required.* Columbia, 1860.

Pettigrew, James Johnston. *Report of the Minority of the Special Committee of Seven to Whom was Referred so Much of Governor Adams Message No. 1 as Relates to Slavery and the Slave Trade.* Charleston, 1858.

Pierce, James. *An Address Delivered in the Chapel of the State Prison in Charlestown . . . to the Convicts.* Boston, 1815.

Pinckney, Charles. *Message of the Governor.* Charleston, 1797.

Plain Facts, Showing the Amount, Expense, and Principal Cause of Delinquency, Vice, Crime, and Pauperism in the City of Boston, for Ten Years. Boston, 1836.

Pressley, B. C. *The Law of Magistrates and Constables in the State of South Carolina.* Charleston, 1848.

Pringle, Edward J. "The Judiciary System of South Carolina." *Southern Quarterly Review* 18 (1850) : 464–86.

Prioleau, Samuel. "Law and Lawyers." *Southern Review* 3 (1829) : 431–50.

"Prison Discipline in the United States." *Nation* 3 (1867) : 147–48.

The Proposed Alteration of Judicial Tenure in South Carolina. Charleston, 1844.

The Proslavery Argument, as Maintained by the Most Distinguished

Writings of the Southern States, Containing the Several Essays on the Subject by Chancellor Harper, Governor Hammond, Dr. Simms, and Professor Dew. Charleston, 1852.

Quincy, Josiah. *Remarks on Some of the Provisions of the Laws of Massachusetts Affecting Poverty, Vice, and Crime.* Cambridge, 1822.

Rantoul, Robert, Jr. *Memoirs, Speeches, and Writings of Robert Rantoul, Jr.* Edited by Luther Hamilton. Boston, 1854.

Remarks on Prisons and Prison Discipline from the Christian Examiner. Boston, 1826.

Remarks on the Existing State of Laws in Massachusetts Respecting Violations of the Sabbath. Boston, 18–.

A Report in Part of the Trial of Thomas Gaynor for the Alleged Murder of His Wife. Charleston, 1810.

Review of Crawford's Report on the American Penitentiaries Extracted from the American Quarterly Review, December, 1835. 1835.

"Revision of the Laws of Massachusetts." *American Jurist* 13 (1835) : 344–78.

Roscoe, William. *Observations on Penal Jurisprudence and the Reformation of Criminals . . . and on the State Prisons in America.* London, 1825.

Royall, Anne Newport. *Mrs. Royall's Southern Tour.* 3 vols. Washington, 1830–31.

Rush, Benjamin. *On Punishing Murder by Death.* Philadelphia, 1792.

Salley, A. A., Jr., ed. *Minutes of the Vestry of St. Helena's Parish, South Carolina, 1726–1812.* Columbia, 1919.

———. *Minutes of the Vestry of St. Matthew's Parish, South Carolina, 1767–1838.* Columbia, 1939.

Sanborn, Franklin B. "North American Prisons." *North American Review* 103 (1868) : 383–412.

———. "The Present State of the Prison Discipline Question." *North American Review* 102 (1866) : 210–35.

———. "The Prison Question." *American Social Science Association Journal* 7 (1874) : 357–74.

———. *Recollections of Seventy Years.* 2 vols. Boston, 1909.

———. "The Reformation of Prison Discipline." *North American Review* 105 (1867) : 555–91.

———, and Ayres, John. "A Preliminary Report by a Subcommittee of the Department." *Journal of Social Science* 7 (1874) : 357–74.

Shattuck, Lemuel. *The Vital Statistics of Boston; Containing an Abstract of the Bills of Mortality for the Last Twenty-Nine Years and a General View of the Population and Health of the City at Other Periods of Its History.* Philadelphia, 1841.

A Short Review of the Project for Uniting the Courts of Law and Equity in This State. Charleston, 1822.

Simpson, William. *The Practical Justice of the Peace.* Charleston, 1761.

Smith, Joseph H., ed. *Colonial Justice in Western Massachusetts (1639–1702): The Pynchon Court Record.* Cambridge, 1961.
Spear, Charles. *Essays on the Punishment of Death.* Boston, 1845.
———. *Plea for Discharged Convicts.* Boston, 1846.
Stirling, James. *Letters from the Slave States.* London, 1857.
Story, Joseph. *Report of the Commissioners Appointed to Consider and Report upon the Practicability and Expediency of Reducing in a Written and Systematic Code the Common Law of Massachusetts.* Boston, 1837. Reprinted in William W. Story, *Miscellaneous Writings of Joseph Story,* pp. 698–740.
Strobel, Martin. *A Report of the Trial of Michael and Martin Toohey, on an Indictment for the Murder of James W. Gadsden, Esq.* Charleston, 1819.
Stuart, James. *Three Years in North America.* Edinburgh, 1833.
Sullivan, William. *Address to the Members of the Bar of Suffolk Massachusetts.* Boston, 1825.
Sumner, George. *Mr. Sumner's Letter.* Boston, 1847.
Taylor, J. H. "Manufactures in South Carolina." *DeBow's Review* (1850).
Taylor, Rev. Timothy Alden. *The Bible View of the Death Penalty, also, a Summary of the Webster Case.* Worcester, 1850.
Thacher's Criminal Cases. Boston, 1845.
Ticknor, George. "Griscom's Tour in Europe." *North American Review* 18 (1824) : 178–92.
Tidyman, Phillip. *Letters on the Pennsylvania System of Solitary Imprisonment.* Charleston, 1835. 2d ed., Philadelphia, 1837.
Trescot, William Henry. *Memorial of the Life of J. Johnston Pettigrew.* Charleston, 1870.
———. "O'Neall's Bench and Bar." *Russell's Magazine* 6 (1860) : 289–97.
———. "Oration Delivered before the South Carolina Historical Society." South Carolina Historical Society *Collections* 3 (1855) : 9–34.
Tudor, William. "On The Penitentiary System." *North American Review* 13 (1821) : 417–40.
Turnbull, Robert James. *A Visit to the Philadelphia Prison.* Philadelphia, 1796.
Washburn, Emory. *Reasons for a Separate State Prison for Women.* Boston, 1874.
Waterston, Robert. *Thoughts on Prison Discipline.* Boston, 1839.
Wayland, Francis. "Prison Discipline." *North American Review* 49 (1839) : 1–43.
Weber, Max. *Max Weber on Law in Economy and Society.* Edited by Max Rheinstein. Cambridge, 1964.
Weld, Theodore Dwight. *American Slavery as It Is: Testimony of a Thousand Witnesses.* New York, 1839.
Wigfall, Arthur. *A Sermon upon Duelling.* Charleston, 1856.
Wilson, John Lyde. *The Code of Honor.* Charleston, 1838.
———. *Codification: Speech of the Hon. John L. Wilson.* Charleston, 1827.

————. *Review of the Court of Equity: Its History, Usurpation, and Tyranny.* Georgetown, 1822.

Wines, Enoch Cobb, and Dwight, Theodore W. *Report on the Prisons and Reformatories of the United States and Canada Made to the Legislature of New York, January 1867.* Albany, 1867.

Winkler, E. T. *Duelling Examined: A Sermon Delivered in the First Baptist Church in Charleston, January 18, 1857.* Charleston, 1857.

Woodmason, Charles. *The Carolina Backcountry on the Eve of the Revolution.* Edited by Richard J. Hooker. Chapel Hill, 1953.

Wright, Henry C. *Dick Crowninshield, the Assassin, and Zachary Taylor, the Soldier: The Difference between Them.* Boston, 1848.

————. *John W. Webster, the Murderer, and John Eveleth, the Hangman: the Difference between Them.* Boston, 1859.

Secondary Sources

Dissertations, Theses, Unpublished Papers

Barnett, Redmond. "A Viperous Brood of Beggars: Concern about Criminal Subcultures in Antebellum Massachusetts." Paper presented to the Annual Meeting of the American Historical Association, 1974.

Beattie, John M. "The Decline of Capital Punishment in Eighteenth-Century England." Unpublished paper.

Bulkley, Robert DeGroff, Jr. "Robert Rantoul, Jr., 1805–1852: Politics and Reform in Antebellum Massachusetts." Ph.D. dissertation, Princeton University, 1971.

Freedman, Estelle Brenda. "Their Sisters' Keepers: The Origins of Female Corrections in America." Ph.D. dissertation, Columbia University, 1976.

Germany, George. "The South Carolina Governing Elite, 1820–1860." Ph.D. dissertation, University of California, Berkeley, 1972.

Murrin, John M. "Anglicizing an American Colony: The Transformation of Provincial Massachusetts." Ph.D. dissertation, Yale University, 1966.

Nicholson, George W. "The South Carolina Penitentiary." M.A. thesis, University of South Carolina, 1922.

Olsberg, Robert Nicholas. "A Government of Class and Race: William Henry Trescot and the South Carolina Chivalry, 1860–1865." Ph.D. dissertation, University of South Carolina, 1972.

Senese, Donald Joseph. "Legal Thought in South Carolina, 1800–1860." Ph.D. dissertation, University of South Carolina, 1970.

Zimmerman, Hilda J. "Penal Systems and Penal Reform in the South since the Civil War." Ph.D. dissertation, University of North Carolina, 1947.

Books, Articles, Pamphlets

Abbott, Edith. "The Civil War and the Crime Wave of 1865–1870." *Social Service Review* 1 (1927) : 212–34.
———. "Crime and the War." *Journal of the American Institute of Criminal Law and Criminology* 9 (1918) : 32–45.
Banner, James, Jr. "The Problem of South Carolina." In Stanley Elkins and Eric McKitrick, eds. *The Hofstadter Aegis*, pp. 60–93. New York, 1974.
Beattie, John M. "The Criminality of Women in Eighteenth-Century England." *Journal of Social History* 8 (1975) : 80–116.
———. "The Pattern of Crime in England, 1660–1800." *Past and Present* 62 (1974) : 47–95.
———. "Towards a Study of Crime in 18th Century England." In Paul Fritz and David Williams, eds., *The Triumph of Culture: 18th Century Perspectives*, pp. 299–314. Toronto, 1972.
Bell, Daniel. *The End of Ideology: On the Exhaustion of Political Ideas in the Fifties.* New York, 1960.
Berlin, Ira. *Slaves without Masters: The Free Negro in the Antebellum South.* New York, 1974.
Biographical Dictionary of the Senate of the State of South Carolina. Columbia, 1964.
Bishop, Joel Prentiss. *Commentaries on the Law of Marriage and Divorce and Evidence in Matrimonial Suits.* Boston, 1852.
Bloomfield, Maxwell. *American Lawyers in a Changing Society, 1776–1876.* Cambridge, 1976.
Bonner, James C. "The Georgia Penitentiary at Milledgeville, 1817–1874," *Georgia Historical Quarterly* 55 (1971) : 303–28.
Boorstin, Daniel. *The Americans: The National Experience.* New York, 1965.
Boucher, Chauncey S. "Representation and the Electoral Question in Antebellum South Carolina." *Proceedings of the Mississippi Valley Historical Association* 9 (1915–16) : 110–24.
———. "Sectionalism, Representation, and the Electoral Question in Antebellum South Carolina." *Washington University Studies* 4 (1916) : 3–62.
Brailsford, Daniel T. "The Historical Background and Present Status of the County Chain Gang in South Carolina." *South Carolina Law Review* 21 (1969) : 53–69.
Brenner, M. Harvey. *Mental Illness and the Economy.* Cambridge, 1973.
Bridenbaugh, Carl. *Myths and Realities: Societies of the Colonial South.* Baton Rouge, 1952.
Briggs, Asa. "The Language of Class in Early Nineteenth-Century England." In Asa Briggs and John Saville, eds., *Essays in Labour History*, pp. 43–73. London, 1960.

Brock, Peter. *Radical Pacifists in Antebellum America.* Princeton, 1968.

Brown, Elizabeth Gaspar. *British Statutes in American Law, 1776–1836.* Ann Arbor, 1964.

Brown, Richard D. "The Emergence of Urban Society in Rural Massachusetts, 1760–1820." *Journal of American History* 61 (1974) : 29–51.

Brown, Richard Maxwell. "The American Vigilante Tradition." In Hugh Davis Graham and Ted Robert Gurr, eds., *Violence in America: Historical and Comparative Perspectives: A Report to the National Commission on the Causes and Prevention of Violence,* 1:121–80. Washington, 1969.

———. *The South Carolina Regulators.* Cambridge, 1963.

Calhoun, Daniel H. *Professional Lives in America, Structures and Aspirations, 1750–1850.* Cambridge, 1965.

Cantwell, Edward P. "A History of the Charleston Police Force." *Yearbook of the City of Charleston,* Appendix, pp. 3–19. Charleston, 1908.

Carleton, Mark T. *Politics and Punishment: The History of the Louisiana State Penal System.* Baton Rouge, 1971.

Channing, Steven. *Crisis of Fear.* New York, 1970.

Chevalier, Louis. *Laboring Classes and Dangerous Classes in Paris during the First Half of the Nineteenth Century.* New York, 1973.

Cox, Archibald. *Report on the State of the Massachusetts Courts.* Boston, 1976.

Curran, William J. "The Struggle for Equity Jurisdiction in Massachusetts." *Boston University Law Review* 31 (1951) : 269–96.

Curti, Merle E. "Robert Rantoul, Jr., The Reformer in Politics." *New England Quarterly* 5 (1932) : 264–80.

Dalcho, Frederick. *An Historical Account of the Protestant Episcopal Church in South Carolina.* Charleston, 1820.

Dalzell, George W. *Benefit of Clergy in America.* Winston-Salem, 1955.

Davis, David Brion. *Homicide in American Fiction, 1798–1860: A Study in Social Values.* Ithaca, 1957.

———. "The Movement to Abolish Capital Punishment in America, 1787–1861" *American Historical Review* 63 (1957) : 23–46.

Davis, William T. *History of the Judiciary of Massachusetts.* Boston, 1922.

Dimond, Alan J. "Congestion in the Superior Court in the Light of the History of the Court since 1859." *Massachusetts Law Quarterly* 38 (1953) : 95–125.

———. *The Superior Court of Massachusetts: Its Origin and Development.* Boston, 1960.

Donald, David. *Charles Sumner and the Coming of the Civil War.* New York, 1960.

Eaton, Clement C. *The Freedom of Thought Struggle in the Old South.* New York, 1964.

———. *The Growth of Southern Civilization.* New York, 1961.

———. "Mob Violence in the Old South." *Mississippi Valley Historical Review* 29 (1942) : 351–70.

Ellis, Richard E. *The Jeffersonian Crisis: Courts and Politics in the Young Republic.* New York, 1971.

Ely, James W., Jr. "American Independence and the Law: A Study of Post-Revolutionary South Carolina Legislation." *Vanderbilt Law Review* 26 (1973) : 939–71.

———. "Charleston's Court of Wardens, 1783–1800: A Post-Revolutionary Experiment in Municipal Justice." *South Carolina Law Review* 26 (1973) : 645–60.

———. " 'That no office whatever be held during life or good behavior:' Judicial Impeachments and the Struggle for Democracy in South Carolina." *Vanderbilt Law Review* 30 (1977) : 167–209.

Erikson, Kai T. *Wayward Puritans: A Study in the Sociology of Deviance.* New York, 1966.

Ferdinand, Theodore N. "The Criminal Patterns of Boston since 1849." *American Journal of Sociology* 73 (1971) : 84–99.

Flaherty, David. "Law and the Enforcement of Morals in Early America." *Perspectives in American History* 5 (1971) : 203–53.

Flanigan, Daniel J. "Criminal Procedure in Slave Trials in the Antebellum South." *Journal of Southern History* 40 (1974) : 537–64.

Fogel, Robert William, and Engerman, Stanley. *Time on the Cross.* 2 vols. Boston, 1974.

Foucault, Michel. *Discipline and Punish: The Birth of the Prison.* New York, 1977.

Frankel, Marvin. *Criminal Sentences: Law without Order.* New York, 1972.

Franklin, John Hope. *The Militant South, 1800–1861.* Cambridge, 1956.

Frederickson, George M., and Lasch, Christopher. "Resistance to Slavery." *Civil War History* 13 (1967) : 315–29.

Freehling, William W. *Prelude to Civil War: The Nullification Controversy in South Carolina, 1816–1836.* New York, 1966.

Friedel, Frank. "Francis Lieber, Charles Sumner, and Slavery." *Journal of Southern History* 9 (1943) : 75–93.

———. *Francis Lieber: Nineteenth-Century Liberal.* Baton Rouge, 1947.

Friedman, Lawrence M. *A History of American Law.* New York, 1973.

Galanter, Marc. "The Modernization of Law." In Myron Wiener, ed., *Modernization,* pp. 153–65. New York, 1966.

Gatrell, V. A. C., and Hadden, T. B. "Criminal Statistics and Their Interpretation." In E. A. Wrigley, ed., *Nineteenth-Century Society,* pp. 336–96. Cambridge, 1972.

Genovese, Eugene D. *Roll, Jordan, Roll: The World the Slaves Made.* New York, 1974.

Goodell, William. *The American Slave Code in Theory and Practice.* New York, 1853.

Goffman, Erving. *Asylums.* New York, 1962.

Grayson, William J. *James Louis Petigru: A Biographical Sketch.* New York, 1866.

Green, Fletcher M. *Constitutional Development in the Southern Atlantic States.* New York, 1966.

———. "Democracy in the Old South." *Journal of Southern History* 12 (1946) : 3–23.

———. "Some Aspects of the Convict Lease System." In Fletcher M. Green, ed., *Essays in Southern History,* pp. 112–23. Chapel Hill, 1949.

Greenberg, Douglas. *Crime and Law Enforcement in the Colony of New York.* Ithaca, 1976.

Grinnell, F. W. "The Constitutional History of the Supreme Judicial Court of Massachusetts from the Revolution to 1813." *Massachusetts Law Quarterly* 1 (May 1917).

Gutman, Robert. *Birth and Death Registration in Massachusetts, 1639–1900.* New York, 1959.

Hackney, Sheldon. "Southern Violence." In Hugh Davis Graham and Ted Robert Gurr, *The History of Violence in America,* pp. 505–27. New York, 1969.

Handlin, Oscar. *Boston's Immigrants: A Study in Acculturation.* New York, 1968.

Hartog, Hendrik. "The Public Law of a County Court: Judicial Government in Eighteenth Century Massachusetts." *American Journal of Legal History* 20 (1976) : 282–329.

Haskins, George Lee. *Law and Authority in Early Massachusetts.* New York, 1960.

Haunton, Richard H. "Law and Order in Savannah, 1850–1860." *Georgia Historical Quarterly* 56 (1972) : 1–24.

Hawes, Joseph M. *Children in Urban Society: Juvenile Delinquency in Nineteenth-Century America.* New York, 1971.

Hay, Douglas, et al. *Albion's Fatal Tree: Crime and Society in Eighteenth-Century England.* New York, 1975.

Haynes, Gideon. *Pictures from Prison Life: An Historical Sketch of the Massachusetts State Prison.* Boston, 1871.

Henry, Howell M. *The Police Control of the Slave in South Carolina.* Emory, 1914.

Higham, John. *Strangers in the Land: Patterns of American Nativism, 1860–1925.* New York, 1967.

Hindus, Michael S. "A City of Mobocrats and Tyrants: Mob Violence in Boston, 1747–1863." *Issues in Criminology* 6 (1971) : 55–83.

———. *The Records of the Massachusetts Superior Court and Its Predecessors: An Inventory and Guide.* Boston, 1977.

Horwitz, Morton J. *The Transformation of American Law, 1780–1860.* Cambridge, 1977.

Howard, George Elliott. *A History of Matrimonial Institutions.* Chicago, 1904.

Hurd, John Codman. *The Law of Freedom and Bondage in the United States.* 2 vols. Boston, 1858.

Hurst, J. Willard. *Law and the Conditions of Freedom in the Nineteenth-Century United States.* Madison, 1956.

Jenks, William. *A Memoir of Louis Dwight.* Boston, 1856.

Jervey, Theodore D. *Robert Y. Hayne and His Times.* New York, 1909.

Jones, Thomas F. *The University of South Carolina: Faithful Index to the Ambitions and Fortunes of the State.* New York, 1964.

Katz, Michael B. *The Irony of Early School Reform.* Boston, 1968.

Katz, Stanley. "The Politics of Law in Colonial America: Controversies over Chancery Courts and Equity Law in the Eighteenth Century." *Perspectives in American History* 5 (1971) : 257–84.

Kibler, Lillian. *Benjamin F. Perry, South Carolina Unionist.* Durham, 1946.

Knights, Peter, and Thernstrom, Stephen. "Men in Motion: Some Data and Speculations about Urban Population Mobility in Nineteenth-Century America." In Tamara Hareven, ed., *Anonymous Americans,* pp. 17–47. Englewood Cliffs, 1972.

Kohn, David, and Glenn, Bess, eds. *Internal Improvements in the State of South Carolina, 1817–1828.* Washington, 1938.

Kutler, Stanley I. *Privilege and Creative Destruction: The Charles River Bridge Case.* Philadelphia, 1971.

LaBorde, Maximilian. *A Tribute to Hon. J. B. O'Neall, LL.D., Being a Summary of His Life and Labors.* Columbia, 1872.

Landrum, John Belton O'Neall. *History of Spartanburg County.* Atlanta, 1900.

Lane, Roger, "Crime and Criminal Statistics in Nineteenth-Century Massachusetts." *Journal of Social History* 2 (1968) : 156–63.

———. "Crime and the Industrial Revolution: British and American Views." *Journal of Social History* 7 (1974) : 287–303.

———. *Policing the City: Boston, 1822–1885.* Cambridge, 1967.

Lasch, Christopher. "Origins of the Asylum." In *The World of Nations: Reflections on American History, Politics, and Culture,* pp. 3–17. New York, 1973.

"The Legal History of Massachusetts." *Massachusetts Law Quarterly* 38 (1953) : entire issue.

Lerner, Gerda. *The Grimké Sisters from South Carolina: Pioneers for Women's Rights and Abolition.* New York, 1971.

Levy, Leonard W. *The Law of the Commonwealth and Chief Justice Shaw.* Cambridge, 1957.

Lewis, W. David. *From Newgate to Dannemora: The Rise of the Penitentiary in New York, 1796–1848.* Ithaca, 1965.

Lewis, Orlando F. *The Development of American Prisons and Prison Customs, 1776–1845.* Albany, 1922.

Lodhi, Abdul Qaiyum, and Tilly, Charles. "Urbanization, Crime, and Collective Violence in Nineteenth-Century France." *American Journal of Sociology* 79 (1973) : 296–318.

McKelvey, Blake. *American Prisons: A Study in Social History Prior to 1915.* Chicago, 1936.

———. "Penal Slavery and Southern Reconstruction." *Journal of Negro History* 20 (1935) : 153–79.

Maier. Pauline. "The Charleston Mob and the Evolution of Popular Politics in Revolutionary South Carolina." *Perspectives in American History* 4 (1970) : 173–96.

———. "Popular Uprisings and Civil Authority in Eighteenth-Century America." *William and Mary Quarterly* 28 (1970) : 3–35.

Messerli, Jonathan. *Horace Mann.* New York, 1972.

Miller, Martin B. "At Hard Labor: Rediscovering the Nineteenth-Century Prison." *Issues in Criminology* 9 (1974) : 91–114.

Miller, Perry. *The Life of the Mind in America.* New York, 1965.

Miller, Wilbur. *Cops and Bobbies: Police Authority in New York and London, 1830–1870.* Chicago, 1977.

Mills, Robert. *Statistics of South Carolina.* Charleston, 1826.

Monkkonen, Eric H. *The Dangerous Class: Crime and Poverty in Columbus, Ohio, 1860–1885.* Cambridge, 1975.

Morris, Richard B. "The Courts, the Law, and Social History." In Morris D. Forkosch, ed., *Essays in Legal History in Honor of Felix Frankfurter,* pp. 409–22. Indianapolis, 1966.

———. "White Bondage in Ante-Bellum South Carolina." *South Carolina Historical Magazine* 49 (1948) : 191–207.

Nash, A. E. Keir. "Fairness and Formalism in the Trials of Blacks in the State Supreme Courts of the Old South." *Virginia Law Review* 56 (1970) : 64–100.

———. "A More Equitable Past? Southern Supreme Courts and the Protection of the Ante-Bellum Negro." *North Carolina Law Review* 48 (1970) : 197–242.

———. "Negro Rights, Unionism, and Greatness on the South Carolina Court of Appeals: The Extraordinary Chief Justice John Belton O'Neall." *South Carolina Law Review* 21 (1969): 141–90.

———. "The Texas Supreme Court and the Trial Rights of Blacks, 1845–1860." *Journal of American History* 58 (1971) : 622–42.

Nelson, William E. *The Americanization of the Common Law: The Impact of Legal Change on Massachusetts Society, 1760–1830.* Cambridge, 1975.

———. "Emerging Notions of Modern Criminal Law in the Revolutionary Era: An Historical Perspective." *New York University Law Review* 42 (1967) : 450–82.

Oliphant, Albert D. *The Evolution of the Penal System of South Carolina from 1866–1916.* Columbia, 1916.

O'Neall, John Belton. *Biographical Sketches of the Bench and Bar of South Carolina.* 2 vols. Charleston, 1859.

O'Neill, William. *Divorce in the Progressive Era.* New Haven, 1967.

Perry, Benjamin Franklin. *Reminiscences of Public Men.* Greenville, 1889.

Phillips, Ulrich Bonnell, ed. *Plantation and Frontier Documents: 1649–1863.* 2 vols. Cleveland, 1909.

———. *The South in the Building of the Nation.* 12 vols. Richmond, 1909.

Polanyi, Karl. *The Great Transformation: The Political and Economic Origins of Our Times*. Boston, 1957.

Pope, Thomas. *History of Newberry County*. Columbia, 1973.

Powell, Elwin H. "Crime as a Function of Anomie." *Journal of Criminology, Criminal Law, and Police Science* 57 (1966): 161–71.

Radzinowicz, Leon. *A History of English Criminal Law and Its Administration from 1750*. 3 vols. London, 1948–56.

———. *Ideology and Crime: A Study of Crime in Its Social and Historical Context*. New York, 1966.

Richardson, James, *The New York Police: Colonial Times to 1901*. New York, 1970.

———. *Urban Police in the United States*. Port Washington, 1974.

Rogers, George C., Jr. *History of Georgetown County*. Columbia, 1970.

Rosenbaum, Betty. "The Relationship between War and Crime in the United States." *Journal of Criminal Law and Criminology* 30 (1939–40): 722–40.

Rosenkrantz, Barbara G. "Booby-Hatch or Booby-Trap: A New Look at Nineteenth-Century Reform." *Social Research* 39 (1972) : 733–43.

Rothman, David J. *The Discovery of the Asylum: Social Order and Disorder in the New Republic*. Boston, 1971.

Rusche, George, and Kircheimer, Otto. *Punishment and Social Structure*. New York, 1939.

Samaha, Joel B. *Law and Order in Historical Perspective: The Case of Elizabethan Essex*. New York, 1974.

Savage, Edward H. *Police Records and Recollections; Or, Boston by Daylight and Gaslight*. Boston, 1873.

Schlossman, Steven L. "The Culture of Poverty in Ante-Bellum Social Thought." *Science and Society* 38 (1974) : 150–66.

———. *Love and the American Delinquent: The Theory and Practice of "Progressive" Juvenile Justice, 1825–1920*. Chicago, 1977.

Schwartz, Harold. *Samuel Gridley Howe, Social Reformer, 1801–1876*. Cambridge, 1956.

Scott, Arthur P. *Criminal Law in Colonial Virginia*. Chicago, 1930.

Sellin, J. Thorsten. *Slavery and the Penal System*. New York, 1976.

Semmes, Raphael. *Crime and Punishment in Early Maryland*. Baltimore, 1938.

Senese, Donald. "Building the Pyramid: The Growth and Development of the State Court System in Antebellum South Carolina, 1800–1860." *South Carolina Law Review* 24 (1972) : 357–79.

———. "The Free Negro and the South Carolina Courts, 1790–1860." *South Carolina Historical Magazine* 68 (1967) : 140–53.

Silver, Allan. "The Demand for Order in Civil Society." In David Bordua, ed., *The Police: Six Sociological Essays*, pp. 1–24. New York, 1967.

Sirmans, M. Eugene. *Colonial South Carolina; A Political History*. Chapel Hill, 1966.

———. "The Legal Status of the Slave in South Carolina, 1670–1740." In

Stanley Katz, ed., *Colonial America: Essays in Political and Social Development*, pp. 404–15. Boston, 1971.

Smith, Daniel Scott, and Hindus, Michael S. "Premarital Pregnancy in America, 1640–1971: An Overview and Interpretation." *Journal of Interdisciplinary History* 5 (1975) : 537–80.

Smith, Timothy L. *Revivalism and Social Reform.* New York, 1957.

Stampp, Kenneth M. *The Peculiar Institution.* New York, 1956.

Starobin, Robert, ed. *Denmark Vesey: The Slave Conspiracy of 1822.* Englewood Cliffs, 1972.

Sullivan, Robert. *The Disappearance of Dr. Parkman.* Boston, 1972.

Sydnor, Charles S. *The Development of Southern Sectionalism, 1819–1848.* Baton Rouge, 1948.

———. "The Southerner and the Laws." *Journal of Southern History* 6 (1940) : 3–34.

Sykes, Gresham. *The Society of Captives.* Princeton, 1958.

Takaki, Ronald T. *A Pro-Slavery Crusade: Agitation to Reopen the African Slave Trade.* New York, 1971.

Taylor, Robert J. *Western Massachusetts in the Revolution.* Providence, 1954.

Taylor, William R. *Cavalier and Yankee: The Old South and American National Character.* New York, 1961.

Thompson, E. P. *Whigs and Hunters.* New York, 1975.

Tobias, J. J. *Urban Crime in Victorian England.* New York, 1972.

Vinovskis, Maris A. "Horace Mann on the Economic Productivity of Education." *New England Quarterly* 43 (1970) : 550–71.

Wade, Richard. *Slavery in the Cities.* New York, 1964.

———. "The Vesey Plot: A Reconsideration." *Journal of Southern History* 30 (1964) : 143–61.

Wallace, David Duncan. *History of South Carolina.* 3 vols. New York, 1934.

———. *South Carolina: A Short History, 1520–1948.* Columbia, 1961.

Warner, Sam Bass, Jr. *Streetcar Suburbs.* Cambridge, 1962.

Welch, Richard E., Jr. "The Parsons-Sedgwick Feud and the Reform of the Massachusetts Judiciary." *Essex Institute Historical Collections* 92 (1956) : 171–87.

Wikramanayake, Marina. *A World in Shadow.* Columbia, 1973.

Williams, Jack Kenny. "Catching the Criminal in Nineteenth-Century South Carolina." *Journal of Criminal Law, Criminology, and Police Science* 46 (1955) : 264–71.

———. "The Code of Honor in Ante-Bellum South Carolina." *South Carolina Historical Magazine* 54 (1953) : 113–28.

———. *Vogues in Villainy: Crime and Retribution in Ante-Bellum South Carolina.* Columbia, 1959.

———. "White Lawbreakers in Ante-Bellum South Carolina." *Journal of Southern History* 21 (1955) : 360–73.

Williams, Raymond. *Culture and Society, 1780–1950.* New York, 1958.

Wines, Frederick Howard. *Punishment and Reformation: A Study of the Penitentiary System.* New York, 1910.

Wood, Peter. *Black Majority: Negroes in Colonial South Carolina from 1670 through the Stono Rebellion.* New York, 1974.

Wyatt-Brown, Bertram. "Southern History Upside Down: Cliometrics and Slavery." *Reviews in American History* 2 (1974) : 457–65.

Younger, Richard. *The People's Panel: The Grand Jury in the United States, 1634–1941.* Providence, 1963.

Index